C0-FYK-721

ÅKE BJERSTEDT

Educational Technology

ÅKE BJERSTEDT

Educational Technology

INSTRUCTIONAL PROGRAMMING AND DIDAKOMETRY

WILEY–INTERSCIENCE
A DIVISION OF JOHN WILEY & SONS, INC.
NEW YORK, LONDON, SYDNEY, TORONTO

Copyright © 1972 by Åke Bjerstedt
First published in Sweden 1972 by CWK Gleerup Bokförlag, Lund
as volume No. 16 in Studia Psychologica et Paedagogica
Published in the rest of the world (excluding Europe)
by Wiley-Interscience Division,
John Wiley & Sons, Inc., 605 Third Avenue, New York, N.Y. 10016
Library of Congress Catalog Card Number: 72-075617
Wiley ISBN: 0 471-07660-0
Printed in Sweden by Berlingska Boktryckeriet, Lund

Preface

The field of educational technology has been defined in various ways, some of which have focused simply on the use of new communications media in the classroom, thus dealing primarily with the equipment, the hardware. Many educators would, however, much prefer a broader definition, emphasizing the process of designing systematic learning conditions, as did the Commission on Instructional Technology in the United States. Instructional technology, this Commission wrote, "is a systematic way of designing, carrying out, and evaluating the total process of learning and teaching in terms of specific objectives, based on research in human learning and communication..." (Tickton, 1970, p. 21). This definition is a good general starting point for our present purpose, although obviously we can only work in detail with some of the many problems within this vast field.

The present book is intended to provide a survey and discussion of some of the basic problems of educational technology, as illustrated particularly in the step-wise construction of instructional methods-and-materials systems, such as self-instructional courses. In a way, the book operates on two levels: the author hopes to give the reader some basic findings and insights applicable within the wide area of educational technology as defined above, but at the same time most of the presentation is devoted to various problems within the rather more limited area of instructional programming as illustrated by the phase-by-phase development of a self-instructional course. The reason for this is fairly obvious: Instructional programming in this sense can be said to be the field where the current type of educational technology was born; during the last decade or so a considerable amount of research and general experience has been accumulated on instructional programming, much of which is basic enough to be more broadly applied.

Professor Susan M. Markle, Chicago, has given me a helping hand in subjecting the manuscript to critical reading. So has Fil. lic. Marie Månsson, Lund. Gillian Nilsson, B.A., Lund, has examined the English text from a linguistic point of view. I am very grateful to all three of them.

The printing of this book was financed by a grant from the Swedish Council for Social Science Research.

Å. B.

Contents

FIRST PART

Introductory Discussion: Basic Principles of Instructional Programming

1. Introductory Points of View

1.1 Notes on the Current Situation

Self-instructional study material became during part of the 1960's—not least in the USA—a focal point of educational interest in a manner that few could have imagined only a few years earlier. The large publishing houses fought to be first on the market with new educational programs. Schools, industries and military departments sent their representatives to attend information courses and seminars. Both the educational and the daily press were flooded with informative articles and equally often—various statements of opinion. Now the situation has partly changed: the boom of interest is no longer so marked, nor the commercial claims so vociferous. This does not mean, however, that there is no interest for the new techniques or that they have been rejected. On the contrary, work is going on all over the world—both in research and in practical product development—using the basic principles of programmed instruction. The experts in the field have increased both in number and in expertise, and—as is so often the case—some of the problems have proved to be more complex than some of the first enthusiasts believed. In commenting upon Skinner's well-known article from 1954, often quoted as the starting-point of the new movement, Markle made this comment fifteen years later: "If there was one great lie in the article, it was the statement in the concluding paragraph 'There is a simple job to be done ... The necessary techniques are known'. The years since 1954 have seen a gradual, often painful, growth in the technology of instructional design." (1969, p. 1.)

The focus has changed from a more limited interest area (a particular type of product) to a broader field: programmers are now more interested in the process, and the products of the process are now conceptualized to encompass different media and media combinations. (This new perspective is clearly seen in recent surveys and discussions, such as Leith, 1969 or Deterline et al., 1970, when compared with early presentations.) It is to keep in line with such developments that some of the journals of programmed instruction have extended their titles to include a broader term ("Programmed Learning and Educational Technology", London, and "Programmiertes Lernen, Unterrichtstechnologie und Unterrichtsforschung", Berlin). And it is to keep in line with the same development that we here look upon instructional programming as a process, basic to educational technology in general.

The construction of self-instruction material is still somewhat of an art, even though it can also be part of a scientific activity, relying on patient and detailed research. Educational and psychological science has been especially made use of in two respects: on the one hand, as a general source of inspiration, in that many of the basic principles can be said to be generalizations of learning-psychological experiences, established in psychological laboratories; on the other hand, as supplier of a systematic method for assessing the results obtained. The possibilities of basing what lies between—the special technique for converting principles into detailed, concrete study material—on scientifically based knowledge have been far more restricted.

Fortunately, self-instructing material in its hitherto most usual form possesses some characteristics that encourage us to hope that such elements of uncertainty will gradually—at least to a certain degree—disappear. For it is the self-instructing material more than any other kind of study material that preserves the individual reactions of the student. And it is the champions of so-called programmed education who more than any other group of study-material constructors have emphasized the importance of constructing the material by means of a series of successive approximations guided by concrete student reactions.

There is reason to suspect that many of the special work techniques initially utilized are whims of fashion rather than rules based firmly on educational experience. Indeed, many educators have felt a certain anxiety that such whims of fashion should by reason of their wide-spread use and the intensive information activity (where persons with little grounding in educational psychology emerge, after a short "workshop", as independent programming experts and preachers of the right faith) acquire more the character of definitive and final truth than was intended by their originators.

But on the basis of the above-mentioned qualities—*the continual reaction-recording* as well as the *successive adaptations based on results*—the adherents of programmed instruction have built up a *self-controlling mechanism.* A program-constructor may start from a particularly crazy special idea; if he follows the principle of successive approximation guided by factual results, he will usually be compelled to correct himself. This relatively unique feature in the self-instructing study-material has in a way facilitated a revival of learning psychology on the basis of data from natural learning situations. If this trend continues, we could perhaps finally pension off the hungry rat and the meaningless syllable as the leading sources of knowledge about human learning.

Even though work during the 1960's has taught us more about how human learning is promoted in self-instructional situations (we might even wonder whether any other educational field has ever been afforded such an extensive and intensive examination within one decade), our knowledge is still rather limited on many issues. In several respects, therefore, a survey of the present kind will be of a preliminary, interim nature. Our hope is that a systematic inventory among other things may serve to give impetus to persons interested in taking part in the continued research and development activities on how to develop adequate instructional situations.

1.2 Selection and Training of Constructors

Who is to carry out the instructional design and construction work, for example, the drawing up of the auto-instructional study material? Here opinions differ sharply. At one extreme there are those who hold that only qualified, educationally and psychologically trained investigators should perform such construction work. At the other extreme are to be found those who optimistically believe that the students in the elementary school can be allowed to construct their own course material!

The answer depends, of course, to a certain extent on what is understood by the two terms "construction" and "programming". I shall subsequently argue that in such discussions it is important to consider a construction procedure in a broad sense. In a *narrow sense,* programming involves the composing of a series of tasks and their arrangement in what one believes to be an instructionally appropriate series following certain special principles. In the *broad sense* programming comprises, in addition to the above, comprehensive preparatory work aimed at, among other things, the analysis of goals, students, and subject-matter characteristics as well as comprehensive following-up with successive testing and revision of the first version.

Only if the latter, more comprehensive procedure is followed, have the inherent possibilities of instructional rationalization been fully exploited. Should we stop at the first-mentioned procedure, we run the risk of getting caught up in less efficient routines. Unfortunately, many of the programs that were marketed during the sixties do not build on much more than this narrow procedure (since this, from the point of view of the rival publishers, takes the shortest time). This fact is, of course, no reason for anyone to deprive himself of the advantages to be derived from a more adequate working method.

In a complete construction procedure, teamwork would seem to be the best solution in the majority of cases. As a rule it is probably easier to teach a physics or language teacher instructional programming than to teach a programmer physics and Russian. The main part of the actual program composition could usually be carried out by a person with good special-subject knowledge as well as teaching experience on the relevant student level (an instructor *and* special-subject expert). This expert-instructor must, firstly, have taken a course in the principles of programming, and, secondly, have constant access to an educational-psychological expert for consultation. Both the preparatory and the following-up phases involve many routine tasks that need not be carried out by pedagogically qualified staff. As a rule, however, this work should be planned and led by instructional experts with access to special-subject expertise. The result can be a set-up of the following kind, for example:

I. Preparatory work:
Led by expert in instructional technology
Carried out by special-subject experts

II. Composing the basic version:
Carried out by instructor and special-subject expert with special training in programming principles
Supervised by educational-psychological consultant

III. Testing and revision:
Led by educational-psychological expert with statistical schooling
Carried out by instructor and special-subject expert with assistants for writing and calculating work

The most time-consuming work in this model is carried out by the special-subject expert-instructor. The educational-psychological expert—an academically trained psychologist or pedagogue specializing in instructional technology—devotes comparably less time to detailed work, but on the other hand leads and supervises the project at all stages. As a rule, it is only natural to take the special-subject expert-instructor from the "purchaser institution", i.e. the school type, the firm or the organisations which will eventually make use of the course. The educational-psychological expert can be a consultant from some external organisation, if the organisation in question has not in its own ranks access to a person with these qualifications.

Another conceivable possibility is to take both special-subject expert-instructor and educational-psychological expertise from outside the purchasing institution for a definite assignment, i.e., to "package-order" a certain course from an institute for programming or instructional technology. In view of the fact that the purchaser gets less insight into the work and less possibility to influence its shaping, and seeing that the school, firm or organisation cannot make use of its experiences for further projected courses, this latter "package model" will often turn out to be more expensive for the purchaser. A great deal naturally depends on the personnel resources, and hence recommendations that are valid in all situations can scarcely be given.

In selecting persons within the organisation attention should be paid to a variety of factors. Persons should naturally—as has already been stated—be *experts in the special-subject sphere,* and they should preferably also possess *teaching experience* (in the special-subject field in question and with students of the kind to which the auto-instructional material is directed). Certain personal qualities should facilitate this work, especially *analytical ability* (cf. Pierleoni & Lysaught, 1970) and *ability to express oneself clearly* and with simplicity in writing. A good deal of enthusiasm for the task, a large dose of patience mixed with a dash of "perfectionism" should also facilitate this time- and energy-consuming work. It is often an advantage if two persons work simultaneously in the same course field. They can then check each other's work and by mutual discussion reach the most satisfactory solutions.

The special-subject experts and teachers, who are to take part in the construction work, must of course have a certain basic training in the principles and technics of instructional programming, comprising, for example (a) a survey of general principles and of various techniques, (b) examination of sample good and bad programs, and (c) construction and discussion of one's own practice material. Naturally the individual conditions vary, and much of the subsequent work must, in all circumstances, take place under careful supervision and thus at the same time entail further training. It would be advantageous if the survey of principles and techniques could be made with the help of a written manual, to which reference can be made, and which can serve as a recapitulation aid and summary. This is one of the purposes behind the present book.

Efficiency in the subsequent work is, of course, intimately connected with the educational-psychological expert's skill as study leader and consultant. His learning-psychological and general pedagogic background should be such as to guarantee to some extent that he will not get entangled too easily in stereotyped routines, that he can keep an eye open for alternative solutions and new instructional techniques, and that he is able to look upon individual procedures not only as ingenious contrivances but also as special applications of more general learning principles.

At the same time, however, he must endeavour to follow up what is happening in his rapidly expanding field so that he can become a progressive rather than a status-quo factor in the pedagogic team-work. He should build up a library of the most important general-survey publications and subscribe to some of the international periodicals which publish the latest research reports and current discussions. Preliminary tips are included in the bibliographic guide given in Appendix 2 below.

2. Some Notes on Basic Principles

This book has been given a double title: "Educational technology" and "Instructional programming and didakometry". By double labelling in this way I wanted to express two things. First: Within the vaguely delineated field of educational technology I have focussed upon instructional programming—the systematic development of instructional programs (especially self-instructional teaching-learning systems)—and the closely related problems of evaluation (assessing the educational outcomes of these programs or systems). Second: While doing this, I have tried to see many of the techniques used as operationalizations of fairly general principles of forming optimal educational approaches. That is, programmed learning is not considered here as just another "aid" to learning (such as various audiovisual devices). It is not primarily any device, machine, or product (to be integrated among other devices, machines, or products). Instead (as already indicated above) we here focus upon instructional programming as a process: a systematic way of exploring the best strategies for solving teaching-learning problems.

By "self-instructional study-material" we here refer to a study-material that does not postulate a teacher's continuous engagement in subject-matter organization, the detailed presentation of subject-matter or examinations, and that in its arrangement endeavours to follow certain principles (partly based on communication theory and the psychology of learning) in order both to make such self-instruction possible and generally to promote the effectiveness and efficiency of the instruction.

In the present section we shall briefly present some general background arguments together with some notes on the basic principles which have hitherto often been followed in the construction of self-instructional materials. Some of these principles are of a very general character equally applicable in other educational settings, others are more specific. Some are relatively generally accepted, while on others opinions are more divided. Continued work with self-instructional materials will probably in due course provide us with a better knowledge of the durability and general validity of the various background principles.

2.1 Some Components in an Instructional Situation

It may be appropriate to start the discussion by trying to outline some main components of a typical instructional situation. First, it may perhaps be tempting to give the outline the following simple form:

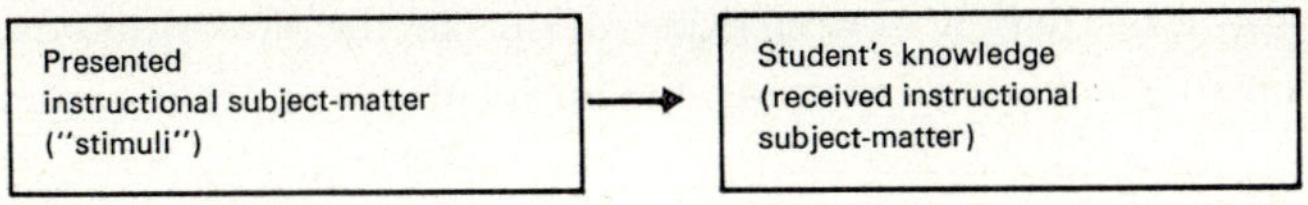

Figure 2.1

But the student, of course, is not a container which can thus easily be filled with knowledge. We understand that the outline gives a far too simplified picture of the knowledge-imparting process, seeing that it does not take into consideration the fact that the ability of different persons to "receive" material varies—owing, among other things, to dissimilarities in previous experience and a fluctuating degree of attention at the specific moment of instruction. Thus, we could schematically imagine the individual student as a receiver with, for various reasons, a reduced receiver-capacity at the moment of instruction or as a "knowledge-filter" that only retains part of the instructional material presented:

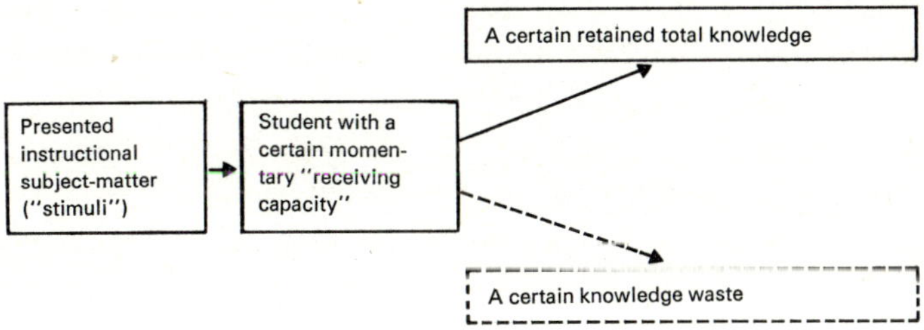

Figure 2.2

Another way of emphasizing this well-known phenomenon is to distinguish, as is sometimes done, between "*nominal*" (or "intended") stimuli and "*functional*" (or "effective") stimuli. The range of "nominal" stimuli can be easily agreed upon a priori; which of these are "effective", that is, produce behavior change in the learner, depends on many factors and may vary from one learner to another.

Our outline, however, still only includes some very crude main components in the instructional situation. The external stimulus situation contains other elements in addition to the specific subject-matter to be learnt. Some of these facilitate learning (such as support information, certain instructions for behavior and stimulating evaluations), other elements are relatively neutral for learning (a number of environmental elements), whereas others again render learning difficult (disturbing environmental elements such as noise or interest-diverting "distractors"). The "external stimuli" can thus be divided up into intended information material (or "focal" stimuli) and stimuli of other kinds.

Similarly, the student's "receptive capacity" is a complex phenomenon: it depends partly on special experiences and expectations in the now-situation, partly also on certain more general reaction tendencies, deriving from earlier experiences.

Finally, we must pay attention to the fact that what is really learnt in the instructional situation is often not only specific information (knowledge of specific subject-matter), but also more general action- and experience-tendencies (study techniques, attitude to the special-subject field and so forth).

These discussions lead, in other words, to a further re-arrangement of our figure:

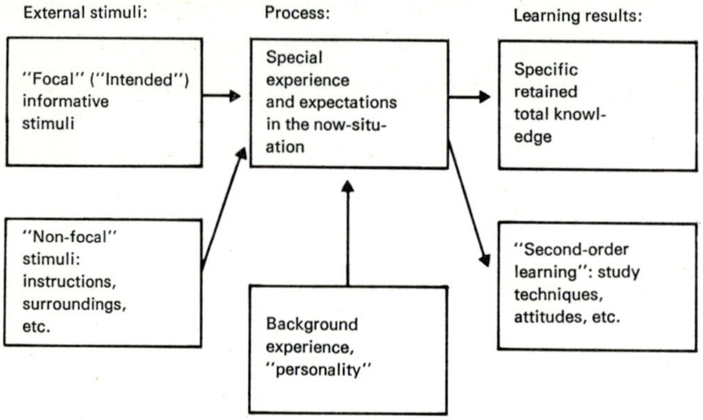

Figure 2.3

In order to be able to carry out a closer analysis of the effectiveness and efficiency in such a "communication system" (that is, the degree to which goals are reached and the time economy of this goal-reaching process) we should, however, make at least a few more sub-divisions so that certain important elements should not be forgotten. We will then arrive at an outline roughly like that of Figure 2.4. At first sight this outline may look terrifyingly complicated. A comparison with Figure 2.3 and a study of our subsequent commentaries should, however, make it easier to understand.

Let us first examine the "*stimulus*" end. By this we mean the external incitement or influences of various kinds that affect the student in the instruction situation. Here, of course, "*the focal informative stimuli*" are of cardinal importance: these are the elements, the very information units that we wish our students to acquire. They should constitute the focus of the instructional

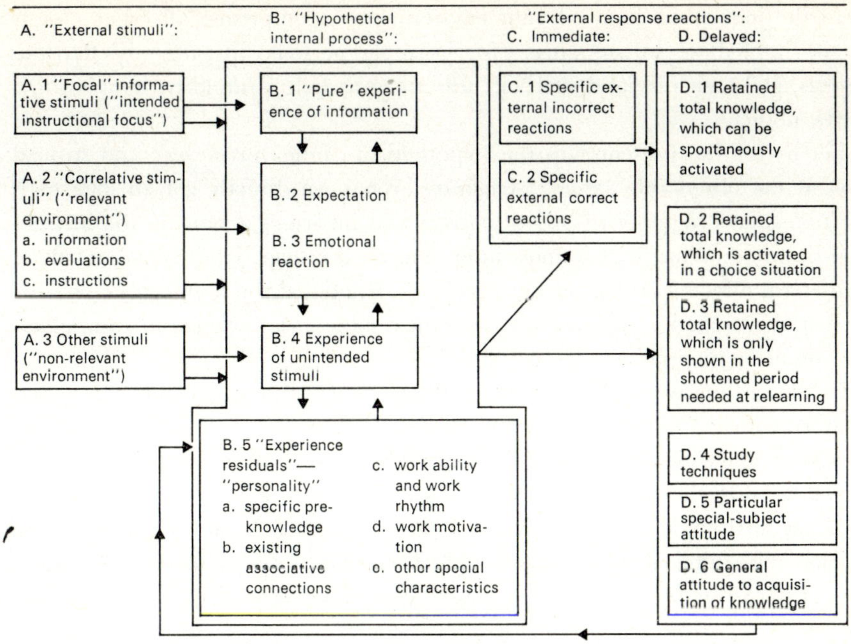

Figure 2.4 An hypothetical sketch of an instructional situation and its consequences (For more detailed explanation of outline, see text.)

situation, whether they be presented in the shape of tasks in the teacher's oral presentation, of data in a book, or of information provided by a tape-recorder or a film. It should perhaps be emphasized here that by the term "focal informative stimuli" we refer to stimuli *intended to be focal* in an effective instructional situation. Obviously, for many students during many instructional situations, the focus of attention is *not* where it is supposed to be (the "personal focus" may be on internal or external "distractors"). One of the purposes of the construction of an effective instructional situation must, of course, be to minimize the difference between intended and actual attention focus.

Besides these stimuli intended to be focal we usually have others, which are essential for learning: accompanying information (not intended to be learnt, but rather to elucidate further or to facilitate the learning of the focal subject-matter), supporting evaluations and instructions closely related to the subject-matter (furnishing the student with directions as to how he should behave in a certain instructional situation or as regards certain parts of the presented subject-matter). We can call these stimuli "*correlative*" in order to make clear that they stand in a certain systematic ("accompanying") relationship to the actual core of the subject-matter. On similar grounds we might speak of them as "relevant environment". The remaining stimuli in the situation then form the inevitable "non-relevant environment", comprising all other factors in the immediate surroundings (for example persons present, miscellaneous objects in the vicinity and such circumstances as light, humidity, temperature, traffic noise etc.).

Let us for the present skip the hypothetical "inner processes" and instead look at the observable *external reactions.* What we directly get an idea of is the *immediate* response reactions: correct and incorrect actions in the instruction situation. What we are most interested in, however, is of course not these short-term effects but instead the "*delayed*" reactions: the *long-term effects* or such student reactions as indicate a certain residue of knowledge in an application situation on a later occasion.

In the outline we have given three different ways in which such "retained total knowledge" might show itself concretely, namely, (a) correct behavior in a situation with a minimum of external guidance, (b) correct behavior in a well-defined choice situation (where the main task is to choose the correct alternative from a series of given choice possibilities), and (c) ability for quicker relearning of subject-matter which cannot be spontaneously activated. The first case entails the highest degree of residual knowledge, the last case the lowest.

What we previously called "second-order learning" has here been subdivided into three categories: teaching effects regarding (a) the student's *study techniques* (the student may have acquired a good study technique, even if he cannot himself activate the special-subject material itself), (b) his *attitude to the special subject* in which he has been instructed (he has perhaps a good residue of subject-matter but has acquired such a negative attitude to the subject that he will never voluntarily take an interest in it hereafter), and (c) his general *attitude to the acquiring of knowledge* on the whole (ranging from the view that study is a privileged pleasure to that of study being something only to be done under direct coercion).

The intermediate links between external stimuli and final reaction—*the hypothetical inner processes*—cannot be observed by us in the same direct manner. But we can study different persons' descriptions of how they experience these processes, and, indirectly, we can draw certain conclusions about them on the basis of experiments and correlative investigations.

We can imagine that the *experience in the now-situation* comprises: *partly,* a relatively *"pure" experience* of both focal and non-focal stimuli (i.e., an experience minimally influenced by factors other than the stimuli themselves); *partly,* a series of *expectations* (created by, among other things, such—previous—experiences) as to what shall further be presented or as to certain connections between different informational units; *partly,* also, an *emotional experience* of the subject-matter and other parts of the learning situation.

Usually, we can only separate these elements in theory. In most situations the interplay between them is in all probability very close. It can, for instance, be extremely difficult to differentiate between expected experience and "pure" experience, something that occasionally is expressed in "incorrect perceptions" on the basis of keen (but unjustified) expectation. Often, in this connection, expectation has both a selective and a reshaping (simplifying, sharpening) function.

Experience in the now-situation is, in addition, influenced by the *student's general experience-background and the more permanent characteristics of his personality*, e.g., by the student's specific pre-knowledge, general ability, motivation and other special characteristics. Certain persons can, for instance, by their personal disposition be more inclined, quite unthinkingly, to attach more importance to the element of expectation than to the recording of unexpected external experiences, whereas others—just as unthinkingly—are more disposed in the first place to pay attention to the realities of the external situation.

The construction of self-instructional study-material starts from the general aim of creating an *effective and efficient learning situation*. By "effective and efficient" we here mean a situation in which, starting from the goal definitions, an *optimal combination of behavioral products* (column D in Figure 2.4) *is obtained in a minimal period*. In shorter courses with well-defined proficiency content this usually indicates—to use a somewhat different formulation—a learning situation in which the greatest possible quantity of the "focal informative stimuli" is retained as easily activated total knowledge in the student as the result of a process entailing a minimum of time-consumption and a minimum of non-desirable side-effects (for instance, negative attitudes).

In order to be able to make an *assessment of a certain situation's effectiveness and efficiency* we must necessarily (a) clearly state in advance the scope and content of the desired total knowledge with a specification of the type of actualization (e.g., alternative D. 1 or D. 2 in Figure 2.4) and (b) decide upon certain tolerance limits for time-consumption and negative side-effects. In certain cases, for instance, the question of time is of subordinate interest, and the demand is for a complete mastery of a certain behavioral repertoire. So, for instance, the driving-licence candidate must train until he reaches a certain acceptable level of performance, regardless of how long this takes him. In other cases we only have a limited amount of time, and it is a question of fitting within this time-frame as much total knowledge as possible within the given field. This is often the case within the framework of the elementary school. Again, in other cases, it is a question of finding the optimal balance between time-consumption and acquired subject-matter so that the learning procedure is broken off at a point in time when further proficiency learning would entail using—according to certain criteria—a disproportionately large period of time.

When assessing learning effectiveness it is of course (as pointed out in our general definition) important to pay attention to *all* links in the teaching product (cf. column D in Figure 2.4) and decide in advance which sub-part (or sub-parts) is the most essential in the event of their coming into conflict with one another or being to varying degrees encouraged by different instructional procedures. Instructional rationalization must not of course trample on the acquired work techniques or study-attitudes in the cases where these aspects are essential to the goals defined for the specific teaching area.

In this respect there is very often a certain difference between shorter training courses for a certain specific post and the more generally oriented training, which, for instance, takes place in the compulsory school. In the former case the goals are comparatively specific and the total knowledge in consequence relatively well-defined or at least in principle easy to define. In this case instructional rationalization can move ahead rather strictly, cutting away irrelevancies and focusing upon the specific proficiency goals. In other cases—as in the elementary school—the goal area is considerably broader: many would agree that in several subjects work techniques and the general attitude to learning are often *more important* than the particular factual subject-matter, which can easily be activated by the student at a certain time. In such a case, the effectiveness definition should also clearly state this in terms of goal priorities so that one does not in ignorant and one-sided zeal rationalize away just that which one most wanted to gain. An assessment of effectiveness without a goal analysis is under any circumstances impossible.

2.2 Some Basic Principles for Self-Instructional Aids

Let us in a few points briefly state the means by which, when constructing self-instructional study material today, we endeavour to increase effectiveness in communication and teaching.

1) By a detailed *goal analysis* we attempt to clear away irrelevancies so that we can clearly *concentrate on the "focal" informative stimuli* ("total focusing") essential to the objectives.

2) By a penetrating analysis of the structure of the subject-matter we facilitate a *break-down of the subject-matter into appropriate presentational units,* which still further contributes to the focusing, the directing of attention on the central information ("itemized focusing").

3) The analysis of the structure of the subject-matter also makes possible better planning and more adequate *decisions on sequences* which facilitates the teaching. In making a sequential decision we pay attention to, for instance, such general principles as that more complex proficiencies are built up on the basis of more elementary ones; also, systematic repetition is built into the

study material itself (and therefore not entirely handed over to the student's own initiative or lack of same).

4) By a *systematic use of "correlative stimuli"* in the earlier stages of the learning process we ensure that the correct "expectation" is created in the student so that he swiftly succeeds in finding the correct solution. This generates an early training of correct behavior (instead of early incorrect behavior with subsequent risk for a more time-consuming training process). Usually it also generates an emotionally positive experience of having succeeded, which in many cases acts in an allround stimulating and "motivation-increasing" manner.

5) By a *successive "fading"* of these accompanying support-stimuli during the progressive learning process we make certain that the student learns to fulfil his task "on his own" (without having to suffer too many defeats on the way to this goal).

6) By the above-mentioned steps, which all have to do with the "stimulus", we do everything possible to prevent irrelevant stimuli from being woven into the course material. By special arrangements—*machine presentation or special types of book presentation*—we sometimes also endeavour to prevent the student from taking such liberties with the material that the projected planning is destroyed.

7) By careful *advance-analysis* of the course material's normal public—the so-called "*target population*"—we try to get to know the students; for instance, their common pre-knowledge, reading ability and special characteristics, so that effectiveness in communication becomes optimal (for example, tasks neither too difficult nor too easy).

8) Knowing that learning becomes more effective when the speed with which the information is imparted can be adapted to the individual, we most often arrange the learning situation in such a way that the student is allowed to *work at his own tempo*. Thus we prevent both the slow student losing important information, and the quick one being bored to death. The not uncommon average-centered or somewhat-below-average-paced instruction is thereby replaced by a more *individual-centered* technique. (It might be added, however, that self-pacing is not always recommended; for certain purposes, group-pacing may be adequate, and programs may also be developed to stimulate certain types of group interaction. See, for instance, Thiagarajan et al., 1970, Gensch, 1971.)

9) In cases where this speed-individualization does not seem sufficient to neutralize the inequalities in the students' experience backgrounds and personalities, we build some *branching technique* into the program. This entails in principle that certain students (on the basis of their performances or attitudes when at work) are streamed along special routes through the study material. This, for instance, can mean that a student with a higher level of

pre-proficiency can take a "shorter route", that a student with a lower level can take a "longer route" with more repetition, or that a student who lacks certain special pre-knowledge gets a little built-in "remedial course" to repair the deficiency in question. Branching can also be shaped in such a way that students with different views or attitudes can study different exemplification materials or be confronted with varied types of argumentation in order to attain by different, individually adapted routes the same conclusions in principle. Finally, we can in certain cases arrange the material in such a way that the student on certain points may himself choose whether he will have a question further clarified by going through a "higher course section" ("voluntary branching").

10) Since learning is as a rule more effective when the "flow of information" is always met by active attention, the teaching situation is usually shaped in such a way as to exploit the *"student-steered stream of information"*. The information does not then continue to flow (as, for instance, is the case during a lecture or at a conventional lesson in a class) if the student relaxes his attention, "goes to sleep" or must go to the dentist. When he concentrates again, "wakes up" or returns from the dentist, he can, in other words, continue where he left off without having missed any important links in the thought chain.

11) In order further to ensure that his attention shall not slacken, we usually arrange the study material in such a way that the student is compelled to give *"external response-reactions" at short intervals* and in immediate connection with the individual presentation units. To read pen in hand has been an old study-technical tip, and a good traditional classroom lesson has sometimes been described as a rhythmic balance between instruction by the teacher and construction by the student. In programmed study material the activity principle is built into the system.

12) With the aid of a *"successive feedback technique"* the student is most often immediately allowed to know whether his response reaction is correct or incorrect. This procedure not only promotes attention but also has certain other advantages. If the student has acted correctly (which is usually the case due to the carefully planned step-by-step presentation-manner), he not infrequently receives an unambiguous progress experience which may increase his pleasure in working. If, on the other hand, he has acted wrongly, he is at once corrected, and the likelihood of the wrong response tendency being retained is therefore lessened.

13) If the incorrect responses are of some fundamental importance ("systematic" errors), and if sufficient correction does not automatically occur in the following work sequence, special *remedial instruction* can be built in. (Remedial instruction of this kind may be thought of as both "micro-branch-

ing" and "extended feedback" and is then more or less a special case of both points 9 and 12.)

14) At the end of the study material or after certain sub-sections of the study material we usually build in *test-tasks* giving a preliminary idea of the retained total knowledge and the acquired work technique, and which at the same time demonstrate to the student what he has learnt.

15) The student's immediate external response reactions in the course of the instructional process have significance not only for the promotion of activity, but also as permanent reaction data for later successive analyses. Thus they can be used for diagnostic information about the student's continued need of supporting material or his ability to benefit from more advanced study material. But they can also be used as a basis for further improvement of the presentation units or the reshaping of the presentation sequence. The latter mode of use is in itself a central point in the construction of self-instructional study-material. The *student's reactions* (including both the immediate responses during work as well as the delayed reactions, which give us information as to the retained total knowledge and resulting attitudes) *are the final indicators of the study-material's effectiveness. Continuous testing and revision under the guidance of the student's reactions* constitute therefore a normal phase in the work of construction.

The above fifteen points can be said to summarize some of the main characteristics distinguishing an effective self-instructional study material as conceptualized by many programmers today (and we have then felt it more important to bring together some fairly common trends than to pinpoint differences between initial "schools"). Several of these characteristics also describe an effective instructional situation in general. It is obvious, for instance, that a detailed goal analysis and a revision of the presentation-forms on the basis of the student's reactions also constitute important factors which promote effectiveness in the usual classroom instruction. Hitherto it has been the champions of self-instructional study material who have most strongly stressed the value of applying procedures of the kind outlined here. The reason—among others—is that the demands on the clarity, unambiguity and effectiveness of the self-instructional material must *always* be high, since the possibility of more improvised improvements and clarifications when required, as offered by conventional classroom instruction, does not exist in the self-instructional situation. While our focus in discussing programmed instruction will be on self-instructional and self-paced materials (representing in a "pure" form many basic problems of educational technology), it should be noted that, since the mid-sixties, there has been an increasing development of group-paced instructional materials that share the systematic development process and validation with the more "classic" forms of programs. In typical cases, students then work with handouts, responding actively to presentations by means of films, TV, filmstrips or audio materials; however, pacing is governed by the presentation device, based on trials with students to determine adequate response time.

The above fifteen points should be examined by the reader both in relation to the hypothetical outline of an instructional situation as given above (Figure 2.4) and as a background to the following concrete survey of different stages in the construction work. The first six points deal mainly with "*the stimulus side*" (column A in the figure); points 7—9 touch on the adaptation to the inner process, especially the student's varying *backgrund-experience* (column B); points 10—15 mainly refer to "*the reaction side*" (columns C and D in the figure). Of course, much of what has been said above may—for one who is not, in advance, at home with the special nature of the self-instructional aids—appear slightly abstract. We hope, however, that the more detailed presentation below wil make our points of view much more concrete and clear.

2.3 Different Motivations for the Use of Self-Instructional Study-Material

We can choose self-instructional study-material for different reasons. Some common motives are the following: (a) There are too few teachers at places where instruction in a certain subject-matter is needed. (b) The programs are seen as vehicles for introducing innovations (the new mathematics, use of contraceptives, etc.) when available teachers may be resistant or at least not sufficiently prepared. (c) The habit of working on one's own with self-instructional study-material is considered important for the student's study technique and training in independent work (an important objective in teaching obviously being to enable the child to get along without the teacher). (d) The possibility of individualizing (e.g. differentiating work-pace) is considered essential in heterogeneous classes with sharply varying background conditions for the students. (e) The self-instructional study-material is considered a more rational and effective instrument, which leads more quickly to intended results.—The reasons must be explicitly clarified, as different motives can and should lead to certain shifts in the center of gravity in construction work.

Thus, the fifth of the above-mentioned points of departure, *e*, places the greatest emphasis on effectiveness and efficiency. In this case the clearing away of irrelevant stimuli and the study of time-consumption and retained total knowledge are particularly essential. Here comparative investigations of the results of different forms of instruction are of obvious interest. Seeing that efficiency is of focal importance, the self-instructional technique should not as a rule be applied in cases other than those which have really been proved to lead more quickly to the goal than alternative instructional forms. These lines of thought often apply to shorter adult courses intended for special, well-defined training goals.

The first-named point of departure, *a,* gives a case, however, in which alternative instructional possibilities need scarcely be considered. It would be rather a question of arranging a kind of "rationalized correspondence instruction". Efficiency comparisons with lesson instruction are hardly relevant in this connection. Reason *b* is similar to *a* in this respect, although changes may with time make such comparisons meaningful.

Motivations *c* and *d* would probably often be of importance in the elementary school. Then it is important that we do not at the same time blindly stare at a one-sided interpretation of the effectiveness demand in terms of subject-matter knowledge learnt. Comparisons between the efficiency and effectivity of different work forms is always of interest, of course, but *knowledge* effectivity is not the only decisive factor. A lower knowledge effectiveness linked with better work-habits or with greater enjoyment of work and pleasanter disciplinary conditions would certainly be considered a fully acceptable goal by many teachers. Here as elsewhere we must not hesitate to declare what we consider to be the most essential—and then keep to the priorities. But naturally we must then not forget to see to it that the new, not merely knowledge-oriented goal is also realized. In other words: we must not relax our efforts in the conviction that self-instructional study-material *may* be useful for study techniques and work training, but we must of course actively strive to get the material so shaped that there will be favorable conditions for this objective to be attained—and subsequently we must also try to check the result. Certain forms of self-instructional material can, for instance, be thought to accustom the students to a far too chopped-up and stereotyped spoon-feeding or to *guessing* their way to their responses rather than *thinking them out.* The fact that we deal with "self-instructional materials" does not mean that we *necessarily* promote good independent study habits (this is a common misconception due to the terms used).

2.4 A Parenthetical Note on the Theoretical Model

Two patterns of thought permeate much of the theoretical discussions within this area: the behavioristic-pragmatic view (common especially in the early American discussions), and a view influenced by cybernetics and informational psychology (common especially in some German and Eastern European research groups). Important insights have originated from both camps.—It has perhaps struck some readers with a knowledge of current works on the subject that the above background discussion has not contained a single word about animal-psychological studies. Nor have we spoken of "reward" or "reinforcement" techniques or of the successive shaping of existing behaviors—terms and expressions that surely play a central part in the discussion about the learning-psychological background. For Skinner—outstanding animal psychologist and one of the leading exponents of self-instructional study-material—it was only natural to formulate the theoretic model in what psychologists are wont to call strictly S-R-theoretic (or R-S-theoretic) terms and together with animal-psychological illustrations. (Technically, Skinner's model is primarily an R-S model, with emphasis on the contingency between response and consequence; although there is concern with the preceding stimulus which may signal the occasion for the response.)

In a historical survey this type of argumentation has its place. I have also to some extent followed a procedure of this kind in another context. But at the same time I think it may be a disadvantage to bind oneself one-sidedly so that one always describes and thinks in these categories. The disadvantages are of two kinds—the one external (communication-psychological) and the other internal:

The external disadvantage is that the animal-psychological illustrations and terms have a tendency among certain listeners to rouse an unnecessarily negative attitude in advance which not infrequently blocks a continued exchange of thought. The rat-psychological perspective thus often becomes an unnecessary communication barrier. If the same basic principles can be demonstrated in experience-material that lies closer to hand, then there is a lot to be said for letting the rat remain in its cage.

The other disadvantage is of a more fundamental nature. I believe—and on this point perhaps many hold another view—that it would be unfortunate for the future development of self-instructional study-material to bind oneself to a strict S-R-theoretical model. This point of departure has already in a few cases led to surprising formulations of experience data and a certain disposition to overlook important realities. Different behavioral theories ought probably to be first seen as different ways of classifying and describing a variegated reality. There is nothing, in my view, that says that experiences and results from studies of self-instructional study material cannot be described just as well in other terms as in those that are typically Skinnerian.

Among research workers interested in programmed learning some do emphasize the development of internal mediating processes between stimulus and response. Landa (1969 a, 1969 b), for example, distinguishes various types of thinking processes. An algorithmic process is characterized by the absence of independent choice. A heuristic process takes place in an indefinite field of choice; creative problem solving would be an example. There are also mixed forms, such as when there is a determined and complete field of possible choice alternatives, but the learner does not have an algorithm for choosing the method of solving the problem. Landa stresses the importance of studying the process by which the learner arrives at a solution. When we are thus interested not only in behavior products but also in internal mediating processes, limited S-R models often seem insufficient as instructional paradigms.

Here I have chosen to start from a simple communication-psychological model including cognitive and personality-psychological elements. In any case, I myself feel this to be a more flexible and more natural way of describing what happens in a human learning-situation, and it seems to me to give greater scope for broad explorations fruitful for the further development of the method. It would also seem to facilitate comparisons between these special instructional forms and other types of human instructional situations. Obviously neither the one nor the other model type should be taken too seriously. Models are convenient data-summarizers and useful sources of inspiration—but they are of course never more important than the basis of empirical facts on which they build, and about which some sort of agreement is usually relatively easily attained.

3. The Three Main Phases in the Construction of a Self-Instructional System

The construction of self-instructional material can, of course, be approached from many different angles—some of which can be described more precisely than others. Concerning the details there is still considerable disagreement among different schools. On the other hand, relatively good agreement has been reached in principle with regard to the broad lines, the main phases of the work. The fact that, for reasons of time or economy, the complete procedure has not always been fully exploited in the concrete tasks, is a different matter.

The presentation which follows is based on a view of the construction process which distinguishes three *main phases* of the work:

1. System analysis: Preparatory work
2. System synthesis: Constructing the preliminary version
3. System modification and evaluation: Testing and revision.

The preparatory work comprises all the important work which must be done before the constructor can sit down with a clear conscience and formulate presentational units intended for direct student work. It includes a detailed analysis of the special goals of the instruction, of its external conditions in the actual situation and of the special characteristics of the relevant subject-matter. Certain preliminary decisions as to presentational media must also be taken at this early stage. In general, the preparatory work focuses upon an "analysis" of the components to be put together later in the "synthetic" phase.

On the basis of the results and decisions of the preparatory analysis, the material-constructor then begins the construction of a preliminary version, in which he must also pay attention both to principles for the shaping of the individual presentational units as well as to guiding-lines for their mutual arrangement.

The quality of the preliminary version naturally varies considerably depending of the nature of subject-matter, the thoroughness of the preparatory work and the constructor's background experience and general aptitude for the work.

The third main phase comprises a gradual testing of the preliminary version with successive revisions and a terminal field-test on representative groups, designed to provide guidance and information for the potential user: a kind of "informative label".

Certain assessments of the *scope* of the different main phases (calculated in working-hours consumed and/or costs) are to be found in the literature. Deutsch (1962, p. 211), for instance, calculates that approx. 25 % of the total investment of time and money is disbursed in preparatory analyses, approx. 30 % in the constructing of the first version, and approx. 45 % in successive tests and revisions. Naturally such statistical information cannot be generalized, since the special conditions of work in each individual case will create a partly unique situation. The scope of the preparatory work varies, for instance, to an extraordinarily high degree depending on whether any kind of preparatory analysis already exists in the shape of detailed course planning or whether the constructors are compelled to begin from rock bottom (starting only from a general and vague formulation of the instructor's goals).

Nevertheless, it can be of a certain interest to note the above-mentioned figures. The beginner in the field sometimes has a feeling that the main part of the work consists of a direct construction of study-material according to a series of rules of thumb, and that what is here called preparatory work and testing together with revision, respectively, are side activities demanding comparatively little time and work. In reality, however, Deutsch estimates that *less than a third* of the total investment is disbursed on such direct construction. (For a more detailed discussion of the economical aspects of work and time, see, e.g., Klaus & Lumsdaine, 1962; Kopstein & Cave, 1962.) Later experiences seem to stress this focus on pre- and post-phases even more. "I have seen estimates of as much as 50 % devoted to analysis and newer modes of programing may spend very little time in writing, with the greatest amount of time going to rewriting (after initial analysis of student input)." (S. M. Markle, 1971, personal communication.)

As is already obvious from the description of the different main phases above, several sub-phases have to be dealt with—for instance, in the following manner:

1. *System analysis: Preparatory work*
    - 1.1 Analysis of prerequisites
        - 1.1.1 Choice of subject-matter area
        - 1.1.2 Goal analysis: Decision on terminal points
        - 1.1.3 Student analysis: Clarification of initial points
        - 1.1.4 Situation analysis
    - 1.2 Subject-matter analysis
    - 1.3 Preliminary decisions on media-method combinations

2. *System synthesis: Construction of preliminary version*
   2.1 Preparatory decisions on sequences and procedures
   2.2 Working out instructional sub-units, deciding on
      2.2.1 Information elements
      2.2.2 Response requests
      2.2.3 Result indications
   2.3 Final adjustment of sequences and media

3. *System modification and evaluation: Post-construction quality control and improvement*
   3.1 Systematic pre-testing examination
   3.2 Successive testing and revision
   3.3 Final field testing
   3.4 Writing of manual

In the following survey we shall broadly follow the work plan outlined here. It might be said that we use a system approach to instruction, but this term should then be understood in a very simple and straight-forward way as the application of analysis and synthesis (based on the analysis) to an instructional system.

SECOND PART

System Analysis in Instructional Programming: The Initial Phases

4. Choice of Area

When an organization or a school begins to consider converting certain courses into a self-instructional form, several questions of choice arise at the very start. Which fields are the most suitable? In which area should we begin? Are there any fields that we should *not* include?

4.1 Trends

An examination of the distribution of published courses for various subject-matter areas may be of some interest in this connection. For instance, reference may be made to the early lists of programmed courses on the U.S. market, drawn up by the Center for Programed Instruction, New York, or similar lists of programs available on the market in Britain, compiled for the Association for Programmed Learning and Educational Technology, London.

Table 4.1 shows that the distribution of subjects in U.S. programs for the three years given is fairly similar despite the differences in the number of courses available. It is easy to see a tendency towards a preponderance of some special subject-matter areas, especially mathematics and science. It is worth noticing, however, that the relative proportion of mathematics decreased from 1962 to 1965. Table 4.2 gives a survey of programs available in Britain in 1969. In spite of a considerable breadth of topics used, mathematics and the natural sciences still form particularly large sub-categories.

Surveys of this kind must not be overrated. What was dominant during an early period need not necessarily be dominant later on in a field developing rapidly. But a statistical survey of this kind gives us some idea of what publishers and course programmers have, up to a certain point of time, *regarded* as the easiest material to convert into self-instructional courses. From this, it need not follow, of course, that other fields are *unsuitable* for programming. The conspicuous increase in the number of programs under the heading "Miscellaneous" in Table 4.1 indicates that the range widened rapidly to include new fields. A quick sample of subject indicators in the index of the 1969 British list of programs in print testifies further to the diversity: Accident

Table 4.1 Survey of the distribution of subjects in American programmed courses (according to the information available for 1962, 1963 and 1965)

Subject	1962		1963		1965	
	No.	%	No.	%	No.	%
Mathematics	52	43	123	35	49	16
Science	24	20	69	20	70	24
English	16	13	51	14	56	19
Foreign languages	10	8	21	6	9	3
Social studies	7	6	16	5	22	8
Business education, economics	4	3	22	6	17	6
Programming	2	1.5	9	3	3	1
Miscellaneous	2	1.5	41	11	65	21
Total	117		352		291	

The figures give a content survey of programs available for purchase in Sept. 1962, Sept. 1963, and April 1965. The data have been obtained from the publishers by the Center for Programed Instruction at the request of the Office of Education (cf. "Programs, '62", "Programs, '63", and "Programed instruction materials 1964—'65").

prevention, Battle of Hastings, Choosing a job, Decision making, Electrocardiography, Frost precautions, Growing adult, Hypnotism, Insurance policy, Julius Caesar, Keybord mastery, Latin, Melodic perception, Neurosis, Ohm's law, Poetry, Queen and parliament, Roentgenology, Smoking, Traffic signs, United Nations, Volcanic activity, and Weft knitting.

4.2 Some Points of View in Choosing Subject-Matter Areas

Some points of view that may be taken into account in choosing subject-matter areas are listed below.

"Subject-matter points of view"

(a) Subject-matter which has a *relatively easily distinguishable logical structure* would seem to lend itself more easily to the usual types of programming for self-instruction than other kinds. It is probably this, among other things, that is reflected in the large number of courses in mathematical subjects, especially during the early period. One might also say that mathematics is one of the subjects in which older teaching approaches have certain similarities with the technique of programming (an alternation of new information, solving problems, result indication). In other words, the step from conventional to programmed techniques may be said to be shorter in mathematics than in

Table 4.2 Survey of the distribution of subjects in programs available on the market in Britain in 1969 (according to subject classification in Cavanagh & Jones, 1969)

A. *Subject headings with more than 50 titles*	
Biological sciences	99
Chemistry	82
Civic affairs	62
Commercial subjects	91
Computers	53
Earth sciences	78
Electricity and electronics	106
Engineering	199
English	130
Industry	51
Management and supervision	67
Mathematics	572
Physics	88
Reading	57

B. *Subject headings with 10—50 titles*

Foreign languages, General subjects, Health education, History, Medicine, Nursing, Programmed instruction, Slide rule, Statistics

C. *Subject headings with less than 10 titles*

Bridge, Carpentry, Dentistry, General science, Librarianship, Linguistics, Logic, Music, Photography, Physical education, Religious education

Total number of programs classified 2004

Note: The editors have tried to list all teaching programs—both industrial and educational—available on the British market in 1969. Of the about 2000 titles, most are of British origin (about 1600 programs); the rest are mainly American programs. In this survey, mathematics programs form the largest single subject category, with 572 titles (or 29 % of the total). The second largest category is engineering with 199 programs (10 %), and the third is English with 130 entries (6 %).—Figures in Tables 4.1 and 4.2 are not directly comparable, since principles of program selection and classification are somewhat different.

some other subjects. The advantages of using subject-matter that has an easily distinguishable logical structure are firstly, that structural analysis and sequential arrangement are easier, and secondly, that there is no great difficulty in deciding what should be considered "focal" stimuli and irrelevant stimuli respectively.

(b) On the other hand, the not uncommon view that routine material with emphasis on pure drilling (unrelated facts: names, symbols) is particularly suitable for the current forms of programming, is based, partly at least, on a misunderstanding. Such material can of course be practised by the student himself, perhaps with the aid of a machine, but as a rule the effectiveness of the learning process cannot be very much increased by the form of systematic constructional work usually associated with the term "programming". The reasons for this are obvious: material that is not structured in itself does not gain anything by structural analysis, and material to be learnt by heart in its entirety and as unrelated items cannot usually be made more meaningful by focusing and weeding out irrelevant stimuli—all stimuli are equally focal! (For experiments related to this argument, see Shettel & Lindley, 1961; Hughes, 1962, p. 58.)

(c) One factor that should be taken into account, on the other hand, is *the degree of permanence of the subject-matter.* It should be borne in mind that conversion to effective self-instructional material requires so much labor that it is important not to expend this labor on a field in which today's problems are out of date tomorrow.

(d) A more tactical point of view concerning subject-matter is that the programmer should not try to embrace connected work units that are too large. It is important for him to arrive at a preliminary test relatively quickly. If the first attempt does not turn out well, not so much time has been wasted, and the constructor of the course can start revision work with equanimity and little loss of prestige.

"Student points of view"

(e) A not unimportant consideration in the choice of area is the estimated *number of students* who are going to use the material. If there is only a very small number, the amount of work required for the programming may perhaps be considered out of all proportion to the returns. (Cf. Kopstein & Cave, 1962.)

(f) If experience shows that sections of a course *present the students with particular difficulties* when conventional teaching methods are used, or when other types of course material available are totally inadequate or do not exist, then these sections would be natural starting areas for programming attempts, providing other circumstances are not clearly contra-indicative.

(g) When it is *difficult or expensive to bring together potential students scattered over a wide area* for a centrally organized course under the direction of a number of experts, there is good reason to investigate the possibility of arranging tuition using self-instructional material on the local level thus avoiding travelling expenses, the costs of living away from home, etc.).

"Instructors' and constructors' points of view"

(h) Subject-matter for courses for which it is difficult to find a sufficient number of qualified teachers naturally suggests itself for programming. For this very reason considerable interest in programmed courses has been shown in countries in which the school system is undeveloped.

(i) Subject-matter for courses for which it is difficult to find experts in a particular subject to act as constructors should, however, be left alone until experts can be found. Considering the total costs of the work on a course, amateurism in the subject-matter area should never be tolerated.

It may be thought that most of the above points are rather obvious. Since labor and resources are very much tied down by large-scale constructional projects of this type, the initial choice of subject-matter areas is by no means unimportant, however. Nor is it particularly unusual for constructional work to be started without careful consideration of the factors mentioned here—motivated only by a casual interest. In order to prevent inadequately planned instructional projects of this kind giving poor initial results, there is every reason to consider these apparently commonplace arguments with a good deal of care.

5. Goal Analysis

5.1 General Aim: Decision on Terminal Points

Once a particular area has been selected, the next task is to analyze the teaching objectives. Analyzing the objectives is, or should be, a vital stage in planning all instruction. The obligation to make such an analysis, however, has usually been more heavily emphasized by those working with self-instructional material than by others.

The use of systematic goal analysis in the field of education is no novelty. Nevertheless, goal-analytic arguments are undoubtedly accorded greater importance in educational discussions and planning today than they were earlier. It is not unknown these days for a student to ask his academic teacher what the aim of the course being taught is; such stimulating direct questions were certainly not common before. But the fact that publishers, textbook writers, teacher trainers, education planners, etc., speak more and more of objectives and goal analysis does not mean that they are in agreement as to what these terms imply.

The terms obviously crop up in discussions with more persistence than accuracy. Those using them have sometimes proved to be comparatively unaware of how a systematic goal analysis functions and, when given descriptions of typical procedures, they often feel rather doubtful as to its value. Increased precision is seen sometimes as a threat, sometimes as a triviality. At the other extreme there are fanatics who believe that they could completely revolutionize teaching results simply by using goal-analytic techniques more systematically. This division of opinion calls for a closer examination of concepts and for empirical studies.

Systematic goal analysis is a *process* with several separate elements. The necessity of some of these elements may be debatable, but the process has a very palpable *product:* a definite series of *goal descriptions* (for a given field). This product will normally have an important role to play in guiding the development of a complete instructional system, as suggested above.

5.2 Some Possible Criteria

We all have ideas about objectives in one form or another, and we have all been forced now and then to formulate these ideas. Occasionally, the term "goal analysis" (or "analysis of objectives") is used to describe these comparatively unsystematic attempts simply to write down or in some other way make explicit our ideas about goals. It would be preferable, however, to keep at least the term "systematic goal analysis" (and "systematic analysis of objectives"; we use these two expressions interchangeably in this context) for work which complies with certain standards. The question then is which criteria should be applied.

There is almost no common practice to fall back upon here, nor any indisputable authority. If we try to summarize various lines of development in current goal-analytic work, however (and primarily take up general criteria which can normally be applied in all fields), it should be possible to agree that the following criteria are at least reasonable starting points (cf. also the survey in Box 5.1):

(1) *a search for empirical information* as a basis for fixing objectives (it is not enough simply to try to formulate one's own goal concepts);
(2) a *comprehensive* search for information (taking data from a single source normally involves a risk of bias);
(3) collection of an empirical *basis for giving priority* to or *evaluating* possible objectives;
(4) firm *rules for decision-making* on the basis of the information gathered (a "firm decision-strategy");
(5) *behavior-orientated precision in formulating* goals (an important phase later is formulating the objectives in unambiguous, simple, communicable terms);
(6) supplementary *logical checks;*
(7) *empirical goal checking* (investigating how "realistic" goal specifications prove to be in concrete cases, assuming certain conditions with regard to resources and initial behavior);
(8) *post-checking revision* of goals (successive revisions can be made of goal formulations on the basis of the checking suggested in point 7).

The order in which the "criteria" have been placed here is at the same time a program, a sequence of *work-phases* within the framework of a complete goal analysis.

Several other sub-criteria could easily be formulated, and it is also possible to summarize the eight points above under more comprehensive headings. A comprehensive three-phase division could be formulated thus: (a) *goal seeking* (points 1—3), (b) *goal focusing* (points 4—6), and (c) *goal adjustment* (points 7—8). Phase 6—8 can also be excluded as a kind of supplementary work which is not always needed, and that leaves two main tasks: (I) *to establish goals* (points 1—4) and (II) to *formulate goals* (points 5—6). In

Box 5.1 What does a systematic goal analysis comprise?

There is at present no generally accepted norm as to which criteria are necessary and sufficient for a systematic goal analysis; and even partial analyses are naturally often worthwhile. Some important components in a more complete process are, however, as follows:

1. *Search for goals*
   - with *empirical* and
   - *comprehensive* methods,
   - providing a *basis for priorities.*

2. *Focusing of goals*
   - with firm *rules for decision-making*
   - *behavior-orientated precision* in formulation,
   - and checking that *goal conflicts* do not occur.

3. *Adjustment of goals*
   - with empirical *goal checking:* testing of "*goal-realism*",
   - and *goal revision:* successive, post-checking revisions.

the following sections some comments and examples will be given for some of the main points in the program outlined here.

5.3 Goal Seeking, Goal Focusing, Goal Adjustment—Some Work-Phases of a Goal-Analytic Process

5.3.1 *Goal Seeking: Empiricism and Comprehensiveness*

The main aim in the introductory, goal-seeking phase is to obtain as comprehensive a basis for decisions as possible. Some obvious questions to start with are:

(1) How is a comprehensive basis for decisions concerning the X field of education to be obtained? What sources of information are to be consulted?

(2) Are there at present any obvious discrepancies between the statement of objectives and the realization of those objectives? Are there discrepancies between the demands made on objectives today and the demands that will be made in the foreseeable future?

Box 5.2 shows different ways in which these questions can be approached. The left-hand column gives examples of a number of possible sources of information, divided into the main categories: texts, "practitioners", contact groups, teachers, students, and other members of society in general. The plus signs in the other three columns are intended to mark some of the cases where a survey of the particular subject-area suggests that information is primarily needed. The signs in the table are naturally only examples, although they have been chosen with a view to presenting a reasonable pattern. (The plus signs in brackets mark secondary sources; and the unmarked sections those which are not relevant here.) In the following we will refer to concrete examples—mostly from current Swedish work—of the various types of analysis.

Text analyses often make good starting-points, and in many cases the official documents are worth a close study. An example of this type of text analysis (focusing on the demands made by society on teachers) can be found in Löfqvist (1969, 1971). The official texts primarily describe the "desired present situation"; what it cannot give any information on is the actual present situation (which can after all sometimes differ considerably from the planned ideal). Moreover, official plans are sometimes formulated in extremely vague and general terms. So additional, more precise information is often needed. A selection of the most frequently used textbooks can in many cases give more substance to the general outlines. They provide a picture which is often closer to the actual present-day situation. An example of textbook analysis can be found in Lindell (1969; focusing on the teaching of the German language to Swedish beginners). At the same time, it should not be forgotten that much of the content of the textbooks is there by tradition rather than as a result of planned analyses (Tingsten's stimulating analyses of textbooks from different countries show how old traditions often cling with remarkable tenacity in schoolbooks that are frequently reprinted; Tingsten, 1969) and that those writing the textbooks have not always fulfilled the aims set out in the curriculum. So a textbook analysis can usually only be yet another small part of the goal-analytic whole. In some fields, documents stating international policy have been issued and may help to clarify the desired trends of development.

One central source of information is those people who can be grouped together under the general heading "*practitioners*": those who, to a large extent, practise skills and apply knowledge within the subject area with which the analysis is dealing. When training for a particular job is being studied, then naturally the job in question is the main object of interest; in many other cases the group is not so clearly defined. Several different methods of collecting data are possible; spot questioning (by interview or questionnaire), personal reporting for a specified period ("diary method"), or direct and detailed observations of behavior. Some of the main questions arising are: Which skills in the field seem the most essential for an adequate total pattern of behavior and for an individual feeling of fulfilling a function well, and on what points do the "practitioners" feel their basic training to be inadequate?

Box 5.2 Goal seeking: Examples of possible sources of information

Sources of Information	Present Situation		Future
	Actual	Desired	(Desired)
1. *Texts*			
1.1 Official documents (curricula etc.)		+	
1.2 Representative textbooks	+		
1.3 International documents on policy		+	+
2. *"Practitioners"*	+	+	
3. *Contact groups*	+	+	
4. *Teachers*			
4.1 Representative groups	+	(+)	
4.2 Special-interest groups	(+)	+	+
5. *Students*			
5.1 Representative groups	+	(+)	
5.2 Special-interest groups	(+)	+	+
6. *Other representatives of society*			
6.1 Representative groups	+	(+)	
6.2 Special consumer groups	(+)	+	+
6.3 "Experts"	(+)	+	+
6.4 "Planners"			+

See text for more detailed discussion and explanations. Points 2—3 are of particular importance in the case of focused job-training, but less relevant in general education, e.g. in the comprehensive school.

In many cases interesting material is revealed by questioning the persons closest to the "practitioners" ("*contact groups*"). This applies particularly in studies of job-training for professions specifically involving contact with others. Studies of "practitioners" and "contact groups" are central to what is known as the B Project in our department, a project involving job analyses of school administrators, lecturers in teaching method and tutors (see e.g. Gestrelius, 1970, 1971).

Both *teachers* and students—those directly involved in teaching—are natural sources of information in many goal-analytic contexts. What in fact are the central ideas on objectives in the teaching world today and what changes seem most urgent? There are two ways in which teachers and students can be studied: either by picking random samples of individuals (perhaps primarily in order to get a cross-section picture of the actual situation, such as it is experienced by representatives of both categories), or by specially choosing groups of people with a particular interest in the subject-area (and then perhaps primarily in order to obtain a broad outline of the changes needed). A study of student preferences in the choice of material is reported, for example, in Lindsten (1969). This aspect can be named "*student-centered need analysis*". Swedish commissions on schools have sometimes made use of this type of need analysis (see Härnqvist & Grahm, 1963).

Representatives of society outside the circle of "practitioners" and outside the school world should also frequently be given a chance to make themselves heard—especially when we deal with final objectives. Random samples can perhaps also be used for this occasionally, but it is more usual to approach special "consumer" groups (the prospective employers or the institutes for further studies). "*Consumer analyses*" have actually played a not unimportant part in the work of Swedish commissions on schools; Urban Dahllöf's work on "Gymnasium" education is an obvious example (see Dahllöf, 1965; cf. also Husén & Dahllöf, 1960). A similar approach is often needed in projects on the development of material (see e.g. a study of foreign language requirements in sections of the Swedish business world in Larsson, 1969). This aspect—in contrast to the student-centered need analysis mentioned above—can be called "*society-orientated requirement analysis*". In addition, it is often valuable for those constructing material to be confronted with some kind of "*expert group*" at an early stage. These people may be experts in the subject (perhaps in the front-line of research with quite different ideas about what is and is not important than those suggested by conventional textbooks). But they could also be experts in method: people who have been particularly intensively engaged in teaching and in teaching innovations in the field in question. Goal-analytic work, based on "expert" opinions, was included in planning the broad outlines of the IMU system, a Swedish methods-and-materials system for individualized mathematics instruction (see Öreberg et al., 1966). When the main purpose is to gather ideas and suggestions from a group with a special interest, a suitable starting-point can be a conference with small group discussions, at which different points of view are confronted, resulting possibly in a closer definition of concepts and a decision on priorities for partial objectives.—When it comes to future developments, information can sometimes be sought from various categories of people specially detailed to plan for the future, simply called "planners" in Box 5.2. Unfortunately, there are all too few persons of this type in the world of education today.

The catalogue of possible sources of information perhaps gives the overwhelming impression of this being an extremely long-term process. It should be understood, however, that these sources are hardly ever all used at the same time. In each separate case a decision has to be made as to which sources are the most important in view of the resources available and the problems to be studied. Often, however, it turns out to be more advisable to explore more than one source less intensively than to concentrate everything on a single aspect: it is easy to become biased if restricted to one single source of information. Some of the criticism directed at e.g. consumer analyses does not claim primarily that such analyses are unjustified, but rather that they are utilized too directly in the planning process without sufficient balance being maintained between different points of view. Similar criticism has often been made of those work analyses which only study the actual present-day situation; it is claimed quite rightly that additional information must be sought, on which desirable future models and objectives can be based.

Let us summarize some of the points covered above, tying them down more specifically to the self-instructional situation. We may then note that existing "source material" in the form of current syllabuses and textbooks (so often used as the sole source of inspiration in programming) is valuable for analyzing objects, but—and this is what we want to stress—that the usefulness of such material should not be overrated. If we rely too much on these sources, we may not make full use of our opportunities to increase efficiency. The shortcomings of these sources stem chiefly from two characteristics. Firstly, syllabuses and similar directions about instruction are often extremely vague and generalized in their formulation. Secondly, existing course material in the form of handbooks and textbooks not infrequently contains subject-matter that is quite extraneous to the objectives in question, being the result of chance, tradition, or personal interests of the author rather than of planned analysis.

In determining the necessary actions and knowledge ("*terminal behavior*" and "*terminal knowledge*") then, some of the better starting-points are: (a) an exact, detailed *description by one or several experts in the subject,* perhaps supplemented by a more extensive *opinion poll,* i.e. a study of so-called "consumer demands"; (b) *a systematic observation of typical behavior* in employees who are recognized as being good at the particular job that the course is designed to train people for. On which of these two approaches the main emphasis will fall, depends partly on the relation between manual-practical and verbal-theoretical aspects in the desired final result. As a rule, the more verbal theoretical factors there are (in a number of typical school courses these predominate), the greater the part played by descriptions by experts in the subject. The more manual-practical factors there are (and these would be frequent in many industrial courses), the better the information derived from observation. Systematic observations will often give a clearer picture of the frequency of various behavioral acts than an individual expert's statements.

In choosing experts in a subject, it should be remembered that the constructor appointed probably often has sufficient qualifications to make an expert description. He was presumably chosen for his competence in that subject. But it is quite possible and often desirable that for this particular part of the work an even more highly qualified person, a top-ranking expert in the field, should be consulted. This applies especially to fields in which there has been rapid development in recent decades. In that case it may be only the outstanding scholar or scientist who is sufficiently qualified to be able to state what is really fundamental at the time, without having to fall back on traditional material.

The expert in a subject, however, needs a certain amount of instruction in how to formulate his survey in such a way as to provide a practical basis for further work. Such instructions would usually be drawn up by a programming specialist in collaboration with the organization's own expert in the subject.

A characteristic of the various knowledge items etc. that the programmer might try to get early information about is the "level of learning" expected from the student. In Figure 2.4 above, some illustrations of various levels were given (column D). Espich & Williams (1967) recommend two interviews with subject-matter experts: the first to obtain a list of relevant facts to include in the program, the second to determine the level of knowledge required of the student for each fact (or group of facts). Levels may be classified in various ways. Espich & Williams use five: (1) exposure level (enrichment material good for reading smoothness etc. but not necessary to retain), (2) recognition level, (3) recall level (non-verbatim recall of definitions etc.), (4) memory level (verbatim recall), (5) concept level (ability to apply knowledge in tasks of generalization, discrimination etc.).

This two-step procedure is sometimes easier to use, since it allows separate focus upon (1) subject-matter and (2) determination of behaviors related to subject-matter.

5.3.2 *Forming a Basis for Priorities and Making Decisions*

After the completion of as detailed and comprehensive a search for information as the particular purpose and the existing resources permit, the question still remains of how decisions are to be made on the basis of the information now available. It is quite conceivable that the total picture given by the information will show a considerable degree of conflict between the different sources (in the discussion of goals for universities, for example, the opinions of "consumers" and research workers often differ), or that the objectives outlined in official quarters are greatly at variance with what powerful tides of public opinion or objective observations deem reasonable. If this type of picture should emerge, it should not be the duty of the research worker to make the decisions or try to conjure away the difficulties; instead he should pass the information to the official decision makers most closely concerned, who will thus be given a more satisfactory basis—with all the facts on the table—for future action. It should be added, however, that such contradictory and unwieldy material is not often obtained. More usually, the various sources of information complement one another, and no real conflict arises between official objectives and the rest of the sources; instead the latter make possible concretion and specification of the comparatively vague and general terms of the official source. In such cases the collection of material has provided a considerably improved foundation for the work remaining to be done.

It is difficult to state general rules for the measures needed for forming a basis for priorities and making decisions, since in the actual transition from the collection of material to the making of decisions the measures vary considerably depending on the type of objective (partial or final) and the type of education concerned. In any case, it is important to decide on firm strategies. Up to now, however, relatively little systematic work has been done here —within the no man's land between research-workers and politicians.

Normally it can be an advantage to keep the two phases clearly separate. Before deciding on priorities the research-worker or the worker in educational development must first gather information; this can be seen as a sub-task under the heading "goal seeking". In some cases the decision-making can be a fairly simple procedure without particularly far-reaching consequences (e.g. in the case of sub-sections of a course area the general outline of which has already been decided, or when the available material is clear-cut); in other cases, on the other hand, it can have considerable political consequences and as a result involve quite different categories of persons. This decision stage is a sub-phase under the heading "goal focusing".

Sometimes the information needed on priorities emerges more or less automatically at an early stage. But it is often an advantage to collect as much comprehensive information as possible first, and *then* find out how it is evaluated or ranked by various interested groups. The main advantage here is that the evaluation or ranking can be carried out more comprehensively, once a primary basis has been obtained. This can mean that some of the groups named in Box 5.2 are contacted twice: first to get spontaneous information on objectives, secondly to get from different points of view evaluations of (rankings of) lists of partial objectives, compiled on the basis of the first collection of data.

It is perhaps rather unusual to incorporate an "evaluation phase" separated in time from the primary search for information in this way. Concrete examples and more detailed arguments can be studied, however, within the framework, for example, of Project B, mentioned earlier (see Gestrelius, 1970).

5.3.3 *Formulating Objectives*

When it comes to formulating objectives, it has proved advantageous (a) to express the objectives in terms of behavior, and (b) to try to combine the formulation of objectives with the working out of "terminal tests" (final tests which contain tasks corresponding to all points stated in the objectives).

Many educational technologists now agree that an effective statement of objectives has the following qualities:

(a) *It does not confuse description of courses (process description) with description of objectives (product description).* A programmer with little experience is sometimes inclined to confuse the description of terminal objectives with the description of what happens while the course is in progress. This confusion may arise from the over-optimistic tendency to obscure the distinction between what the teacher goes through in class and what the student actually learns. Obviously, however, there may often be a considerable difference between what is "taught" (if by this is meant what is presented during a course) and what is "learnt" (if by this we mean demonstrable additions to or changes in the student's behavioral repertoire).

It is a somewhat trivial, but important fact that "initial behavior", "course process", and "terminal behavior" are three separate phenomena (distinct both logically and in time). Sometimes it is necessary to formulate "starting requirements". In that case we describe what the student must know before taking a certain course. In other situations there are grounds for formulating a "description of the course" (as often happens in a syllabus or a prospectus). But when, in planning self-instructional material, we have to draw up a "terminal description" we are attempting something quite different. Then we have to state what a student is able to do after he has completed the course (if the course functions the way we want it to).

To take an obvious example: The statement "The principles of programmed instruction are discussed on the basis of an historical survey and a detailed account of Skinner's theory" presents us with a "course description" ("process description"). A "terminal description" ("product description"), on the other hand, might look like this. "Should be able to describe at least three basic principles of programmed instruction and state at least two essential features of Skinner's theory correctly."

(b) *The description of objectives concerns, to the greatest degree possible, observable* (and thus clearly communicable and verifiable) *behaviors.* It thus avoids terms which can be given varying interpretations by different readers. It is not enough, for example, to say that a student should know a law of physics A, or that he should understand a mathematical argument B. We must try to explain *how* the student is to *demonstrate* that he "knows" A or "understands" B. We prescribe a "mastery repertory" (Gilbert, 1969).

Many words commonly found in syllabuses are on a low level of precision, that is, different interpretations are often possible. Among the terms which occur very frequently, but which are somewhat ambiguous in the description of a course are words such as "understand", "know about", "appreciate". It is obviously not wrong to say that the student should "understand" a certain situation, but it is often not specific enough to provide a good starting-point for preparing material. Unless we indicate some explicitly observable signs of comprehension, it is difficult for us to agree whether a student has attained the desired objective. Examples of words which have a more unambiguous meaning than those cited above are: "construct", "enumerate", "give examples of", "identify", "reproduce", "write down" etc. As a rule, then, such words referring to observable behavior, are preferred in our terminal descriptions. The five words "identify", "name", "describe", "order", and "construct" are considered to cover most goals within the cognitive domain and thus to be broadly useful for these purposes (Gerlach, 1971).

Let us look at the following descriptions: (a) "The student should be able to appreciate fully Swedish poetry of the 'forties'." (b) "The student should have gained a complete understanding of the causes of the Cuban Revolution." Do these two statements satisfy the requirement of "communicability" set up above? Obviously not. Neither of them identifies clearly observable behavior. Strengthening additions (such as "appreciate *fully*", "*complete* understanding") do not usually make it easier to give such statements an unambiguous interpretation.

(c) *The description of objectives also states the prerequisites, which define more closely the demands made on the student's behavior.* We do not simply say, for example, that the student should be able to type out a French business letter. We must also state if he is to be able to do it both from oral dictation and from a handwritten manuscript (type of stimulus), if he is to be able to do it both on an ordinary office typewriter and on an electric typewriter (type of tool), if he is to be able to do it with or without the help of dictionary (type of aid permitted) etc. (Among other things, a clear definition of the stimulus situation is important in order to prevent what unfortunately often happens: that we unconsciously lower our standards and make do with indirect simulation of the type verbal answer to verbal stimulus instead of a more direct response in a complicated concrete problem situation.)

We distinguished above between a volume of knowledge which is activated "spontaneously" (that is with minimal cues) and a volume of knowledge which is only activated when a choice of specific alternatives is to be made. A given series of alternative answers is an example of one kind of situational prerequisites, and such prerequisites—if they are acceptable to our purpose in the course—should be stated in the description of objectives since their acceptance in fact makes the objective different. The behavioral requirement can usually be made quite clear by using such phrases as "Without a dictionary the student should be able to . . ." ("aids"); "Using log. tables the student should be able to . . ."; "If the student is presented with a list of . . ., he should be able to identify . . ." ("alternative choices given"), etc.

One method of checking to see whether the situational prerequisites have been made specific enough is to let someone go through a collection of test items in the subject-matter area and sort them into two piles: those covered by the given description of objectives ("the plus category") and those not covered ("the minus category"). If there are too many test items in the first category, more than the programmer intended, or if there is considerable hesitation in making this classification, then the description of objectives must be made more specific (i.e., more restrictions must be introduced). If there are too many test items in "the minus category" (more than the programmer intended), then the description of objectives must be changed so as to include fewer restrictions (the number of aids allowed must be increased, etc.).

If such a check is to work satisfactorily, we must assume that the programmer himself knows precisely what the goal is. In other words, in this case the check does not apply to the suitability of the goal, but only tests how well the programmer has succeeded in making his goal clear to others in his terminal description. If the check works out well, we may say that we have adequately described the conditions necessary for excluding irrelevant student behavior (behavior that cannot be taken as evidence of the goal having been attained). Nor have we excluded too much.

(d) *As soon as we are dealing with a continuum of possible achievements in the relevant behavioral field, the description of objectives should give a "pass criterion",* or liminal value, i.e. the lower threshold value which the student ought to attain. What is meant, for example, by typing out an English business letter? What demands do we make on speed? How many errors are we prepared to tolerate? (This demand for a clear statement of liminal values contrasts strongly with the numerous expressions to be found in traditional curricula, such as "some knowledge of . . .", "deeper knowledge of . . .".)

Such a threshold value or "minimum for success" can be expressed in many different ways. Two of the most common are to state a time-limit or the error tolerance. The error tolerance may in turn be expressed either as an acceptable deviation from a certain standard ("negative formulation") or as the smallest percentage of a given series of problems which the student should be able to solve ("positive formulation").

(e) Finally, *the description of objectives should be inclusive; it must not exclude any part of the total goal area,* even if one particular part should prove more difficult to formulate in terms of specific behavior. Non-cognitive (e.g. attitudinal) objectives can be difficult to describe precisely; this fact must not be used as an excuse for not including them in the goal-analytic phase.

If another person conversant with the subject can, after reading the description of objectives and seeing the test results of a number of students, state which of these students have succeeded in attaining the objective and which have not, and if this person's classification of the students agrees with that of the person who drew up the description, then the description has been successful in communicating the objectives unambiguously, and the main purpose has been achieved. If this is not so, then communication has broken down. The various features of a good description referred to above are neither absolutely essential in themselves, nor necessarily entirely adequate. However, experience has shown them to be useful *aids for increasing communicability.* It might therefore save time and trouble to bear them in mind.

The explicit specification of precise and behaviorally formulated objectives are certainly an important part of the total process of instructional programming. The discussion around this procedure has, however, been somewhat ambiguous and controversial, and some people have rightly resented the notion that all other types of goal description should be taboo. Objectives can well be thought of as being on various levels of abstractness or inclusiveness, levels which are related to each other and useful in different connections. For instance, Jenkins & Deno (1970) talk about four such levels, with different degrees of distance from observable data. *"Level A" objectives* are global educational objectives, referring to future states; subsumed here are such expressions as "becomes good citizen", "becomes well-adjusted member of society". *"Level B" objectives* refer to hypothetical dispositional states (knows, understands, appreciates, values etc.) and bridge the gap between global educational objectives and specific item forms. *"Level C" objectives* refer to inferred generative capabilities of the learner in such a form that they specify "item types" (classifies, defines, produces examples, predicts). *"Level D" objectives,* finally, have the form of specific test items (writes, checks, points to, says etc.). Whereas society (especially its visionaries) is responsible for setting level A and B objectives, curriculum developers and educational psychologists have to deal with the links between B and C. Test writers and instruction designers would have to cooperate on level D. Teachers often have to operate at all levels.

Obviously, there would be other ways of describing the continuum from more abstract and inclusive objectives to more concrete and specific ones; the important thing is that several levels are legitimate, depending upon the particular situation, and that they are closely related to each other. When writing a catalogue of performance specifications, it may often be worthwhile (for instance, in discussions with teachers) to add statements on the significance of the objectives, that is, to indicate the larger or ultimate objective, of which the more specific one is a sub-item. (Cf. Mager, 1968.)

5.3.4. *Logical Goal Analysis and Other A Priori Checks*

As one sub-phase within the process of "goal focusing", we might wish to include a "logical goal analysis" for the purpose of studying the final formulations of the various goal components in relation to each other. Difficulties can arise, for example, if some objectives conflict with others. In such cases of conflict, the person responsible for analyzing the objectives usually has to refer the question back to the decision-making level for a new decision on priorities. A preliminary logical analysis is naturally made during the goal-seeking stage, e.g. in the text analyses, but the final logical check should be made at the same time as the descriptions of objectives are given their final form.—Other a priori checks can also be made, e.g. expert opinions on how realistic the descriptions of objectives are in the light of earlier experience of the target-groups in question.

5.3.5 *Adjustment of Objectives: A Posteriori Checks and Revision*

In one sense the goal-analytical work is complete once the final version of the objectives has been precisely defined and operationalized in the form of a terminal test. After that it is up to the teachers (or the constructors of instructional materials) to attain the objectives. If the first attempts achieve little success, it is usually not the objectives that need revising, but the methods or time schedule. Normally a teaching system cannot be considered ready until the given objective has been reached.

The chances of carrying out this ideal strategy, however, depend largely on resources: time for teaching and time for systematic improvement of methods. There is a strong possibility that in some cases (and despite what are above called a priori checks) we have aimed unrealistically high and that a revision of the levels of the objectives is well-motivated. Resources can also change in a way not predictable at the start, such as when the time allotted to a course is reduced. (Even though one in principle does not want to accept the present all too dominant role played by time schedules, there are naturally often sound reasons for this kind of limitation of resources.)

The normal techniques for checking the quality of methods and material in a new teaching system can in some situations also be used to check how realistic the objectives are, allowing for a certain initial level in the target-group and certain resources. If empirical tests of this kind suggest that the level of the objectives is unrealistic, then it may be necessary to revise the objectives and undertake new tests.

It would take too long to discuss this supplementary work in detail; what has been said above must suffice to make it clear that work on goal analysis can also involve a gradual adjustment of objectives, making use of empirical feed-back.

Another potential adjustment that *could* be made is to lower the general "level of success" for the program. A criterion often mentioned in the U.S. is that 90 % of the students should achieve 90 % of the objectives before the programmer stops revising. This may be difficult to attain, for example, when the programmer has no control of the entering skill of older students and those entering skills are in basic areas (such as, ability to write or ability to think analytically).

5.4 A Few Queries

It is obvious that often when people say that they are carrying out goal analyses, they are in fact only working with a relatively small part of the spectrum of tasks outlined here. The reasons for this are sometimes sound; on other occasions they simply seem to be unaware of the opportunities available.

Among the influences which have served to bring goal-analytical work much more noticeably to the fore in general educational discussions, has been the interest in programmed instruction and in systems of educational technology (see e.g. a "classic" like Mager, 1961, or discussion reports like Popham et al., 1969). But the point that is most heavily stressed in these contexts is often the precise formulation of objectives. Presumably the process of instruction can be speeded up if teacher and students have a clearer idea than is usually the case of where they are going; irrelevant behavior then tends to diminish and the student trains more intensively what is later going to be tested. On the whole, this emphasis on the value of formulated objectives as an instrument of guidance and focusing has had a very beneficial influence on both the general discussion of objectives and the work being done on systems of material and methods. Nevertheless, it is surprising how indifferent some of those urging the need for precision can sometimes be to the relevance and significance of the given objectives seen from other points of view. In such cases our criterion 5 (the formulation of objectives) has been allowed to weigh so heavily that there is a risk of other points of view (the seeking of goals and decisions on goals) being neglected entirely. This state of affairs has led to some rather strange contributions to educational discussions, which sometimes give the impression that one is forced to choose between precise trivialities or diffuse but significant objectives. If it could be made clear that the setting up of objectives and the formulation of objectives are *two stages*—both very important—in one and the same goal analysis, then the debate would become less muddled.

There are other examples of an unhealthy bias. The demand for empirical foundations has among other things resulted in extensive and extremely useful consumer analyses being made. These analyses have sometimes, as was hinted above, aroused criticism. This criticism has occasionally been expressed in political slogans ("we shall not let education be manipulated by the business world and high finance"), but has all the same contained an important core of insight, namely that objectives should not be set up on a one-sided basis. Short-term utilitarian perspectives (dredged from consumer analyses) should naturally not dominate educational planning to such an extent that we deprive ourselves of the chance of developing completely new ways of achieving such a reconstruction of society which we agree to be desirable. Fundamental values must in some way be inserted in the equation, so that we are not tempted to equate consumer analyses with educational planning. The work carried out on consumer analyses has been very important, to some extent pioneering, but those interpreting it have perhaps on occasion been over-eager in generalizing the results. They then strongly emphasize our criterion 1 and at the same time tend to forget criterion 2, which balances it, and are not always particularly interested in the other criteria.

Considering these various tendencies towards what has here been called one-sidedness, the following question seems self-evident: If we accept the criteria given above as a description of a complete, systematic goal analysis, to what extent does this paragon actually exist in our hurried and stressed environment? This question would be worth studying more closely, but at the present time the answer would probably be that such complete analyses are at least not common. And what then is the reason for this? One important factor is naturally that the technique is not widely known. But can there be other reasons? Is their value perhaps doubted in relation to the amount of work involved?

In fact, this field, which has attracted increasing interest and activity, contains a whole series of subjects suitable for research and developmental work. It would be of interest, for example, to set up a series of alternative models for goal-analytic processes and for statements of objectives. Many questions then follow naturally: How common are the various models and the various types of goal descriptions in different educational developmental contexts? What goal concepts and goal descriptions exist at present in the sphere of practical education (among those working on curricula, writing textbooks and training teachers, among administrators, teachers and students)? In what ways do these goal concepts and goal descriptions differ from the norms most commonly recommended by experts on goal analyses? Which advantages or disadvantages do various categories see in the more exact methods? Which arguments occur most commonly against the use of increased precision? And to what extent can one show, by means of experiments, clear-cut effects of strict goal analyses in various practical situations?

This problem area of goal analyses, so hastily touched upon here, is of central importance and can have practical consequences for several aspects of educational planning. There is good reason, therefore, for making it the object of further conceptual analyses and discussion and increased empirical investigation.

5.5 Special Aids: Terminal Charts, Terminal Cards, and Terminal Tests

It is often helpful to describe "terminal requirements" in the form of a "terminal chart" (or a series of "terminal cards") and a representative "terminal test" based on these.

Specifier: / Terminal behavior:	A Conditions given (incl. aids permitted)	B Minimum speed	C Maximum error tolerance
T_1			
T_2			
T_3			
⋮	⋮	⋮	⋮
T_n			

Figure 5.1 Basic principles for a "terminal chart"

A "*terminal chart*" is simply a system of cells in which the horizontal rows represent the desired objectives and the columns give the special conditions in which the student should be able to give evidence of the behavior in question, e.g. (a) the aids with which the student should be able to solve the problem and (b) the degree of proficiency with which he should be able to do it.

The appearance of the chart will vary considerably depending on the particular subject-matter dealt with, but some of its major aspects are illustrated in Figure 5.1.

A few examples. If the terminal behavior is the ability to work out a correlation coefficient of a certain type, the question of "aids permitted" is important when presenting the course material. Under some circumstances we may require the ability to make these calculations without any aids at all. In that case we put "0" in *column A* in the table and then we must make sure that the study material gives the student the kind of training that will enable him to work out these coefficients independently and confidently without using formulae or models. In other cases perhaps we only require the calculations to be made with the aid of formulae. In still other cases, when a job requires less independent calculations, we do not even ask this much, but only that the student has a certain amount of practice in following a step-by-step model. This model then comes under the heading of "aids permitted".

In many tests of proficiency, the speed of working (*column B*) is very important. We do not convey much information if we state only that a pupil should be "able to transmit a Morse telegram" or be "able to receive a Morse telegram". An indication of the minimum requirements for the transmission speed and the receiving speed (e.g., the number of signs per minute) would be much more to the point.

The error tolerance to be allowed (*column C*) must often be considered together with the requirement of speed. In several cases, absolute perfection is so essential that the error tolerance must be considered 0. This applies, for instance, to certain instrument readings in flying an aeroplane, where even slight mistakes can endanger life. In other cases, of course, we can be a little more tolerant, e.g. slight mistakes in typing a running text.

As the number of terminal objectives is often large, and as it may be useful for further work to have descriptions of these terminal objectives in a form that readily allows rearrangements, additions etc., it is often convenient to work with "*terminal cards*", at least initially, instead of a fixed "terminal chart". Each card then corresponds to a horizontal segment in the "terminal chart". The card should thus include the same data as is contained in one row of cells even though the information need not necessarily be presented in the same format (column distribution).

To obtain further guidance for the construction of the study material and to get clear-cut instruments for estimating the effectiveness of the material from the very start, it is useful, even at this stage, to draw up a representative "terminal test", i.e. a series of tasks containing sample tests of the proficiency and knowledge which the student is expected to have acquired in the terminal situation. The "terminal chart" and the "terminal cards" provide the basis for the construction of the test. All the essential part-objectives will normally be represented in the test; the conditions given (including aids), the requirements of speed, and the error tolerance should be taken into account.

5.6 Goal Analysis and Taxonomies

During recent years various classifications of behaviors (often called taxonomies) have attracted considerable attention among educators, such as the classification systems proposed by Bloom (1956), Guilford (1958), Krathwohl et al. (1964), Gagné (1965, 1970), and Merrill (cf. Tennyson & Merrill, 1971; Tennyson & Boutwell, 1971). Sometimes educational technologists wonder whether these various classification schemes are sufficiently realistic and useful to deserve this widespread attention. However, for the instructional designer they may be of value in at least three respects:

(1) In so far as they intend to be and are inclusive of all behaviors of interest to instructors, they can be used during the goal-analytic stage as a mapping instrument to check that no areas of real concern to a particular project for development of instructional material have been neglected.

Box 5.3 A comparison between the classification systems of Bloom and Gagné (as perceived by Gagné, 1971)

Major terms in the Bloom system	General category terms as used by Gagné (1971)	Corresponding "verb labels"
Psychomotor Domain	Motor Skills	"execute"
Cognitive Domain:		
Knowledge	Verbal Information	"state"
Comprehension etc.	Intellectual skills*	"demonstrate"
Synthesis, Analysis	Cognitive strategies	"originate"
Affective Domain	Attitudes	"choose"

* The eight forms of learning as described earlier by Gagné (1965, 1970) are considered to be eight types of "intellectual skills".

(2) In so far as they intend to be and are built up to describe a psychologically valid hierarchical sequence of forms of learning (from simple to complex), they can be used during subject-matter analysis and the building up of instructional materials as a guide for sequencing. If two terminal objectives, X and Y, are on different levels of the hierarchy in such a way that behavior X is a necessary prerequisite to Y, the obvious learning sequence would be: first X, then Y. If a particular terminal objective T cannot be adequately dealt with, unless the learner first reaches a lower-level behavior S (not mentioned in the goal catalogue), this "enabling objective" S should be taught before the terminal objective T.

(3) In so far as they intend to be and are expressed in operational language, they may be used as an aid in the construction of valid and inclusive measurement instruments.

It should be noted, of course, that not all classification systems have all these three intentions, and that even where such an intention is stated, the result may still be debatable in some respects.

It may be of interest to note in particular that the two criteria of (1) inclusiveness and (2) guidance for hierarchical sequencing may be impossible to reach at the same time for the whole area. According to a recent communication by Gagné (1971), his well-known eight types of learning all fall within one area out of five more general areas of learning outcomes, viz. the area of "intellectual skills"; and he considers this particular area to be the only one among these five to be characterized by sub-skills to be learned in hierarchy (cf. Box 5.3).

It should be reasonable to expect that the present high interest in the area of taxonomies, not only in the U.S. but also elsewhere (cf. a Swedish proposal in Klingberg, 1970, and such examples of related German discussion as Flechsig, 1970, Boeckmann, 1971, and Weltner, 1971), will hasten developments to make the schemes better empirically underpinned and more useful to instructional designers. In so far as a classification system is used as a checking aid in the goal-analytic stage (and this is what is most relevant to the present chapter), it is obviously desirable that not too few behavior categories be used. Systems which are both broad and detailed would seem to be best suited for this particular purpose.

6. Student Analysis and Situation Analysis

6.1 Student Analysis

The basic analysis of prerequisites also includes a student analysis, i.e. a survey of the special characteristics of the intended target population. We have particular reason to study the students' *"initial repertoire"* (the behavioral repertoire they take to the study situation: previous knowledge and existing skills etc.) and their probable "*medial situation*" (the experiences that await them and the opportunities for training which are available *between* the study situation and the terminal situation proper.

In general, we start from what has sometimes been called a Characteristics × Prescription interaction model, expressing our differential instructional hypotheses as "if—then" statements (Stolurow, 1971). The "if" clause states the diagnosis, and the "then" clause gives the prescription. "If learner L_1 has characteristics C_1, then treat him T_1."

6.1.1 *Expanded Terminal Chart*

The result of the student analysis should preferably be incorporated into an *"expanded terminal chart"*. The data on the target population are introduced as extra "specifiers", which provide further information on the prerequisites for the training course. As shown in Figure 6.1, these data can, for example, be placed in a Column D ("initial prerequisites") and a Column E ("medial influence").

The initial prerequisites we are thinking of here are primarily previous knowledge and already existing skills (certain other prerequisites will be mentioned further on). "Readiness" is obviously one of the most important predictors of success in learning. When the *entire* target population has certain pre-knowledge, significant cuts can naturally be made in the study material. This often happens in courses for adults, which recruit people with basic vocational training. When a large part but *not* the entire target population is thought to have previous knowledge, a special "supplementary course" is needed for those who have no previous knowledge and in addition a "filter test" to extract this group, in the cases when it is not obvious in advance.

Specifier: / Terminal behavior:	A Conditions given (incl. aids permitted)	B Minimum speed	C Maximum error tolerance	D Initial prerequisites	E Medial influence
T_1					
T_2					
T_3					
⋮	⋮	⋮	⋮	⋮	⋮
T_n					

Figure 6.1 Expanded terminal chart

Column D ("initial prerequisites") is thus concerned with the past. An assessment should be made for each separate desired terminal behavior, stating to what extent it may already exist as initial behavior for the target population as a whole or in part.

Column E ("medial influence") attempts instead to take a look at the future. In some cases the individual's ordinary occupation (which he practises between the study occasion and the terminal situation) makes it easier for him to retain the knowledge acquired. In other cases, however, it can make it more difficult for him ("interference"). A probability assessment of this is made in Column E. To what extent does "medial behavior" (the existent behavior between the study situation and the terminal situation) reinforce the desired terminal reactions? To what extent does it interfere with the retention of skills? Any attempt to make such an assessment on the basis of acquaintance with the target population can often of necessity be no more than approximate.

Let us suppose that we are dealing with behavior for which the terminal situation is mobilisation and the study situation a military course. If the particular target population consists of people who can in their normal occupations maintain the acquired skills, then we can say that the medial behavior forms a *supporting connecting link* between study behavior and terminal behavior (and we might signify this with "+ +" for "strongly supporting" and "+" for "rather strongly supporting" when it comes to individual skills). In many cases the medial behavior is neither supporting nor interfering. We then put "0" in Column E and perhaps count on the acquired knowledge and skills gradually diminishing as time passes.

Finally, in other cases we must take *interference* into account. It can be a question of individual skills: e.g. if two different methods of notation are used in civilian and military practice, or if the students use two different shorthand systems (one in the study and terminal situations and another in the medial situations). But it can also involve more general behavioral roles connected with a certain position in society. A man who in his everyday life is used to leading others and acting independently may often find it more difficult than someone who has a more subordinate civilian position to enter into the role of the submissive and obedient private soldier, which he practised for a few months in his youth and which he is expected to resume in the event of mobilisation.—The idea of having the right man in the right place in a mobilisation context means—using our present terms—making sure that the "terminal role" and the "medial role" are mutually "consonant", so that the medial behavior becomes a reinforcing factor rather than an interfering one. In many cases, however, *general role dissonance* or *special behavior dissonance* must be accepted as unavoidable and this should then be marked in Column E (e.g. with one or two minus signs to denote a lesser or greater degree of interference), and then measures must also be taken in the training situation to make the effect of the training maximally resistant to interference.

The *interference phenomenon* can sometimes occur *simultaneously as an "initial prerequisite" and as a "medial influence"* and thereby have an increased effect. This kind of dual-effect often has to be taken into account, for example, in the teaching of foreign languages. An English student comes to the course in French or German with deep-rooted English language habits, including patterns for the combination of language categories, a set of well-trained sounds and special intonation series. Some of these combination patterns, sound and intonation sequences are parallel in the student's mother tongue and in the new language. These cause relatively little difficulty. In other cases, however, there is a lack of agreement and this is where the established language habits make learning more difficult. This interference continues both during and after the course, since training in the mother tongue goes on all the time.

Opinions are divided on the best way to counteract the effect of the interference factors. No-one can deny, however, that they do exist and that they exert a strong influence. This is shown most clearly in the fact that school children from different countries make very different mistakes when learning a particular foreign language. This should in its turn mean that when training any one language, the main emphasis should be placed on different points for different groups of students (representing different language areas or sometimes even different dialectal regions).

Linguistic interferences should, therefore, be considered a matter of central importance when self-instructing aids are being constructed. For that reason it is often advisable, when working out courses in foreign languages, to use a slightly *different form of expanded terminal table, where the interference phenomenon is given a separate column.* It is naturally *possible* to learn languages with the help of courses which have not been adapted on the basis of existing interferences. The courses which are often arranged in a country for mixed groups of foreigners prove this, as do the cases when a course originally intended for use in another country has been "borrowed". There is reason to believe, however, that this often leads to a considerable loss of efficiency. Some students are given unnecessarily long training on points which cause them no difficulty, while others get far too little practice on the items which are the most problematic for them.

6.1.2 *"Modified Terminal Test"*

The expanded terminal table might also lead to certain modifications being made in the terminal test. The types of behavior that can with certainty be said to exist as initial behavior in the student group in question naturally need not be tested, but can be omitted from the test. This means that the data in Col. D must be taken into consideration. Furthermore, we must often try to estimate the immediate effect of a particular study material, even when the terminal situation is remote in time. In that case we should also, when constructing the test, heed the circumstances stated in Column E, together with the interval of time which is relevant in this context. Thus the immediate test becomes a *"pseudoterminal"*, and there is often good reason for making these immediate demands somewhat higher than the terminal table otherwise declares to be necessary.

Some readers perhaps think that this two-stage procedure (*first* establishing a terminal table in general terms and a subsequent terminal test and *then* a terminal table extended on the basis of student analysis and a subsequently modified terminal test) is unnecessarily circuitous. Would it not be just as easy—with some general information about the student group—to concentrate directly on the second stage of the goal analysis? There are naturally quite a lot of cases in which the use of this shorter procedure is plausible.

There are two main arguments, however, in favor of sometimes using the more detailed two-stage procedure. The process becomes more explicit, which reduces the risk that hitherto unexplored possibilities are neglected simply because of tradition (the usual pattern for teaching a particular student group, e.g. a particular age group). Secondly, it is not necessary to start working from the beginning again as soon as one wants to build up a new course in the same field for *another* group of students (the first stage remains intact, as a foundation for future work).

6.1.3 *Further Points to Be Considered in the Student Analysis*

So far we have for the most part only discussed student analysis from the point of view of concrete previous knowledge in the field to be dealt with in the course. The student naturally has many other important sides, which should as far as possible be known and taken into consideration from the start, when the course is being planned. Examples which can be given are the students' level of intelligence, reading ability, general background experience together with their purpose in studying (and subsequent study-motivation).

Some early studies (see e.g. Little, 1934 and Porter, 1959) seemed to show little connection between the *intelligence* of the students and the results they achieved in programmed teaching. This gave rise to optimistic ideas that programmed teaching would wholly eliminate the significance of varying levels of intelligence in learning. The only difference would be in the length of time taken to learn by those with greater or less ability. The correlation between intelligence and student results in current teaching was seen as an expression of that teaching's lack of instructional effectiveness: what a student got out of a course depended most on what he "took with him" to the course. It was thought that if the course were planned more adequately, it should communicate its message regardless of the level of intelligence of the students.

Experienced teachers found it difficult to accept this excessive optimism and later studies (e.g. Silberman, 1961; Shay, 1961) seemed to show that the conclusions mentioned above were premature. Naturally, the individual rate of work and the student-guided flow of information can result in the disappearance of some "unnecessary" failures. The inability to grasp an account quickly should have *less* significance in the use of self-instructing study material than in conventional teaching. But the idea that general intelligence should suddenly, as if by magic, cease to have any relation to the ability to learn must, for the time being, be dismissed as wishful thinking. But the case is not closed; and the degree of optimism permissable is a matter for research.

At the present stage of knowledge it seems reasonable that the average intelligence of the target population must be taken into consideration both in the wording and in deciding the "density of information" (more about this in a later context), and also that an attempt should be made to judge whether or not the target population is very heterogeneous with regard to intelligence. In many cases those taking part in a course form a relatively homogeneous group and then there is usually no reason for working with parallel courses. In some cases, however, the variation is exceptionally great. It can then be worthwhile to consider either *parallel courses* with varying degrees of "information-density" or *a course with branching* (e.g. with additional built-in repetition for those students who prove to need this). This point will be discussed further below in connection with the concept of "flow model".

Reading ability, perhaps in particular the command of vocabulary, is obviously of great importance if the student is to be able to assimilate a certain study material. Even the ordinary textbooks are usually carefully adapted to the reading ability of the target population. But in self-instructing material this aspect is of even greater importance. Here, unlike in ordinary classroom teaching, there may be no teacher available to explain the parts that are difficult to understand. Reading comprehension tests for representative groups of the target population can in this context play a useful part at the planning stage. This question should naturally also be kept in mind during the successive testing of the preliminary version.

Acquaintance with the general background experience of the students is important because it makes it possible to provide meaningful illustrative material and "correlative stimuli" (to make use of the terminology used above) which promote learning.

Certain series of associations are natural in some "symbol environments", but completely foreign in others. If one is acquainted with the target population's common symbol environment (determined partly in an adult group by education and vocational experience), then it is easier to formulate the teaching material in such a way that it fits in with the conceptions the students already have. This is the best way of using the "net of associations" which the students have already acquired to bind the new material in the "repertoire of associations". If possible, one should try to get some idea of the natural "symbol environment" at the preparation stage and then all later revision work should obviously be guided in part by how well one has succeeded in making use of the student group's background experience.

The target population's particular purpose in studying is naturally of significance for the level of motivation. If there is *no* intrinsic motivation behind the studies, i.e. if they are experienced as compulsory, it may be necessary to incorporate special measures to promote motivation. In such cases, it becomes even more important to associate to the student's own experience and to use examples which make him feel that the material can—despite everything—be relevant to him personally. Sometimes an item should be treated from different angles for people with different study-purposes and different interests. If such groups with clearly separate interests occur within the student group in question, it may be necessary to construct parallel versions of the course material for some sections of the course (for more on this, see below). In general, the main aim—both when the group is relatively homogeneous in purpose and when various sub-groups have different purposes—should be to make the study material as "consonant to purpose" as possible. If this is done consciously and according to a clear plan, there is a greater chance of achieving positive gains in motivation and thereby also making the process of learning more efficient.

Less essential—but not without importance in some contexts—is the fact that the purely external form of presentation can create an interest in studying which the study-material in itself does not provide. An example of this is the mechanical form of presentation which, by the process of manipulation involved, creates an additional interest in the same way as a gambling machine. The most important thing is naturally always to make the study-material interesting in itself, but these devices used to heighten interest should not be despised if they really prove to be effective and are at the same time easy to produce. Often it is not the mechanical manipulation in itself which is interesting, but the fact that the machine gives continual information on what has been achieved. Like an automatic target, it shows immediately—sometimes by means of a dramatic light or sound signal—how an attempt to solve a problem has succeeded. The value of such obvious praise-signals for the motivation of students who are nervous and anxious to succeed should not be underestimated. But naturally the individual differences should not be forgotten here either. A process which amuses and heightens the motivation of a boy in the lower forms of the comprehensive school can very well be an unnecessary source of disturbance and irritation to an educated adult with an intrinsic motive for his studies and who is used to dealing with complicated tasks independently (without the support of someone who shouts 'Bravo!' at every stage).

In general, increasing basic knowledge of differential psychology will probably give us useful hypotheses for designing instruction differently for many specific sub-groups within our target population, using also *personality variables*. Stolurow gives a list of examples of such hypotheses, based on available research findings (1971). We may quote a few tentative contingency statements: If the learner's anxiety level is high, give him: (a) a highly structured learning environment; (b) non-ego-involving directions; (c) positive feedback; and (d) an opportunity to work by himself.—If the learner's anxiety level is low, give him: (a) ego-involving directions; (b) negative feedback; and (c) an opportunity to work with a partner.—If the learner has a high need-achievement, give him a task he perceives to be moderately difficult. —If the learner has a low need-achievement, give him a task he perceives to be either very easy or very difficult.

To summarise, the main questions which anyone constructing study material must ask himself in connection with the student analysis are: a) Does the group have "previous knowledge" which makes some of the items included in the goal-specification unnecessary? b) What limits do the general intelligence and reading ability of the target population set for the degree of difficulty which can be used in presenting the material? c) In what way can knowledge of the students' background experience and purposes of study be used to make the material more efficient? d) In what way must the nature of the "medial situations" (what the student does in the interval between the study-situation and the terminal situation proper) be taken into consideration when the course is planned? e) To what extent can an analysis of probable "interferences" help us to pick out the items in the course which need most practice? f) Does the student group vary in different respects—intelligence, reading ability, background experience, personality, purposes of study etc.—to such an extent that differential treatment, such as parallel courses or courses with different branches are indicated or even necessary? We may also at this later assessment be forced to accept that some parts of the content of the goal-specification are *too* difficult for some section of the student group under given conditions.

It may be added (as a soothing remark to readers who tend to feel that the area of student analysis seems to be so vast as to be unmanageable) that some learner characteristics which happen to be overlooked during the analytic stage will lead to revisions when the program gets into testing. In this sense, there is a safety valve for student analysis that is not always available for other aspects of the preparatory analyses.

6.1.4 *Special Aids for Tentative Discussions on Goal-and-Student Characteristics*

In some situations we are faced with an interaction between a curriculum or program specialist (with technical know-how, but little information on subject-matter and learners) and a person (or group of persons) with intimate practical experience of subject-matter and learner, but with little knowledge of program development. The program specialist then uses the "practitioners" as a source of information in the goal-seeking phase as well as in the student analysis. In this case, however, and especially when the "practitioners" in question are not only an information source, but also important decision-makers (perhaps the managers who have requested the construction of the programs), it may be worthwhile to use special survey aids in tentative discussions on goals and learners before finally deciding on the program content. These aids will make possible any corrections needed in an early phase, especially important when the factual information on goals and students is sparse. Zielke (1970, p. 61 ff.; 1971) who has considerable experience of construction of programs for adults within firms recommends a procedure (what he calls "Faktenanalyse") which we will describe in a slightly abbreviated and modified form here as an example of what might be done under such circumstances.

The first step would be to collect whatever material is available as basic information on relevant course content (work norms, books, articles, interviews, etc.). From these the program designer writes a first-draft text ("Urscriptum"), condensing what seems to be the basic content, but naturally with both irrelevancies included and important things forgotten. From this

	Need not be included		Should be included				Should not be included	
	1 "Knows"		2 "Side inform."		3 "Must know"		4 "Not"	
	a	b	a	b	a	b	a	b
Question 1 Answer 1								
Question 2 Answer 2								
⋮	⋮		⋮		⋮		⋮	
Question *n* Answer *n*								

Figure 6.2 A question table for tentative discussions between program requester and program designer on goal-and-student characteristics

he constructs a "*question table*" (cf. the outline in Figure 6.2), including for each information unit of the preliminary text a question with its supposedly correct answer. The program requester, when confronted with this table, will be able to correct or improve each single formulation. In addition, the programmer and program requester can indicate the importance and program use of each item, for example, in the following respects:

Column 1: "*Knows*". Here those questions and answers with which the learner is already familiar in advance are checked. The content of these items should obviously not be programmed, although it might be used for illustrative or motivational purposes.—Column 2: "*Side information*". Things that should be mentioned in the program, but which are not central items on which tests are constructed.—Column 3: "*Must know*": Under this heading the central items are marked. These should be used for the final "basic text", make up the main thread of the learning program and be tested for in the terminal tests.—Column 4: "*Not*". These are items that should *not* be used in the program (for various reasons: information that is superfluous, out-of-date, or that might interfere).

In the column-parts marked *a* the proposals of the program designer are entered (using cross marks), whereas the column-part *b* is used for any proposals for change from the program requester. All change proposals are discussed, and this discussion forms the basis for a final decision.

6.2 Situation Analysis

We should, on the basis of the prerequisites given us by the goal analysis and the student analysis, try to create an adequate teaching situation. If on this basis we can decide upon the most effective forms of presentation, we should acquire the aids we need in order to present the material in this particularly effective way. And if, on the basis of goal analysis and student analysis, we can establish the time needed to reach the goal, then we can use this in deciding the time-structure of the course. In other words, we let the external organisation of the teaching situation emerge naturally from the analysis of what is most rational instructionally.

The educational "rationalization expert" seldom works, however, in an environment that is so flexible that he can immediately have all his wishes fulfilled; no matter how well-documented they are. On the contrary it is usually so that financial resources, available aids and specified lengths of time for courses are already fixed or can in each case only be influenced to a limited extent at the moment when the course is being planned. While plainly declaring what in his opinion would have been the most rational procedure, he must nevertheless see it as his task to make the best possible use of the resources available (with regard to time, aids and money, for example).

This means that an analysis of these external restrictions on the use of the study-material must also be included in the original preparatory work as factors to be remembered in the final selection of material and in assessing which presentation media etc. are economically feasible. But these assessments should be kept clearly separate from the goal-related and instructionally more rational considerations.

External restrictions must not gain such a foothold in the construction of the course that accidental circumstances at the beginning of the course gradually become tradition and are afforded the status of definite principles. This is possibly one of the greatest difficulties involved in constructing self-instructing material. The course must often be started in a very special "compulsory situation". The work of constructing the material is extensive and costly and one has no desire suddenly to tear up what one has created. And then as a result one has perhaps helped to preserve an unfortunate initial situation instead—as the intention was—of making a contribution to the continuing pedagogic development. If only one is aware of this danger, however, it should be easier to avoid it. One way is to keep a special record of emergency measures, measures taken because of external organisational circumstances, not based on pedagogically rational considerations—and then to use the record continually in the battle for a more rational state of affairs. This also leads naturally to revision of the working program as soon as this battle succeeds on some front.

7. Subject-Matter Analysis

The analysis of objectives gives a general survey of the terminal behavior which a specific instructional material is intended to lead to and involves thereby, at least implicitly, a preliminary delimitation and determination of its content. But before proceeding from this first delimitation to the actual writing of study material, however, a more detailed analysis of the subject-matter should normally be made. The main purpose of this analysis is to obtain a more thorough understanding of the *logical and psychological structure of the subject-matter,* with a view to deciding on the most effective instructional presentation.

The detailed procedure of this analysis must differ to some extent from case to case, depending on the general aim of the particular course and the suitability of the subject-matter in question for a particular analytical procedure. The following description, therefore, gives only a few *examples* of methods which can be useful in this connection. It should be added that in certain cases it is also possible to proceed more directly from the analysis of the objectives and the analysis of the students to the writing of study material. While a detailed goal analysis is almost always necessary, a subject-matter analysis of the type we shall illustrate here should be regarded rather as an aid and check than as an absolute necessity.

7.1 Examples of Procedures for Analyzing Logical Structure of Content

An analysis of the structure of content is obviously most easily applied to those subjects in which the logical structure is relatively fixed and fundamental. This is especially true of mathematics and certain scientific subjects. But sometimes this analysis can be more *useful* for subjects in which the logical structure is not so readily apparent in our conventional textbooks. In the latter case it is sometimes possible to make a radical improvement, after a study of the central structure of the subject, by getting rid of much unnecessary and distracting matter which is neither relevant to the objectives nor fulfilling any clear function as "instruction facilitators" on the route to the goals.

Some natural stages in such an analysis can be: (a) working out a list of the basic units of the area covered by the course, usually "concepts"; (b) trying to arrange these basic units in a logically meaningful sequence, normally within a hierarchical system; and (c) studying other relationships between the basic units in order to choose such "relational pairs" as are particularly significant from an instructional point of view.

7.1.1 *The "C-Catalogue" and the Preliminary "S-List"*

From a logical viewpoint it is normally natural to break down the content of a subject into fundamental *concepts* (here referred to as "*C*") and *statements* of different kinds about these concepts (here referred to as "*S*"). In a course on grammar, for example, one could regard such terms as "noun", "pronoun", "subject" and "predicate" as *"C units"*, and a statement of the type "Nouns and pronouns can function as a subject" could be regarded as an "*S unit*" or "statement" as it is used here. The "statements" often express relationships between the basic concepts.

Among the advocates of a logical analysis of course material we can mention Evans, Homme and Glaser (1962), whose analytical procedure is usually called the "Ruleg" system, since it is built up on "rules" and "examples". A number of ideas from the "Ruleg" system have been incorporated in the present discussion, but we have thought it natural not to limit the analysis to "rules" and "examples" (which are often relatively complex from a logical point of view) but prefer to start from somewhat more basic elements ("low-level units"). It should be added that the term "concept" is used here in a fairly non-technical sense, in so far as the catalogue system is assumed to be broadly useful for various types of low-level units, some of which may not meet the usual criteria of "concept" (as put forward in some psychological contexts). Hence, it may sometimes be better to use a term with fewer established associations, such as "C unit".

It is often expedient to have an expert in the particular subject area work out a detailed "*C-catalogue*" for the area delimited by the list of "terminal behaviors" decided upon. Every item of behavior in this list is examined, in this process, with the following question in mind: Are there one or more concept-units of which the students should have knowledge to be able to act correctly (and with sufficient flexibility)? Each item of behavior can imply a large number of different concept-units, but on the other hand, of course, a whole series of items of behavior may be connected with one concept or the same group of concepts. In other words, no one-to-one relationship exists between behaviors and necessary concepts. It may be worthwhile to draw up a simple table to show the relationships. Related to each terminal behavior description (T_1, T_2 etc.) there may be one or more terminal concepts (C_1, C_2

etc.). To reach some of these terminal concepts, some additional "enabling concepts" may also have to be included (C_{e1}, C_{e2} etc.):

$T_1 \rightarrow C_1, C_2, C_3 + C_{e1}$

$T_2 \rightarrow C_4 + C_{e4.1} + C_{e4.2}$

etc.

We should like to be certain that this analysis is made in an unprejudiced manner and without reference to current textbooks and similar study sources. The work at this stage should therefore be carried out as far as possible by experts at the highest level.

As a practical matter of technique, it would be an advantage if each separate concept were noted down (by means of a "key-word" together with any necessary explanation) on a separate card ("C-card"). The obvious advantage of a card-index here is that later on it will be so much simpler to handle the basic units when it comes to examining the relationships between them. This collection of C-cards constitutes the *"preliminary C-catalogue"* and thus implies a breaking-down of the total content into logical units.

Before this collection of concepts is used for structural studies, it would be advisable to check and supplement it by comparing it with existing source material in the field, as it is possible that the subject specialist may have overlooked certain significant concepts. But this *"source confrontation"* should be the *second* stage in the work, not the first. (If one starts from source material, one risks losing the advantage of the survey of essentials made by the expert and runs the risk of being unnecessarily restricted to traditional approaches.)

Then the subject expert makes a *"preliminary S-list"*, i.e. writes down the special relationships (rules or laws) which, in his opinion, should be taught in order to prepare the students adequately for reaching the instructional goals listed.—(Besides "concepts" and "rules" the appropriate specific "facts" and "terms" might be listed separately.)

7.1.2 *The "Sorted C-Catalogue"*

The next stage is to try to arrange the basic units (the "C units") in a logically meaningful sequence. One of the simplest and most natural ways of doing this is to systematize the basic units into a hierarchical system, i.e. by grouping the cards within a system of superior and inferior classification categories.

A simple procedure is as follows: The total content is divided up under a number (perhaps between ten and fifteen) main headings. In choosing the main headings, one is partly guided by an examination of the data from the goal analysis and partly by going through the unsorted C-catalogue. The

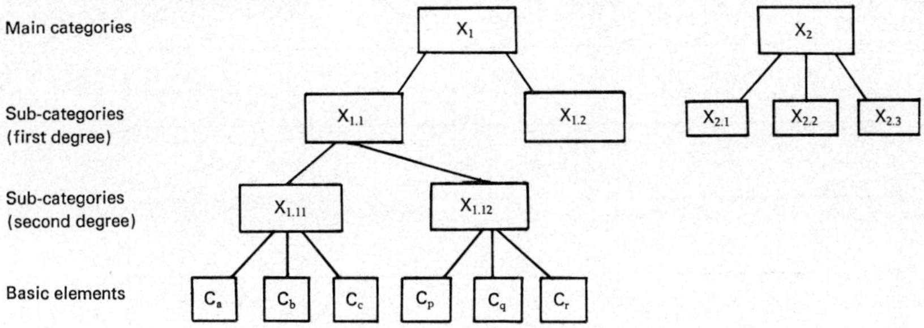

Figure 7.1 Example of the principle for constructing the "Sorted C-catalogue"

Note: For the sake of surveyability, categorization has been completed for only a small part of the structure (proceeding from $X_{1.1}$)

main headings are written on demarcating colored guide-cards, and the single C-cards are sorted under these different headings. Each of these main sections is then split up into a number of sub-sections, each with its own sub-title. The sub-titles are written on guide-cards of a different color and the C-cards then sorted into these smaller divisions. A further sub-classification is then carried out, in which a third color is used for the headings of these new sub-categories. This sub-dividing is continued as long as it appears to be fruitful for the particular material being handled. Finally, the individual cards are arranged in a logically meaningful sequence within each category.

The result of this procedure is that the basic units in the "Sorted C-catalogue" have been arranged in a hierarchical scheme of the general type shown in Figure 7.1.

As an aid to finding one's way quickly about the catalogue, one might use a predetermined color scale for the guide-cards, e.g. from "warmer" colors for the broader categories to "colder" colors for the more limited ones (in accordance with a suggestion by Mechner; cf. Glaser, 1962). Such working details are, however, a matter of individual preference, and are obviously of no critical significance for the main purpose.

7.1.3 *"C-Matrix" for Exploring Relationships*

It is convenient to number the individual cards in the sorted C-catalogue in the order which has been established. Starting from this fixed sequence, a "C-matrix" is then built up. This consists simply of a system of cells whose row and column headings are designated by the key-words of the individual C-cards. In other words, the key-words on the C-cards are entered in numerical order from top to bottom in the left-hand heading column of the matrix and in the same order from left to right along the upper edge of the matrix.

	C_1	C_2	C_3	...	C_n
C_1	X	C_1—C_2	C_1—C_3	...	C_1—C_n
C_2	C_2—C_1	X	C_2—C_3	...	C_2—C_n
C_3	C_3—C_1	C_3—C_2	X	...	C_3—C_n
⋮	⋮	⋮	⋮	⋰	⋮
C_n	C_n—C_1	C_n—C_2	C_n—C_3	...	X

Figure 7.2 General characteristics of a "C-matrix"

A cell in the matrix is taken as symbolizing all conceivable relationships between two basic units as shown schematically in Figure 7.2. The main diagonal is of little interest in this connection and has been marked with an X. The first row gives the relationships between concept C_1 and other concepts. The second cell in the first row thus gives the relationships between concept C_1 and concept C_2. In the same way, the third cell in the same row gives the relationships between concept C_1 and concept C_3, and so on. The lower left-hand half of the matrix forms a mirror-image of the upper right-hand half, in so far as the same pairs of concepts are repeated. For some purposes, however, the "direction" of the relationships is significant, and in these cases the two halves are not identical: in the upper right-hand half of the matrix the "first" component of each pair is the unit with the *lower* sequence number, while in the lower left-hand half the "first" component is the unit with the *higher* sequence number.

The *main purpose* of the C-matrix is to serve as a starting-point for *systematic exploration of the relationships.* The basic question which should be considered throughout the examination is: Is this particular relationship such that it should be used for instructional purposes? The constructor can, for example, go through the matrix cell by cell asking himself: What connection is there between these two concepts, and is the connection of a type which can be used in teaching? Or perhaps he can ask: Is there a basic *difference* in character between these two concepts of such a kind that it can and should be used instructionally in preparing the study material?

A separate matrix could be used for each type of relationship one wishes to explore in this way. One would then produce a *matrix book,* in which the individual pages represent different types of conceptual relationships. Usually, however, such a procedure is unnecessary, and in many cases it would be of practical value to record the different types of relationship on one and the

	C_1	C_2	C_3	C_4	C_5	C_6	C_7	C_8	C_9	C_{10}
C_1	De		Ca						Ca	
C_2		De				Di				
C_3	(Ca)							(Ca)		
C_4				De		Ca	Ca			
C_5										
C_6		(Di)		(Ca)					(Di)	
C_7				(Ca)			De			
C_8			Ca					De		
C_9	(Ca)					Di			De	
C_{10}										

Figure 7.3 An example of a C-matrix with markings for relationships judged to be important for instruction

Note: The marking of this matrix shows that the constructor considered it important

a. to give a detailed *definition* (De) of concepts C_1, C_2, C_4, C_7, C_8, and C_9;

b. to use instructionally a certain type of *causal relationship* (Ca) between concepts C_1 and C_3, C_1 and C_9, C_4 and C_6, C_4 and C_7 etc.; and

c. to use instructionally *differences* (Di) between concepts C_2 and C_6 and between C_9 and C_6.

same matrix, so that they can be seen at a glance and readily compared. One perhaps decides first of all to mark with "*Ca*" on the matrix those cases in which a certain type of *causal* connection is of instructional interest and with "*Di*" those cells in which a *differential* relationship is pedagogically interesting. At the same time one can decide to enter a "*De*" in the main diagonal of the matrix for concepts for which it appears especially important to give a clear and detailed *definition*. A C-matrix used in this way might after the exploration look like that shown in Figure 7.3.

A well-executed exploration of the C-matrix guarantees to some extent that the original sequence order according to the hierarchical pattern does not lead us to forget important and instructionally valuable relationships of other kinds. Thus the two ways of studying the material supplement each other. It should also be noted that some subjects do not lend themselves easily to conceptual hierarchies; in some such cases an "unprejudiced" matrix exploration may be of considerable help.

As suggested by Thomas et al. (1963), matrices similar to the ones discussed above may also be used more directly as guides in *ordering* subject-matter logically. When cells for key comparisons have been marked, their pictorial distribution is studied. *If* the units have been listed in a logical presentation order, then the cells marked for comparisons will cluster around the diagonal. If they do not, various rearrangements for better sequence may be indicated.

7.1.4 *Comparison Between "C.C-Cards" and the "Preliminary S-List"*

Working from the C-matrix which has been marked up in the above way, the constructor makes a series of additional cards. Each of these takes up *one* of the conceptual relationships which has been marked on the matrix as instructionally interesting. The extra cards—called "C.C-cards"—are then compared with the previously mentioned "preliminary S-list". The latter can be regarded as a "C.C-catalogue" which is based on general teaching experience, but has not been examined in detail from a logical point of view.

A comparison of both collections should in many cases be instructionally rewarding. In a number of cases—especially when the subject material in current text-books has been logically well worked out—the difference between the collections is perhaps not particularly great, and the contribution of the C.C-catalogue is then more modest. In these cases it is primarily an extra check and confirmation that no important logical connections have been missed. In other cases—perhaps especially when there is relatively little instructional experience in the particular field—the differences between the two categories can be rather numerous.

A number of these discrepancies will probably indicate that certain of the statements recorded in the preliminary S-list have no equivalents in the C.C-catalogue. One should then ask oneself: Has this gap in the C.C-catalogue occurred because, when going through the C-matrix, one has omitted to record an important relationship (this kind of thing naturally does happen), or is the discrepancy a more important one? Perhaps certain propositions in the preliminary S-list are, on second thoughts, hardly fundamental and deal with only superficial connections? But most often the majority of the discrepancies between the S-list and the C.C-catalogue will probably be in the opposite direction, that is, several relationships which do not appear in the S-list will come up in the C.C-catalogue. This would also be the most valuable result from the instructional point of view. Under optimal circumstances, such an addition can mean a really fruitful collection of suggestions for fresh pedagogical approaches.

In many cases the final step in this stage of the work would be to insert the C.C-cards (after possible corrections and additions through reference to the preliminary S-list) in suitable places in the "Sorted C-catalogue". A good method of doing this is, for example, to insert an individual C.C-card immediately after the C-card which describes the last component of the relationship (in other words, at the earliest point in the sequence at which both components have been introduced).

7.2 Some Reflections on Psychological Supplementation of the Logical Analysis

Some readers may perhaps by now have a feeling that the treatment of material we have just described places far too much stress on logic, and are perhaps inclined to object that it is not after all the logical approach that is most important. The essential thing is to present the material in a psychologically suitable and instructionally effective way. It is not at all certain that what has been broken down to its logical essentials is necessarily the most effective type of material for teaching purposes. Is there not a risk of involving ourselves again in a "pedagogical logicism" corresponding to the exaggerations of the Herbart-Ziller teaching methods—a logicism which has rightly been rejected by modern educational reformers on grounds of developmental psychology? Getting rid of what is logically unnecessary can perhaps mean that one removes both extra material which arouses interest and "redundant" material which promotes the learning process, i.e. which is superfluous from a logical point of view, but is essential for teaching because it gives the students the necessary repetition and time for familiarization.

Such objections would certainly be valid *if* the intention had been to restrict the constructor's work to logical analysis and to let this decide the final form of presentation. But this is certainly not the purpose. It is intended instead that the logical analysis should be a first step, giving a better understanding of the structure of the subject-matter, so that the constructor of study material is perfectly clear about his intended "focal stimuli", i.e. what basic concepts and fundamental relationships he should accentuate. This is obviously not the same as saying that the study material should be *presented* in this way (pared down to logical fundamentals). The method of presentation has to be treated in a second step and is a question of instructional suitability, which is likely to be answered in different ways for different groups of students.

Obviously, additional "interest-arousing" material must often be introduced to increase motivation and for illustrative purposes. Similarly, it is clear that repetitive material must usually be included. But such additional material should be inserted consciously and systematically. Any form of "padding"—material which is not in itself focal—should have a clear instructional motivation and *not* be there by chance or because one has only a hazy notion of what one really wants to achieve. If this degree of rationality and awareness is to be attained, it is frequently necessary to begin by "logical stripping". But, of course, this does not mean that one stops at this point and adopts mere logical nakedness as an instructional ideal.

It may be of interest to note in this connection that studies comparing "logical" and scrambled sequences of didules have surprisingly often ended up with "no significant difference" (cf., e.g., Payne, Krathwohl & Gordon, 1967). In commenting upon these results, Stolurow (1971) makes the observation that they "raise the question of whether logical presentations elicit logical thinking and some would go further and ask if they elicit thinking at all. It could be argued that logical presentation elicits memorization and facilitates recall and recognition more than problem solving". And he continues: "Information processing which produces logical organizations of information is a type of skill that might be the objective of an instructional program. However, are logical presentations the kinds of structures to use if we want learners to achieve these objectives?" This does not seem very probable. Instead, "only partial organization or no organization in the presentation but a response demand to organize would be a way of eliciting information processing activities that produce organization".

We shall return to the question of the educationally and psychologically most suitable form of presentation at several points in our discussions below of how the preliminary version of the study material should be constructed.

In the present section, however, it is possibly worthwhile to stop and consider briefly the more general question: Is it possible to make a psychological analysis of the subject-matter in such a way that it will give a better starting-point for choosing instructional procedures; and which methods of analysis will be most fruitful? Unfortunately our psychological knowledge in this field is still scanty, and many problems await deeper study.

In general, we can say that a psychological analysis of a particular subject-matter for teaching purposes will often amount to an analysis *of the possible and desirable interactions between a student and the subject-content.* In other words, it involves a study of the relationships between the specific subject-content as stimuli and the student's response reactions. If the *logical* basic unit can in most cases be considered to be the "concept", the psychological unit would normally be the individual *stimulus-response connection,* i.e. a behavioral unit with its stimulus conditions.

In such an analysis, however, it should not be forgotten that the human learning process is characterized to a high degree by its complexity and by parallel learning on different "levels". To describe the learning process simply in terms of separate S-R connections often implies, therefore, an over-simplification, which is not well suited to guide our decision on teaching strategies.

From the point of view of instruction it may often be worthwhile to observe four different types of learning that go on more or less simultaneously: (a) the learning of separate "subject-matter items", (b) "field articulation" or the learning of "subject-matter systems", (c) the learning of "subject-matter treatment techniques" (study habits, problem-solving approaches etc.), and (d) the learning of "subject-matter attitudes".

To make our reasoning clearer and more precise, let us introduce some simple symbols and give some examples:

US = undifferentiated stimulus
FS = focal stimulus
CS = correlative stimulus
NS = non-relevant stimulus
PR = pupil's reaction (response behavior)
→ = associative connection (with the general meaning "is followed by", "gives rise to" etc.)
- - → = temporal development (from before learning to after learning)

We should then be able to exemplify some common types of learning in the following way:

a. *Learning "subject-matter items", I: One-way connection.* Here the learning process consists of practising the correct reaction to a given stimulus without reference to its sequence or position in a system.

$FS_a \rightarrow PR_a$

b. *Learning "subject-matter items", II: Reversible connection.* Here again it is a question of reacting adequately to the correct stimulus. In this case, however, the association can take place in both "directions". What at one moment is the response Z to stimulus A should be able to function, when necessary, as stimulus Z and then result in response A. A typical case of this reversible association, to give a concrete example, is obviously the learning of vocabulary in a foreign language, when a normal requirement is skill in translating both ways. When teaching English to a Swedish child, for example, not only must a Swedish word (sw) be able to produce the English equivalent (eng), but the English word must also produce the Swedish one.

I.e.: $FS_{sw\ 1} \rightarrow \left| \begin{matrix} PR_{eng\ 1} \\ FS_{eng\ 1} \end{matrix} \right| \rightarrow PR_{sw\ 1}$

c. *Learning "subject-matter items", III: Disconnection of supporting stimuli.* Learning often implies a development from a correct response after maximal help to a correct response with a minimum of assistance. Expressed in terms we have used elsewhere, we are here concerned with a gradual withdrawal of "correlative stimuli".

I.e.:

$$\left(\left.\begin{matrix} FS_1 \\ CS_1 \end{matrix}\right\} \rightarrow PR_1\right) \dashrightarrow \left(FS_1 \rightarrow PR_1\right)$$

It is often, of course, a question of a procedure with several intermediate stages of this general type:

$$\left(\left.\begin{matrix} FS_1 \\ CS_{1.1} \\ CS_{1.2} \\ CS_{1.3} \end{matrix}\right\} \rightarrow PR_1\right) \dashrightarrow \left(\left.\begin{matrix} FS_1 \\ CS_{1.1} \\ CS_{1.2} \end{matrix}\right\} \rightarrow PR_1\right) \dashrightarrow \left(\left.\begin{matrix} FS_1 \\ CS_{1.1} \end{matrix}\right\} \rightarrow PR_1\right) \dashrightarrow \left(FS_1 \rightarrow PR_1\right)$$

d. *Learning "subject-matter systems", I: Sequences.* A common form of learning, which goes beyond learning one item at a time, is the practice of "chain connections". In this case we have a series of stimulus-reaction connections, in which the internal order is important, and in which the response in the first stage becomes the stimulus for the next:

I.e.:

$$FS_1 \rightarrow \left|\begin{matrix} PR_1 \\ FS_2 \end{matrix}\right| \rightarrow \left|\begin{matrix} PR_2 \\ FS_3 \end{matrix}\right| \rightarrow PR_3 \ldots \text{etc.}$$

e. *Learning "subject-matter systems", II: Refined discrimination.* Even one-way association implies a certain form of discriminative learning (practising the right reaction to the correct stimulus, when this stimulus must be selected from among a large number of other stimuli which are irrelevant for the response). What we are considering here is something else: a differentiated reaction to separate parts of a larger complex which has previously been experienced as a single unit as far as reaction is concerned. In the uncomplicated association, we have a simpler figure-ground relationship, in which a focal stimulus is given a certain content and is brought sharply into focus while other stimuli recede into the background. In this refined discrimination we get an increased differentiation within the focal sphere. We proceed from undifferentiated wholes in focus to differentiated wholes in focus (while retaining experience of the whole).

e.g.:

$$\left(US_8 \rightarrow PR_8\right) \dashrightarrow \left(\left\{\begin{matrix} FS_{8.1} \rightarrow PR_{8.1} \\ FS_{8.2} \rightarrow PR_{8.2} \\ FS_{8.3} \rightarrow PR_{8.3} \end{matrix}\right.\right)$$

Continued differentiation can naturally also result in the sorting out of some part of the whole as not being relevant:

$$\left(US_9 \rightarrow PR_9\right) \dashrightarrow \left(\begin{matrix} \left\{\begin{matrix} FS_{9.1} \rightarrow PR_{9.1} \\ FS_{9.2} \rightarrow PR_{9.2} \end{matrix}\right. \\ NS_{9.3} \rightarrow PR_0 \end{matrix}\right)$$

f. *Learning "subject-matter systems", III: Increased generalization.* Another type of learning implies the ability to see the connection between phenomena which have previously been experienced as separate.

I.e.: $$\begin{pmatrix} FS_{1.1} \rightarrow PR_1 \\ FS_{1.2} \rightarrow PR_2 \\ FS_{1.3} \rightarrow PR_3 \end{pmatrix} \dashrightarrow \begin{pmatrix} FS_{1.1} \searrow & \\ FS_{1.2} \rightarrow & PR_4 \\ FS_{1.3} \nearrow & \end{pmatrix}$$

The above descriptions should be looked upon as exemplifications, and not as an exhaustive survey. In addition to these types of learning, there are of course, as we have already indicated, the learning of the techniques of handling the material (methods of study) and attitudes towards the material, commonly going on simultaneously.

It would be useful in several respects to carry out, at the preliminary stage, analyses of the types considered here, and in doing so the possibility of an empirical study of students' reactions should be borne in mind. An examination of the desired stimulus-reaction connections prevents the importance of some type of connection being overlooked. For example, if it is necessary for the student to be able to behave in terms of reversible connections within a particular area, the training should normally be so designed as to give room for training in both "directions". Empirical data also indicate that this is a correct procedure. Usually there is not much transfer from "one-way training" to behavior in the "opposite direction".

Let me here add some brief remarks on critical thinking, concept learning, transfer, and creative problem-solving, that is, on some of the more complex learning problems that our programmer will often have to plan for.

Critical thinking is obviously a very large area, including many different types of problem which we cannot enter into here. However, basic to many instances of "critical thinking" is the case where somebody (the propaganda man, the advertiser, the political manipulator) arranges stimuli in a way that easily leads to nonadequate generalization (too little discrimination). Training in critical thinking would in such cases involve making the receiver of such loaded information aware of the techniques and train him to make the required discrimination, in spite of the "manipulation" offered. While the "manipulator" presents a specific focal stimulus (FS_1) together with some other stimulus known to evoke positive reactions ($S_2 \rightarrow R+$) in the hope of getting an undifferentiated, but positive reaction to his basic stimulus (perhaps a commercial product):

$$\left(\boxed{\begin{matrix} FS_1 \rightarrow R_1 \\ \\ S_2 \rightarrow R+ \end{matrix}} \rightarrow UR+ \right) \dashrightarrow (FS_1 \rightarrow UR+)$$

the training will focus upon the need to keep the two things separate, "looking through" the manipulator's intent and rejecting it:

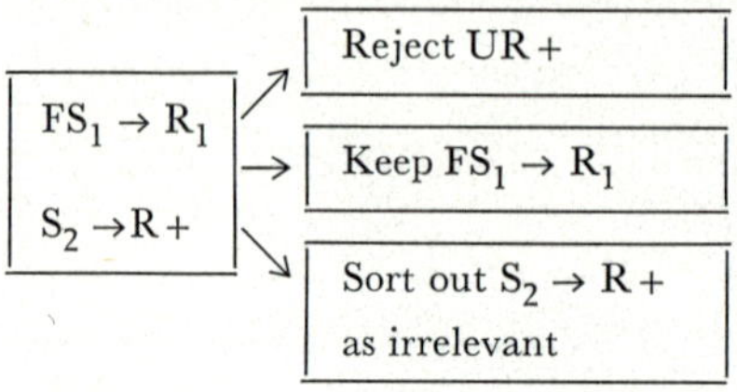

Conceptual learning is central to many subject areas and at the same time relatively complex and therefore not easy to bring about both adequately and quickly. Programmers not analyzing the problem of concept learning carefully may lead their students astray by insufficient or inadequate sampling of illustrations. Let us briefly summarize a few general points to be observed, emphasized in more detail by Markle & Tiemann (1970). There is considerable agreement that a concept (in a technical sense) is a class (category) the components of which share a particular combination of critical properties not shared by any other class. When a student has "fully grasped" a concept, he can generalize to relevant instances and discriminate non-instances. Ability to verbalize a definition, on the other hand, is no reliable sign of being able to respond conceptually adequately to individual illustrations.

Normally, concepts cannot be taught by one example or by a narrow range of illustrations; if too few or too narrow examples are used, the likely result will be "under-generalization" (the student includes some irrelevant attribute and makes the relevant area too small). With insufficient discrimination training, learners may not attend to all critical attributes and make the relevant area too large. The result will be "over-generalization". The remedy should then be better training in discriminating easily confusable non-instances from "real" instances of the concept (useful non-instances are those which share all but one critical property with the category under scrutiny). Hence, a good set of examples and non-examples should be used during the program, and a comparable (but not identical) set chosen for testing. The learner who demonstrates, in the final test, that he is able to generalize and discriminate appropriately within this set of new instances and non-instances has reached the goal. If he does not, the reason may well be an inadequate analysis and inadequate choices of illustrations during the instruction.

Planning for transfer. Closely related to this discussion on concept learning is the notion of transfer. In a recent presentation, Pikas (1971) referred to two important dimensions in educational planning: the interaction dimension and the transfer dimension. The end points of the interaction continuum would be authority power (low interaction between educator and educand in selecting and using materials) vs. divided power (high interaction). The end points of the transfer dimension would be preparing for a low degree of transfer (need of concrete skill, rote learning, few variations but many rehearsals of the same elements etc.) vs. preparing for greater transfer (need to be prepared for changing tasks in the future, concept-type learning, many variations but fewer rehearsals of the same elements). According to Pikas, programmed instruction has so far focused too one-sidedly upon exercises characterized by low interaction between educator and educand on the one hand and by a low degree of transfer on the other. While such exercises have their place, the area of programming should not exclude the perhaps difficult, but important task of introducing more interaction and planning for greater transfer. If we want to prepare the students for mastering the unexpected events of life, we should obviously try to design programs where applications of rules are illustrated by a broad range of examples (but with comparatively few rehearsals); then the common structure, illustrated by the examples, is not distracted by the repetition of particularities of individual illustrations. This general type of goal presents an interesting challenge to programmers.

Too often programmed learning has been thought of as being suited only to the learning of facts or organized sequences. Many traditional programs also are, in fact, most capable of teaching those behaviors in the cognitive domain which Bloom called 'knowledge' and 'comprehension'; whereas, in these cases, an integration of teacher and traditional program may seem needed to promote 'analysis' and 'synthesis' (cf. Noble, 1969). For such goals, then, traditional programs should be used as a supplement to conventional instruction. However, there seems to be no hindrance to constructing programs with explicit emphasis on more complex or "higher-level" objectives. For example, it has been demonstrated that such skills as creative problem-solving, can be taught by programmed instruction materials (cf., e.g., Crutchfield & Covington, 1965). The instruction designer then uses the basic paradigm of explicit training of the activities desired as terminal behavior. It takes some psychological knowledge and skill to arrange suitable activities, but we have no reason to believe that this would be impossible or alien to the programmed learning situation.

It is particularly important not to concentrate so closely upon learning subject-matter items that simultaneous parallel learning processes of other kinds are neglected. It is often the case that the learning of items can take place in many ways with greater or lesser efficiency (time taken). But some of these ways demand simultaneous learning of subject-matter systems (e.g. generalization or differentiation), while others do not. Similarly, some learning processes are valuable for the development of individual study techniques, while others can be less valuable from this point of view.

Frequently a method which results in a relatively small increase in effectiveness as far as the learning of items is concerned may well at the same time lessen the possibility of learning a good study technique. In subject-matter analysis, therefore, the questions to be considered are not only: What material should be chosen? In what order should it be presented? We must also ask: What type of behavior do we require from the student when he is confronted with the study material? Do we ask him to copy given information, do we let him guess the answers, or do we help him to think out the solution to a problem? If the programmer is constantly aware that he must ask himself this double question ("Which way to the information?" *and* "Which information?"), he should run less risk of finding himself imprisoned in a one-sided programming routine. For programmers not afraid to talk about intermediate processes, this point is rather obvious. For example, Landa (1968, p. 116 ff.) criticizes many programs for "unsatisfactory control of the intermediate processes"; here the programmers often seem to be exclusively interested in particular behavioral *products* of the student's mental activity and not to care much about the *process,* that is, *how* the student obtains the particular result, how he thinks, reasons and acts to arrive at it.

8. Choosing Means of Presentation

8.1 Some Problems in Terminology

Like many other terms in the field of educational technology, the word "teaching machine" has caused a great deal of confusion: (a) The term has aroused undeserved negative reactions because in the minds of many it is strongly associated with automation and "soulless" mechanization. (b) It has, in innumerable discussions, been difficult to distinguish between "teaching machine" with its special meaning for the programmer and the teaching machines of other types which have already been in existence, such as presentation aids in the audio-visual field. (c) It has sometimes been difficult to define a clear boundary between "teaching machines" and program presentations in book format. In some contexts, consequently, the programmed textbook has been presented as one type of "teaching machine".

The first-mentioned point, *a,* is perhaps of least importance in principle, although it still has a certain bearing on our communication to teachers and other groups. We can be fairly safe in assuming that mechanical aids of different types will gradually become so much a part of our surroundings (and hopefully so well adapted to human needs) that they will lose their "threat" image. The two other points, *b* and *c,* concern, on the other hand, tangible conceptual obscurities which it would be advantageous to have cleared up. In this presentation we do not want to give definitive suggestions for general use. But when we, within the frame of our present discussions, wish to achieve a fair degree of precision, we shall use the following terms with the meanings set out below:

The term "*presenter*" is used for arrangements whose main function is to present to the student a certain pre-arranged stimulus sequence. Certain presenters have tangible mechanical components (ex. wheels and/or levers). To this group belong projectors for lesson material on film strips, tape recorders for lesson material on soundtapes, TV sets for TV lessons, etc. Several so-called "audio-visual aids" can be considered mechanical presenters when used as they normally are at the present time. Presenters of a non-mechanical type have long been in use in teaching. Large pictures and maps (for group demonstrations) and textbooks (for individual use) can usually be counted as belonging to that category.

The term "*reactor*" is used for those arrangements whose main function is to offer the student the opportunity of making a response reaction. The "question book" in the form of practice tests or work sheets illustrates a non-mechanical system. We find the mechanical type in various so-called "feedback systems" (or "teletest systems") which include student sets for response reactions (press-a-button type, making possible individual and group combined "reaction totals"). Simpler forms (which do not offer the possibility of getting individual reaction totals) are also available.

Of principal importance for the auto-instructional system is, however, that the question is *not* one of presentation only or of reaction alone, but of a *constantly alternating sequence of presentations and reactions.* An arrangement or system, mechanical or non-mechanical, the purpose of which is to offer the student programmed teaching with such an alternating sequence, could be described by the general term "*integrator*". If the arrangement in question is built up of mechanical parts, then we are correct in referring to it as a "*teaching machine*". If it does not have any mechanical parts at all, it will suffice in many cases to speak of a "*programmed workbook*". If we wish to avoid entirely the term "teaching machine", and if we in any case want more specific terms and are not afraid to coin new words, then we might use the term "*tutofor*" as a general name for an arrangement based on programming and facilitating systematic alternations between presentations and reactions (= integrator) and use the terms "*tutomat*" for mechanical arrangements and "*tutoprint*" for the non-mechanical. See Figure 8.1 for an outline of our terminological suggestions.

It might be added that there is, of course, nothing in lectures, texts or any of the visual media (TV, films, etc.) which prevents applying programming techniques to them. As used in the *traditional* and so far most usual way, they are "presenters". By appropriate adaptations (including, for example, adequate pauses for student responses) they may very well be *transformed into* "integrators".

8.2 Choosing Between Mechanical and Non-Mechanical Arrangements

The author of auto-instructional course material must decide in the preparatory phase the form which he intends to use in offering the program to the student, since different forms of presentation require to some extent different patterns in detail work. It is, of course, desirable that the choice of the form of presentation be based on data from the current goal analyses and the student analyses, and that the actual technical aid situation at the time is not taken into consideration until the final round. In order to make a judicious choice, the person who has this responsibility must keep up-to-date with the rapid developments in the field of teaching aids and must try to choose critically from

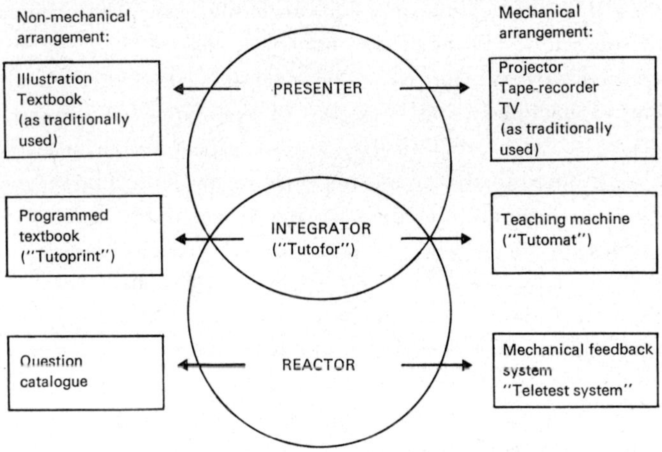

Figure 8.1 Diagram of relationships between some of the main types of teaching aids

the announcements of the hawkers in that particular market, who are more often than not considerably louder than they are informative.

What, in principle, are the advantages which mechanical program presentation has to offer? In which respects can it increase effectiveness in the auto-instructional context?

Obviously the debate for and against mechanical teaching systems has often raged with more intensity than objectivity. At one extreme are those who believe that programmed teaching *cannot* function without mechanical help. In this group we find—besides some manufacturers of machines—principally those who lay great stress on the machine's function as a discourager of cheating. At the other end of the continuum are those who claim that mechanical aids are an entirely superfluous "frill". In this group we have most likely a considerable number who react negatively and emotionally to instructional innovations in general and to instructional apparatus in particular. In this group can be found persons who quite simply find it "inhuman" and "soulless" to place a student in front of a teaching machine (but who seldom call constant use of sarcastic criticism from a teacher "inhuman" and seldom or never consider it "soulless" or meaningless to force students who have already mastered certain material to listen to the teacher's repetition of it for the benefit of those in the group who are not so advanced).

But this group resisting machine teaching also includes more reasonable critics. They are above all anxious that that which is good in the basic principles of programming and which often can be put into effect in a well-planned and adequately tested workbook should not be lost in misplaced enthusiasm for the surface glamour of the impressive machines with all the pushbuttons (which can, of course, easily be shown off to admiring and not so well-informed visitors, thus giving the organization or school an easily earned reputation for keeping up with the times). Through the industrious use of such expressions as "complicated page-turners" (for branching machines) and "hard plastic book-covers" (for linear machines) and by means of the somewhat tiresome but helpful refrain that "it is the program that is most important", a number of these critics have contributed to a more realistic view of mechanical arrangements. They have brought teaching machines back down to earth again and have prevented the myth of the "emperor's new clothes" from spreading in too wide circles.

The most reasonable attitude at the moment seems to be that many types of existing programs should function very well for many student groups without any mechanical components at all—and this has also been demonstrated by repeated empirical tests. This does not mean, however, that mechanical aids for other types of programs and other groups of students cannot increase effectiveness and even be essential for certain types of programs. Those participating in these discussions have too seldom taken into consideration the great *differences in the terminal situation,* both as to type of *stimuli* and type of *reaction.*

For example, it is quite obvious that a self-instructional program in a foreign language could not be made very effective if only visual presentation of word pictures and objects as well as written answers were used. Here the auditive *stimuli* as well as the auditive-oral interaction between the tape-recorder unit and the student are a fairly obvious mechanical supplement.

Mechanical components are often just as natural and as essential when the *terminal reactions* are of a *manual-motor* type. We can no more renounce mechanical components in teaching manual proficiency in an auto-instructional teaching situation than we can in an ordinary teacher-instructional situation. For instance, we do not train a typist without a typewriter or a punching-machine operator without a practice punching-machine.

One of the best known "student-adapted" types of teaching machine is "SAKI" (constructed by Gordon Pask; cf. Lewis & Pask, 1965, and Figure 8.2). "SAKI" was designed for learning different types of keyboards. The special keyboard on which the student is going to practise is connected to the system which, in addition, has a presentation unit and a program-and-registering unit. If the student is to practise card punching, then a punch-card keyboard is plugged in to the circuit. The presentation unit has two parts: the upper with rows of numerals in sequence and the lower with numbers arranged as they are on the keyboard. The student presses down on his keyboard ("response unit" in the figure) that key which has the same marking as the light signal which flashes on the upper part of the presentation unit. As an extra aid for the student in identifying the right key, an extra light signal is given in the beginning in the lower part of the presentation unit (from

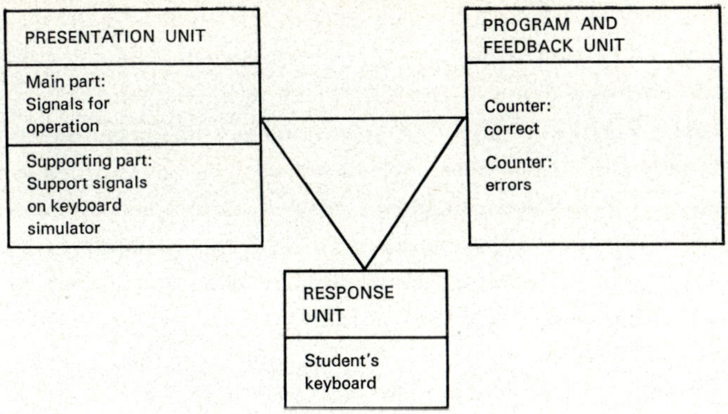

Figure 8.2 The principal components of a SAKI-type system. (Further explanations in text)

which, of course, the position of the key is easily seen). When the student has pressed the key, both lights go out and a new pair of stimuli is offered. The number of correct and incorrect reactions are registered, and can be seen on the feedback unit. The tasks increase successively in difficulty as the student gains in assurance and speed, partly through faster presentation, partly by successive fading, and finally by complete disconnection of the lower part of the presentation arrangement. (It has been demonstrated that this set-up can produce good results in teaching without an instructor, although not necessarily better than the results attained with a combination of instructor plus practice punch; Randell, 1964.)

The manual training situation can also in an *indirect* way lead to the decision that it is desirable to use some sort of mechanical presentation. Many manual practice situations are such that the student's hands and eyes are busy performing a certain task (for example, that of putting together parts of a machine). It would be both impractical and ineffective to present simultaneously to the student repeated visual instructions in a programmed workbook. He would be forced to shift his visual attention unceasingly back and forth between the page of the book and his work. In a situation of this kind it is natural that the programmed instructions are given auditively through a recorder, possibly with appliances which could prevent disturbance of others (earphones), but which still do not interfere with the mobility of the student (wireless transmission).

For the teaching of many kinds of skills, "simulators" of quite a complicated type are used (perhaps best known in pilot and driver training). Ordinarily these provide a versatile imitation of natural situations, including also representative stimuli as well as the usual reaction possibilities (with the exception of some of the expense and the danger of the real situation). The student is trained, when he receives certain stimuli (e.g. picture of moment of danger on the road), to react in a certain manner (e.g., with special maneuvers with levers). Usually teaching in simulators is carried out by individual instructors. It should in many cases be possible, however, to rationalize the procedure by successive machine-presented instructions. If, moreover, the mechanically-offered stimuli sequence is built according to a plan from simpler to more complicated tasks, and with some degree of adaptation to the student's speed of progress, we have a typical example of a programmed teaching situation in which the mechanical components play a natural role.

In all of the examples now given, the introduction of the mechanical factors depends upon the presence of essential stimuli and/or essential types of response in the terminal situation, which cannot be translated naturally or with maximum effectiveness into written-verbal or static picture symbols alone. There is a tendency to forget that terminal situations of this type play an important part in ordinary school teaching (e.g., in teaching languages) and that it is most significant in many adult education programs (in industry, for example). Once attention has been directed to the existence of these special situations, however, it is usually quite clear that mechanical arrangements can be of basic importance here.

Using the machine to discourage "cheating" is another story. Many of the machines presented during the early sixties had that more or less as their *only* purpose. The usual technique here is, as we know, that the machine presents one task at a time (via a "task-window", for example). When the student has answered it (possibly by writing in an answer blank), he draws forth, by some means, a key answer so that he can compare his answer with the "model answer". On many types of machines it is impossible for the student to change his own answer afterwards or to see the key answer before. The feeding mechanism of the machine moves in one direction only, and the student's own answer glides in under a transparent cover as soon as the model answer is turned forward.

Are these special anti-cheating functions sufficient reason for acquiring these simple, but often fairly expensive machines? Is it not a mistake to introduce the thought of cheating during the learning process? (When it is not a question of a final examination, a look at the key answer can sometimes be both sensible and practical, and above all, it is both sensible and practical to be able to look over material which has already been done.) Is it not simply a case of provoking a less desirable attitude to the work if this is always presented in "cheat-proof" form (which might in some cases lead to an attempt to "fool" the machine)? These questions are meant to be thought-provoking; it is difficult to give them a definite answer valid for all kinds of situation.

It might be well to point out, however, that the role of the machine in this connection cannot always be completely covered by the possibly somewhat misleading term "anti-cheater". Actually that term ordinarily covers three different functions: (a) The student is prevented from seeing the key answer *before* he tries to reply himself. (This is, of course, the most typical of the "anti-cheating" functions.) (b) The machine guarantees that the carefully planned work sequence is followed by the student, who does not have the opportunity of taking any undesirable short cuts or zigzagging through the material (this could be called the "sequence-guarantee" of the machine). (c) The machine limits the number of distracting stimuli and facilitates, thereby, the focusing of attention on the focal stimuli in each stage—unlike, for example, the welter of intertwining items of information to be found on one page of an ordinary book (this could be called the "focusing" function of the machine).

It is easy to speak disparagingly of "page-turning" machines, but it is not impossible that these three simple functions in certain cases *can* have a not insignificant influence on furthering effectiveness. At the beginning of this century—long before teaching machines in the modern sense had even been thought of—Thorndike, one of the leading figures in the study of the psychology of learning, mentioned how advantageous it would be for learning if textbooks could be so constructed that they did not allow the reader to proceed to page 2 before he had completed all that he was supposed to do on page 1 (Thorndike, 1912). Obviously it is just something of that uncompromising stage-by-stage presentation and stage-by-stage control which the program tries to achieve and which the simple machines, moreover, try to *guarantee.*

Let us consider a typical correspondence course taken by a student during the vacation period. The course offers informative material and a long list of practice problems in a "letter" which the student is supposed to read through before answering the test items. A conscientious student reads the letter carefully and solves the problems scrupulously in the prescribed order. A less conscientious student does not read so carefully, skips some of the problems which seem to be difficult, or takes a peek at the key in order to get through them as soon as possible. A capable student feels, perhaps, that he can take considerable short cuts, and sometimes goes directly from the information in the letter to the final assignments. In some cases, naturally, this skipping technique on the part of the student can do no harm, especially since current corespondence courses are not often designed for the individual and therefore can contain entirely unnecessary repetition material for certain groups of students. But in many cases, this "shortcut behavior" (whether it derives from a desire to get through as quickly as possible or quite simply from the student's overrating of his own knowledge and ability) leads to a less satisfactory end result.

Some form of "sequence guarantee" should logically reduce to some extent the danger of a deterioration in final results. And if such a sequence guarantee can be desirable even in an ordinary textbook or a correspondence course, it is reasonable to suppose that a guarantee would be of even greater importance in a programmed course where the order of assignments and number of assignments are the result of careful preliminary planning and testing, and where, therefore, "skipping behavior" is more seldom motivated. On the other hand, students may feel a healthy sense of control when working through a programmed text in that they can back up when necessary; machines usually prevent "self-programming" of that sort. The *possibility* of "self-programming", even when rarely used, may be of emotional importance to some students: the individual has more "degrees of freedom", is not *only* influenced, etc.—Hence, there is obviously good reason for further testing of programs both *with* and *without* various simple "sequence-guaranteeing" devices. We can only hope that later on we will be able to make a more definite statement about the value of these two modes of procedure. So far, much empirical research seems to have ended up by being unable to demonstrate significant differences between machine and text versions. (The "anti-cheating" component is—regardless of what one thinks of its importance for instructional effectiveness—of special value in connection with research, since it facilitates interpretation of the student's running performance; the student cannot, for example, complicate the work protocol with later changes.)

If we sum up what has just been discussed and add to this some other points of view often expressed, we have the following list of common arguments for mechanical set-ups:

1. When the instruction material, in order to achieve full effectiveness, must contain *stimuli* of a type other than the printed word and the static picture (for example, moving pictures or auditory stimuli), then mechanical components are usually needed. A special case, which we will deal with in more detail below, is when we need to *amplify or modify the observation area.*

2. When the instruction situation, in order to achieve full effectiveness, must give the student other *reaction possibilities* than those offered by pen and paper (such as is the case when training many manual-motor skills), the mechanical components are usually equally necessary. (This can sometimes mean construction of special teaching apparatus such as SAKI, while in other cases it may mean only the use of a programmed workbook in combination with an ordinary working machine.)

3. The instruction material in a typical auto-instructional course is designed to be presented step-by-step, unit-by-unit, in a sequence carefully planned and fixed in advance, with the key solutions immediately following the student's own response attempt. The machine can be a *guarantee* that this planned, *step-by-step* and well-focused *presentation* can be realized, so that the student does not take forbidden short-cuts, skip tasks or look at the key answers before he has written down his answer.

4. When more complicated *systems of individualization* are desired, a me-

Box 8.1 Some notes on computer-assisted instruction

A computer may sometimes be given the role of a teaching machine. We then talk about computer-assisted or computer-directed instruction. In some general discussions the two concepts of "programmed instruction" and "computer-assisted instruction" have wrongly been considered to be in opposition to each other or to deal with widely different strategies. Often it would be more correct to consider computer-assisted instruction as a special case of programmed instruction: a case where one for one reason or another has found it convenient to have the computer take over information storage, answer comparisons, and feedback to the student. The computer is better than more conventional teaching machines in two main respects: (a) It can store large data collections and thus hold both detailed student profiles and several different courses at the same time. (b) It can handle a great number of analyses and "decisions" more easily and more quickly than other arrangements.

Let us take a look at the "conversation" between computer and student during a logic game in which the task of the student is to identify a letter the computer is "thinking of", using as few questions as possible. The student is allowed only to put one question at the time, and the questions may deal with the number of curves, loose ends, obliques etc. (For instance, the letter X has no curves, but four loose ends, whereas R has one curve and two loose ends.) This is how a conversation may proceed:

Computer: Start.
Student: Curves?
C: One.
S: Loose ends?
C: Two.
S: Obliques?
C: Zero.
S: C. (Meaning C is the correct answer.)
C: You don't have enough information yet to get the right answer. How do you know it isn't J, for example?
(Note: The computer will not accept a guess from the student, if he does not have enough information to back up a final decision; this is not a guessing game, but a logic game.)
S. J.
C: You don't have enough information yet. How do you know it isn't C, for example?
S: Horizontals?
C: Zero. That was a wasted question. It did not eliminate any possibilities.
S: Verticals?
C: Zero. Good question.
S: G.
C: Wrong. Your guess is not consistent with the information you have been given. You must have forgotten that the right letter hasn't any horizontal lines. The letter you guessed can't be right—it has too many loose ends.
S: Curves?
C: The answer is still: one.
S: C.
C: Yes, you have done it. Good work. If you want to play again, start right in.

The example shows how the storage capacity and ability for quick analysis of the computer can be utilized to demonstrate to the student when he is asking an unnecessary question or comes up with a conclusion not consistent with information given. This high degree of individualization is quickly felt by the student to be both effective and exciting.

In principle the instruction of the computer follows this design:

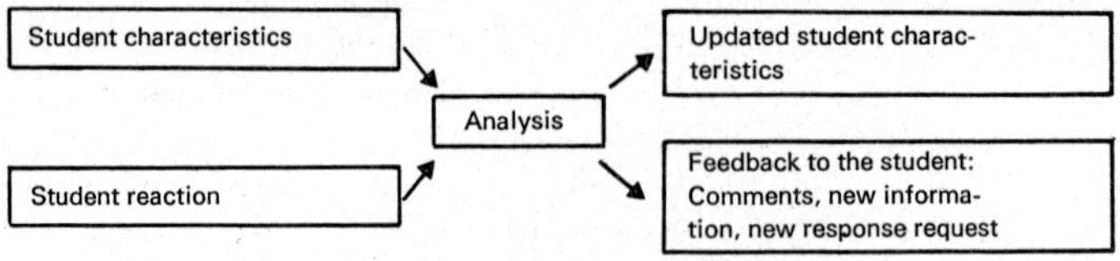

The difficulties involved here are most often neither technical, nor economical, but educational-methodological. Technical solutions are available, and the costs need not necessarily be forbidding (if many students can utilize the equipment; also it seems reasonable to predict diminishing costs in the future as a consequence of the development of electronics). But the construction of the highly individualized program involves difficulties of a kind that teachers and education experts so far have only to a very limited extent dealt with systematically.

It is not at all self-evident what kinds of feedback are educationally most fruitful for various combinations of student characteristics and student reaction. Today, therefore, the problem is not so much what the computer is able to do, but to what extent we as behavioral scientists have sufficient knowledge of complex human learning and sufficient valid models of Attribute × Treatment interactions to compose effective instructions for the computer.

(The example above of logic games is based on Swets & Feurzeig, 1965.)

chanical presentation can sometimes simplify the alterations needed within the total bank of instructional units and thus save time.

5. When it is desirable to obtain "*reaction summations*" quickly as an indication of student achievements, mechanical devices for the registration of correct and incorrect answers can save a certain amount of work.

6. In some cases machines probably increase motivation among certain students for whom the physical manipulation and the gambling-type set-up may create an atmosphere of fun and play.

When it is a question of choice between the *tutomat arrangement* and the *tutoprint arrangement,* arguments 1—3 should be the decisive ones, while arguments 4—6 are usually of secondary importance. If a detailed student-adaptation is desired (argument 4), mechanical aids are sometimes desirable and can—as a number of experiments have demonstrated—be brought about by systems including a computer. For reasons of economy, among others, these arrangements have so far mostly occurred in research situations. Innovations and quick changes are likely here, however (cf. Box 8.1 and the discussion in Richter, 1971).

8.3 Various Mechanical Arrangements

When there is a question of choice between different types of *tutomat arrangements,* a number of other factors must be taken into consideration. In several cases (especially where special manual skills are concerned) a "*special tutomat*" must be constructed for that particular purpose. Pask's "SAKI" for card-punching is an example of this. Simulator-arrangements with programmed instructions provide other examples. In many cases, however, a more generally applicable arrangement can be considered. Most of the so-called teaching machines on the market during the sixties seemed to be "*general tutomats*" in this sense of the word, and were chiefly suitable for advancing verbally communicable knowledge and skills.

Examples of the factors to be taken into consideration in choosing among the machines for more general use on the market are presented below. (Points 1—4 deal chiefly with the stimulus phase, points 5—7 with the reaction phase, and points 8—10 with certain forms for interplay of reactions and stimuli. Points 11—12, finally, contain some practical-economic considerations).

1. Is *visual presentation* sufficient (as many of the constructors of apparatus seem to assume) or is *auditory presentation* also necessary? Auditory presentation is obviously of importance if the terminal behavior demands sound discrimination, or if the focusing of the behavior is substantially facilitated by auditively communicated instructions (compare our example above); this is also quite obviously true in the case of students who can neither read nor write.

Sound presentation is technically not especially difficult to arrange and occurs in many tutomat systems. But since it often involves a substantial increase in the cost of materials, it should not be used unless necessary. In certain cases the auditory unit is separate so that visual presentation only can be used at first, and the sound unit brought into use later on if the need for it becomes apparent.

2. Is it most advantageous in the teaching situation under consideration to choose *the printed page* or *projected still pictures* as a means of presenting information? Those apparatus which use printed sheets are often cheaper. Moreover, the printed sheet is, as a rule, easier to produce within the frame of existing resources, for example in a school (where ordinarily you are more likely to have access to a stencil apparatus than to a developing laboratory). On the other hand, a supply of paper programs often demands a great deal of storage space. In addition, paper programs, if they are to contain illustrations (especially colour photos), can be considerably more expensive than programs on microfilm. If the projection apparatus is chosen, care must be taken that the projected pictures do not create special "tiring" effects.—(These comments are most relevant to individual use. If group-paced situations are considered, the relative cheapness of re-usable projected materials for large groups might be an important factor.)

3. Is "*focusing*" on one task at a time essential to the program?

4. Is it desirable to be able to try out stenciled versions of new programs directly without encountering problems with *paper format or type of paper?* If so, machines

using odd sizes of paper are less suitable, as well as apparatus which work with different types of running paper, lengths (folded fanwise or rolled).

5. Is it essential to have *self-constructed answers* (with reference to the special terminal behavior which one hopes to achieve), or is it sufficient (perhaps even more natural) to work with *choice reactions?* Machines which work with written student answers are best suited to the former, whereas most machines which work with keyboard responses are better for the latter. It should be noted, however, that certain keyboard machines can be used for self-constructed answers (using combinations of letters or of numerals).

6. Is it desirable that the student be able to work on a *special "answer strip"* to make possible repeated use of the same program sheet? If so, apparatus without separate answer arrangements are not suitable. Is it desirable to be able to use the machine both *with* and *without* a special answer strip? (In research one may want the answers included in the program, while for practical use it is perhaps desirable to save paper.) If this is the case, then apparatus with both possibilities are worth considering.

7. If some form of *error summation* is desired, it is usually necessary to use some kind of keyboard apparatus (these often have error counters, e.g. "Auto-Tutor Mark II"). There are also machines with written answers and some "semi-automatic" error-counting operated by the student. In the latter case, however, one must be sure that the student does not "forget", either wittingly or unwittingly, to mark all errors.

8. Is it enough to work with *linear progression,* that is, the same system of instructional units for all students, or is it desirable to have possibilities for "*branching*" within the unit sequence? Most tutomats are designed for linear progression. There are a few, however, which offer good branching possibilites; among the best-known of these is "Auto-Tutor Mark II". (The principal questions with regard to various branching-off procedures will be discussed below.)

9. Is there a need for a mechanical "*skimming*"-*device* as a time-saver in later repetition? Very few apparatus have any such possibility. In principle, an arrangement of this type can be built into a tape recorder unit. The student thereby enters a high frequency tone on the tape every time he makes a mistake. When the tape is run back quickly afterwards, it slows down to normal speed just at those points.

10. Is there any need for a *mechanical pace-accelerator?* It is usually considered one of the advantages of programmed instruction that the student may set his own pace. In *certain* cases, however, successively increased demands—still fitted to the individual—can be even more advantageous, since they may force faster performance. The Pask-machine "SAKI" described above suggests how an arrangement of this type can be worked out. Ordinarily these arrangements are expensive, however, and it is not at all certain that their instructional value is in proportion to the cost.

11. Which is more important, low *cost* or *durability?* Many variations are available, from the cheap and disposable paper devices to expensive and fairly durable metal constructions. Unfortunately, many of the existing apparatus are both expensive and easily damaged.

12. Which is more important, *capacity for program storage* or *space saving* (and possibilities for stacking)? The well-known problem of the lady's shoe—it must be large inside and small outside—has turned up again in a new version. The supply of machines for one class should not take up too much space. On the other hand, they should not hold so little continuous material that they must constantly be opened (by the teacher, for instance) in order to change the material. Naturally, the storage capacity in principle is greatest in those apparatus which use micro-material for projection. Because of the space needed for the projector itself and the power supply, however, these apparatus can seldom be listed among those most easily handled.

8.4 Amplifying and Modifying the Observation Area: Some Notes on CCTV and Video-Recording in Instructional Systems

Among the training situations for which some sort of mechanical arrangement seems indicated, we mentioned above the special case where there is a need to amplify and/or modify the "observation area". Good techniques for doing this are now available in the form of closed-circuit television systems and video-recording. Since such systems are now increasingly being used as major components of instructional systems, it seems pertinent to make a brief digression here from our main theme with some notes on these aids. We shall focus on some general principles, illustrating various ways of amplifying and modifying the observation area, but we shall also try to make our comments concrete by relating to a particular area of application.

8.4.1 *General Character of CCTV and Video-Recording*

Before we try to answer our main question here, namely how closed-circuit television can be used to amplify and modify the observation area in a way that will be helpful to instruction, it would perhaps be as well to recapitulate briefly some main characteristics of these aids.

"Closed-circuit television" (CCTV) commonly means the transmission of sound and pictures to receivers within a closed system, e.g. by means of cables (as opposed to the open "broadcast television"). Thus a CCTV system is usually clearly defined in its range, which does not, however, necessarily mean that it is small. It can be a very small class-room system (where camera and receiver are both in the same room for demonstration purposes, sometimes called "desk TV"), but it can also be a system which embraces a very wide geographical area.

A minimum installation for transmission from one room to another entails having for picture transmission a TV camera in the sending area which is connected to a TV receiver in the viewing area and for sound transmission a microphone and loudspeaker respectively.

There is, however, comparatively limited use for such a simple system. Instead, one usually considers a larger installation of the general type outlined in Figure 8.3. (It should be emphasized that the figure gives only a general sketch and not a complete technical diagram.) In the sending area (S)—for instance, a classroom—there are two or three cameras, of which at least one can be worked by remote control, both optically and for direction, and a number of microphones, one of them perhaps a neck microphone for the teacher. Picture and sound impulses go first into the control room (CR), where they can be both recorded by means of the video-tape recorder and also transmitted further either completely or partly to one or more viewing areas (V_1, V_2 etc.).

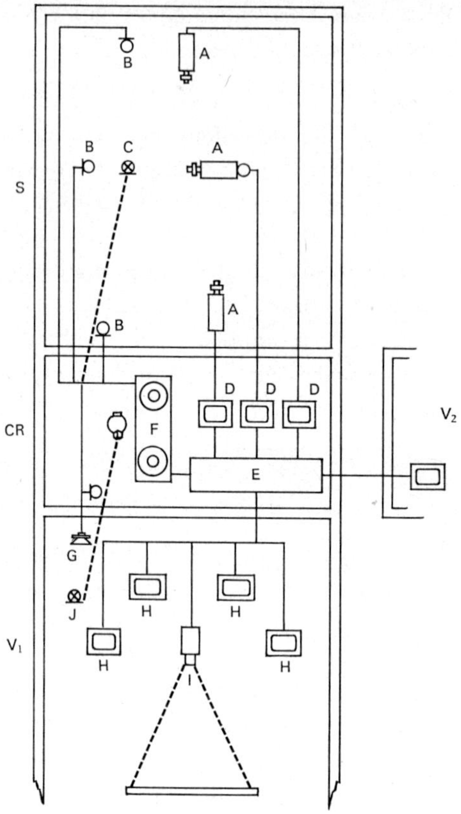

Figure 8.3 Typical installation of CCTV

In the *sending area* (S) there are three TV cameras (A), one of which can be directed by remote control, three fixed microphones (B), and one portable teacher's microphone (C).

In the *control room* (CR) there are monitors (D), a control board for picture selection etc. (E), and a video-tape recorder (F) etc.

In a large *viewing area* (V_1) there are, in addition to loudspeakers (G), either a number of TV receivers (four in the picture, H) or an enlarging projector (I). Viewing can take place simultaneously in separate rooms (e.g. V_2). A tutor/supervisor in the viewing room can communicate with the control room via a portable microphone (J).

In the control room there is a picture receiver for each camera (monitor). In certain cases pictures from each camera are transmitted, so that there is one receiver for each picture in the viewing room. In other cases, the pictures are selected in the control room, and only one picture is transmitted to the viewers, i.e. the one which seems most valuable at a given moment. If the viewing space is large, it can be equipped with a large number of receivers so that the viewers can form small groups for unhindered observation. But there is also the alternative possibility of using a special projector which shows an enlarged picture.

Within the framework of a system of this kind there are many possibilities for variation. The cameras can be fixed without operators, operated manually within the sending area, or manipulated by remote control. The microphones can be fixed, worked by remote control, or portable. The portable ones can be wired to the control room or be of the wire-less type etc.

The video-tape recorder included in our figure is not, of course, a necessary ingredient. However, as we shall see, video-tape recorders are a very valuable addition to the arsenal of aids whose further development should be followed with great interest by those engaged in the construction of training systems.

8.4.2 *CCTV and Video-Recording as "Observation Amplifiers"*

Numerous advances in science, education and production are the result of man's success in constructing new aids which have increased his capacity to receive information or process it, or both. The microscope is an example of an aid which has increased man's capacity to collect information, while a computer is a machine which has increased his ability to process it. Without making general comparisons, it would be useful to regard CCTV and video-tape recording as "observation-amplifying" aids of potential value for education in general. Let us, however, for the purpose of illustration, focus upon a special area of application and ask ourselves: Which types of observation-amplifying arrangements, using these aids, are most adequate for use in teacher training: Figure 8.4 gives some main examples, which I will here briefly explain and comment on.

By "*micro-showing*" (Figure 8.4, a) we mean here the possibility of demonstrating small objects and events to a large group of observers simultaneously. This is perhaps one of the most frequent uses of television in education, e.g. in medicine. A dental or heart operation can be followed in detail by a large group of dental or medical students via the TV screen. A demonstration which would otherwise be limited to a very small group of direct observers can now be observed by a very large group. This means that the events which the individual student would perhaps never have the opportunity of seeing because of their comparatively low frequency in the training or practice institution in question can be illustrated concretely in the course of teaching.

Several of the difficulties experienced in teacher training could well be minimized if wider use were made of the micro-showing qualities of CCTV and video-tape recording. The possibility of giving a concrete demonstration of events within the framework of theory teaching is considerably increased, which should contribute to narrowing the gap between the worlds of theory and practice. Similarly the possibility of the student teacher's seeing and hearing details during the course of an observation lesson is also increased. The possibility of spreading information about infrequent phenomena to large groups is obvious. For this purpose we can use very simple arrangements of the "desk TV" type, by which a theory lecturer can demonstrate an individual child's work with self-instructional material or with a test (in this case the child is present in the

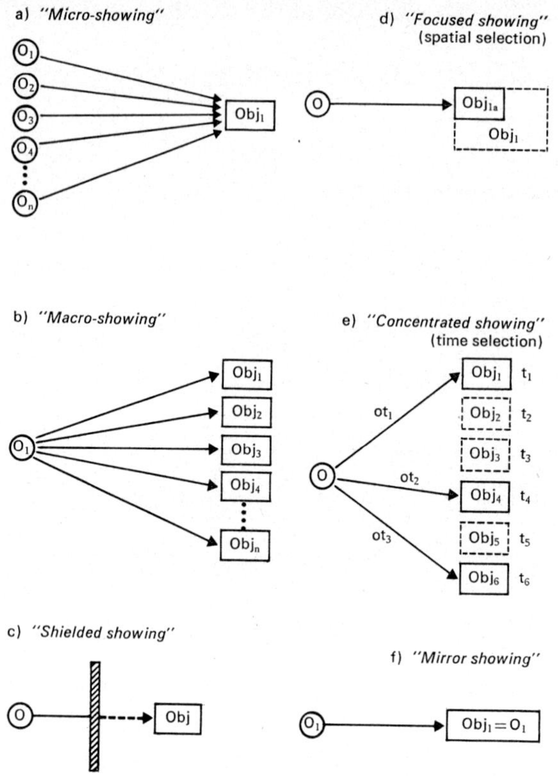

Figure 8.4 Schematic examples of different types of "observation amplifying" arrangements possible with CCTV and video-tape recording

Symbols: O_1, O_2, O_3 etc. = observers
Obj_1, Obj_2 etc. = objects for observation
t_1, t_2 etc. = time 1, 2 etc. in a sequence of events
ot_1, ot_2 etc. = time 1, 2 etc. in a sequence of observations

lecture room). But it can also be used for demonstrations of test and study material from a studio or classroom (where, for example, a child and a tester or a child and teacher can work undisturbed by the presence of an observation group) or for the showing of a previously recorded demonstration. In this way the methods used in a laterality test, individual pronunciation training or in working with small groups can advantageously be demonstrated. Finally, it could be used for something more like the normal observation lesson, where the student teachers can follow a whole class at work, while a manually or remote control operated camera can take close-ups of interesting details in the course of the teaching.

"*Macro-showing*" (Figure 8.4, b) means that an observer can watch several separate observation areas. Signals from different sending areas are led into a common viewing area (with several TV receivers). We find this method used in supervision of traffic areas, prisons and factories; a single supervisor can by this means keep his eye on a large area without leaving his post. A comparable method can be used in teacher training for simultaneous or almost simultaneous observation of several different classes in which, for example, the same step in a given subject is being handled in different ways. Here it is not usually the case that *one* observer sees many observation objects, but instead that a group of observers, gathered in one place for tutorial discussion before and after the observation, can see picture material from two or more classrooms at the same time. Sound signals from the different classrooms can be switched on alternately to avoid disturbing the observer too much (alternating rather than completely simultaneous observation). Such observations should in many cases give a good background for evaluative and comparative discussion.

"*Shielded showing*" (Figure 8.4, c) means that the viewer and the object are shielded from each other. One of the most obvious examples of this type of use is in atomic laboratories. Processes which would be highly dangerous for an observer to study *in situ* because of radioactive radiation can be studied at a suitable distance or behind protective lead walls. Only the TV camera is in the actual location. In teacher training it is not, of course, necessary to protect the observer from the observed object. On the other hand, there is an obvious need to protect those observed (the children and their teacher) from disturbance by the observing group. It is true that classes under observation do become *relatively* easily accustomed by experience to having a small group of observers in a corner of the classroom. But—and this is a particularly important reservation—oral commentaries (by e.g. a teacher of method or education) during the course of the observation are out of the question. Furthermore, an observation group inside a classroom must always be small, whereas a group of observers can be of almost any size if shielded viewing is used. These two factors combined (the possibility of simultaneous commentary and of increasing the size of the group of observers) obviously mean a considerable improvement in the observation situation and can theoretically help to avoid several of the difficulties involved in observing lessons. It will be possible to make the observation more meaningful by carefully directing the observers' attention during the observation. All will obtain the same background of experience, which will also make it possible for the teacher of theory to give more detailed and adequate comments afterwards. A large group of student teachers can more easily be given the opportunity of observing even the less frequent phenomena. Administrative and schedule-making difficulties are reduced and teacher students waste less time in travelling.

Another method of facilitating observation by student teachers is to direct their attention by means of a selection of pictures to what the lecturer in education or method considers most interesting at a particular moment ("*fo-*

cused showing": Figure 8.4, d). Technically, this works mainly in two ways: a roving camera is directed at the desired point of interest at the given moment, or a choice can be made in the control room between several incoming pictures (which are continually being studied in the monitors) of what is most profitable to distribute to the viewing room. This procedure has the instructional and psychological advantage that the confusing mass of possibilities for observation are cut down, what is considered important is brought to the foreground, and the rest which from the point of view of informational psychology can at that moment be considered as irrelevant "noise", is cut out. If the choice is made skilfully (and this naturally makes great demands on the person selecting the pictures), this kind of technical device might considerably increase the educational effect of the observation period.

With the aid of the video-recorder, this spatial selection can be supplemented by selection in time. "*Concentrated showing*" (Figure 8.4, e) means that the raw material is cut and only certain essential points are shown. There are plenty of examples of this type of "reduced" sending in the conventional TV programs on sports or parliamentary discussions. Every football kick and every word said by a member of Congress are certainly not pearls, and skilful selection saves a great deal of time while still giving sufficient information. The same thing can be done with classroom observation material. Student teachers sometimes experience an observation period as somewhat unproductive "sitting-in" partly because they are unaccustomed to observation and it is not possible to direct their attention, but partly also because a certain amount of what happens is naturally comparatively uninteresting, at least as far as the specific point being studied is concerned. A solution to this problem can be obtained by means of the video-tape recorder. Technically this can be arranged either by making a partial recording or by making a selection later (e.g. by partial copying from another tape). The latter method allows a better planned selection to be made; the former, on the other hand, saves time and tape. What we get is a rationalized demonstration situation in which, in addition, we are not bound by time and space. To take one of many examples, there is nothing to prevent our using the material for evening refresher courses for teachers.

Once the observation material has been recorded on video-tape, there is moreover scarcely any limit to what can be done by editing. It would often be an advantage to produce a demonstration tape in which short illustrations of procedures are shown for comparative analysis (different ways of beginning a lesson, different ways of handling a breach of discipline, different ways of concretising abstract conceptions etc. etc.). Such "contrast-illustrating demonstration tapes" should obviously provide excellent starting points for tutorial discussion on many topics. By inserting a preparatory and/or subsequent commentary by the lecturer in method or education, the illustration tape can be built up into independent teaching material which can also be used by a less experienced group leader ("commentary-interfoliated demonstration tape").

An even more important opportunity is perhaps that of inserting tasks for the observers. The possibility of stopping a lesson in mid-action to allow the student teachers to consider and make their own decisions about a teacher's possible behavior when faced with concrete classroom incidents and *then* see what the teacher actually did and what the results were has sometimes been described as wishful thinking. But video-tape recording makes it possible to conjure with time in this way. Such activation of the observer could have several good effects: it compels him to pay close attention, to think more deeply and to take a more personal attitude. It can also be arranged so that misunderstandings are immediately corrected. Such tasks could therefore help to make the observation more meaningful and lessen the gap between it and what the students would do themselves in practice. "Task-interfoliated demonstration tapes" will in this way be very similar to other self-instructional material and also to the "classroom simulators" which have sometimes been used (usually with the aid of filmed material). They could be used not only for *training* in adequate decisions and teacher-behavior, but also as a *test* of the student teacher's repertoire of behavioral tendencies relevant to the classroom role. They could also perhaps pave the way for better methods of selection and better aids to grading than those we now have.

Finally, "mirror-showing" or "*self-confrontation*" (Figure 8.4, f) means that a person can study himself and his own behavior patterns by means of video-tape recording. This method has been used in athletics teaching, for example, where high-jump or stroke techniques are studied by the athletes themselves afterwards. (Cf., e.g., Weltner, 1970 b.) A similar technique can be used in teacher training; to observe one's own lessons would become, with the aid of the video-tape, not something supernatural, but a highly practical aid in our attempts to make the student teacher aware of his shortcomings and merits.

So far we have mainly considered different ways of using closed-circuit television and video-tape recording in order to make students' lesson observation and teaching practice more effective. Obviously the advantages of these two aids as "observation amplifiers" can also be used in other ways in teacher training. In a situation where there is a lack of teachers of educational theory, CCTV can thus be used for "multiple direct teaching" (lectures and demonstrations are simultaneously transmitted to several different lecture rooms, perhaps even from one School of Education to branches in other places). Lecturers in education and method who are going to give lectures, demonstrations etc. on public television can, with the aid of the video-tape recorder, give themselves teaching practice ("rehearsal with play-back"). The technique of judging lessons could well be practised by means of group evaluation of recorded material followed by discussions. The reliability of teaching marks could also possibly be increased by using a technique whereby a number of independent assessors judge the same lesson (which should not be administratively impossible with the help of recorded material: "objectivised behavior assessment"). There is not room here to go more deeply into the advantages and disadvantages of these different possibilities. They should, however, be borne in mind for further research work.

One of the often mentioned difficulties in teacher training is our lack of basic knowledge as far as teaching methods are concerned, and the fact that these problems are connected with insufficient research and the earlier difficulties in recording actual events in the classroom objectively. There is no doubt that here too CCTV and video-recording have opened up new possibilities which should gradually contribute to more definite basic knowledge. The advantages of video-recording as a "data-storage research aid" should not be forgotten in this connection. (Cf., e.g., Cartmell, 1971.)

8.5 Various Non-Mechanical Arrangements

After this excursion, dealing with an important but rather special aid in instructional system building, let us return to the question of mechanical vs. non-mechanical arrangements. Since tutomat arrangements are often comparatively expensive and since many of them, in spite of the fact that they are meant for general use, have their special limitations, it is often a good idea to *begin with* an attempt to manage without a tutomat system. Only when experience has shown that mechanical components really *are* desirable, is it advisable to buy one or to have one constructed. (This general recommendation does not apply, naturally, in those cases discussed earlier, where the character of the terminal situation shows immediately that some sort of tutomat arrangement is necessary.)

It can be reported parenthetically that about two-thirds of all U.S. programs commercially available in the year 1965 had been produced *only in a tutoprint version.* The relative number of programs which were produced *both* for mechanical and non-mechanical use dropped noticeably from the year 1962 to 1965 (see Table 8.1).

Table 8.1 Mode of presentation in U.S. programs: Three surveys

	For non-mechanical use only	For mechanical use only	For both methods
Programs, 1962	31 %	7 %	62 %
Programs, 1963	56 %	20 %	24 %
Programs, 1965	66 %	21 %	12 %

(Percentage figures are based on information in "Programed instruction materials 1964—'65", covering 102 programs in 1962, 333 programs in 1963, and 291 programs in 1964—65.)

In this respect, however, there are interesting international differences. In Britain we find a predominance of machine programs (see Table 8.2). In 1966, more than four out of five of the American programs available in Britain were in book form, while just over one in five of the British-made programs was designed as a book.

Table 8.2 Mode of presentation: Programs available on the British market (Total figures, 1960—66)

	British	American
Text	156 (20.8 %)	410 (87.4 %)
Machine	593 (79.2 %)	59 (12.6 %)
Total	749	469

Later on a decrease is seen in British machine program figures. Nevertheless, in the 1969 survey (Cavanagh & Jones, 1969) they still represent the majority of British programs (1079 out of 1553, or 60 %).

It should be observed that all figures of these types should be taken with a large pinch of salt. They can be very unreliable, since bibliographers have had to include in their listings also "pseudo-programs" (if a publisher submitted the title). By "pseudo-programs" we refer to those texts that *look like* a program, but that have not gone through an adequate development process. Unfortunately, no known bibliography so far contains solely "real programs".

If we want to try out a simple tutoprint arrangement to begin with, what are the possibilities? Among the most common methods of procedure are the "panel-books" (in which the presentation units consist of shorter parts of one page, panels, and where these units are arranged in some form of succession) and "scrambled books" (in which the presentation units ordinarily consist of entire pages, and where these units are arranged in a more "scrambled" fashion). Panel-books can also appear in different forms (among others, different "reading directions"). Here are some examples of different tutoprint arrangements at the present time:

(a) *Panel-book with vertical progression ("The vertical panel-book").* This arrangement differs least from an ordinary textbook. The pages are read as usual from top to bottom and in the usual order. That which *in appearance* distinguishes this type of book from conventional books is chiefly the more widely spaced printing. Every instructional unit is usually demarcated from the others with heavy horizontal lines. The student writes his answer as a rule within the frame of the instructional unit, often on an empty line which leaves blank one or more key words from the text. The model answer appears relatively near the response request, perhaps in a special column in the margin either right beside the response request or—in order not to be too conspicuous—beside the following unit (see Figure 8.5).

The method of procedure is quite a common one (see, for example, an early and well-known introduction to programming techniques: Markle, 1961). The printing and editing techniques are simple. The greatest drawback is that the temptation to look at the key answer immediately is so great. But with certain types of students and certain kinds of assignments, this is undoubtedly not of very great importance.

Type A:

Task 1	Answer 1
Task 2	Answer 2
Task 3	Answer 3
Task 4	Answer 4

Type B:

	Task 1
Answer 1	Task 2
Answer 2	Task 3
Answer 3	Task 4

Figure 8.5 "The Vertical Panel-Book"

Some studies have even shown faster work with the *same* degree of knowledge, when the students are specifically instructed to read the answer at once (instead of first writing down their own answer and then looking at the key answer). This method can undoubtedly function well in some situations, especially when the percentage of correct answers is high in any case and the model answer is, therefore, a relatively "unnecessary" confirmation of something which the student understands immediately. This should be an interesting field for further research, since it concerns one of the fundamental principles of programmed teaching. Some of the early programmers emphasized strongly the significance of the overt answering behavior and seemed even to have difficulty in acknowledging that learning *can* take place *without* this overt reaction. On the other hand, many interpret research experience in this area to mean that increase in effectiveness in programming is more dependent on the improved focusing of the stepwise presentation and the cognitive working over of these well-focused stimuli than with the observable response behavior in itself. The latter can be of value as a *guarantee* for the cognitive working over, but it need not be *essential to learning* for that reason.

Various ways of diminishing the risk of looking at the correct answer too early by chance or all-too-obvious temptation have been tried with vertical programs. The answers may appear in the margins in scrambled order, for example, but with a key given after the item. Or they may appear at the foot of the page in some kind of matrix arrangement (cf. Leith et al., 1966).

(b) *Panel-book with horizontal progression ("the horizontal panel-book")*. Here an attempt has been made to avoid the difficulties with the great "cheating temptation" discussed above by setting up the book horizontally. The pages appear much the same as those in the vertical panel-book with a row of clearly demarcated test items. The student does not read the book page by page, however. Instead he usually goes from the upper section of the first page to the upper section of the next page, etc. In other words, he reads a certain section of the pages throughout the whole book (or in any case through a part of the book) before he goes over to other sections of the same pages.

The simplest arrangement would be, therefore, to let the first item on the

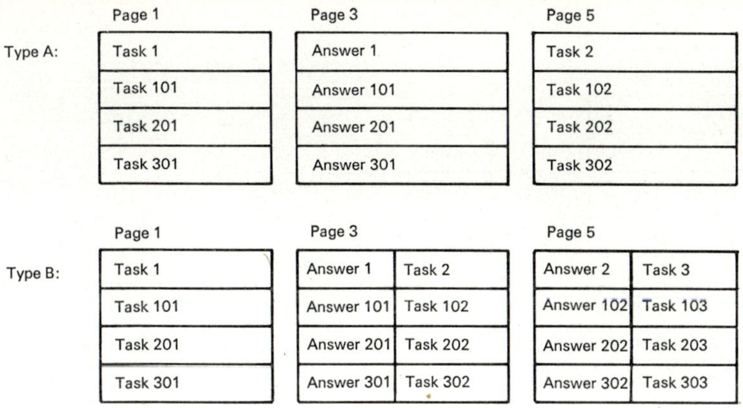

Figure 8.6 "The Horizontal Panel-book"

Note: Even-numbered pages need not be left blank, but can as a rule be used for new tasks and answers, for example, as follows (for Type A): page 2 upper: Task 51; page 4 upper: Answer 51, etc.

first page have its key answer in the first section on the second page, after which the new item at the top of the third page would have its key answer in the first section on the fourth page. Cheating is still easy, it is true, since it is just a matter of turning the page, but the temptation is less than when the key answer information is placed right next to the test item. In order to avoid disturbing factors from the answer to the preceding test item, it is probably better to allow the student to turn the page after every presentation unit. By this means the first test item on the first page has its key answer on the *third* page, after which the new test items on the *fifth* page have their key answers on the *seventh* page (compare Figure 8.6, Type A).

One constructional disadvantage of the horizontal panel-book is that editing is more complicated (the addition of just one unit can involve rearranging large sections). One disadvantage in respect to teaching effectiveness is that the students might possibly have difficulty in "navigating" the transition from one page to the new page and can easily land on the wrong "track". In some cases an attempt is made to prevent this by printing every other section in a contrasting style (for example, on a grey background). An economic drawback, finally, is that this method of procedure involves the consumption of a great deal of paper, since the key answer panel uses as much paper as the test item panel. In order to save paper, therefore, the second unit is often allowed to follow directly after the key answer to the first unit (within the same section and on the same page; compare Figure 8.6, Type B). This has been done, for example, in one of the best-known, "classical" programmed textbooks, namely Holland & Skinner: "The Analysis of Behavior."

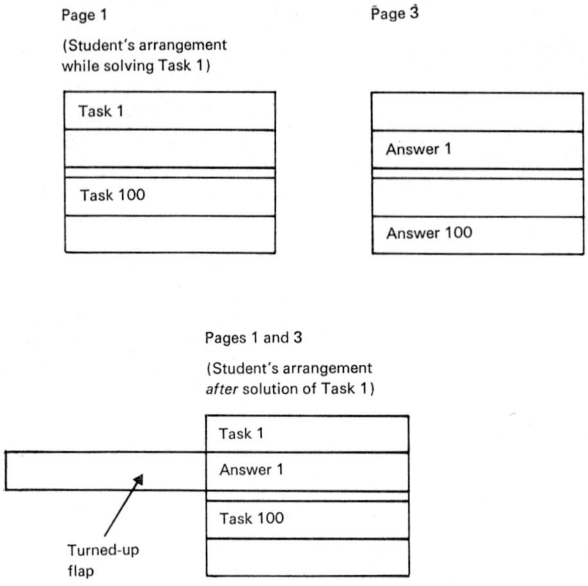

Figure 8.7 "Zigzag Book"

One difficulty with the last-mentioned method can be that focusing on the new items can be disturbed by the preceding answer. In theory it is naturally better to have response request 1 and key answer 1 within the field of vision simultaneously (as often is the case with machine presentation), than to see key answer 1 and response request 2 at the same time (which is more often than not the result of an effort to save paper in the horizontal panel-book). The latter arrangement can be no small source of disturbance, especially when the aim is to teach a special type of response with varying stimuli and gradually fading prompting assistance in a certain task sequence. In some programs at least it would undoubtedly be a case of injudicious zeal to use this paper-saving technique.

(c) *Panel-book with zigzag progression* ("Zigzag Book"). One way of solving the problem—to have the response request and key answer in the same field of vision *after* the student answer without their also being in the same visual field *before*—would be to work with "cut" sections which can be turned forward and backward independently. Then, for example, item 1 can be given in the first section of the first page, and key answer 1 be given in the second section of page three. While the task of the item is being solved, the key answer is concealed. When the problem *is solved,* the answer is made visible (by folding down the upper flap of panel 2), but the response request is still within the visual field. (See Figure 8.7 and Figure 8.8.)

(d) *Panel-books with extra aids.* The temptation to cheat can be diminished

Type of arrangement	'Within the visual field'	
	At stage A (ex., solving Task 3)	At stage B (ex., answer control for Task 3)
Vertical Panel-Book	*T_3+K_3*	T_3+K_3
Horizontal Panel-Book, Type A	only T_3	*only K_3*
Horizontal Panel-Book, Type B	*K_2+T_3*	*K_3+T_4*
Zigzag Book	only T_3	T_3+K_3

Figure 8.8 Principle differences with reference to "focusing balance" between four types of tutoprint arrangements for linear program

In the above chart the letter T is used to symbolize the given tasks (with or without student answer affixed), while the letter K represents the "key answer". The stimuli arrangements which most likely are less suitable (since they bring about inadequate focusing-balance) are in italics. The vertical panel-books provide too *little* screening in the first work stage, while the horizontal panel-book Type A provides too *strong* screening in the second stage. The horizontal panel-book Type B gives too *little* screening in the first stage (when Task 3 is solved, the answer to Task 2 may furnish an inadvertant prompt) and an *inadequate* shielding in the second stage (too great, inasmuch as Task 3 should still be accessible; too little, inasmuch as Task 4 is not relevant to observation of key to Task 3). Of the four arrangements shown here, only the "Zigzag Book" seems to fulfil the demands of focusing balance.

to some extent and, in any case, focusing increased with the vertical panel-book if some type of aid is used for covering the key answers while the test items are being solved. It can be a separate cover stick or one which glides along a groove in the cover, or perhaps a separate outer cover equipped with a series of side flaps which can successively be turned up.

(e) *The Scrambled Book.* One of the best-known types of programmed textbooks is Crowder's so-called "scrambled book". In this version a whole page is used, as a rule, for each information unit with its response request. On one page appears first information and then a control problem. The student must then choose between a number of alternative answers, after which he is referred to one of a number of different pages, depending on which alternative he has chosen. If he has made the correct choice, the new page presents new information and the new unit. If his choice has been wrong, he finds an explanation of the mistake. In the latter case he is usually then referred back to the previous page with the recommendation that he choose a better answer alternative (see Figure 8.9).

That arrangement is, therefore, especially adapted to individualization of content, and it also functions in discouraging the temptation to cheat. (It is

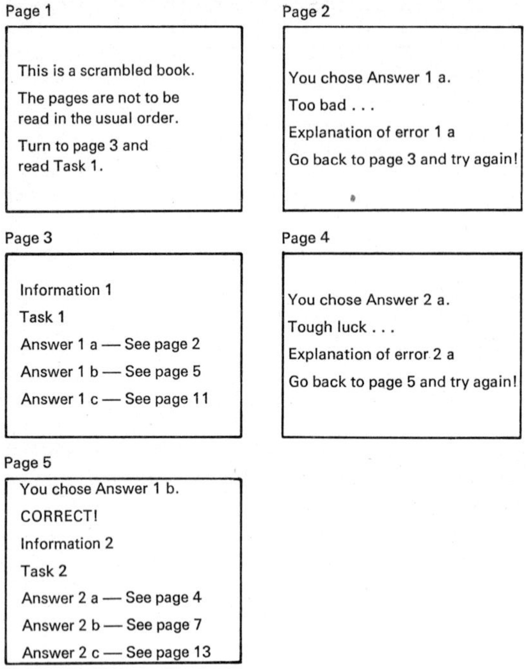

Figure 8.9 Scrambled Book

possible, of course, to peek at all the pages to which reference is made *before* beginning to think, but for most students it is more satisfactory—and often faster—to think first and turn pages later.) One disadvantage can be, however, that in the usual format we are forced to present to the student completed answer alternatives, which under some circumstances is perhaps less desirable. Considering the terminal behavior at which we are aiming, the choice reactions may not be sufficient, and it is not always wise to present confusing misinformation in the earlier phases of the teaching process (a more detailed discussion of these problems will be presented below in connection with an analysis of different "flow models").

(f) *"Cheat-proof" tutoprint arrangement.* None of the tutoprint systems mentioned above is cheat-proof even if the degrees of temptation and opportunity may vary. Attempts have been made to devise more cheat-proof systems. These usually have the drawback that they deal with choice reactions (multiple-choice answers). If this is acceptable with reference to the terminal behavior, then one of the following arrangements may be worth trying—surface covers, perforations, embossed key answers, or chemically prepared answer sheets.

The first technique means that the student selects one of the answer alternatives by *erasing an opaque cover* either directly after or under the alternative in question. Under

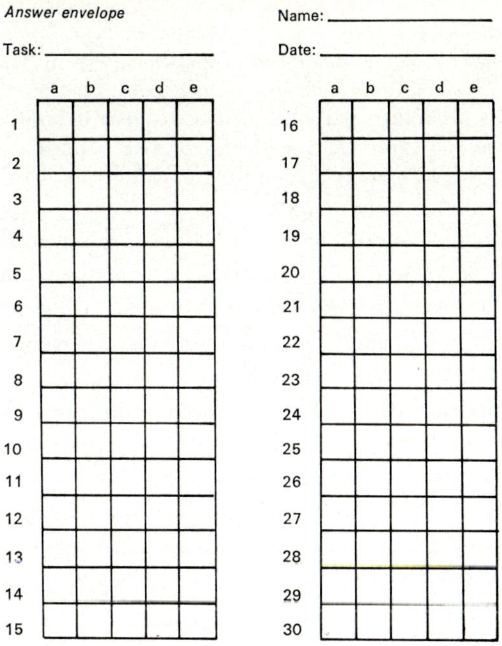

Figure 8.10 Example of attempt to devise "cheat-proof" tutoprint arrangements (raised answer technique)

Each work sequence is represented by an answer envelope printed somewhat like the above, an answer plate with raised letters, numerals, etc., as well as a carbon and a copy-paper. When the answer plate plus a carbon and a copy-sheet have been placed in the envelope, the squares printed on the front of the envelope match up to the symbols on the answer plate inside. If the student now rubs a certain square with a pencil, the symbols from the answer plate are visible in that square; at the same time they are also registered on the copy paper in the envelope.

One way of using this arrangement is to work with a question list with choice of answers. The student marks on the sealed envelope the answers he thinks are correct. The symbols which then become visible let him know whether he is right or wrong. The symbols can, moreover, also provide page references (for explanations of the errors, for example) or can give information in the form of words or numbers. The student knows that he cannot change his answer without its showing on the enclosed copy.

this cover he can find the information which tells him whether he has chosen correctly or not. At the same time the student has, naturally, no possibility of invalidating his selection. The second method—*perforation*—can take a number of forms. In principle it means that the student answers by making a hole with his pencil in the answer sheet at the alternative he considers correct. Through this hole he gets, by one means or another (e.g. with different colors), a report as to whether he has answered correctly or incorrectly. The third method—*the embossed* answer technique—makes use of a response unit consisting of an answer sheet printed on the outside of an envelope which contains the answer plate with raised symbols as well as carbon paper. The student answers by rubbing the blunt end of the pencil over the selected answer pane, which makes visible the information on the accuracy of the answer (Figure 8.10). The fourth—*chemical*—technique involves the use of a special pencil or paintbrush with which the student either touches or dampens an answer sheet, thus indicating which choice he thinks is the right one. The answer sheet is chemically treated in such a way that it turns a certain color (e.g. blue) if the answer is correct, and another color (e.g. red) if the answer is wrong.

To sum up, among the questions which should be considered before selecting a tutoprint arrangement are the following: Is a linear or a branched unit sequence desired? Is a self-devised answer essential for the terminal behavior, or are choice reactions sufficient (or even more natural)? How much weight should be placed in our special student groups on possibilities for cheating and the temptation to cheat? How important is it to be able to have the response request and the key answer *simultaneously* in the visual field *after* the student response? How important is it in our special programs *not* to have distracting elements from previous items in the visual field while a new problem is being solved? If the answers to these questions are unequivocal, then the selection of an arrangement for the special purposes can be relatively simple. But it is also possible that none of the existing systems is entirely satisfactory. Efficient arrangements which work with self-created answers and at the same time have low risk for cheating, or none at all, do not seem to be available at the present time. Neither are a number of the compromises between good focusing and economizing on paper especially successful. In these areas new and better ideas are needed.

THIRD PART

System Synthesis in Instructional Programming: The Intermediate Phases

9. Preparatory Establishment of Sequences: Choosing "Flow Models"

After analysis of prerequisites and subject-matter, but *before* preparing the individual instructional units for the student, the constructor of instructional material should provisionally establish the sequences; this will include choosing the "flow model" (e.g., deciding on possible branching in order to individualize the content).

9.1 Two "Old" Prototypes: The Skinner Model and the Crowder Model

During the first period of interest in instructional programming the best-known types of "flow model" were the two which are called, after their inventors, the *Skinner type* and the *Crowder type*. The main characteristics of the former are (a) that all students go through the study material in the same way, i.e. work through all the tasks in the same order (*linear model*) and (b) that the students give self-constructed answers (either by means of a system of levers controlling a series of letters or numbers, as in certain types of teaching machine, or, more usually, by writing their answers on the work sheet). The characteristics of the *Crowder type* are (a) that branching occurs in the material for error treatment and sometimes to individualize the amount of work (*branching model*) and (b) that the students respond by choosing between ready-made alternative answers (either, when using a teaching machine, by pressing buttons representing different answers, or by turning to different pages in a book, depending on which alternative solution they choose).

A good deal of the early discussion about the preparation of material concerned the advantages and disadvantages of these two main types. Both gave rise to somewhat aggressive schools of thought in defence of the advantages of each of them. Some research projects have also studied the question, but mostly without coming to any definite conclusion clearly favoring one side or the other. It is obviously difficult, in any case, to generalize from the results of this type of research. Presumably different models suit different topics and varying groups of students. Furthermore, so many other factors affect the effectiveness of the material that, in the research which has been done, it has

		TYPE OF ANSWERS	
		Self-constructed answers	Choice between alternative answers
FLOW MODEL	Linear model	A Linear model with self-constructed answers (Skinner type)	B Linear model with alternative answers
	Branching model	C Branching model with self-constructed answers	D Branching model with alternative answers (Crowder type)

Figure 9.1 Different possibilities of combining "flow model" and "type of answer"

often been difficult to isolate the effect of the flow model used. It must be added, and indeed emphasized, that the two models most commonly used during the first years are by no means the only possibilities. Many other forms are certainly conceivable and probably just as effective. The usual combination of flow model and type of answer found in these two "old" prototypes is also by no means self-evident (cf. Figure 9.1).

It might be added that fairly irrelevant characteristics of the early programs were sometimes interpreted as vital components of the two schools. As Markle (1969, p. 1) aptly comments: "Since each new convert to programming tended to imitate the programs he saw, a couple of bad apples in the barrel could spread their influence far and fast . . . much of the real activity in applying techniques of behavior analysis to education is, like the mass of an iceberg, below the surface and not visible in the final product. Copying the surface characteristics does not produce a program." Gradually, programmers have felt more free to depart from the models provided by the pioneers. Gradually, they have realized that much in these models ought to be seen as exemplifications rather than as prescriptions.

9.2 Some Basic Concepts

Even if the early "schools" of programming did not agree about the best type of flow model or answer, they did agree on many basic points. Thus most of these programmers had no doubt that the material should be divided up into small units for presentation (although the word "small" might be somewhat differently interpreted) and that, in addition to new information, these units should also contain some form of request for an answer and be followed by some kind of report to the student about the correctness of the answer.

Unfortunately there is no generally accepted terminology for these basic components which at the same time (a) is unconnected with some special form of presentation, (b) does not favor a particular theory, and (c) is sufficiently exact to be used unambiguously.

Thus the term "frame" is often used for the basic unit, in spite of the fact that it is really only suitable for certain types of presentation (it does not seem suited, for example, to an auditory presentation). In addition, the term has not been used consistently, since certain writers use it about the whole complex: information + response demand + indication of result, while others use it only for information + response demand (regarding the indication of results as a separate phenomenon, which in fact it is in certain forms of presentation). In other words, the expression "frame" vacillates between its original meaning as a technical term referring to a specific presentation method and a later, broader interpretation.

/The word "frame" also tends, unfortunately, to lead to a restricted understanding of what is meant by an instructional step. Many people think that the "small steps" so often talked about in programming are more or less identical with what can be presented in the small rectangular opening of a simple teaching machine (perhaps 1 1/2 × 3 ins.). (For problems of the size of steps, see below.)/

Similar difficulties arise with other words which are used in this connection. The terms "stimulus" and "response" are so general that they are difficult to use in the sense of component parts of a single unit of presentation in teaching material of the above type. The word "reward" is misleading because of its everyday meaning. The term "reinforcement" is theoretically "loaded" and should in principle not be used *a priori.* In other words, it should be used only when it *has* been demonstrated that a certain report of the correctness of behavior does in fact "reinforce" that behavior, i.e. make it easier to produce.

At one of the early international conferences on programmed learning (Berlin, 1963) there was a Terminology Committee whose task was to examine critically existing terminology in the field of programmed instruction. From the discussions in the committee it became evident that the main problem was not to find adequate translations from one language to another (although that aspect of the problem could certainly be important), but to arrive at a sufficiently unambiguous and functional terminology in English, the initial language. Several people, and especially the specialist on learning theories, E. K. Hilgard, expressed the opinion that this terminology should be fairly neutral from a theoretical and interpretative point of view, so that educational psychologists with different theoretical points of departure could nevertheless agree on a basic descriptive vocabulary as a common point of reference.

As an illustration of this endeavour we can mention the attempt to find a series of simple starting terms in English, German and French for five key concepts or stages in the instructional situation: (a) what the student is offered in the way of information and tasks; (b) the processes thereby set in motion in the students, together with the preparatory behavior which can be registered, but which does not constitute the actual response reaction; (c) the

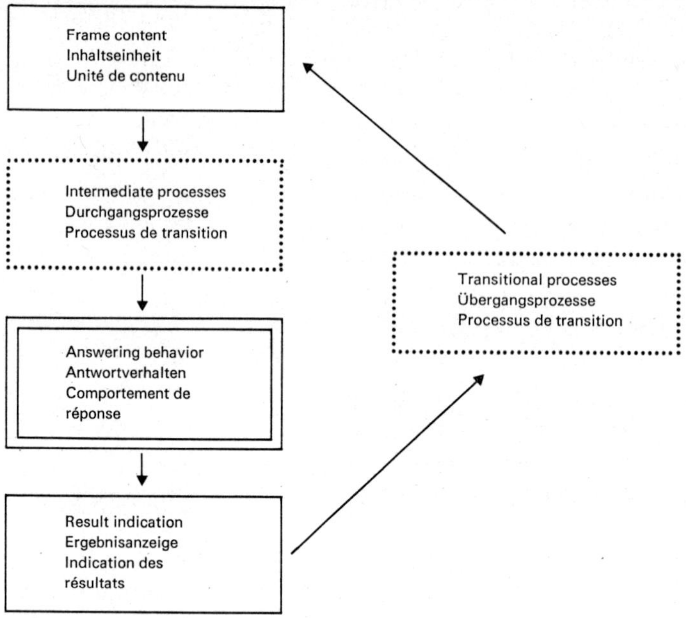

Figure 9.2 Terminological description of some basic stages in a typical self-instructional situation

Note: The student's direct response behavior is marked by a double line (═══════). Other student processes are shown by a dotted line (.....). Stages in the program are marked by a continuous line (————).

response reaction itself; (d) the indication given by the teaching program of the correctness or incorrectness of the response reaction; and (e) the (partly hypothetical) processes which register the result for the student together with the necessary manipulations (if any) for proceeding to the next unit of study (manipulation of levers, turning the pages of a book etc.). The suggested terms and the operational sequences referred to are shown in Figure 9.2.

The examples of terms given here can naturally form only a modest beginning for a descriptive terminology. In many cases there is a need for a fairly specific terminology, for which existing linguistic usage is not felt to be sufficient. In such cases, it is naturally often necessary to introduce completely new terms. In the following we present a few terminological suggestions which, at least within the framework of the present survey, should serve the purpose of referring unambiguously to some basic concepts.

In what follows we shall thus when needed use the term "*didule*" (pronounced: di'dju:l) for the typical instructional unit in programmed study material, to include "information", "response demand" and "feedback" to the student. The term is assumed to include both what is called "frame content" (stage 1) in Figure 9.2 and also "result indication" (stage 4). (As already indicated, the term "frame" is not completely satisfactory as a description of stage 1, since certain programmers also use it for stage 4 and since it has some undesirable side-associations. It will be noticed that the representatives for both the other main languages avoided corresponding words in the terms they recommended.)

Within each didule we can differentiate three more specific components, for which we shall use, for the present, the following technical terms: (a) *stimule* for that part of the teaching unit which presents focal stimuli (central teaching material) plus support stimulation; (b) *respule* for the response demand connected with it and (c) *corrule* for the feedback connected with the student's response, i.e. usually the indication to the student of the correctness of his answer ("result indication" in Figure 9.2).[1] Thus a typical "didule" consists of "stimule" + "respule" + "corrule". When wishing to express these concepts by brief symbols, we shall refer to them by the letters D, S, R and K.[2]

We shall use these concepts in our discussion of the characteristic properties of the different flow models. To begin with we classify the different flow models into *two groups*: (1) *linear models* (with a sequence independent of the responses) and (2) different *branching models* (with a sequence dependent upon the responses).[3] Branching models may in turn be said to be of two main types: (2a) micro-branching models, in which differentiated treatment occurs only within a didule, while the didules themselves are arranged wholly linearly; and (2b) macro-branching models, in which branching also occurs with respect to the didule sequence and/or the number of didules.

9.3 Some Basic Models

9.3.1 *The Simple Linear Model*

The simple linear model is represented by the best-known form of the Skinner program. In this, all the students in the target population go through all the didules in a pre-ordained order. This can be done by means of presentation in book form (one of the most well-known courses of this type is the psychology course which Skinner worked out in co-operation with Holland) or by presentation by a simple type of machine.

[1] The term "result indication" can in some cases be far too general, as it can also be used for the final result as shown e.g. by the error counter of a teaching machine.

[2] K is used here instead of C in order to avoid duplicating the meaning of our basic letter symbols. C is used in this book for basic content unit or "concept".

[3] The linear model has been the most used. Among 749 British programs during 1960—66, 68 % were linear; and among 468 American programs, commercially available in England, during the same period, 84 % were linear. (Cf. Cavanagh & Jones, 1966.)

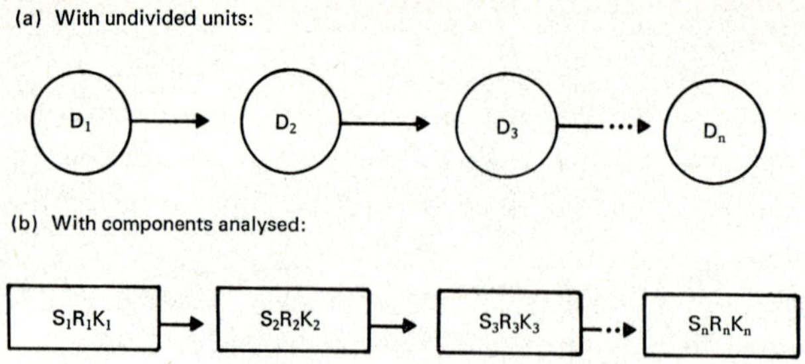

Figure 9.3 General diagram of the simple linear model

Box 9.1 The simple linear model: An example

37. DE- is a negative prefix that is put in front of verbs.
DE- means "do the opposite of" the verb's meaning.
HUMANIZE means "make human". The opposite of making something good for humans is making it bad: the opposite of HUMANIZE is ________

— —

DEHUMANIZE

38. An army is called together and trained for action: it is *mobilized.* When the time of service is over, the men are let go.
They have been ____________

— —

demobilized

39. If the laws of a country are "made fit for humans" (or changed to what is favorable for man), we say that they have been *humanized.* If the changes are unfair to man, we would say that the laws have been *dehumanized.*
HUMANIZE is the
________ of DEHUMANIZE.

— —

opposite

40. DEHUMANIZE, DECENTRALIZE, DEMORALIZE, DEODORIZE—All these words have the n ________ prefix DE-.

— —

negative

41. A hundred years ago, young boys worked in factories and in mines. Boys as well as men worked twelve hours a day for very little money. Before long, such treatment of children was considered *inhuman.* There now are laws against it. The laws have ______________ (dehumanized/humanized) the treatment of working children.

— —

humanized (Things are better now)

Sample units, slightly edited, from S. M. Markle: "Words. A programed course in vocabulary development." (1962)

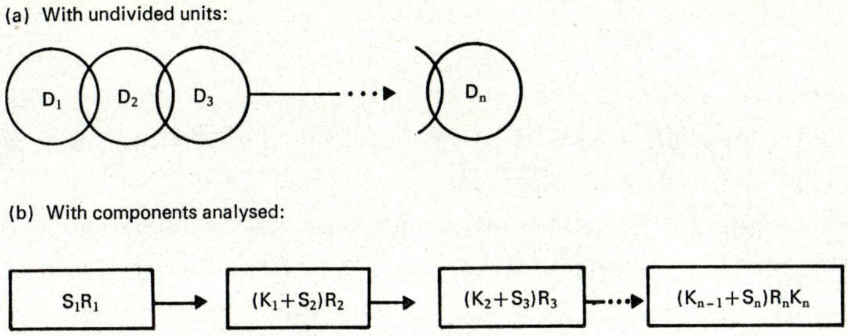

Figure 9.4 General diagram of the chaining model

Box 9.2 The chaining model: An example

37. DE- is a negative prefix that is put in front of verbs. *Humanize* means "make human". The opposite of making something good for humans is making it bad: the opposite of *humanize* is ___________

38. DEHUMANIZE, decentralize, demoralize, deodorize.—All these words have the n ___________ prefix de-.

39. Using the NEGATIVE prefix de-, you can often express the opposite of a verb's meaning. An army is called together and trained for action: it is *mobilized*. When the time of service is over, the men are let go. They have been ___________
etc.

In principle, we get a build-up of the kind shown in Figure 9.3 (and in Box 9.1). The student responds to one task at a time and immediately gets information about the correct answer. If he has given the wrong answer, he is made aware of it, but nevertheless goes straight on to the next task. The response request functions as part of the learning process and does not constitute any "test" of what has been learned. Fairly often, rather short didules have been used in these programs, but this is not, of course, a necessary consequence of the flow model.

9.3.2 *A Variation of the Linear Model: The Chaining Model*

A variation of the linear model is the "chaining model", advocated by John Barlow (1960). In both models all students go through the same didules in the same order. In the chaining model, however, the didules are "chained together" in such a way that the corrule component in one task is incorporated as a part of the stimule component in the next (cf. Figure 9.4). The student is first presented a task in the ordinary way and gives his answer. Instead of getting information about the correct answer separately (as is usual in the simple linear model), the right answer is incorporated in the next task unit as one or more words in different type (e.g. capitals). See Box 9.2.

This special technique can have two advantages, (a) *the student* can experience greater continuity in the material, and (b) it prevents *the constructor* from making too large leaps in his thinking and can therefore act as an aid in reminding him of the "small steps" principle. The special form of writing is obviously of great importance, for there may sometimes be a risk of reduced "focusing" and lesser "readability". Few studies seem to have used the method in research (but cf. Trittipoe et al., 1963, and Greenberg, 1968).

9.3.3 *The Micro-Branching Model: Branching for Error Treatment*

The most usual kind of branching seems to have been that special type of error treatment most often used in the Crowder program which has already been summarily treated above. It consists mainly of a branching within the individual didule without alteration of the total didule sequence or number of didules.

This error treatment in general takes the following form (cf. Figure 9.5 and Box 9.3). In study unit 1 the student is given information and the accompanying task. He will answer by choosing one of a number of alternative possible answers. If he gives the correct answer, he immediately gets the next information and task. If, on the other hand, he gives the wrong answer, he gets instead an explanation of his mistake, which shows that he has made a mistake and explains why the answer was wrong. As a rule, the student is then directed back to the first study unit with instructions to choose another alternative ("stimule and respule repetition") before continuing.

This procedure can be expressed in another way thus: All the students get the same basic stimule and respule components, but as a result of the student's answer, the corrule can take various forms. When a wrong choice is made, the corrule consists of error treatment (different for different errors) and, when the correct choice is made, of an indication to this effect and direction to the next didule. This indication is sometimes only *implicit*: the student knows that he has given the right answer since the next task is presented. But frequently it takes the form of a "pat on the back", e.g.:

"Right you are."
"You are correct, of course."
"Excellent."
"You are doing fine."
"Grand."

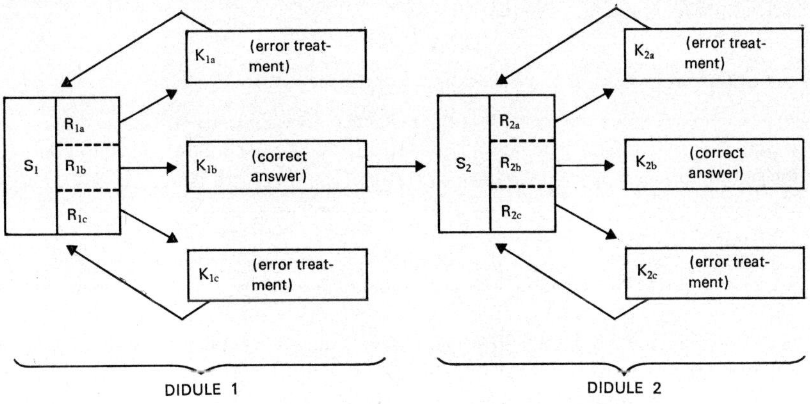

Figure 9.5 General diagram of the micro-branching model

Error indication in a typical Crowder program often begins with some form of chaffing:

"Now, wait a minute!"
"Now, you really know better than that."
"Oooops!"
"Oh, come on now."
"Sorry, bad guess."

The latter phrases, however, always lead to a more detailed explanation, and it is this explanation which is most characteristic of Crowder's micro-branching. Other constructors have worked with multi-choice alternatives *without* error treatment (e.g. Pressey). In these cases it would be more natural to speak of a linear program with alternative answers (cf. Figure 9.1, cell B) than of micro-branching.

9.3.4 *The Macro-Branching Model (1—2): Sequence Differentiation of the Repetition Type*

The ability of different students to profit from something new varies greatly, depending, among other things, on their background experience. The need of practising the application of certain rules is therefore also very varied. From the point of view of time and effectiveness, it can be uneconomic to suit the construction of self-instructional material to the "lowest common denominator", i.e. to build into it as much repetition for *all* as for the student with the greatest need for repetition. An alternative possibility worth considering is therefore a sequence variation in the material with more repetition for the students with the greatest need of it.

Box 9.3 Micro-branching: An example

Note to the reader:

This is not an ordinary book. Although the pages are numbered in the ordinary way, you must not try to read them consecutively. You must follow the directions at the bottom of each page. Now start with page 1.

PAGE 1

What Is a Poem? Few writers are in complete agreement, but many seem to agree in one area: a poem must at least be honest, consistent, and complete.—Almost everyone has read some poetry, and we can all recognize a poem when we see one. Or can we?

Which of the following statements is true?

I?
Why?

is not a poem. (See *page 7*)

abcdefg
hijklmnop
qrs and tuv
w and xyz

is not a poem. (See *page 9*)

Both of the above are poems. (See *page 11*)

Neither of the above is a poem. (See *page 13*)

PAGE 2

You have reached this page by mistake, for you could not have arrived here by following directions. You must not try to read the pages serially. On each page there are clear instructions directing you to the next page you are to read.
Now go back to the page you just came from, and follow directions.

PAGE 7 (from page 1)
YOUR ANSWER:

I?
Why?
is not a poem

Why not? Do you think that a poem must have a specific number of lines or look regular or contain a certain amount of material? If so, you are wrong. "I? Why?" has been called the shortest poem in the English language because its two words rhythmically express a complete thought. It asks a question that has plagued men since the beginning of time: "Why do I exist?"

During this century poetry has undergone a period of experimentation. Changes in style and subject matter have sometimes produced oddities. But language is flexible, and you must expect poets to utilize its versatility. However, the poem can still meet the three requirements mentioned earlier: honesty, consistency, and completeness.

Return to page 1 and select another answer.

PAGE 9 (from page 1)
YOUR ANSWER:

abcdefg
hijklmnop
qrs and tuv
w and xyz
  is not a poem.

Careful. It is a poem, for it well exemplifies the requirements of honesty, consistency, and completeness set forth earlier. The alphabet, although commonplace, is not an unfit subject for poetry, even though its poetic possibilities are limited. In fact, the alphabet, in its normal order, was actually used in the 1920's as a poem entitled "Suicide".

Poets often experiment, and you should be willing to accept variances from what you might consider traditional forms. In experimentation, however, the poet need not violate the requirements of honesty, consistency, and completeness.

Return to page 1 and select another answer.

PAGE 11 (from page 1)
YOUR ANSWER: Both are poems.

Yes, you are right. "I? Why?" could perhaps be entitled "A Metaphysical Introspection of Myself in Terms of the Universal". The alphabet, so presented, has a rythmical completeness that a reader may find attractive.

But you would have a difficult time justifying your view that the two examples are poetry unless you defined your terms. Most disagreements about poetry stem from a failure to do just this.

Therefore, it is desirable to clarify further the meaning of the three key terms mentioned above: honesty, consistency, and completeness. If we have a poem . . .

(Note: Here the program gives a new task with different response alternatives, leading on to different pages.)

PAGE 13 (from page 1)
YOUR ANSWER: Neither is a poem.

Are you willing to back up this belief with evidence? Can you define for yourself what a poem is? Try it. In 25 words or less, complete the following statement: "A poem is . . ."

Could you do it? If so, did your definition contain references to rhyme and rhythm? Both texts contain rhyme and rhythm, don't they? If the two arrangements are not poems, what else are they? Just because a group of words does not appear to have a clear meaning at first glance does not preclude its being called a poem, if the three requirements of honesty, consistency, and completeness are not violated.

For the moment, I suggest that you accept both of these examples as poems. If you had selected the answer "Both are poems", you would have been directed to page 11. Go to that page now, and we will clarify the definitions further as we go along.

Sample units, abbreviated and slightly edited, from J. C. Pratt: "The meaning of modern poetry" (1962).

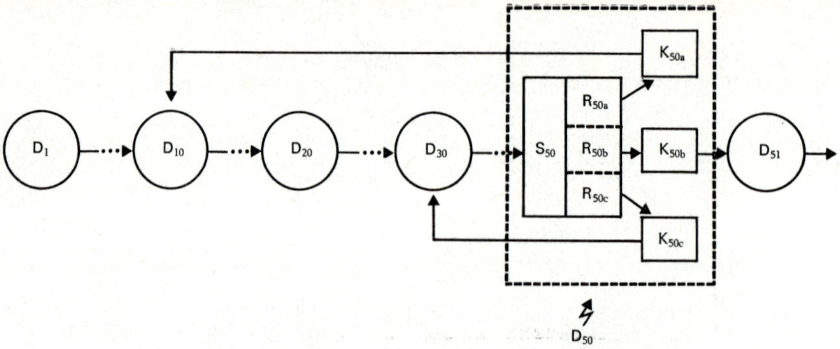

Figure 9.6 Macro-branching model 1: Sequence differentiation of repetition type—simple direction back after wrong answer in a post-checking didule

Note: The student has got as far as didule no. 50, which is a checking didule for the immediately *preceding* study section. If he answers correctly (alternative *b*), he gets the next task (D_{51}). If, however, he answers with alternative *a*, we perhaps consider this a serious mistake, which shows that the student has missed important information. The student is therefore directed back so that he repeats a long section, e.g. from D_{10} to D_{50}. If he answers with alternative *c*, which is considered a less serious mistake, he need repeat only a shorter section, e.g. from D_{30} to D_{50}.

A simple example of such macro-branching is shown in Figure 9.6. Here a special "post-checking didule" has been introduced into the task sequence. If the student solves the test part of this well, he simply goes on to new study material. If, on the other hand, he fails to complete it satisfactorily, he gets instead a larger or a smaller repetition task. In the simplest case, he is directed back to a certain earlier task number and instructed to repeat a series of didules which he has already gone through.

If one is dealing with subject-matter which is not sequential in character, e.g. the learning of individual associations (vocabulary in a foreign language etc.), the repetition can mean that the student goes back to the tasks in which he earlier made mistakes and works through them again. This post-check is often arranged so that the student has to go through the tasks to which he has given the wrong answer until he has answered each task correctly at least once. It should be noted that Skinner, in his earlier experiments with the so-called "disc programs" (discs inserted in an apparatus similar to the old memory psychologists' "mnemometer") worked with study material of this type. Skinner's name has in the discussion been almost exclusively connected with strict linear programming. It is therefore interesting to observe that he also worked with highly individualized repetition programs (cf. Figure 9.7).

Figure 9.7 Macro-branching model 2: Sequence differentiation of repetition type—direction back to individualized repetition, including previous wrongly-answered didules

Work criterion: Each task answered correctly once.

Initial sequence for all students:

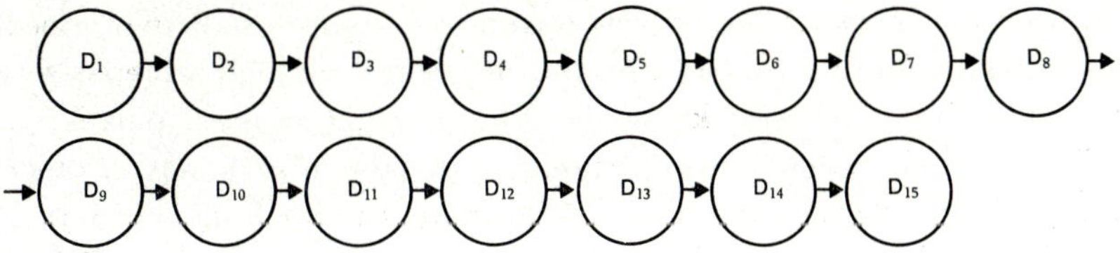

Student A's work (completed in 18 stages)
Result of student A's work in first working:
r_1, r_2, r_3, r_4, r_5, w_6, r_7, w_8, r_9, r_{10}, w_{11}, r_{12}, r_{13}, r_{14}, r_{15}
(r = right, w = wrong)
Student A's individual work sequence, second working:

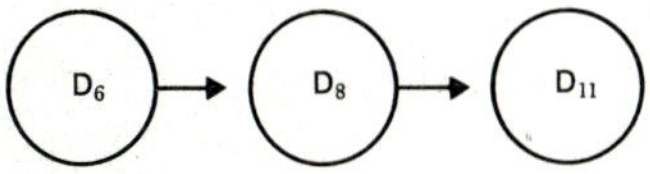

Student A's result in second working:
r_6, r_8, r_{11}

Student B's work (completed in 26 stages)
Result of student B's work in first working:
r_1, r_2, w_3, w_4, w_5, r_6, w_7, w_8, r_9, r_{10}, w_{11}, w_{12}, r_{13}, r_{14}, w_{15}
Student B's work sequence, second working:

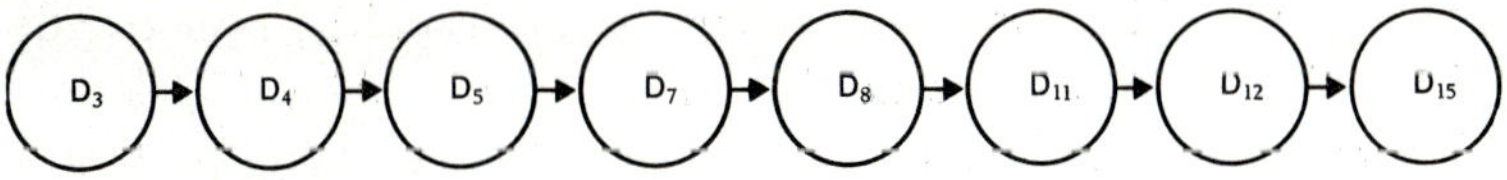

Result of student B's work, second working:
r_3, w_4, w_5, r_7, r_8, w_{11}, r_{12}, r_{15}
Student B's work sequence, third working:

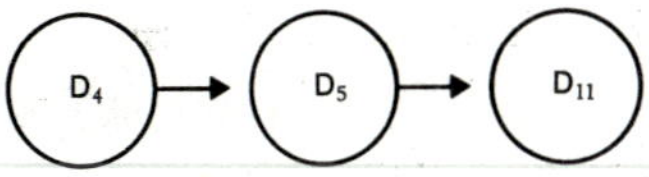

Student B's result in third working:
r_4, r_5, r_{11}

9.3.5 *Macro-Branching Model (3): Sequence Differentiation of the Rapid-Track Type*

As a counterpart to simple "direction back" at a wrong answer in a post-checking didule, we can obviously devise a simple "direction forward" for other circumstances. Let us assume that we cannot presuppose, among the majority of the target population, a certain type of mathematical knowledge which is necessary so that a certain new stage in the course can be performed. We must, then, before we can start on this new stage, arrange a preparatory sequence to teach the necessary knowledge. However, the target population in all likelihood contains a few students who have already, in some way or other, acquired this knowledge and thus do not need to work through the preparatory didules. If we believe that this is so, we can arrange a "pre-checking" item which tests the students' knowledge in this respect. If this check is successful, i.e. shows that individual students really have this knowledge, we direct them to skip the preparatory sequence and instead let them start straight away on the next stage of the course. (Figure 9.8 and Box 9.4.)

Both pre- and post-checking items can be thought of as "filter tests", which give information about the best possible flow track for the individual student. To avoid guess-work and chance playing too great a part at such important check points, it is often a good thing not to be content with just one checking task, but to use several of this type. If they all give the same result, we can naturally be more certain that our recommendation of a flow track is based on reliable information about the student's qualifications.

9.3.6 *Macro-Branching Model (4): Parallel Track Type*

Both the repetition type and fast track type of sequence differentiation imply in a way only manipulation of a basic model of a "linear" type, a fixed chain of study units which we "shorten" or "lengthen" according to the needs of the individual student. We either make the student go back and go over certain sections again, which we believe he needs to repeat, or let him skip certain sections, which we think are unnecessary for him. But there are also possibilities of macro-branching with tracks which run parallel. (A general diagram of such a model is given in Figure 9.9.)

A parallel track arrangement can be used for very different purposes: (a) repetition or practice material of different kinds for groups of students who show varying retention of material previously worked through, (b) informative material of varying scope for groups of students with varied pre-knowledge, or (c) treatment of the same set of problems from different angles depending on the students' various attitudes and opinions.

The first of these uses has a purpose very similar to that of the above-

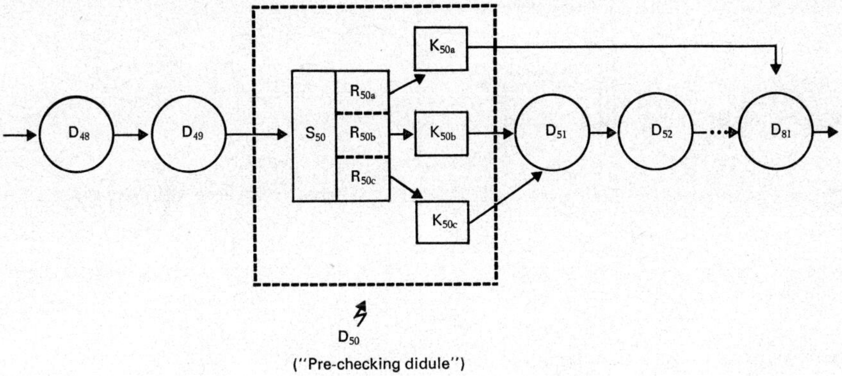

Figure 9.8 Macro-branching model 3: Sequence differentiation of the rapid track type

Note: The student has reached didule no. 50, which constitutes a pre-checking didule for the next study section. If he chooses a wrong answer (*b* or *c*), he simply goes on to the next task. If, however, he answers correctly (*a*), we perhaps estimate that the student already has the knowledge the next section is supposed to give. He can then make a jump forward (skip the material he already knows) and begin studying, for example, didule 81.

Box 9.4 Rapid track model: Example of a pre-checking didule

41. To be able to go through our next section in German grammar, you must be quite sure about what is meant by "subject", "dative object" and "accusative object".

    Mark the *subject* with an S.
    Mark the *accusative object* with an A.
    Mark the *dative object* with a D.

    a. The girl gave the boy a ball.
    b. He bought an ice-cream.
    c. He gave it to her.

Solution to No. 41:

a. The girl gave the boy a ball.
   S D A

b. He bought an ice-cream.
   S A

c. He gave it to her.
   S A D

Instruction:

If you made a mistake, or if you do not feel sure about it, go on with No. 42 next. This will give you more practice with parts of the sentence.

If you did not make any mistakes and feel certain that you can recognize the "subject", "accusative object" and "dative object", go on to No. 71.

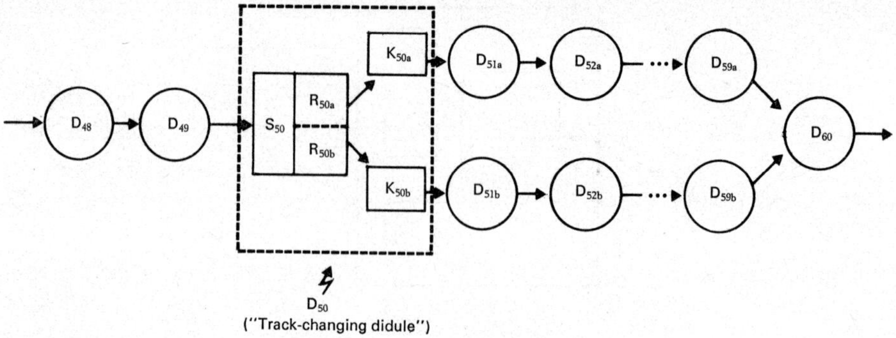

Figure 9.9 Macro-branching model 3: Parallel track type

mentioned branching model with repetition. There is sometimes a risk, however, that a strict repetition of material which has already been worked through (not least in the form occasionally presented by machines which "reverse back") can be a disagreeable experience for the students. Since a positive learning climate is essential when self-instructional material is being used, it would be well to try to arrange it in a more pleasant way. All the students can, for example, get "new" practice tasks, so that those who have shown that they have not mastered previous material get a *longer* parallel series of practice tasks than the others. It is then a question of further training in the form of new tasks instead of strict and manifest repetition of the same tasks.

The last-named method—treatment of the same set of problems from varying angles depending on different students' varying attitudes and opinions—is perhaps the one that has been least used. If self-instructional material is to be made really effective in areas where different opinions exist and should be clarified, for example, a parallel track arrangement of this kind should be an excellent method.

9.3.7 *Directed vs. Voluntary Choice of Track*

It is worth mentioning here that there are many ways of choosing a track at the point of differentiation in a multi-track model. The most usual is perhaps that the choice is made on the basis of the student's *response to a filter test.* He is directed to different study sequences according to the alternative answer he chooses. Another possibility is to choose a track as a result of some kind of *reaction summation.* If, for example, the student gives more than 90 % of the correct solutions in one section, he may continue directly with the next section. Otherwise he first has to work through a special review section.

Side by side with these two types of *directed* choice, there is also the possibility of a *voluntary* choice. The student chooses at a certain point (a)

Box 9.5 Choice according to direction of interest or attitude: Two examples

Example A:

50. In our study of developmental psychological principles and their importance for the teacher's handling of the student in school, we shall now give a series of concrete illustrations. Here you should choose the section you read according to your interest or area of experience.

Instructions:
If you teach in grades 1—3, study next tasks 51—60.
If you teach in grades 4—6, you can skip the next tasks and concentrate on Nos. 61—70.
If you teach in grade 7 or higher, you can concentrate on tasks 71—80.

Example B:

100. When we describe the target for our teaching, it is usually not enough to say what kind of behavior the course is intended to teach. We must also state clearly how well the student should be able to do. In other words, we should state a lower limit for an acceptable performance. Now choose the pages you will read, depending on your attitude.

a. "Show me how I should set about describing the limits for acceptable performance."—turn to p. 103.
b. "Much of what I teach cannot be evaluated or measured."—turn to p. 101.

(The students who choose p. 101 will get the starting-point further clarified and motivated. It is hoped in this way to avoid possible misunderstandings and, if possible, to create a more positive attitude to the suggested procedure. These students are then directed to p. 103 to continue.—A procedure closely corresponding to this example will be found in Mager, 1961.)

whether he wants to repeat a section or continue, (b) *whether* he wants to study a certain problem more deeply by going through our "extra course" sequence or skip this material, or (c) *whether* he would like to have a certain type of problem illustrated by examples from one special area of experience rather than from another (Box 9.5, Example A).

A certain number of such opportunities for voluntary choice may often give the students, especially if they are more adult, a valuable feeling of greater freedom in their work. Apart from the fact that such a choice of illustrations from a personally relevant area of interest can in itself *directly* promote effectiveness on the particular point to be illuminated, being encouraged to make some sort of choice often increases motivation generally. Hence, this technique may increase effectiveness *indirectly,* too. (Obviously, the area of choice is still rather limited in this design. Models with considerably extended "degrees of freedom" will be dealt with below; section 9.4.2.)

In certain cases such a voluntary choice inserted at an early stage helps a student to clear an "emotional block" caused by misunderstanding of the instructor's presentation of the facts and his intentions. This means that an unnecessary barrier to communication is broken down, thus making a further contribution to increased instructional effectiveness (cf. Box 9.5, Example B).

9.3.8 *The Completely Student-Adapted Model*

Even if branching models of the type now under discussion result in greater attention being paid to the individual differences than the linear model admits, they hardly mean that one proceeds in every single task as a really effective private teacher would have done. Sometimes a particular student is given unnecessarily many examples. Sometimes he is given too few. It is, however, quite possible in principle to build up considerably more student-adapted models in which each unit of presentation is chosen on a basis of the student's reaction to the one immediately preceding it as well as in line with a series of basic student characteristics. This type of highly individualized treatment is sometimes referred to as "idiographic" programming (Stolurow).

Computer techniques can be used for this purpose. However, this demands comprehensive preparatory work to create instructionally suitable patterns of "machine behavior" (cf. Box 8.1 above). Advanced computers within the school system are still not very frequent, and initial costs are high. This means that while such possibilities are certainly of great theoretical interest, they have *as yet* limited practical value for many teaching situations. (Readers interested in developments of this kind may refer to Stolurow & Davis, 1965, Bushnell & Allen, 1967, and Lehnert, 1970, among others.)

9.4 Two Special Arrangements

9.4.1 *The "Tail Model"*

If the completely student-adapted model belongs to the uncertain future, what is called here the "tail model" belongs to the past history of the teaching machine. The first well-known experiments with teaching machines were carried out in the twenties by Sidney L. Pressey, Professor of Education at the Ohio State University. The machines he used were primarily intended for the correction of tests. They saved the teacher the work of correction by adding up the number of correct answers to test questions which the student answered by pressing buttons.

According to Pressey, these machines could also be used for teaching purposes. In this case, the machine did not go on to the next question before the preceding problem had been correctly solved. The student had to go on attempting until he found the correct alternative answer. Since the student worked actively and always got the right answer, Pressey maintained that this type of work had considerable value for effective teaching. The ideas of creating a totally self-instructional course in the form of a chain of small tasks, to arrange course material in an instructionally detailed sequence, to work with small steps and try to keep the error rate low;—these ideas did not lie within the scope of Pressey's aims, simply because his teaching machines were not primarily intended for teaching in the ordinary sense of the word, but for checking results and a certain amount of "post-teaching". The *real* teaching, the basic inculcation of information, was done in other ways, e.g. in the form of traditional lessons and by reading textbooks.

When the idea of completely programmed courses was worked out later, many thought Pressey's technique primitive and ineffective by comparison. Nor was it built up from the thorough preliminary work which is nowadays considered natural in preparing the material for a self-instructional course. But it must be remembered that he had a different purpose in mind. It was not a question of complete study material, but material for checking and correcting. However, Pressey has argued, with some success, that such "tail models" may have a special value. In many cases, we have neither the time nor the possibilities for constructing completely programmed courses. In some cases we are perhaps more interested in giving the student good habits of study and the ability to work with refractory material than making certain that, by pedantically thorough spoonfeeding, certain subject-matter has been completely learnt. It would then be quite natural to let the students work independently with textbooks and other source material and, after they have done this, check and correct their work by a device of the "tail model" type. On the other hand, if one does construct material of this "tail" type, one should naturally not deceive oneself or others into believing that one *has* a completely programmed course with its special advantages and area of use.

9.4.2 *The "Intermittent Model"*

A compromise between Pressey's "tail model" and a more completely programmed course is the "intermittent model". In the preparation of the study material one then differentiates between the subject-matter, the instructions for treatment of the subject-matter and the checking tasks. The newly constructed study material thus mainly takes the form of a detailed study plan interspersed with self-correcting tests, while the actual material for study is taken by the students from a variety of other sources, to which he is directed from his study compendium. The source material can consist of different sections of textbooks and reference books, diagrams, tables, maps, etc. The study compendium gives him directions as to where to find his material and how it is to be treated.

When he has followed the instructions and used the material in this way, he goes back to the compendium where he is tested on his knowledge. If the result is satisfactory, he is directed to new material. If it is unsatisfactory, he is directed to study the earlier material again or to go to another source which in principle presents in another form the same material to be learnt.

The change-over between reading the instructions, independent work from sources and self-testing afterwards which the "intermittent" model offers should in many cases give the teacher a useful instrument in his striving to create good, independent habits of study. However, there may be a risk of lazy reading and direct copying, and this should be borne in mind when the material is constructed. It will naturally be important to formulate the instructions in such a way as to encourage a critical and active form of study. The method may also mean that the individual student gets inadequate help in his studies, unless special preparatory training has got rid of the difficulties.

Both the "tail" and "intermittent" models can be said to consist mainly of checking didules. In the tail model, the whole checking section comes at the end of the work, and the necessary subsequent direction of the student is left entirely to the tutor/teacher. In the intermittent model, this checking takes place at suitable stages in the work sequence. *On the basis of the test result* the student is then directed to new tasks without the immediate intervention of the teacher. Self-instructional study material, consisting mainly of source material, instructions and checking didules, very closely resembles the kind of study material traditionally used by correspondence schools. There are also considerable similarities between what is here called the intermittent model and the working techniques used in the Winnetka plan and the Dalton plan (both in operation in the 1920's). In both, students proceeded at their own rates and took diagnostic tests as entrance tickets to new units. It should be possible to increase effectiveness in the technique of teaching by correspondence or the working procedures in the Dalton and Winnetka plan by following, to a greater degree than has been customary in the past, the stages of preparation we have outlined above for constructing self-instructional material (and also, of course, by submitting the material to the empirical testing procedure which we shall deal with later on).

9.5 Choosing a "Flow Model"

9.5.1 *Starting from the Subject-Matter*

In one of the many introductory works on programmed teaching published in the USA, the author (Cram, 1961) concludes his chapter on linear and branching programs with a self-test (p. 64) which, somewhat shortened, looks something like this:

Which style of programming would you consider first if you were to program a lesson or book on the following topics?

1. Household budgeting
2. How to mount a butterfly
3. How to find the square root of a number
4. Methods of psychoanalysis
5. Should you be in a mental institution?

The reader could well ponder a moment on possible answers and motivations. It would then perhaps be of interest to compare your own conclusions with Cram's suggestions and reasoning, of which we give a slightly summarized version in Box 9.6. We do not maintain, obviously, that Cram's suggestions are necessarily better than the reader's! It depends on the special purpose of the teaching, the special group of students one has in mind and the concrete form the flow model takes, whether one or other type of model will be most effective for a given subject area. In other words, it is not necessarily the subject which determines the flow model. But in the choice between different models, the subject may naturally play some part; and the points of view put forward by Cram can perhaps be summarized thus (cf. p. 141):

(a) If the subject matter has a very fixed structure and consists mainly of facts, definitions and basic skills founded on such facts and definitions, a linear approach is natural. Many mathematical subjects are examples of this. The example given above ("How to find the square root of a number") is a case in point.

(b) If the subject-matter contains a great many comparisons, assessments and opinions, i.e. matter apart from the basic facts and definitions, the branching technique is often very suitable. It is easier in a branching program to work from the student's previous understanding of the subject and to deepen and/or correct it. The comparative discussion of various psychoanalytical methods mentioned above is an example of this.

(c) If the subject matter most relevant to each individual student varies within the framework of a larger area of subject matter, the branching technique can quickly lead the student's reasoning to what is relevant to him personally. An example of this is the subject about household budgeting.

(d) If the material is suited for treatment in a personal way or in the style of popular journalism, the freer branching technique is often suitable. It more easily permits personal commentary and author—student interaction on a basis of individual reactions. The above-mentioned example "Should you be in a mental institution?" might illustrate this type.

Logically, *style* and branching should not be closely related. Nevertheless, historically there seems to have been a slight correlation, probably connected with the size of didule and the "space" for humor and good writing and the more individualized feedback opportunities (cf. d above). Susan M. Markle, one of our best examples of programmers with a personal style, has these comments to make:

"When you are limited to 30 words, as we were with the old Skinner machine, there is no opportunity for fun and each word must count. The programed textbook has allowed us more freedom. There is a side issue I tease my students with—is it possible for someone who is capable of being so totally rigorous and analytical to at the same-time have an interesting way with words? There is no doubt that many programs are dull and boring even if effective. Knowing as many programers as I do, I can also say that many of them are dull and boring—not a spark of wit anywhere. Crowder was not an analyst—he turned the textbook into a student-responsive device, but he wrote texts. And the guy is funny as a person. Since new programers tend to model what they see or choose what they prefer, I notice that witty writers model on Crowder, if they can. If they have not seen wit in a program, they tend to be dull and boring, thinking that they have to, since we programers lecture them on the necessity for relevance and striking out all irrelevancies." (1971, personal communication.)

9.5.2 *On the Basis of Terminal Behavior Characteristics*

Unfortunately the question of the "flow model" has often in discussions become too closely bound up with the type of response reaction. The reason is, of course, that many branching programs have for practical reasons used multichoice alternatives. This is certainly true of the well-known Crowder programs. Even if the connection as we have pointed out above is not logically necessary, it must be taken into consideration, since it is such a usual and simple one.

It is quite easy to find criticisms of the multi-choice technique. We have already referred to some of them in passing when we were discussing different media of presentation. The following criticisms are among those most frequently directed against the alternative choice method: (a) The student can be tempted to guess without thinking out the problem. (b) The knowledge registered is of a fairly passive kind. The activity he engages in can easily be superficial. It is so easy to tick an alternative or press an answer-button. (c) The correct answer can be obtained by means of elimination. That the student has eliminated a couple of obviously wrong alternatives, does not necessarily mean that he has understood the correct answer. The likelihood of being correct is often "unnaturally" great. A lucky guess or elimination also prevents the student from getting the benefit of the error treatment which would otherwise usually act as a corrective. (d) The continual reading of plausible incorrect alternatives can reduce learning effectiveness. If we work with five alternatives, the student reads four times as much incorrect information as correct information. This can lead to unnecessary confusion for some students, at least in the early learning phases before knowledge is properly absorbed. (e) The use of the multi-choice technique can in certain cases also have a negative side-effect on the work of constructing the program. As the constructor thinks that he has guarded against error reactions from the student (by error treatment), he is perhaps less inclined to test the program empirically, to make error analyses etc.

Can the multi-choice technique be justified, in spite of objections of this sort? A study of the characteristics of the terminal behavior can be one deciding factor when answering this question. In many cases we prefer a more "spontaneous" solving of a problem as the behavior in the terminal situation. If so, it is also natural to make the same type of demand in the teaching situation. Not to demand a "self-constructed" solution in such a case often means setting too low a target. In other cases, however, it is sufficient for the student to recognize the correct alternative. For example, a doctor who reads a cardiogram should be able to distinguish between healthy and unhealthy curve patterns, but he need not necessarily be able to draw them. In other words, in cases where ability to distinguish between different complexes of stimuli is central (discriminatory learning), the multi-choice technique is admissible and natural.

It should perhaps be added, that the multi-choice technique in some instances only superficially indicates an immediate choice procedure. In some cases, for example, the solution requires that the student, in order to be able to make his choice, first constructs a solution (as when dealing with more complicated problems of calculation). In these cases, the difference between both types of response should not be particularly great, and the risk of the student's remembering some of the incorrect answers is minimal.

Two things should, however, be borne in mind by the constructor. *Firstly,* there is nothing which says that a whole program must consist of multi-choice alternatives just because it is practical to use multi-choice alternatives in the checking didules (so that branching can easily be introduced in certain sections of program). There is nothing to prevent multi-choice questions being used at *particular* points to channel students into separate streams, while questions which demand self-constructed answers (taking into consideration the type of terminal behavior) are used in the other parts of the program. *Secondly,* it is quite possible to introduce branching on a basis of self-constructed answers (even if in some cases it can be less practical). A student who has given incorrect self-constructed answers to two or three questions may be branched off, for example, to a remedial section. One who has answered a couple of specially difficult questions of the construction type correctly can skip a section. One who gives a certain type of answer is directed to a special review, and so on. It should be obvious that these branching possibilities based on constructed answers exist, but the fact has sometimes been forgotten in the heat of the discussion for and against the special Crowder technique.

9.5.3 *On the Basis of the Characteristics of the Target Population*

Although the type of subject matter and terminal behavior are important facts to be considered in choosing the "flow model", the most significant factor is usually the characteristics of the group of students. If the target population is homogeneous as far as previous knowledge, intelligence, experience and interests are concerned, it is often natural to work with a linear program. If it is markedly heterogeneous as to previous knowledge, checking didules should be inserted at an early stage in the course material and "remedial courses" given to those who lack the knowledge to proceed directly to the main matter of the course. If the group is very variable in intelligence, it may sometimes be adequate to insert, in certain sections, parallel branching with greater or lesser density of information. If there are subgroups with special experience and interests, one could similarly use branching to illustrate a particular problem from a variety of personally relevant viewpoints. Procedure in these and similar cases has already been outlined in dealing with the various models.

In this connection, however, we should urge caution. If one has observed that the group of students is heterogeneous and has for this reason introduced branching, one can sometimes be tempted to go too far in this direction and so do unnecessary extra work. This is perhaps not so true when it is a question of special previous knowledge. In that case it is often a fairly simple matter. Either the student has the previous knowledge and does not need to be taught it, or else he has not and must work through a special section. But the risk is more obvious when it is a question of different levels of intelligence. Although it is often quite true that a more intelligent student may go successfully through the program using fewer steps, it can *sometimes* be just as well to let the more intelligent go through every task all the same. The learning process is often more stable in this way and the time gained in performing fewer tasks is anyhow often minimal. Minimizing branching for levels of intelligence may also mean minimizing the risks that some less fortunate students interpret their position as underprivileged. (Obviously, if some "tracks" are experienced to be for "the stupid ones", it may not be very exciting to follow them.)

It might be added that it is, of course, not always necessary or even the best strategy to choose a final model before beginning construction of the exercises. In practice, many programmers branch when developmental testing indicates the necessity for it (often having rather limited information on the students in advance).

Box 9.6 Motivation for choice of "flow-model" (after Cram, 1961, p. 65; cf. text above, p. 137).

Here is the style I would consider first:

1. *Household budgeting.* I would use a branching program, because the rules for budgets vary with income and needs and therefore are not suited to a restricted linear approach.
2. *How to mount a butterfly.* This suggests a linear approach, since the procedure is rather fixed and would be memorized.
3. *How to find the square root of a number.* Again, I would try a linear approach for the same reason as in No. 2.
4. *Methods of psychoanalysis.* Here it would depend on whether it is a tabulation or a comparative discussion. In the first case I would try a linear approach, in the second a branching technique.
5. *Should you be in a mental institution*? One could have a lot of fun with this one—a branching program could consist of situations and a variety of ways of reacting to them, each branch leading closer to a self-imposed diagnosis!

9.6 Preparatory Structuring of Subject-Matter

9.6.1 *General Viewpoints*

Some early empirical studies (such as, for example, Evans, Glaser & Homme, 1962; or Roe, 1962) showed that in general a carefully established sequence of subject matter can be instructionally more effective than a less carefully established one. This may seem to be rather self-evident from a common-sense point of view, and it is not difficult to find theoretical support for such observations. In his review of a decade of work in educational technology, Skinner stated that an important contribution of technology to education has been its emphasis on the "construction of carefully arranged sequences of contingencies leading to the terminal performances" (1965, p. 6).

On the other hand, a surprisingly large number of empirical studies on programmed instruction have *not* been able to verify the importance of sequencing. In several cases, random-order arrangements have seemed to be as effective as carefully sequenced materials (cf. discussion in Niedermeyer, 1968, for example). Obviously, however, the studies made deal with many different types of educational goals, various subject-matters, and different groups of learners. From discussions and results in the field it can be assumed, among other things: (a) that sequence effects depend upon the type of sequence used in relation to the behavioral goals set (memorization of structured material may be facilitated by logical organization, whereas skill to organize logically may be better elicited by requests to organize poorly structured material; cf. Chapter 7); (b) that sequence effects depend upon the age and ability level of the learners (older learners and high-ability students are probably more immune to the effects of "poor" sequencing); and (c) that sequence effects depend upon the character of the subject-matter involved (intellectual skills built up hierarchically, cf. section 5.6 above, would presumably be more severely affected by random sequencing than many other subjects). Support for the last-mentioned assumption is found, for example, in a study by Brown (1970), where sequence seemed to have an important effect upon learning when the tasks involved complex problem-solving.

Even though we may conclude that sequencing *is* important in many cases (perhaps especially with low-ability students, young learners and in the building up of complex intellectual skills), we still have rather little empirical knowledge about *which type* of instructional sequence arrangement is instructionally *most* effective for different purposes.

Most educational psychologists would nevertheless agree on some very general formulations about sequence of subject matter: (1) Complex concepts are usually built up out of simpler concepts, and more complicated knowledge structures often represent a combination of simpler knowledge structures. Therefore a logical progression from simpler to more complicated phenomena is normally more effective educationally when it is a question of training a student to master a range of concepts. (2) Distributed learning often means longer retention, and integration and generalization are made easier if the student has the opportunity of working with a certain section of subject matter from different points of view and putting it in relation to a series of other subject areas. It is therefore often an advantage to use a "spiral" sequence (cf. Glaser, 1962), in which one deals with the easier sections of *several* parts of the subject matter before the more difficult sections of the same parts (as outlined very schematically in Figure 9.10).

Another example of sequence guide may be mentioned. When two sets of concepts, A and B, are taught in succession, one of which (A) fits an already existing pattern of concepts while the other one (B) conflicts with this, we will usually expect interference effects. A will interfere with B, unless mediating material C (serving to distinguish between the sets and placing them in some wider context) is learned in addition. It has been shown, that the best effects are achieved, when the mediating material is interposed, and when the conflicting material is introduced first. That is, the best treatment in such cases seems to be using sequence B—C—A ("difficult"—"mediating"—"easy"; cf. Leith et al., 1966, p. 112 f.).

But although we can perhaps agree on such principles, we know too little about how to translate them into concrete arrangements. We are in many cases uncertain as to how far individual variations are important here. More applied learning research of a specific type would probably be useful here. It could be

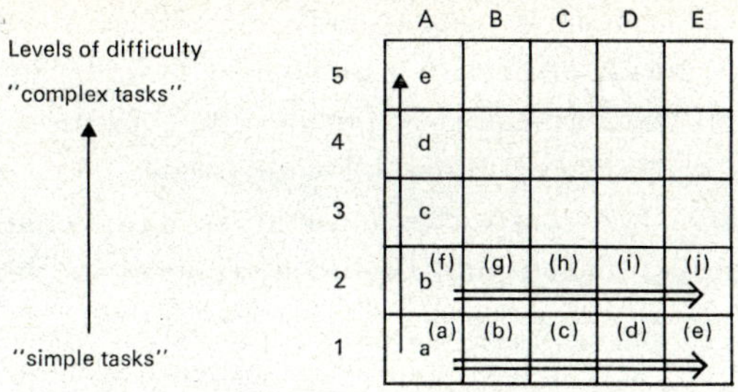

Figure 9.10 Schematic outline of didactic "spiral progression" as compared to "simple difficulty progression"

"Simple difficulty progression" means that the student, in each separate part of the subject matter (A, B, C, etc.), goes from easier to more difficult tasks: steps a, b, c, d, and e. The single arrow shows such a sequence.

"Spiral progression" means that the student goes through all the requisite part areas (subject matter areas) at a low level of difficulty before going on to a higher level of difficulty: steps (a) to (j). This form of procedure is indicated by the double arrow.

helpful to study the working sequences chosen by experimentees themselves when they have been informed of the terminal behavior the course is intended to teach. The experimentees should then be allowed to make their own decisions on the learning situation and to "steer" its sequence.

In some cases such experiments are naturally not very fruitful, since students without previous knowledge of and with little interest in a particular subject area will probably often use a planless trial and error technique. Experiments with "student-steered" learning can probably never be a *sufficient* source of information. But they are definitely worth trying, as far as research is concerned, taking into account the fact that most didactic experiments have been started in a very "dictatorial" way, with a number of rough-hewn types of sequence handed out by the leaders of the project, and their effectiveness assessed afterwards by the average result. Programmed teaching is, of course, adapted to the students to a much greater extent than most conventional teaching methods, as the programs are revised as a result of empirical experience. But it would be even more adapted to the student, if the construction of the program could be influenced by the student at an earlier stage. This would presumably be useful both for the individual course and for our knowledge of basic teaching principles. One of those who have experimented along these lines is Mager (cf. Mager & Clark, 1964). "Learner-controlled instruction" is the term sometimes used for such techniques; the learner leads the instructor.

But even if the programmer does not at present know as much as we would like about the instructionally most suitable sequence of material, he is forced, like the lecturer, teacher and textbook writer, who are all faced with the same problem, to come to a decision about sequences and to do so from the best possible hypotheses. We have already dealt with a number of the relevant viewpoints in this chapter. The question of sequences pursues the constructor through several stages of his work and crops up in the following forms:

(a) *Preparatory macro-sequence.* The constructor must at an early stage make up his mind about suitable flow models and the main sequence of the total subject-matter.

(b) *Micro-sequences.* During the actual writing of the program a large number of micro-sequences must be built up, within the framework of the main sequence, for the successive learning of single concepts and functions.

(c) *Review with special regard to sequences.* After the first detailed work it is often advisable to carry out a series of checks regarding sequences: Have we sufficient and suitably spaced repetition? Have we provided for continuity? etc.

(d) *Changes of sequences during the try-out phase.* The constructor naturally gets some idea of the effectiveness of the sequence arrangement during the successive empirical try-outs of the study material on typical representatives of the target population. Re-arrangement of sequences may then be necessary because of error analyses and analysis of final results.

While preparatory planning of macro-sequences (a) has been dealt with in the present chapter, the other problems referred to will be touched upon in various discussions below.

9.6.2 *Some Examples of Concrete Aids*

Transformation and completion of the S-list and the C-catalogue: "Basic text", "didactic statements" and "examples". From the analysis of the subject-matter we obtained a C-catalogue (a collection of fundamental concepts within the subject area) and an S-list (a collection of "statements" about the concepts and their relationships). The constructor can now "translate" these concepts and statements into a connected "*basic text*", i.e. a very brief, but complete text ("condensed textbook"). This gives the constructor one starting-point for his further construction work. At the same time it might be used for certain analyses of "information amount" and "information increase" (which we will not deal with in detail in this context; cf., however, e.g. Weltner, 1971).

Such a "basic text" may, of course, take various forms. It might be given a fairly "*target-free*" character, whereby the emphasis is upon brief, complete information, written without consideration of any particular target group. But it might also be given a "*target-directed*" form. In this case the purpose is not only to get a connected text, but to "translate" the concepts and statements (from the C-catalogue and S-list) into "didactic statements" (DS), i.e. preliminary formulations more suited to the age and experience of the particular group of students. These should contain "critical words" which can be regarded as the kernel of the new information, around which the student's response in the didule should center. The individual units of information in the next stage of work can then be constructed using these "didactic statements" as a basis. In this case, it may sometimes be unwise, however, to complete this target-directed basic text (or DS-catalogue) at one time (especially if we deal with a very large subject-matter area), since one can get into the habit of making formulations in certain ways, which may not be practical bases for the writing of didules. It can therefore be advisable to work out only a part of this catalogue at a time and then try to translate that into didules before going on to develop it further. At this stage it is also desirable to collect numerous and varied "examples" of the main didactic statements.

Didactoplan. Each main section of the planned course contains several "didactic statements". The order in which these are to occur must be preliminarily established. (This may be done partly from the inherent structure of the subject-matter. Some tentative rules for such a procedure have been illustrated and discussed in Lahn, 1971.) It is natural at the same time to indicate possible branching as the course progresses. It can be valuable to illustrate this more detailed structure diagrammatically. We then obtain a relatively detailed flow-chart, which could be called a "didactoplan". The working sequence is indicated by arrows. It is perhaps as well to differentiate between those didactic statements which everyone could be expected to handle in the same way ("the main course"), those which will be supplied to certain students only (extra or remedial courses), and those supplied in different ways to separate groups of students (parallel courses). Various symbols can be used, e.g. circles for "common" units, triangles for specially directed units, and squares for units which vary in form for different groups of students. (The chart thus obtained can, in addition to its function of assistance in the writing of the program—after due revision and additions—be used as a basic scheme for mapping the students' reactions to the course; cf. separate discussion below.)

The DS-catalogue (or target-directed basic text) and the didactoplan will be the direct starting point for the working out of the concrete details, which can now be started on.

10. Working Out Instructional Units: Information Component

10.1 Introduction: Components and Types of Didules

As we have already had reason to point out, in many self-instructional materials the "instructional unit" is characteristically made up of three main components: the presentation of new instructional information, the response request, and the result indication. Our task now is to examine more closely a number of problems that arise when the designer of the material proceeds to transform his preliminary plans into concrete instructional units. We shall study each of these main components in turn.

We should, however, emphasize at the outset that the designer is by no means tied to working out a didule of this special three-component type (stimule + respule + corrule) even if this still may be the most common kind and in its pure form often exemplifies the problems that may be encountered in the self-instructional teaching situation. In other words, we can regard the three-component didule as a natural basic pattern (or the "atomic sentence" of the "instructional grammar" to use an expression from Stolurow, 1971) which we should, however, be free to modify in various ways. This may apply to both "shortened" and "extended" didules (cf. Figure 10.1).

"Shortened" didules, for example, can consist of instructional units *without the corrule-component.* In certain cases we may consider any separate result indication unnecessary, since the program is of such a type that the student is more or less certain to answer correctly anyway. In other cases the "shortened" didule may *lack any request for an explicit response.* On the basis of a special test we may sometimes consider the implicit reaction to be equally effective and at the same time quicker. Didules that *lack any proper new instructional information* are quite common and with new response requests serve to consolidate further previous information.

On the other hand *"extended" didules* introduce new types of components. At present the most common additional components seem to be those that contain (a) a *special instruction* to the student (to move about in the program in a certain way, to study certain material outside the program, to operate his apparatus in a particular way or something similar), or (b) an *imitation request* (the student is to repeat the answer in order to consolidate it further in his repertoire).

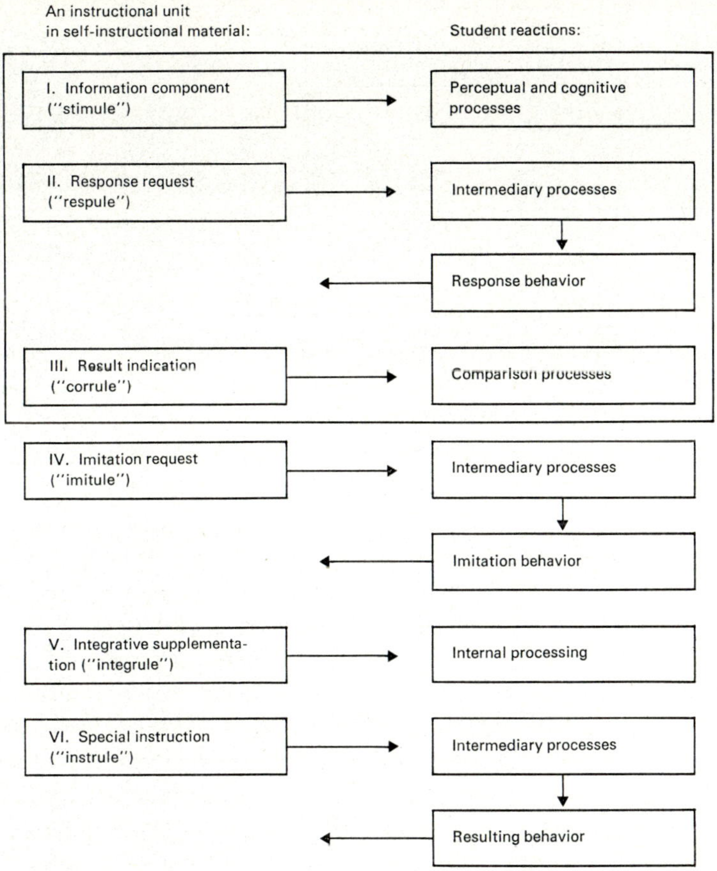

Figure 10.1 Outline sketch of some part-components in an "instructional unit" (didule) in interplay with a student

(Components I—III are fundamental, while components IV—VI only occur in special contexts. The Roman numerals denote the typical sequence.)

Instruction components are common especially in certain types of branching program, for example in the interplay between student and computer. In linear programs explicit instructions are rather rare during the course of the work: of course, the end of every exercise implies in some ways an instruction to go on further (to turn the knob or something similar). Imitation requests occur above all in those types of program where the border-line between a correct and an incorrect answer is less distinct (with the possibility of the continuous variation of "better and better" response reactions) and where the extra imitation stage therefore offers the opportunity of "polishing" the response

TRACK 1 (model track)	Stimulus material ("stimule")	Instruction + pause or only pause ("respule")	Key answer ("corrule")	Pause ("imitule")
TRACK 2 (student's track)		Student's response		Student's imitation
	Phase 1	Phase 2	Phase 3	Phase 4

Figure 10.2 A typical four-phase didule in language instruction (twin-track arrangement)

Example:

The student's task is to put in "ne . . . que" in French sentences.

Phase 1: *Nous lui donnons 100 francs par mois.*
Phase 2: Nous lui ne donnons que 100 francs par mois.
Phase 3: *Nous ne lui donnons que 100 francs par mois.*
Phase 4: Nous ne lui donnons que 100 francs par mois.

The student makes a mistake in his first response (phase 2), after which the key answer (phase 3) is drilled in by the student's repeating it (phase 4).

behavior further. We probably find the most typical examples of this in language programs of the kind presented in our language laboratories.

A very common language laboratory didule (twin-track arrangement, cf. Figure 10.2) consists of four components: (a) stimulus material on the teacher's track, (b) response request, marked by an instruction + pause or simply a pause on the teacher's track (at which the student reacts on the student's track), (c) a model response given on the teacher's track as feedback together with (d) an imitation request, marked by a pause on the teacher's track (at which the student repeats the model response on the student's track).

Other types of extended didules occur, though less frequently at present. An interesting technique proposed and used by Schröter (1970) may be mentioned in this connection. Often the result indication is followed in his programs by some supplementary information ("Ergänzungsstufe"). The psychical tension built up by the comparison process (comparing answer and feedback information) is thought to be better utilized by including some additional information related to the answer (e.g., further explanation of the solution, additional aids for memorizing, additional side information to back up the central information). This technique, which is not always used in Schröter's programs (for example, not in easy passages where the number of correct solutions is very high), may perhaps be described briefly as an "integrative supplementation" (attempting to integrate better the particular response in the response repertoire of the student) and may be thought of as one possible component among others within a didule (see Figure 10.1). It may be added that Schröter considers his "two-level" technique to be a kind of bridge between the pure Skinner and Crowder techniques, retaining some advantages of both.

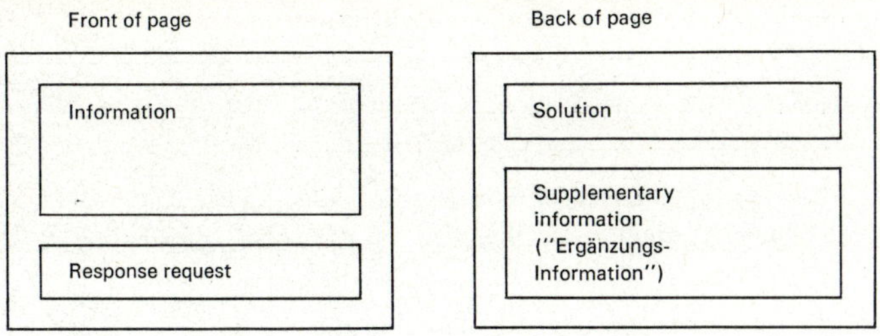

Figure 10.3 A schematic illustration of the two-stage presentation of the four components in a typical didule of a Schröter program

It may be worth mentioning in passing that a "didule" ("instructional unit") in the sense indicated here does not necessarily involve simultaneous presentation. The didule is the program's contribution to a fundamental interactive unit: an interaction between the instructional material and the student, having a distinct initial-final character (the unit begins with the presentation of the information and the task, continues with the student "returning" his answer and most usually ends with the feedback of the program in the form of result indication). This instructional unit usually, however, corresponds to *two* presentations: as a rule components I and II are presented first (cf. Figure 10.1), and *then* either component III on its own or components I + II + III together. The term "frame" has sometimes been used in the sense of "simultaneous presentation" (a sense which, after all, is closest to its basic meaning), and sometimes in the sense of "didule". This varying usage is, as was indicated above, one of the reasons for avoiding this term and its closest equivalents in other languages. A concrete illustration of a didule with a typical two-stage presentation is given in Box 10.1. (A schematic picture of the presentation sequence in the specific Schröter-type program is seen in Figure 10.3.)

10.2 The Problem of Step Size

One of the most persistent refrains in the programmers' message has been the advice to work in "small steps". In the early days of programming, the principle of "small steps" was considered to be one of the very pillars of programming. Both theoretical reasons and empirical results suggest that there is also much truth in this. Smaller steps mean, among other things, a better focus on what is essential, more opportunities for activating the student, and greater ease in ordering suitable sequences.

However, this demand was more often made with parrot-like persistency than with analytical clarity and precision. What exactly is meant by "small steps"? How does one distinguish "small steps" from "large steps"? In other

Box 10.1 Example of a didule, divided into two presentational units

Presentational part A:

11. According to the National Board of Education's regulations the following applies to the size of the school site: "The size of the school site must be calculated on the basis of 1000 sq. m per class when the school premises are developed to their maximum. In the central parts of towns the area can be reduced to 800 sq. m and if the site is in or by a park, the use of which can be granted to the school, to a minimum of 600 sq. m per class. For schools in towns intended only for the junior stage a site area of 500 sq. m per class is accepted."	I Information section
How large a school site should be calculated according to the National Board of Education's directions for a school with combined junior and intermediate stages in central Malmö, which, when fully developed, is estimated to take 30 classes? Answer:	II Response request

Presentational part B:

Correct answer: 24,000 sq. m.	III Result indication
If you answered correctly, go on to exercise 15. If you answered wrong, go to exercise 12.	IV Special instruction

words how does one measure the size of a "step"? When challenged thus, the advocate of "small steps" will sometimes begin to falter. In any case it is easy to find in specialist literature widely differing opinions on how to assess what "small steps" are. It should be of advantage for the discussion if the existence of these alternative methods of assessment were more generally recognized and it were explicitly stated which of the possible points of view have been adopted in any particular case.

It may perhaps be wise to distinguish between *"a priori" criteria* and *"a posteriori" criteria.* The former represent view-points which can be applied to the program material as such without first studying individual students' reactions. The latter, on the other hand, are based on an empirical assessment. *"A priori" criteria* can in their turn be divided into two categories, linguistic-formal and conceptual-psychological assessment types. Let us take some examples of these various types of assessment.

(a) *The number of words presented to the student in the didule* is perhaps one of the most clear-cut linguistic-formal bases for assessment. Quite plainly the abundance of words in the units of the Crowder program is one of the reasons why most reviewers say that Crowder works with "larger steps" than Skinner. Crowder's stimule and respule phase as a rule takes up nearly a printed page, while the corresponding components in a typical Skinner didule take up only one or two sentences (for example, one stimule sentence and one respule sentence).

(b) *The average length of response expected from the student* is perhaps a somewhat less common, but quite feasible basis for assessment. An exercise which demands that the student shall write down ten terms that are used in a certain field is, in one sense, obviously "larger" than one that only demands that the student shall tick one of ten given terms, the one, for instance, which does not belong to a particular field, even if the quantity of words presented to the student in the didule is larger in the *second* case. The assessment can, however, still be made on purely linguistic-formal premises.

(c) *The number of response requests in relation to the number of new concepts or in relation to the number of new statements about concepts.* It is evident that, when starting from a given number of units in the C catalogue and S list (cf. the section on subject-matter analysis above), one can construct a comparatively small or large number of didules. The more didules one has made, the smaller, in a sense, the steps must be. This is, then, primarily an example of a conceptual-psychological criterion. In this connection we should be able to speak of varying degrees of "concept density" (or more generally "*information density*"). When, in empirical experiments, the effect of the size of the step has quite simply been studied by starting with an already existent program and eliminating a certain number of didules from it (presumably those that do not destroy the sequence too much, i.e. review items and practice items) and then comparing the educational effect of the longer program (with "smaller steps") and of the shorter program (with "larger steps"), it is precisely on "information density" that the size of the step has been assessed. (Incidentally, these experiments have often shown the advantage of comparatively small steps—in this sense—for the learning result. The longer program has, in other words, often been more effective with regard to the level of knowledge. But at the same time it has sometimes—but not always—taken more time, which makes the overall results somewhat less distinct. In addition, the reader should note the reservation implied in the word "often". There are conflicting results. This should not be surprising, however, since different programs obviously vary in the amount of redundancy. Some give very ample practice, much more than needed, others almost too little. Eliminating items from such different programs easily leads to variation in results.)

(d) *The number of stages in the intermediary process between perceived response request and final response behavior.* Usually we do not with any certainty know very much about what the intermediary process looks like in individual cases. It is, however, easy to establish that certain demands on the intermediary process are appreciably smaller than others. Sometimes it is a matter of the student just "copying" given information: repeating a phrase in a language laboratory, for instance, or writing down a new term. In other cases, however, a long series of intermediate activities have to precede the final response, as, for example, when the student's task is to solve a complicated mathematical problem. The more complicated the intermediary processes are, the larger, in a sense, is the step which the student is to take.

The four examples just given are all of the "*a priori*" type. Let us also give some examples of "*a posteriori*" assessments.

(e) *The average working time of the student group per didule.* The faster the students finish a didule, the smaller, in a sense, the step can be said to have been.

(f) *Frequency of mistakes.* When Markle et al. define a small step in the following way: "A small step is a step toward mastery that the student is capable of taking without making errors" (1961, p. 10), they obviously let themselves be ruled entirely by the occurrence of incorrect answers, and they also separate large steps from small ones on an all-or-none basis. A small step is a step which the student *is able* to take; a large step is a step he *cannot* take. —As a result of such a view, the appropriate step-size will, in fact, vary from individual to individual. This is stressed, for example, by Landa: "Thus the problem of the size of the . . . steps of programmed instruction turns out not to be a problem of formal criteria of step-size" (1968, p. 86). Instead it depends upon, for example, "the individual peculiarities and the level of development of the pupils" (ibid.).

(g) *Reduction of mistakes after the addition of information.* An interesting, but rather specialized interpretation is offered by Björkman (1963) when he asks himself whether by small steps is meant tasks with low empirical information value (small reduction of uncertainty). In order to assess this reduction of uncertainty one ought to investigate whether the student can give the correct answer to the response requests *before* the information section of the didule has been presented, and similarly whether he can do this *after* the information section has been presented. Tasks in which the difference between the frequency of correct solutions before and after the presentation of information is small may be said to imply, in a sense, small steps. In this case we can speak of small steps on the one hand when practically everyone is able to solve the exercise in advance, and on the other hand when practically no one can solve the task afterwards. Even if the suggestion that we should study the probability of the problem being solved *before* information is given, is in itself interesting, it is fairly evident that as a rule the programmers do *not* use the term in this sense. For if you use the definition discussed by Björkman, the best-designed programs obviously prove to consist of maximally *large* steps!

For the sake of illustration, let us look at our example of a didule in Box 10.1 above. Reasonably enough most people answer the question correctly. So according to Markle's conception mentioned above—which is probably representative for several programmers—we are dealing with a small step. If, however, we first tried out the exercise without the information section and only asked how large a school site should be according to current regulations for a school of the type quoted, in typical target populations (without previous special knowledge of school building regulations etc.), we should probably receive extremely *few* correct answers. (We would otherwise have either removed the exercise after our first try-outs or included it in a "special branch".) Thus the "reduction of uncertainty" is likely to become large (perhaps from nearly 0 % correct answers *before* the presentation of information to nearly 100 % correct answers *after* the presentation of information). So according to the definition discussed by Björkman, our students have taken a large step. (Cf. further our discussion below.)

There is obviously an interesting field for research here: what is the empirical relationship between the various types of assessment of the size of the step, and what is their relationship to final effectiveness? Can a certain combination of assessments ultimately be shown in an empirical way to be particularly significant for instructional purposes?

We may end this discussion by noting that instructional designers today are less likely to emphasize "small steps" as a necessary condition for useful instructional material. They are more likely to talk about "steps appropriate to the learner", that is, step size should be set to match the capacities of the specific learners involved. In fact, it may often be better initially to *overestimate* this capacity slightly than to underestimate it, since overestimation is more easily detected and more easily corrected in the process of trying out the program than is underestimation (and the programmer may often learn more during the development process about how to guide learners efficiently, if the early versions of the programs overestimate steps eliciting some error material for use in the refinement of the material). The term "*lean*" *programming* is sometimes used to refer to a process in which you start by overestimating the students' capacities (with steps too large to take, discriminations too fine to make, a minimum of practice etc.). The idea is to end up with the "leanest" version you can that will work, adding or revising only where data show it to be necessary. (Cf. O'Day et al., 1971, p. 198.)

The concept of "appropriate steps" may be less easy to work with than the notion of "small steps", since the appropriateness has usually to be tested out, whereas the smallness notion may somewhat more easily be dealt with in apriori judgements. In fairness to the early programmers who so heavily stressed the smallness concept it should be said, however, that the notion of appropriate steps obviously very often means "much smaller than has traditionally been used in instructional materials".

10.3 The Problems of Prompting

10.3.1 *General Character of Prompting*

As we had reason to point out above (chapter 2), different types of stimuli occur in a teaching situation: focal, correlative, and non-relevant ones. *Focal* stimuli represent the central information which we wish the student to acquire. *Correlative* stimuli are of a "concomitant" nature. They are not intended to be drilled in, but can illuminate the focal subject-matter and make it easier to learn. *Non-relevant* stimuli are various kinds of influence from the environment or in the subject-matter that can be classified neither as focal nor as correlative.

The effectiveness of the information component of the didule depends to a large extent on suitable dosage of these types of stimuli. Most didules should contain vital focal stimulation—but no more than the student's attentiveness can cope with. Furthermore, the didule should contain as few non-relevant stimuli as possible. All superfluous material that serves no specific educational purpose should be removed. A moderate dose of "correlative" stimuli, on the other hand, is often valuable. These correlative stimuli not infrequently have the character of "hints", i.e. stimuli that make the correct answer more likely.

Historically speaking, the extreme frequency with which many early programmers used the hinting technique or prompting is connected with Skinner's theories on behavioral shaping through the gradual reinforcing of certain elements in the already existent behavioral repertoire. The skilful animal trainer "shapes" the animal's behavior by rewarding the animal when it comes close to a movement that makes up an element in the desired behavioral chain. By systematically rewarding all desired behavioral elements one can gradually produce the entire behavioral sequence desired: the pigeon learns to walk in a figure-of-eight or to pick at tangents in a certain pattern. When these ideas were transferred to the programming of verbal material for human beings, it therefore seemed reasonable to regard as justified all stimuli that make the desired reaction likely. Once one has produced the correct reaction, one can in fact "reinforce" it and successively bring it out by more adequate means.

The point can also be formulated as follows: The student's terminal reactions must, of course, be given in their proper contexts and on the correct basis. But when one *begins* to teach the student the reaction in question, one may be satisfied with his being able to copy (repeat orally or copy out in writing) the correct answer, or with his being able to supply it when one has given him a start or with his being able to supply it in a context that is *approximately* right. Let us take an example from the world of the infant. Let us suppose that one wants the child to be able to use the word "gee-gee" for "horse". At first the mother and father are exceedingly proud if the child can produce the word "gee-gee" at all by mimicking, or when it utters a happy "gee-gee" after the mother has given it a start with an encouraging "gee . . .". It is also great fun when the child starts to point at certain moving objects—whether they are dogs, cats or horses—and call them "gee-gee". But in the end one wants, of course, a more correct and precise terminal reaction. Then "gee-gee" has to be a horse and nothing else.

In programmed instruction (as of course in other teaching) we can often obtain in abbreviated form this gradual process of shaping and becoming more accurate which we observe in the child's way of dealing with our conventional world of symbols. When we want to teach our student a new, difficult symbol, we may perhaps let him just copy it using a model within his field vision.[1] Then we may ask the student to remember it—at least from one didule to another and if we give him a start. We gradually teach him then to use it correctly, to start with in almost self-evident contexts (where the logic of the context does not allow many alternative solutions), but later in a more independent manner. All the technical moves we employ in the early stages of the learning process in order to make it easier for the student to produce the correct answer reactions (whether we do it by means of more formal tricks as in nursery rhymes, or by means of rather more logical aids) may be called by way of summary "hinting techniques" or "prompting".

Three main rules are worth remembering when using these aids: (a) Do not give more prompting than necessary! (b) Whenever possible choose logical and meaningful hints rather than formal and mechanical prompts, and avoid mechanically repeating the same type of hinting technique! (c) Do not assume

[1] Providing a model for copying was especially often used in early programs. It is still considered to be an appropriate first step in several cases when dealing with difficult symbols that the student has to master exactly. However, copying as a routine form of teaching new terms is considered undesirable. Markle's manual "Good frames and bad" devotes a whole section to avoiding this design (1969, p. 250 ff.).

too much previous knowledge and too large a common background of experience when selecting illustrative prompting!

10.3.2 *The Problem of Over-Dosing Prompting*

The *first rule mentioned* may seem self-evident, but the fact is that prompting has often been regarded as such an integral part of programming technique that certain program writers seem to use special hinting procedures as a regular work-routine whether it is called for or not. Thus there are a number of programs that keep on and on informing the student which letter his answer-word begins with (or ends with) or how many letters it contains without the programmer seeming to have really investigated whether all these hints are necessary. As a rule it should be advisable to use only a minimum number of hints in the first version of a program and then to increase the hints only to the extent that the first empirical tests show to be necessary (for example, on account of a too high percentage of mistakes in certain exercises). Admittedly, it is easy by constantly giving hints to guarantee a low percentage of mistakes, but the latter is no end in itself. A too regular use of hints may accustom the student to a passive attitude in his studies and/or to a distorted kind of attentiveness (concentrating on the "form" of the instruction rather than its "contents") so that there may also be a risk of the overall benefit diminishing.

One way of not over-dosing the prompting can be to individualize it in such a way that the student first receives the opportunity to give his response reaction *without* prompting. A hint is introduced at a second stage. If the student does not succeed in answering correctly the first time, he can usually manage it the second time. But if he has already answered correctly, he does not need to bother about the hint, but can go on to the next exercise. This two-step technique (with no prompting until the second step) can be built systematically into a program, and machines have even been specially designed for simplifying a two-step presentation of this kind.

10.3.3 *Formal-Mechanical vs. "Thematic" Prompts*

As our *second rule* suggests, over-dosing might well be particularly undesirable if it is a matter of formal and mechanical hints. These methods include underlining the most important words in the information section or stressing these words in some other way by, for example, printing them in italics, using capital letters or placing them in inverted commas. Special techniques of this sort are not in themselves objectionable, of course. Indeed they are sometimes particularly effective as focusing aids. But if such a procedure is used as a matter of routine so that the important words that the student is to reproduce in some form in his response are underlined in didule after didule, the risk arises that the student will quite soon adopt a special approach to the answers which is irrelevant to the subject-matter ("The idea is obviously that I am meant to fill in the words that are underlined in the text"). A response technique of this kind may give him many correct answers but little knowledge.

Programmers sometimes tend to show with some delight how it is possible to produce correct answers from a school child in very complicated fields that the child was not familiar with before. It is fairly obvious this is possible if one uses a hinting technique of this kind, but little is gained if one receives a correct answer which is not accompanied by increased knowledge or understanding. An example may perhaps make this plain. Read the following exercise and try to fill in the right answers!

Example 10.1

The longer you let the TABLATE dismeliate in hexicave dacrane, the more difficult the adclosion of the *plasylene* becomes.

In order to facilitate the adclosion of the pl_________ne it is therefore advisable not to let the T_________E dismeliate in hexicave dacrane for too long.

As in many programs the student's task is to fill in the missing words. First and foremost the first and last letters are given as hints. In addition the keywords are specially indicated (by capital letters and italics respectively). Did you succeed in solving the exercise? The correct answer should read, as the reader has of course seen, as follows: "In order to facilitate the adclosion of the plasylene it is therefore advisable not to let the TABLATE dismeliate in hexicave dacrane for too long." Fine! But did you understand anything contained in the exercise? There is every reason for your not having understood it since the sentences are strings of nonsense words.

This demonstration of how one can perfectly well supply a correct answer without gaining any knowledge if the hints are too obvious should stand as a warning. We must beware of teaching our students to answer mechanically or on an incorrect basis. The habit of mechanically following hints instead of using critical reflection is after all the very opposite of what most of us want to teach. We do not want conformistic puppets that have learnt to respond according to a mechanical pattern. Instead we should try to promote critical thinking, power of combination and curiosity. But is it at all possible to achieve this with programmed study-material? I believe that one can do it, but I also believe that it is very important to fight the frequent tendencies towards the mechanization of program production according to certain trade routines. Included in these trade routines are quite obviously the so-called "formal prompts", the mechanical and formal hints which may sometimes be justified, but which should never become a standard technique used in a routine way time and time again. This in no way has to mean that prompting is rejected altogether. It only means that one preferably chooses hints of a more meaningful character (sometimes called "thematic prompts"), hints that make use of empirical illustrations, analogies and logical connections instead of mechanical and formal tricks.

The following simple example adapted from a physics course illustrates this kind of more meaningful prompting:

Example 10.2

Now that we know that most metals expand or contract according to changes in temperature and that the oscillation rate of a pendulum depends on its length, we can expect that if there is a very great drop in temperature a pendulum clock ________

The two facts mentioned by way of introduction have presumably been taught previously. But in the special exercise the student is guided by logical prompting towards actually making a small "discovery" himself. Exercises of this type often lead to both better working technique (familiarity with logical and critical thought) and greater satisfaction. The degree of difficulty has, of course, to be adjusted to the students' knowledge and other background factors for we are naturally anxious for the student really to succeed with the exercise. We check this point especially in the test phase. If an exercise proves to be too difficult, we must make the prompting more obvious. The exercise quoted above about the pendulum clock becomes easier if, for example, we describe the background facts in greater detail and if we state more distinctly the alternatives which the student has to choose between:

Example 10.3

We know that most metals expand when heated and contract when cooled. We also know that a short pendulum swings faster than a long pendulum. How is a pendulum-clock likely to be affected when there is a very great drop in temperature? Will it become too fast or too slow?

Answer: It will become ___________

The exercise has now become easier without our waiving the rule that it is preferable to work with logical rather than with formal and mechanical methods.

One of the most natural types of prompting is the *example*. Above we recommended compiling a rich and varying collection of example cards as an important ingredient in preparation work.

It is usually as well to give an example of almost every new "didactic statement" including the easiest of them.

Example 10.4

To take the SQUARE of a number means to multiply the number by itself.
The square of 3 is equal to 3×3 or 9.
The square of 6 is equal to 6×6 or 36.
The square of 4 is equal to _____ × _____ or _____.

Example 10.5

Instead of writing out the words "square of" you usually write a small figure two to the right above the number you are to take the square of.
The square of 3 is thus written as *3^2*
The square of 5 is written as 5^2
The square of 4 is written as _____

Of course it is possible to give the same information by means of a shorter procedure and without the prompting contained in the examples, as here for example.

Example 10.6

To take the SQUARE of a number means to multiply the number by itself. A small figure two is usually written to the right above the number you are to take the square of.
The square of 4 is written ________ and is equal to ________

It is, however, clear that the percentage of mistakes in the latter case (among students who did not previously know the concept concerned) will probably be considerably greater and the instruction is also likely to be less effective when measured by retention over a period of time. Not infrequently the program *writer* feels detailed exemplification to be "repetitive" and "childish" because he is himself well-versed in the matter. The program *reader* in the particular target population often feels the exemplification to be necessary. But this is difficult to judge in advance. Only empirical testing can show definitely what the students' reaction is.

In some cases one can make a simple additional branch of the "fast track type" (cf. chapter 9 above), i.e. let the students that require them have more examples than the others. Box 10.2 gives an illustration of this kind of procedure. In somewhat modified form it reproduces a piece of an American dem-

Box 10.2 Fast track arrangement for the variation of prompting (more or less exemplification for different students)

1. We shall now teach you a trick in mental arithmetic that enables you quickly to work out the square of a two-figure number ending in 5. When you have gone through a couple more exercises you will be able to say what 55×55 or 95×95 are in a few seconds. Go on to the next exercise!	
2. You can work out what 35×35 is in the following way:	
a. First note between which multiples of tens the number 35 comes. It comes between 30 and 40.	
b. Multiply these two multiples of ten: 30×40= ________	2 b. 1200
c. Add 25 and you get the final answer ________	2 c. 1225
Don't you believe me? Check it in the usual way!	
3. Now try with 65×65!	
a. 65 comes between the multiples of ten ________ and 70	3 a. 60
b. Multiply these numbers: ______ × ______ = ______	3 b. 60×70 =4200
c. Add 25 and the final result is ______	3 c. 4225
Can you work out in your head what 45×45 is? Or what 85×85 is? If you can, go straight on to exercise 6. If you feel uncertain, continue with exercise 4.	
4. You multiply 45×45 in your head in the following way:	
a. 45 comes between two multiples of ten, i.e. between ______ and ______	4 a. 40, 50
b. When you multiply these multiples of ten by one another, you get the number ______	4 b. 2000
c. When you then add 25 to this number, you get the product of 45×45 or the number ______	4 c. 2025
5. 55×55?	
a. 55 comes between the multiples of ten ______ and ______	5 a. 50, 60
b. Multiply ______ by ______ and you get ______	5 b. 50, 60 3000
c. Add ______, and the final result is ______	5 c. 25 3025
6. Work out in your head!	
a. 15×15= ______	6 a. 225
b. 85×85= ______	6 b. 7225
c. 95×95= ______	6 c. 9025
If you have made a mistake, go back to exercise 4!	

onstration program. In this case the student learns by means of examples (item 2 and 3) a special trick in mental arithmetic, aided by a careful step-by-step explanation. In conjunction with item 3 he receives special instruction. Anyone who thinks he can now manage arithmetical exercises of this kind on his own is sent on to item 6 in which this ability is tested. Anyone who feels uncertain is instead given some more demonstration examples first with more detailed (no. 4) and then with less detailed (no. 5) prompting. If a student who has gone straight to item 6 finds that he has estimated his skill too optimistically (in other words if he makes mistakes), he is sent back to more practice examples. (The program example given in Box 10.2 is only intended to illustrate the possibility of providing examples in a differentiated way and not to constitute a model in any other way. In many cases one does not want to stop at a superficial presentation of a trick in mental arithmetic, but to try to give the student insight into *why* the trick works.)

The *third rule* for prompting we gave above was that one should not assume too much knowledge or too much common experience. This is of importance especially when giving examples. After all, the examples are to be gateways to new knowledge as the student passes from familiar to unfamiliar material, from concrete to abstract material. But it is, of course, important that what one assumes to be familiar is in fact familiar. Otherwise the examples are of no help but an unnecessary difficulty. Here one must keep one's eyes open for individual variations in background experience and not use illustrations that can only appeal to part of the target population. In this case, too, trial testing will show to what extent one's choice has been successful.

10.3.4 *Linguistic-Semantic Prompts*

We have chiefly touched upon two main types of prompts: on the one hand those we have called *formal and mechanical* (for instance, the first letter of a word or a number of letters in a word) and on the other hand more meaningful hints in the form of examples or logical conclusions—so-called "thematic" prompts. A third main type can be said in a way to come between these two: linguistic-semantic prompts. The latter make the response easier by reducing the number of possible answers with the aid of the structure of the language. In this case it is a matter of making an appropriate choice. One should avoid both sentence structures that are *too "open"* and allow for too many possible answers and do not therefore clarify the problem, and sentence structures that are *too "closed"*, leaving too *few* possibilities open and therefore coming close to mechanical hints. Look at the following examples!

a) Cold air ________________________________

b) Cold air moves in a(n) __________ direction

c) Warm air moves upwards, cold air ________________

d) Warm air moves upwards, cold air ________ downwards.

We can probably agree that the first phrase, *a,* leaves too many answers open. We risk the student's simply not knowing what we want. "Cold air is found in the mountains", for example, is after all a conceivable answer. Most of us can probably also agree that the last phrase, *d,* leaves too few possible answers so that we receive a pseudo-answer of doubtful value. In this case, however, some programmers are of a different opinion and use this type of sentence without any further ado following the maxim "everything that produces a correct answer is permitted". The two other examples, *b* and *c,* represent an intermediate degree of "answer guidance". The number of possible answers is smaller than in *a,* but an incorrect answer is possible. In the concrete case the particular choice should, of course, depend on what precedes and follows it in the program (i.e. what knowledge there is and in what way one intends to continue the line of reasoning).

When it is a matter of teaching new systems of symbols (for example, foreign languages), one can utilize the "redundancy" of the linguistic-semantic system for educational purposes. A very specialised but interesting demonstration of this has been given by Schaefer (1963). The procedure is based on the fact that most verbal expressions contain "redundant" parts which can be removed without any real loss of meaning (something that we do, for instance, when writing telegrams). These parts can, for example, be replaced by nonsense words without the student losing the meaning of the text. If instead of the nonsense words we put in corresponding words in a foreign language and do this in a systematic manner these foreign words should gradually take on the correct values of association. In other words the student learns foreign words by seeing them used over and over again in their correct context. "The context" becomes the actual prompt for what we wish to teach. What is characteristic of this technique is among other things not *presenting* the foreign words to start with as *focal* stimuli for drilling. They are instead relatively unimportant *correlative* stimuli *in the student's world of experience.* This is where the difference lies between this kind of prompting and more usual types of "thematic" hints in the form of examples or logical argument.

Schaefer's procedure was of the following nature: The students who were to learn German were given thrilling detective novels by Edgar Allan Poe to read. In these certain of the words in the native language (English) were exchanged for corresponding words in the foreign language (German). In the initial phase this was done very cautiously. It was only a matter of odd words that bore little meaning (for instance, articles and pronouns). In the second phase the foreign elements were increased in number. Among other things the special foreign word-order was introduced. It was thought, however, that the

First phase:

"True!—nervous, very, very dreadfully nervous, *ich* had been, and am; but why will you say that *ich* am mad? The disease had sharpened *meine* senses—not destroyed, not dulled them. Above all was *der* sense of hearing acute. *Ich* heard all the things in *dem* heaven and *der* earth. I heard many things in hell. How, then, am *ich* mad? Hearken! *Und* observe how healthily—how calmly *ich* can tell *die* whole story."

Second phase:

"*Der* second *und* third day went by *und* yet showed himself *mein* tormentor *nicht*. Again could *ich* as free man breathe. *Das* monster was apparently in great terror run away! Never again would *ich es* see! *Meine* happiness was complete! *Die* guilt *der* black deed disturbed *mich* but little. Some questions were asked *und* readily answered. *Eine* search was even undertaken, but, of course, could *nichts* be found. *Ich* looked *einer* safe future toward."

Third phase:

"*Die* slope *seiner Wände wurde von Moment zu Moment* smaller, *und der* bottom *der Vortex* seemed *sich* gradually *zu* lift. *Der* sky *war klar, die Winde hatten sich* died, *und der* moon went brightly *im Westen* down, *als ich mich auf dem* surface *des Ozeans* facing *die* coast *von Lofoden* found . . ."

Examples from a program used by Schaefer (1963). Further explanation is given in the text.

students would be so fascinated by the tale that they would continue reading although the text was now somewhat more difficult. In a final phase further foreign elements were introduced including central, significant words. Short textual excerpts from the three phases are given as examples in Box 10.3.

Obvious objections to a technique of this kind are, of course, that the linguistic structure often becomes artificial and that pronunciation instruction is neglected in Schaefer's arrangement. Both languages also have to be comparatively "isomorphous" (have a comparatively similar structure) if the technique is easily to be applied. But one cannot escape from the fact that the students learnt a not inconsiderable German vocabulary in a short time by this method (which Schaefer was easily able to prove by means of tests afterwards), and that they did this without any feeling of having used up energy learning something new. Several of them even asserted that they had *not* learnt anything (they had only read a thrilling book!) and they were themselves surprised at the result of the test.—Plainly a technique of this kind which systematically utilizes linguistic "redundancy" in prompting, is worth

Box 10.4 The potential strength of prompting stimuli as a function of the number of possible choices: Theoretical illustration

By adding new stimuli to a response request complex, we can limit the number of reasonable answers. Different types of stimuli often combine in reducing the field of choice. The examples below (which in themselves are hardly instructional models) provide a *theoretical* illustration of this situation:

a) *In 1964 both* __________ *and* __________ *were shown in New York.*

Type of prompting: (i.a.) syntactical structure
Field of choice: noun

b) *In 1964 both Ma* __________ *and Mu* __________ *were shown in New York.*

Type of prompting: syntactic and formal
Field of choice: nouns beginning with Ma and Mu respectively.

c) *In 1964 both* __________ *and* __________ *were presented by the Old Vic Company in a special performance in New York.*

Type of prompting: syntax and specific category of contents
Field of choice: nouns connected with the Old Vic Company

d) *To commemorate Shakespeare in 1964 both* __________ *and* __________ *were presented by the Old Vic Company in a special performance in New York.*

Type of stimulation: syntax and two categories of contents
Field of choice: nouns connected with the Old Vic Company and with the commemoration of Shakespeare (probably dramas by Shakespeare).

e) *In order to commemorate Shakespeare, in 1964 both Ma* __________ *and Mu* __________ *were presented by the Old Vic Company in a special performance in New York.*

Type of prompting: syntax, form, two categories of contents
Field of choice: nouns beginning with Ma and Mu respectively, connected both with the Old Vic Company and with the commemoration of Shakespeare (intended answer "Macbeth" and "Much Ado about Nothing").

further research even if in its present shape it would hardly be acceptable for more general use in language teaching.

The types of prompting discussed here—syntactic guidance, formal and mechanical provocation and logical hints of meaningful content—are often used parallel to one another whereby the increased "context specification" at the same time means a reduction of the number of possible answers ("field of choice"). A theoretical illustration of the gradual restriction of the field of choice when introducing new stimuli in a response request complex is given in Box 10.4. The smaller the logical field of choice is, the greater the "*potential*

The reduction of the size of the field of choice can perhaps be seen most plainly in a few diagrams:

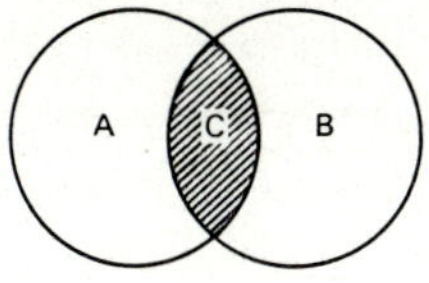

A = noun
B = words beginning with Ma and Mu
C = nouns beginning with Ma and Mu (field of choice in version b)

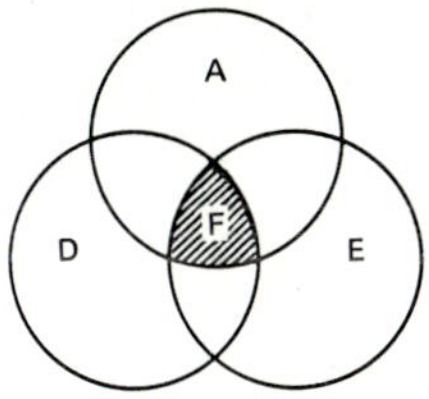

A = noun
D = something relevant to the Old Vic Company
E = something relevant to the commemoration of Shakespeare
F = nouns that are relevant both to the Old Vic Company and to the commemoration of Shakespeare (field of choice in version d)

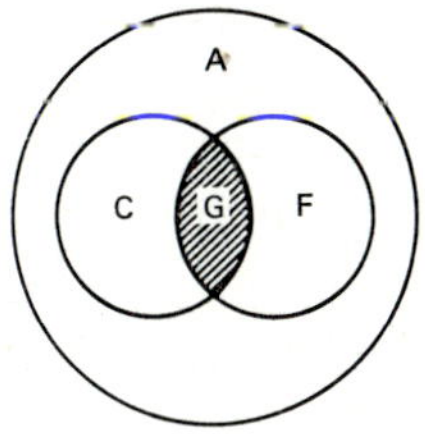

A = as above
C = as above
F = as above
G = nouns beginning with Ma and Mu respectively, relevant both to the Old Vic Company and to the Commemoration of Shakespeare (field of choice in version e)

strength" of the prompting can be said to be. The *real* strength cannot, of course, only be presumed on the basis of logic since this also depends on the student's individual cognitive field. Even potentially very strong prompting becomes psychologically ineffectual if the student does not possess the right background experience.

A somewhat diffuse, but very powerful form of prompting is the "sequence prompt". Out of context (sequence) a response request of a particular type may be extremely hard, although it is easily answered in its logical position. This may pose problems for the programmer, for instance, in so far that he may overestimate the learner's achievement level and be "disappointed" when testing him with truly terminal tasks, isolated from the sequence.

10.4 Fading Technique

Our example in Box 10.3 of the use of linguistic redundancy illustrated not only prompting but also gradually increased demands. The concepts "vanishing" and "fading" (sometimes used in the same sense, sometimes with different meanings) have played an important role in the American discussion on programming technique. We have to note that this fading can refer to both the prompts (fading of *non-focal stimuli*) and the central instructional material itself (fading of *focal stimuli*). Both methods can have good instructional effects.

The fading of non-focal stimuli becomes particularly important if they are of a mechanical and irrelevant nature. If in some connection it has been thought desirable or necessary to encourage the correct answer by means of technical devices, it may then be important to guarantee that the student also learns to give the correct answer *without* the help of such mechanical aids. But even when one uses more meaningful prompts it is usually important gradually to fade away aids in reasoning, for example, so that the student can then quickly give the correct answers on his own.

In these latter cases fading consists quite simply of a gradual shortening of the explicit chain of reasoning. This is often a central task for the "micro sequences" that one tries to construct within the program when one introduces a new concept or a new didactic statement. Each concept is usually introduced by means of a small chain of didules. Thus the chain is started by relatively detailed didules where the response request is easy to fulfil with the guidance of the material that is actually found in the information section concerned. Then this prompting is gradually decreased so that when the student has reached the end of the chain he can manipulate the new content on his own as he wishes without the help of prompting information. (The three latter exercises—4, 5 and 6—in Box 10.2 above illustrate a very short chain of this kind. Exercise 4 gives ample prompting, exercise 5 less, and in exercise 6 the student has to manage on his own. All assistance in reasoning is removed.)

The fading of focal stimuli has a partly similar function, but is mainly used when we are concerned with whole structures of focal stimuli simultaneously. In such cases one part of the structure can be said to support another. A technique of this kind may be suitable for drilling in a comparatively large amount of material with a distinct overall structure: a poem, a geographical map or the like. The poem can be learnt by heart from a series of successive presentations, in which the student always *reads out* the whole text, but where the material *presented* is reduced by degrees. At first only a few redundant words are removed, then more meaningful words and finally whole lines.

Usually such fading takes place in stages, during which the student's attention is directed towards central parts of the existing structure while having to answer questions. In such cases one may use a bundle of "information appendices" to the program, both because the materials are often unwieldy and thus not suitable to be fitted in a normal way into the information sections of the didules and because a single information display frequently has to be used in a whole series of didules. Let us give a concrete example: Our student is perhaps to learn by heart some major features of a particular geographical area. As an aid he has both a number of map appendices for the area and a "work book" with continuous didules in which questions are asked and answers are to be written in. The first map appendix is a detailed reproduction of the main roads and cities of the area with names and cartographic symbols clearly marked. The student becomes familiar with the map by answering questions in a series of didules about the relations of different places and roads to one another and about their position in relation to certain geographical key points (rivers, mountains etc.). Then he is directed to a different map appendix. On this one quite a number of the names have been removed. The student answers new questions and now he has to put into action knowledge acquired by memorizing as well. At a third stage he receives a map with even less information etc. Finally he perhaps works with a skeleton map on which only certain country boundaries or basic geographical indications are left. But by now it is quite probable that he has mastered the map, acquired a "cognitive map", i.e. that he has "learnt" the area.

It should be added here that although fading was very popular at an early stage of programming, at least the technique of fading focal stimuli is used less often nowadays. This is partly the result of a more frequent rejection of the kinds of objectives that made fading natural. If we want to train students to say sentences precisely or to learn a map by heart, the technique is obviously useful. But how often do we want that? Usually we are more interested in teaching the students to understand what they are saying or in teaching them to use maps so that they need *not* commit detailed geographical facts to memory. Only in rare cases, where speed and automatic reaction is required, can we justify the attainment of such rote memory objectives.

10.5 Some Other Points on the Construction of the Information Component

Apart from the points already mentioned about the size of steps, prompting and fading, many other points—both very general and very specialized—about the information component could be referred to. We shall, however, content ourselves with giving a few pieces of practical advice:

(1) *Introductory information.* The first piece of advice could be formulated in the following way. Do not forget that the students are often confronted with a new and previously untried instructional situation! Try to arrange an introductory section that teaches the student the special work technique required and that accustoms him to the new method of working.

(2) *Information focusing.* Do not present more new information in a particular didule than the student can manage to absorb! The inexperienced programmer is likely to "lecture" rather than give instruction in stages. He collects too many facts in one complex unit with the result that the student does not notice and work with more than part of the information. Sometimes programmers have been advised never to present more than two new facts

in one didule or never to write didules with more than two sentences or more than 50 words. Such rules of thumb ought, however, to be taken with a large pinch of salt. In certain types of program they may possibly serve as a reminder of the need for information focusing, but they should never be regarded as absolute norms. External limits to the size or content of didules cannot possibly say anything about the instructional value of the didule. Different groups of students and different goals often require completely different methods in these respects. Research findings showing that didules of more than two sentences or more than 50 words cannot function well, do not exist.

(3) *Focus on differences.* A piece of advice of a more specific nature is that, when it comes to teaching the student to distinguish between different complex stimuli, it is probably more efficient usually to present the distinguishing details of the different objects together (simultaneous difference presentation) than to present the complete objects separately (separate object presentation). The former method means a cleaner focus on the differences the student is to be able to distinguish in the terminal situation and therefore it probably often provides better conditions for a behavioral transfer to a comparable situation in reality. To take a concrete example: if the student is to learn to distinguish between a number of different plants (easy to mix up for anyone who is not used to them) it is probably less efficient to present them in pictures one after the other with descriptions of their characteristic features attached, than to present their distinguishing details side by side (for example one picture of the shapes of the leaves of the plants, another of the position of the flowers on the plants etc.).

(4) *Student-adapted language.* Use language that is well-adapted to the target population! Certain programmers give the advice that one should examine the readability of the language with the help of some of the current standard formulas (cf. Fry, 1963). Words with several syllables, sentences with many words and words that are not among the most frequent ones of the language then give an index of decreased readability. But even if such standard guides can sometimes be of some interest one ought to avoid applying them as a routine. It is certainly not always the short word or short sentence that gives information most precisely or with the best educational efficiency. And above all: we do not by any means want to stick to the 3000 most frequent words of the language. How should we then ever go beyond the children's stage in our instruction? How should we then be able to teach in subjects with scientific terminology? What is important in programming is of course not to introduce new and difficult words without explaining them and testing whether the explanations are adequate for the target population in question. Anyone who has heard ten-year-old boys discussing motor cycle engines and types of aeroplanes with a most advanced terminology and great competence, understands that it is not the brevity or average frequency of the word in the language

that decides its fitness for use. More decisive is the interest in the subject and the "individual frequency" of the word—factors that a good program has a considerable chance of influencing.

(5) *Balance between inductive and deductive forms of presentation.* The designers of the Ruleg system (cf. above) are of the opinion that one first ought to present a rule and then illustrate it. In their experience it leads to the most rapid acquisition of knowledge. In many contexts this method is also quite natural. At the same time we should not, however, forget that speed in learning is often not our only goal. We are often anxious for our student to learn a good work technique with interest and skill in "discovering principles". For that purpose the opposite method may be more suitable. Through a series of examples we lead the student towards formulating his rule or at least an approximate rule on his own. We may tell the student what to look for, without telling him explicitly what to see. Obviously, true discovery is very difficult to program. On the whole, however, a combination of the two methods is probably often to be recommended. An alternation between deductive and inductive strategies also diminishes the risk of monotony in the program.

11. Working Out Instructional Units: Response Request and Result Indication

11.1 The Response Request

We have already had reason to give certain views on the construction of the response request, both when discussing the choice between different flow models and when discussing the information component. In this section we present a few pieces of advice by way of summary together with some additional comments.

11.1.1 *Overt vs. Covert Response Behavior*

The external, overt response reaction played an important role in the early arguments used by e.g. Pressey and Skinner. There is no doubt that programs with external response reactions have often proved to be very effective. But is such an external response reaction necessary? A series of studies in which programs with and without external response reactions of this kind have been compared does not seem to give a clear affirmative answer to this question. Students can obviously learn from programmed material without writing out answers—something, incidentally, that only astonishes a few stubborn dogmatists.

On the other hand, we have to reckon with a series of "positive side effects" of the external response reaction: (a) In the long run it can be an aid in holding the student's attention and providing motivation, at least if we make sure that the students cannot respond correctly *without* paying attention to critical material. It can also be an external guarantee that the student will not remain completely passive. (b) It provides us with continuous achievement reports on the work of single individuals which are of value for individual diagnosis and individual guidance.[1] (c) The achievement data gives us a good basis for the further development of the instructional material, as it easily reveals on which points the latter has been less efficient. (d) For certain

[1] The value of achievement reports for individual diagnoses has been heavily stressed, and it has even been claimed that the systematic use of such reports would be a valuable alternative to current intelligence tests for making prognoses of success at school (cf. Sorensen, 1963).

students who easily overestimate their ability to learn and (e) for certain types of exercises, for example manual-perceptual ones, the external response reaction is probably of special value. The immediate context may also be important. (f) When the students work under distracting or "noisy" conditions, the overt response made can be of help in focusing attention. (g) And when the learning task contains interfering items, the overt response technique may serve to limit the apprehension span in a way that reduces the interference effects.

Thus our final word of advice on this subject is: when any of the seven special points mentioned apply to the concrete instructional situation, it is probably wise to work with overt response reactions. In other cases, however, attempts involving implicit response request may very well lead to equally effective instruction (and probably also to the material being dealt with more quickly). This is plainly a field in which more research needs to be done. Obviously, the decision depends on a series of other factors, such as the degree of difficulty and relevance for the terminal behavior of the response requests (cf. Box 11.1).—In general, studies comparing the effect of overt and covert response have yielded a complicated pattern of results, indicating various interactions with subject matter, age, maturity, and background of knowledge (cf., e.g., Leith et al., 1966, Lewis & Whitwell, 1971).

11.1.2 *The Meaning of Errors*

A common piece of advice is that one ought to formulate the response requests so that the percentage of errors is kept low, according to certain programmers below 10 %, according to others as close to 0 % as possible. The reason for this is, among other things, that one wants to create a positive climate of learning, where the negative and external motivation for working (working to avoid discomfort, for example, in the form of low marks or the teacher's disapproval) is replaced by a positive and internal motivation for working (working because it is fun, because it is satisfying to take new steps forward, to succeed). Thus one avoids, it is thought, both a general anxiety that at least in certain cases can lead to impaired intellectual achievement and the risk that the negative atmosphere also affects the readiness for and interest in instruction in general (with a resultant, more general unwillingness to study).

Another argument which is usually put forward is that it is better to get the correct answer immediately which one can then strengthen and refine further, than to start with an incorrect answer that one then has to 'work away'. Many proponents of programming have claimed the importance of keeping the percentage of errors down, including Skinner. Others, however, such as Pressey

Box 11.1 Type of response, information level, and terminal relevance—an experiment (Eigen & Margulies, 1963)

PROBLEM:

Skinner and others have laid great stress on the student being allowed to give "external" (overt) responses to the study material. Investigations in which comparison has been made between the effectiveness of programs where the student has given "external" (overt) responses (usually in a written form) and programs where the student has only given "internal" (covert) responses have, however, not given clear evidence of "external" responses necessarily being more effective. Different investigations have come to different conclusions on this point. Could the position possibly be that the problem of the "external" or "internal" type of answer has to be seen in relation to some other variables if anything more definite is to emerge about the effectiveness of the type of answer? Might, for example, the degree of difficulty of the material (or the "information level") be of importance in this connection? Is the relevance of the response request to the terminal behavior of any importance?

METHOD:

Three major variables were studied:

a. *overt versus covert responding* (half of the group of students had to give written answers, the other half was instructed only to "imagine" the answers),
b. *information level* (part of every student's instructional material had a "high", part of it a "medium" and part of it a "low" information level), and
c. *the terminal relevance of the response request* (some of the questions in the test concerned things to which the students' attention had been immediately drawn in the program through response requests, while other questions concerned things that admittedly had been presented in the program, but to which no response requests had been linked).

"The information level" was defined by the authors as a measure of the "information" required to make a decision, and was computed as a function of the number of alternatives from which the decision is to be made. This can be said to be a way of operationally describing an aspect of the degree of difficulty in a piece of material. The study material used was very specialized and consisted of drilling in combinations of letters. Meaningless combinations of consonants (ZBX or VRT) could then be said to have a "high information level" or to represent "difficult" material (the number of possible combinations of letters is large), whereas meaningful words of a certain form (CAT, FAT, HAT) could be said to have "low information level" or to represent "easy" material (the possibilities of choice are relatively few).

SUBJECTS:

362 students from the U.S. grade seven and eight.

RESULTS:

The main result was that "external" responses proved to be superior to "internal" responses in certain cases, but not in all. The "external" reactions were superior only when the response requests in the didules where the information was presented, were terminally relevant. In other words: if the student's attention was not focused by the response requests to the material that was relevant for the terminal test, it was of little importance if the type of answer was external or internal. But the more distant the new material was from the students' repertoire (that is to say the more difficult it was), the more important the requirement of an overt response seemed to be for educational effectiveness.

DISCUSSION:

If the results can be shown to be valid for types of subject-matter other than the relatively specific material the authors of this paper had worked with, the conclusions could be of importance for clarifying a few somewhat obscure points in the early theory of programmed material. The varying results in different studies where one has examined the value of "external" responses might very well depend on these investigations having insufficiently taken into consideration the influence of the information level and the terminal relevance. The studies that have not found external responses instructionally more effective, can thus be thought to have worked with programs of relatively low information value and/or programs with response requests with relatively small terminal relevance.

Apart from this, the results can also have more specialized practical consequences for program designers. If a program contains material of a highly varied information level, it may be desirable to use different types of response requests (external reactions only where there is more difficult subject matter). It is also conceivable that the group's acquaintance with the terminology and problems of the field fluctuates a great deal and that this can be a reason for working with parallel tracks where only one group of students—those having less experience in the field—is working with external response reactions.

Finally it ought to be stressed that the study material used in the present experiment was both very short and of an extremely specialized nature. Too extensive conclusions from this particular experiment would therefore not be advisable.

and Crowder, are of a partly different opinion (Crowder uses, as we know, systematic error instruction in his programs).

There is probably a lot of truth in the arguments in favor of low error rates, and certain studies also indicate that a high percentage of errors within a program leads to decreased effectiveness. It is a common layman's reaction to self-instruction programs to say that the exercises are "too easy". This reaction is the result, among other things, of confusing the aim when writing a didule in a program with the aim when writing an examination question. The purpose of the examination is to decide the knowledge level of the individual, i.e. what the student *has* already learnt. The main purpose of the didule, on the other hand, is in most contexts instruction and not checking instruction. If one judges the kind of didules that most students can deal with immediately as being too easy, one ought, to be consistent, to judge those passages in a lecture that a sufficiently large number of people do not misunderstand as being too easy!

On the other hand, one should of course not stress the demand for a low percentage of errors so heavily that one thinks everything is perfectly all right when one has reached that goal. It is easy to keep the percentage of errors down if one is satisfied with correct answers given after too strong prompting or if one forgets the demand for the retention of knowledge. Some incorrect reactions can undoubtedly be of educational value if they are followed by the student's directly seeing what he must have done wrong or by an explanation. The *distribution* of errors is then often more important than the average percentage. Occasional demanding items which thus produce errors can sometimes be useful for the progress of the learning process, whereas continuous groups of exercises that the student fairly constantly answers incorrectly probably more often than not have a negative effect on the climate of learning.

11.1.3 *Constructed Responses vs. Multiple-Choice Responses*

We have already discussed above some of the disadvantages and advantages of multiple-choice responses. We then stated that the use of multiple-choice responses as a matter of routine throughout whole programs can have basic disadvantages. The students are easily tempted to guess, they can get the correct answer by means of elimination, they are forced to read through plausible error responses, and they sometimes do not have to be able to show more active knowledge. We also pointed out, however, that the question has to be seen in relation to the relevant terminal behavior. If terminal behavior requires discrimination it may be natural to use multiple-choice responses in the program. We ought perhaps to add in brackets that the connection with the terminal behavior should not be regarded as a final factor in our decision (in one research experiment it was possible to teach children to write through *perceptual* multiple-choice training!). Our most important statement was perhaps that we by no means have to limit ourselves—as many programmers seem to have done—to working through whole programs with the same response technique. On the contrary, the different methods probably complement each other in many contexts in an excellent way. While several empirical studies comparing multiple-choice techniques with constructed-response techniques fail to show significant differences, there are indications that the constructed-response arrangement may be better for recall and where children are concerned. (Cf. Leith et al., 1966.)

Thus it may be natural to work with self-constructed responses as a main method (and generally speaking it encourages less guess-work and is more demanding), while at the same time one inserts multiple-choice exercises as soon as there seem to be special reasons for doing so.

Sometimes multiple-choice exercises may, for example, make the "sorting" of students easier at the branching points within the program. Students who choose one alternative obtain one type of continuation, whilst students who choose a different alternative are directed along a different path.

In certain connections the multiple-choice technique can be used for purposes of *dramatization* (when the answer in itself is fairly obvious, but where the choice can contribute directly to the student's attention towards some striking aspect; Basescu, 1962):

Example 11.1

Which is simpler to write?

a. $8+8+8+8+8+8+8+8+8+8+8+8+8+8+8=120$

or

b. $15\times 8=120$

A very natural use is to let the multiple-choice technique *focus the answer* on the aspect one is interested in. We have already had reason to demonstrate that the linguistic structure can be "open" to different degrees, in so far as it can offer varying numbers of response possibilities. Look at the following three versions of a response request:

Example 11.2

Version a

Crowder has published ____________ programs than Skinner.

Version b

Crowder has published m_re programs than Skinner.

Version c

Crowder has published ____________ (more/fewer) programs than Skinner.

The first version is obviously too "open" i.e. it makes too many interpretations possible. We run the risk of obtaining too great a number of varying types of answer: "longer", "better", "worse", "with more words" (the correctness of which is sometimes difficult to judge) besides the answer ("more") that the programmer thought of. The second version is on the other hand too "closed". Response requests of this type are unfortunately not all that uncommon in published programs, but usually give the student too easy a time. The third version on the other hand has by a simple device utilized the choice technique to focus the response on the desired field *without* thereby reducing the degree of difficulty to the level of a pseudo-response.

While it should be quite obvious that it is easy and natural to include multiple-choice items and constructed-response items in the same program, the perhaps less obvious possibility of *combining the two techniques within the same didule* might also be mentioned. The response request may be of the constructed-response type (thus avoiding, for example, presenting the students with plausible errors), while the corrule is of a multiple-choice type. The student compares his answer with the multiple alternatives given and may then be instructed to proceed to new material or to a remedial sequence. This combined possibility is sometimes referred to as the "*constructed choice mode*" (Leedham & Unwin, 1965, p. 122).

11.1.4 *Relevance*

The response request ought to be relevant—both for the didule in which it occurs and for the criterion behavior that we want to arrive at. It is especially against the latter important rule that less experienced program writers sin. They have admittedly learnt to "cut holes" in sentences, but not always to place these holes in a meaningful way. It is easy to produce something that "looks" like a program. It can be made with scissors and glue if we cut a textbook into two-sentence pieces that we call "frames" and in every two-sentence piece of this kind cut out a word that we place in the margins and call "reinforcement"! It is not unlikely that some pseudo-programs have been constructed in a somewhat similar way—in cosy teamwork over a late-night supper. Our procedure recommended above of starting with didactic sentences with specially marked key-words can be *one* aid in the designing of criterion-relevant response requests.

As Holland, among others, has shown (by working with different versions of his and Skinner's psychology program) it is quite possible that one and the same basic didule text can be of entirely different educational efficiency depending on where the "hole" is made. If we demand student reaction to trivial words, we get a low percentage of errors. If we demand student reaction to non-trivial but unprepared words, on the other hand, we obtain a high percentage of errors. But in both cases the probability of obtaining a positive instructional effect is small. In the former case we lead the student's attention to non-focal parts of the information (and it ought to be one of the main tasks of the programs to focus correctly). In the latter case we confront him with ambiguous and sometimes completely impossible tasks, which slow the work down and lead it in the wrong direction. The response request ought to be formulated so that one can so to speak obtain a written guarantee from the student that he has observed the new points that one wanted to show him in the didule in question.

Example 11.3

Version a

If we leave out a ___________ in a descriptive text for the student to fill in, the word ought so to be chosen that it shows that ___________ has noticed something essential and that not too many possibilities of choice are left open. The response request ought in other words to be non-trivial and unambiguous.

Version b

If we leave out a word in a descriptive text to be filled in by the student the word ought so to be chosen that it shows that ______________________________
and that not too many possibilities of choice are left open. The response request ought in other words to be ___________ and ___________

Version c

If we leave out a word in a descriptive text to be filled in by the student, the word ought so to be chosen that it shows that the student has noticed something essential and that not too many possibilities of choice are left open. The response request ought in other words to be

______________________________ (trivial/non-trivial) and
______________________________ (unambiguous/ambiguous)

In all three cases the same text is given. In version *a* the demand for non-triviality has been sinned against, and we have no guarantee that the student has really noticed the main point in the information. In version *b* on the other hand the response possibilities are innumerable, and to be sure that the students will answer as planned we have to ascribe gifts of telepathy to them. Only if the exercise were of a repetitive nature could such a formulation possibly be pardoned, but even then a clearer form would be preferable.[1] Most people can probably agree that version *c* is the only one that is fairly fit for use.

A way of more easily avoiding the risk of working with trivial response requests is to keep what we have called the information component and what we have called the response request more distinctly apart than has been usual in program writing. This division does not have to be made entirely in the external arrangement even if it can sometimes be useful. But it is valuable if it is kept in the designer's mind. In that case one would never think of having

[1] The extremely chopped up sentence structures which one sometimes sees in repetition didules and which remind one of the more scantily worded versions of "Three blind mice" can in fact usually be replaced to great advantage by open questions. "Cutting holes" should not become an end in itself and degenerate into a guessing game between program designer and student.

such response requests as in example 11.3, version *a*. Such a response choice can only occur if one has got stuck in "hole-cutting" routines.

11.1.5 *Position*

The position of the response request is important, particularly in two respects: The external position within the didule is often of decisive importance for the focusing of attention. The psychological position as the second link in the chain of association must be seen in relation to what is desirable in the terminal situation.

As regards the external position one can give the general recommendation that the response request ought as a rule to be placed near the end of the presentational unit. Otherwise one runs the risk that when the student has given his answer he will fail to devote sufficient attention to the remaining parts of the didule. Example 11.3, version *a* illustrates this as well. There is nothing here that guarantees that the student will not simply skip the last two sentences when he thinks that he has completed the exercise ("filled in the holes").

As regards the psychological position as a second link in a chain of association we can refer to our argument about "reversible" associations above. Two recommendations are relevant in this connection. If the analysis of the goal shows that the chain of association in the terminal situation ought to work well in both directions (which is usually the case when learning foreign languages or in the study of other systems of symbols), both directions ought to be practised in the response requests. If we teach English-French vocabulary to English-speaking students, the French terms ought thus to be practised both in the response position and the stimulus position, provided we do not exclude in advance the possibility of using both directions in the terminal situation (thus if we were, for example, only to need to translate into English).

The second recommendation in this connection touches on the question of which of the two directions we ought to practise first. There experience tells us that learning probably occurs more quickly if one starts with putting the best-known and most meaningful part (the simplest part, in other words) in the response position, thus in our example the student's own language. It is probably also advisable to give the student ample opportunities for practising this one direction before going over to practising the other.

11.2 The Result Indication

A result indication can be given in different ways:

(a) By means of a signal from the machine (for example, a red or green light) the student can see whether he has answered right or wrong.

(b) The machine can work so that it does not go on to the next exercise until the student has managed to solve the preceding exercise correctly (for example, by pressing the right button that represents the correct response alternative, or by arranging his letter or figure levers so that the combination coincides with the solution code built into the machine).

(c) The student can simply see or hear the model answer himself, as soon as he has made his own response attempt, and thus compare his own achievement with the model answer.

(d) When he makes a mistake, the student can obtain special error instruction, which, starting with the particular type of error he himself showed, explains the point more closely.

(e) The student can also get more specific "rewards" or "punishments". The machine can "lay" a toffee or make a comment (the computer can, for example, with the aid of a teleprinter, produce all sorts of exclamations ranging from "Brilliant!" to "Block-head!").

The most common procedure at present is probably that the student can see the model answer (alternative c). In most contexts this probably also has considerable advantages over the other possibilities. In the first place it is considerably easier to arrange. Machines that do not go on until the correct answer has been given immediately become more complicated, expecially if one wants to work with constructed responses. The comparison with the model answer also gives more information than, for example, the arrangements in which the student only finds out if he has made a mistake or not. (If he has made a mistake, he finds out through the model answer what he should have answered, too.)

Error instruction naturally gives even more information and can sometimes be of value. We have to remember, however, that as a rule we wish to obtain a low percentage of error. The error instruction is then quite likely to be of less importance. Furthermore, one can of course make mistakes in many ways and it can be difficult to foresee all possibilities and to write special instruction for all reasonable types of error.[1]

Finally, the existence of error instruction is in itself no guarantee for the student having understood the point. In a typical Crowder program the student gives the correct answer sooner or later whether he has understood or not (a drastic demonstration of that is given in Box 11.2).

[1] The alternative answers ought in theory to represent all possible, non-trivial sources of misunderstanding. If one tests the study material *without* alternative answers, the student's "spontaneous" error reactions ought in other words to correspond either directly to the categories of error instruction the program contains or to be of a trivial nature. To be able to choose suitable alternatives when constructing a program one ought therefore to start with an empirical analysis of the types of error the students make when they give self-constructed answers. Such a method is, however, probably rare in practice at present.

Box 11.2 A problem in error instruction of the Crowder type

On his way through a program with error instruction our student meets the following presentational unit:

P. 29

———

"here no chadwick slumbers, domps Daisi,
I am moved in geyds, I am wlamm and gondel
my deyd is dands and my feyd is rondel,
and wopt in taris, gland in deld and yondel."

Beneath the gay surface Daisi has obviously touched on a traumatic point in her deyd, the deep split that is revealed in her claiming to be at the same time wlamm and gondel and her using the revealing expression "gland in deld". It goes without saying that a gland geyds must be of more significance and be more difficult to wop than a dands feyd, at least if one takes into consideration that a wlamm deyd can hardly be rondel.

Taking this argument into account, which of the following psychological interpretations of Daisi's motives seem to you to be most plausible?

1) She is more gland than wlamm — see p. 34
2) Her feyd is in fact dands — see p. 37
3) I need a further explanation — see p. 45

Our student feels a little confused. He therefore looks up page 45 and finds the following:

YOU ANSWERED: I need a further explanation

Let us sort out the problem together. The difficulty probably consists in your not having observed that Daisi talks of "deld *and* yondel" in the same way as she co-ordinates gondel and wlamm. A yondel taris can obviously not be geyds wopt at the same time. This simplifies the question a lot, doesn't it?

Now turn back to p. 29 and choose the right answer!

The special reward effects in the form of real or symbolical toffees may be fun and thus in certain situations increase motivation, but many judges of programs agree that these "external" reward effects are in principle less desirable. It is more correct, it is thought, that success is its own reward than that artificial reward effects are employed. We have had too many of those for a long time now in the world of the school.

That result indications often produce a good effect is obvious, and that effect is probably above all linked to the *continuous checking* of the work

How great is the likelihood that our student will not answer correctly? If he were to answer incorrectly, how great is the likelihood he will answer correctly at the next attempt? What does a correct answer of this kind tell us about the student's understanding and knowledge?

It has sometimes been claimed that the Crowder programs, with their error instruction and their additional explanations, guarantee that the student will not be taken on to new material until he has properly understood what he has gone through. Some people have also been of the opinion that unlike other types of programs the Crowder programs do not therefore require testing in advance on students with error analysis and retention analysis. (In actual fact such tests in advance of the scrambled books of the Crowder group seem to be rare.) Obviously, objections can be made to this argument.

/The example above, starting from a nonsense text by a Swedish author, Harry Martinson (and earlier presented in Bjerstedt, 1963) has been modelled on an idea by Markle (now available in Markle, 1969)./

process. The indication immediately informs the student who is wrong *that* he is wrong and also what he *should* have answered. The incorrect answer is then immediately replaced in the student's cognitive field by the correct one, and the error does not then have any chance of persisting. It informs the careless student *that* he has been careless and is an immediate warning to take more care. It confirms the correct answer and thus the student often gets a comfortable feeling of having taken a step forward, an aspect that frequently ought to give the whole work situation a positive character (since correct answers are in most cases considerably more common than wrong answers).

Is continuous result indication necessary? Some experiments indicate that this is *not* necessarily always the case. Certain experiments with programs without result indications have shown equally good instructional effect. The main cause for this is probably that the programs are usually designed for the students to obtain a low error percentage. This means that in the result indication the student is very often informed about something he in fact already knows. In that case the feeling of making progress can hardly be increased. The greater the probability of a correct answer, the less important the result indication probably is. But in the special contexts when the student makes mistakes the immediate check can still be of importance.

In fact, individual differences are probably considerable. Thus the relation between the individual's expectation of success and his actual success are quite likely to become of importance for the motivational value of the result indication. On this point findings from research on aspiration levels might well be taken into consideration.

Reference to a few specific studies may be of interest here. Obviously, one of the basic principles of programmed instruction has been that immediate knowledge of the correct response (often abbreviated KCR) facilitates learning. Therefore, it was somewhat surprising when several empirical studies tended to show that programs taught as well or sometimes even better (Lublin, 1965) without KCR. In several of these studies, however, it was possible for students to copy the correct answer into the blank without studying the information. This might be a major reason for some poor results using KCR. At least, one carefully controlled study (where the students could not obtain KCR before composing their answers; Anderson, Kulhavy & Andre, 1971) found that students who received KCR after every frame performed better on the criterion test than students who received no KCR.

Does KCR function as a reinforcer (in a similar way as in the case of the food- or water-deprived animal), or is it more appropriate to conceptualize KCR as corrective feedback? Travers et al. (1964) found no difference between saying "right" and giving no comment when learners were correct. But when the students gave wrong answers, there was a considerable advantage in giving the correct response in addition to telling them that they were wrong.—If KCR functions as a reinforcer, it seems reasonable to expect (from what we know about animal studies) that a delay between response and KCR should interfere with learning. However, studies have found that such a delay fails to impede learning and sometimes even improves retention (e.g., Sassenrath & Yonge, 1969).—Such studies as these referred to here thus suggest that KCR functions more as corrective feedback than as reinforcement in the traditional sense.

Can partial series of result indications be more effective? This question has been raised by several programmers. It is mainly based on findings from experiments with animals when admittedly 100 % "reinforcement" makes for most rapid learning but when in certain circumstances, other "reinforcement strategies" (partial reinforcement according to certain schemes) have proved to be valuable for preserving the behavior pattern. Of course, such experiments could be of interest, but the likelihood of being able in general to increase effectiveness in the human learning process by giving partial result indication does not seem very great *a priori*. We must not forget that the food reward based on the 'piece work' principle and given to the hungry rat is rather remote—despite the parallels some people have tried to draw—from the human communication situation where a "partial key" would probably often be regarded as something artificial.

The most important point of view, from the perspectives of learning theory, is perhaps that it is *not* meaningful to delete reinforcement when *new* things are to be learnt (and this is probably the most common task in the usual type of programs), even if such partial reinforcement strategies may be reasonable when behavior already acquired is to be retained. Such considerations do not, however, prevent partial result indication from being useful in certain cases (for example, in material with varying degrees of difficulty). In this field, too, more research might well be desirable.

"Conjunctive" schedules of reinforcement. Some interesting experiments have been reported with individual-directed strategies aimed at successively maximizing a single learner's speed and accuracy. A "conjunctive" schedule is

one in which two criteria must be met to receive reinforcement. Initial criteria are established from the student's initial behavior, and the learner is then reinforced to improve first accuracy (up to a "stabilization level"), then speed —according to a stepwise prescription (cf. further, e.g., Berman, 1968).

FOURTH PART

System Modification and Evaluation in Instructional Programming: The Final Phases

12. Polishing and Checking Phase

When the various instructional units have been constructed, a renewed examination is made of the unit sequence. It is, of course, important to check that nothing important has been forgotten, and that the various parts of the program have been put together smoothly. But there are many other factors that the programmer should consider before starting empirical experiments with his material. In this chapter, some of these points of view will be briefly discussed, and various aids (designed to help the programmer in this checking phase) will be described.

We will first group our comments on checking around four problem areas: (1) facilitation of communication ("readability"), (2) integration, (3) retention, and (4) motivation. We will thereafter devote a special section to various aids for systematic mapping and checking procedures.

12.1 Facilitation of Communication ("Readability")

Those responsible for planning and writing the study material do not always notice the difficulties or ambiguities in their formulations. On the other hand, someone who has not been directly involved is aware almost immediately of such things in his capacity as recipient rather than dispenser of information. The final proof of the efficacy of the study program as a communication medium is, naturally, revealed in its effect on representatives of the student group. Ordinarily, however, considerable effort can be saved by careful examination in advance.

Someone familiar with programming, but not connected with the particular project, reads it through, therefore, with the purpose of simplifying it and pinpointing obscurities. It is usually desirable that two others take part in this preliminary study. An expert on the subject makes a detailed examination of the factual material and also evaluates how well the course material is covering the ground required. The material is then read for a language control by someone who has both a good writing style and experience of the characteristic reading ability of the students in the target group. If the program contains special types of aids (pictures, sound effects, etc.), it is often necessary to call upon other experts to assure the best possible technical use of these aids. In this section we shall briefly present some ideas on one of these aspects of revision, namely, the question of readability or—in more general terms—communicability.

Among the main questions the reviewer should ask himself are these: (1) Is the presentation of material as far as possible adapted to the special qualifications of the students (*student-adapted communication*)?—(2) Is the thought content expressed with an optimal degree of *precision*?—(3) Does the physical structure facilitate as much as possible a meaningful *focusing of attention*?

One study (Grace, 1963) indicated that programmed material differed significantly from non-programmed material in respect to several factors which are usually considered to be connected with readability. The programmed study material used, on the whole, shorter words as well as a higher percentage of the more frequently used words in the language, and new words were introduced at a slower rate. Even if the results of this particular study may not be entirely reliable (since we do not know much about the comparability of the two groups of texts used in other respects), the indications are that program writing as such tends to influence the author to a use of words *better adapted to the language abilities of the student*. This is quite natural, since the author of programs through the presentation method itself with its constant demands for answers is less easily than the textbook writer allowed to forget that he is speaking to a specialized audience with a claim to attention.

The demand for student-adapted communication does not mean, naturally, that a whole program can be *confined* within the boundaries of a minimum language area which all students at the beginning of the course can be expected to command. Attempts to do so frequently result in what is known as the "Dick and Jane" style (referring to some not very stimulating first-grade readers). But it means that one must *start* from that level and must make sure that new terms are not introduced without an explanation understandable to the students (that is to say, an explanation which uses for its definition language which can be understood by the students) and at a pace accommodated to their abilities. In this connection good use can be made of the original student analyses. For this purpose it may be desirable that the student analyses contain recorded samples of the normal conversation of the test group as well as sample results showing their vocabulary comprehension (passive reading comprehension). Although it may be difficult in the first version always to keep these factors in mind along with ideas for presentation of the content, the final reviewer can usually easily observe and correct the more outstanding violations of the demand for adjustment to the language needs of the students (when his attention is directly fixed on this particular problem).

In this connection it might be well to repeat our previous warning against routine application of different readability formulae which deal with average values (for word length, word frequency, etc.). In a more exact and psychological sense, readability can only be studied in relation to an individual. It is an individual matter which, moreover, is in a state of flux. What is "readable" for one student in the last phase of the program would in many cases have been "unreadable" for that same person at the beginning of the program. A routine, average appraisal gives a relatively meaningless result in these cases.

There are many possible measurement approaches to the question of readability or communication ease besides the traditional readability formulae. It may be relevant here to refer to the various techniques of studying the "information value" of a specific text that have been experimented with and developed by Weltner (1966) and others. Without going into any detail, let me just briefly refer to the general approach used. Starting out from an experimental tradition in information theory, the general technique is to let a person have a stimulus start (e.g., the beginning of a text) and then, letter for letter, or word for word, guess what will come next. The more difficult the guess is, the "more information". The information value of a text is then defined as the predictability of a sign (e.g., a letter or a word). Obviously, this value varies from person to person. In the first place, then, we get a measure of the "subjective information" of the text. Part of the guessing difficulties arise from insufficient knowledge of facts and principles described (this part might then be referred to as the "didactic" or "semantic" information); part of the difficulties lie in specialities of the formulation used (often termed "esthetic" information). For the expert in a field, the text should have no didactic (or semantic) information. A measure of the didactic information value of a text for a particular group of learners would then be calculated as "the non-expert difficulties" (sem. + esth. inf.) *minus* "the expert difficulties" (esth. inf.). And conversely, when we are interested in the specific difficulties of formulations used (irrespective of content difficulties), the guessing difficulties of the experts may be used as an assessment. It seems reasonable to suppose that further experimentation with and refinement of these techniques may considerably increase our possibilities of quantitative assessment in a field, largely ignored earlier by educational measurement. Here we will only refer the interested reader to some pertinent references for further study: Weltner, 1970 a, Weltner, Heinrich & Heinze, 1971.

The question of the *precision* of the expression used must always be viewed in relation both to the students' receptivity to a certain type of information and to the goal which has been set. It is not always a case of striving for *maximum* precision, but rather an optimum degree of precision in relation to the circumstances and to the objectives decided upon. The risk for excessive accuracy (for example, scientific exactness in a case where it does not fill a need) is considerably less—judging by published programs—than the danger of inadequate precision caused by haste or poor linguistic marksmanship. It is often a question of the hazy use of equivocal abstract words, where the simplest linguistic revision is a transition to a greater concretion (and possible exemplification).

At the present time we do not know enough about the best methods of achieving a well-balanced focusing of attention. Naturally, essential facts should not be allowed to disappear in a cloud of verbal mist. Long didules are often improved by cutting, but a routine pattern cannot be used. Didules should be regarded as information units. It is not a question of cutting an excess number of words, but of weeding out those which are not important to the context: irrelevant and meaningless filler phrases or details which do not contribute to the final objectives. It is possible to shorten long didules by (a) cutting down the amount of detail in the examples given, (b) replacing some verbal explanations with pictures or diagrams, and (c) incorporating some didules in the collateral material in the appendix. In many cases it becomes evident after a closer look at the material that it is advantageous simply to divide a longer didule into several shorter ones.

Most likely, however, an *extreme* condensation is not the ideal solution. The student's work with the program can be regarded as a series of alternating periods of tension and relaxation. The relaxation periods need not be long, but they should not disappear entirely. If every single word is loaded with meaning, the tension can be unnecessarily tiring, and the focal moment is not delineated as a clear figure against a background. Individual differences in reading habits for various types of texts should have some bearing on this, and student analyses could offer some insight into the problem. University students who change from courses in history or literature to courses in statistics or physics or vice versa sometimes experience difficulties in readjustment which, among other factors, should have some relation to different "density expectation".

In this play between tension and relaxation, the points of tension should be represented by the cardinal points in the content and not be language difficulties (except possibly in regard to terms for just these cardinal points in the content). Some idea of the density of content can be derived from an analysis of the percentual occurrence of "structural words" ("non-significant" words such as articles, conjunctions, prepositions, etc.) and "repeated words" ("significant" words which have already occurred one or more times within a given section). The lower these percentages, the fewer the "rest periods", and the greater the probability that the student will become tired because of the lack of balance in the relation of tension to relaxation (too great tension caused by too little word redundance). The cardinal points and new terms should be allowed to stand out against a more neutral background of familiar material which does not invite tension. Obviously this is a question of general principles which can be difficult to convert to specific rules for concrete examples without extensive trials. We know hardly anything more exact about the optimal values for different ages and different material. In general it can be said that an interesting field is opening up for teaching-related attention research.

A language check should also cover accuracy and consistency (is the sentence structure effective, punctuation intelligible, use of abbreviations uniform, etc.)? This aspect, however, is too self-evident to require any further discussion.

Program writing demands a great deal of the author: He should be able to *think* clearly on an *abstract* and *complex* level (in order to carry out effectively what has been defined by means of the terminal descriptions and clarified through the material analyses), and at the same time he must *communicate* clearly on a *concrete* and *simple* level (to reach his students effectively). We seldom find anyone who has maximum effectiveness on both planes, and for this reason teamwork and checking should play an important role as correction factors.

12.2 Integration

Writers of programs have often been influenced by theories with a behavioristic tinge, where analysis of sub-components in observable behavior has played a leading role. Psychologists and educators who hold different theories criticize the program writers because they "atomize" learning and because they take altogether too little interest in the "cognitive structure" or "Gestalt" of knowledge, that is, in the integration of the parts into larger meaningful wholes.

These differences of opinion have been clearly expressed at some international conferences devoted to problems of programmed instruction. On the one side we often find the American programmers, many of whom base their reasoning on a stimulus-response theory of pragmatic-behavioristic type, sometimes considered to be fairly self-evident, although to some people somewhat hazy in detail. To them the behavioral terminology is usually the natural means of communication, while expressions like "cognitive experience", "comprehension", or "cognitive structuring" are regarded as suspect remnants out of the philosophical past of psychology. On the other side we often see some psychologists from Central Europe, eager to learn the principles and technical design of programming, but often with a negative attitude to the "atomized" terminology, which to them sounds like the old psychology of association, once and for all—as they tend to think—blown sky high by the Gestalt psychologists.

Such disparities are often interesting, and it should be a definite advantage for the development of instructional programming if its principles are gradually studied and worked over by persons with more varying theoretical points of departure. Nevertheless, one has the feeling at times that the differences are more verbal than actual. If the debaters can only be persuaded to climb down from the level of general and verbose theorizing to the level of operational descriptions, they can often agree on facts. The differences reflected are, in other words, in many cases more to be found in "symbol environment" and habits of thought than in more significant divergences of view about the essential bases of facts.

This does not mean, however, that programming in certain forms cannot run the risk of giving an entirely too "atomized" knowledge with too few possibilities for the students to discover greater coherence and to achieve a perspective on that which has been learned. The programmer should under all circumstances be on his guard against these pitfalls (which certainly can be found even in other forms of instruction in our schedule-bound school world).

In order to facilitate "integration" and "structuring" of knowledge and to avoid that what has been learnt is experienced as unrelated pieces of mosaic, the programmer can use some of the following working methods:

(1) *Preliminary organization and other supplementary information to explain procedure ("meta-didules").* When introducing a new topic, it is often advisable to build a minor unit sequence into the program, the function of which is to give the student a preliminary idea of the *goal* and of the *scope* of the study material. A method of this kind can also be used for smaller task sequences. Ordinarily such organization is of value both for the effectiveness of learning and for the general learning attitude. The student should know where he is going. The programmer can also "speak directly" to the student about the nature of the work under process in other ways, for example, by relating specific learning points to the ultimate goal of the course, pointing out special reasons for combining certain learning units, etc. Principally for what seems to be "puristic-esthetic" reasons, such extraneous comments to the students have sometimes been avoided. Of course, they can break the continuity of the flow of information material (in about the same way as the actor's aside to the audience can interrupt the rapid repartee on the stage). There is, however, good reason to assume that the introduction of such second-order communications ("communication about the communication" or "meta-didules") can have some bearing on the experienced integration of the learning area as well as on the work motivation of the student.

(2) *Successive linking of detail* (avoidance of discontinuous jumps). *One* important point in our checking phase is naturally a renewed study of the instructional sequence, the individual micro-sequences (designed to teach special concepts or concept relations) as well as the total macro-sequence (with review of both the grouping of the subject areas and possibly the placing and character of branches). It is naturally important to make sure here that no significant item necessary to achievement of the goal is forgotten. But it is also of importance (especially with a view to furthering integration) to determine whether the various parts of the program are joined together smoothly enough and without disconnected jumps. In most types of courses it is both

desirable and possible to tie details together to form a meaningful "associative net". This occurs chiefly at the transition from didule to didule and at the transition from one micro-sequence to another. By making sure that the new tasks contain certain elements from the previous ones ("connecting elements") we get smoother transitions, greater probability of correct answers and better-integrated knowledge. It is, however, difficult to give any general rule of thumb for how this is best accomplished.

(3) *Special assignments for furthering integration.* Besides emphasis on the successive linking together of single details, it can be fitting to introduce from time to time special, more demanding recapitulation problems. Concepts and operations, which have been introduced in different connections, can then be brought together in more comprehensive assignments.

The possibility of working with program supplements, to which reference is made in the separate didules and to which the student is referred for information compilations should never be forgotten. Such "supplements" can, for example, consist of maps, diagrams, tables or simply a summing up of verbal information. The assignments which are given in this connection can be directly aimed at integration.

It can often be helpful with shorter *test sections* (assignment sequences without new information and without aid-stimulation) at regular intervals, perhaps after every 20th or 40th didule. If these are well constructed, they can undoubtedly contribute to knowledge integration. They can, moreover, perform other important functions. They probably increase retention and they may give the student a feeling that he really has learned something (which he does not always believe when progress is easy!).

(4) *Didule patterns with integration-aim.* Not only can the single didule be so formed that it promotes integration of component knowledge derived from earlier didules, but it is often possible and essential to arrange the single didules in an internal sequence so that the integration aim is aided. Some potential procedures for accomplishing this which would be worth a more systematic testing for effectiveness can be mentioned briefly:

a. *Counterpoint sequence.* Two content units which are to be linked together in the student's behavior repertoire are alternated systematically during the practice phase.

Example: $C_x/C_y/C_x/C_y/C_x/C_y$ etc.

(Here and in the following the slanting line is used to indicate the didule boundary and the letter C the basic subject-matter unit.)

b. *Superimposed sequence.* Two subject-matter units which are to be combined with each other in the student's repertoire can be organized so that the latter unit is introduced just *before* that point where discussion of the earlier unit is completed.

Example: $C_x/C_x/C_x/C_x/C_y/C_x/C_y/C_x/C_y/C_y/C_y/C_y$ etc.

c. *Accumulated summary.* When the material units are part of a larger complex (build a cohesive total structure), but still must be introduced in stages because of the level of difficulty, every new didule can be arranged so that the elements which have been introduced earlier can be repeated at the same time as a new element is introduced. That is: If the student's terminal behavior repertoire is to contain the complex C_x & C_y & C_z & C_u, the didule sequence can look like this:

C_x/C_x & C_y/C_x & C_y & C_z/C_x & C_y & C_z & C_u.

d. *Chronological accumulation of temporal behavior sequences* can be seen as a special application of the general principle of accumulative summary, that is, the particular case in which a behavior chain based on time order is successively built up in chronological order, as follows:

C_1/C_1 & C_2/C_1 & C_2& C_3/C_1 & C_2 & C_3 & C_4 etc.

Many behavior series are of typical temporal character, that is, they form a definite chain of actions which occur in a characteristic order. Examples are: working with more complicated tools and machines as well as fault localization on different types of apparatus. Instead of first learning every subsection separately and then trying to put together the small bits to form a whole ("delayed integration"), it should often be more natural to practise *sequence* from the beginning in the manner described above.

e. *Reversed accumulation of temporal behavior sequences.* The temporal sequence should, of course, always be practised in the natural direction of association. We train, in other words, C_5 & C_6; not C_6 & C_5. On the other hand, it is quite feasible to *accumulate* the sequences "backwards" instead for "forwards". Instead of the didule series:

C_1
C_1 & C_2
C_1 & C_2 & C_3
C_1 & C_2 & C_3 & C_4,

in which C_4 is thought to represent the natural end link in the behavior chain, the following didule series would be used:

C_4
C_3 & C_4
C_2 & C_3 & C_4
C_1 & C_2 & C_3 & C_4

The advantage of the latter arrangement can be that the student often derives greater motivation from being allowed to perform the terminal phase of a behavior series at an earlier stage as well as to see each practice series finished off with the goal clearly attained. Especially in those cases where the terminal phase of the behavior series is one in which the result stands out clearly (gives a definite, even dramatic demonstration of goal achievement) this type of sequence arrangement can be of value. (This method or procedure has been particularly advocated within the frame of the so-called "mathetical approach" represented by Gilbert and his disciples; see, for example, Gilbert 1969; Pennington & Slack, 1962; cf. also Balson, 1971.)

(5) *"Information maps" and adaptation of study material to divergent study behavior motivated by diverging initial repertoire or aims (with gains in integration when used for review).* Our ordinary textbooks and handbooks can be used in many ways. Besides being successively learned as course literature, they can be "skimmed" or "read diagonally" by someone who has already mastered the principal contents of the subject (in which case "skimming" provides a quick survey and the possibility of discovering any new points). They can also be used as reference literature by those who have a more specific end in view than that of learning the subject as a whole: by use of the table of contents or the index, it is easy to look up a special part which is relevant to the current object without studying the other material in the book. One criticism of programmed study material has been that the specialized form (for example, the fixed arrangement of "small steps", arranged in "scrambled" order or in horizontal "bands") makes it difficult or impossible to use the study material in a flexible way, and that the reader is bound to using it for only one single reading method—according to the rigid pattern of careful memorization. This means too that those who want to brush up their knowledge after a period of time and once more get a comprehensive view of the material which has been covered have difficulty in doing so—unless they take the time consuming way of again going through all the material in the prescribed order.

Anyone who tries to read through a finished program for a familiar subject area can easily be persuaded that these objections are valid. It is true enough that the programmer can defend himself with the argument that the program is designed for persons with a certain type of initial repertoire and is meant for a certain type of goal, and that because of this the programmer has no reason to take into consideration the fact that persons with a different initial repertoire (greater knowledge) and/or different goal (covering only certain parts of the field) think that the study material is not practical.

On the other hand, it can reasonably be argued that difficult surveyability, with the rigidity in usage which follows, is often greater than necessary and that the writer could by relatively simple means make the total structure considerably more transparent—to the benefit of, among other things, later reviews for improving retention. Even though, naturally, the primary usage should determine the presentation and arrangement, the secondary usage (as review or reference book, for example) should not be made more difficult than necessary.

One technique which could easily be used to increase the structural surveyability is that of working out detailed tables of contents with references to didules as well as drawing up a list of essential terms and ideas (also with references to didules), and also printing the integrating main sections (preliminary introductions and outlines, for example) in italics, in another color, or emphasizing them by some other means. Ordinarily it is an advantage if the main sections ("chapters") are clearly separated from one another by page. It is usually easiest to set up separate chapter sections in programmed books with vertical progression, but this can very well be done in programmed books of other types.

Whatever the structure of the program, separate pages for surveyable summaries are valuable (both for an immediate summing up during the step-by-step work and for later reviews). The term "*information map*" is sometimes used for such single-page overviews (see Horn et al., 1969, and the example in Box 12.1).

12.3 Retention

"Forgetting" is naturally affected by many factors. Several of the points on readability and integration which were presented above are also of importance in connection with retention. For example, the well-integrated material has—other things being equal—greater resistance to obliteration than the not so well-integrated. In this section we shall confine ourselves to summarizing some brief rules for repetition:

(1) *Avoid both too much and too little repetition*! Many a programmer includes too little repetition since the construction of repetition assignments is often boring for him and—since he himself is so familiar with the material—may also seem unnecessary. The student, on the other hand, who meets for the first time a number of new ideas and associations, is normally in great need of repetition. Retention of that which has been learned depends, naturally, to no small degree, on the "overlearning" which takes place in the instruction set-up. In this connection, however, the time-lag between the instruction occasion and the terminal situation must be taken into consideration as well as the student's opportunities for natural repetition or practice during the intervening period. Any possible dangers of interfering factors ("competing behavior patterns") must also be noted. As a guide for these judgments, the initial student analysis is of value and also the "expanded terminal chart" worked out in conjunction with it (cf. discussions on initial system analysis). As mentioned

Box 12.1 Integration by means of "information map": Example of a summary map

Below we illustrate a summary map dealing with basic concepts of conditional probability. It serves as a quick capsule integration of what has been presented up to that point of the course. Some of the main features are: (a) An introduction underlines the importance and usefulness of the topic; (b) Simple questions paired with concrete illustrations are presented to help the learner remember the distinctions; (c) Formulas are accompanied by verbal descriptions.

POSTVIEW OF CONDITIONAL PROBABILITY

Introduction Conditional probability is one of the most useful tools in probability theory. We have seen how the equation can be rearranged to give the multiplication theorem and the independence definition, both important concepts.

The inter-relatedness of these ideas is a great boon to memory. If the conditional probability definition is thoroughly understood and stored in memory, it can serve as the key to unlock recollection of how the other formulas can be derived.

For review, we re-state the definition of conditional probability along with the concepts derived from it.

QUESTION	CONCEPT AND FORMULA
What is the probability of A, *given* that B has occurred? (Given a red-haired person, what is the probability that he has blue eyes?)	*Conditional Probability:* $P(A \mid B) = \dfrac{P(A \cap B)}{P(B)}$ the conditional probability of A, given B = the probability that both events will occur divided by the probability of B
What is the probability that both A *and* B will occur? (What are the chances of winning Olympic medals in both track and swimming?)	*Multiplication Theorem:* $P(A \cap B) = P(B) \cdot P(A \mid B)$ the probability that *both* events occur = the probability of B times the probability of A, given B
Are the events A and B *independent*? (Is the event "flunking math" independent of the event "flunking history?")	*Independence Definition:* Two events are independent if and only if: $P(A \cap B) = P(A) \cdot P(B)$ the probability that both events occur = the product of the separate probabilities
Given two independent events A and B, what is the probability that *both* of them occur? (If Tom and I both roll a die, what is the probability that we both get sixes?)	*Multiplication Rule for Independent Events:* (This is the independence equation just above.)

(Example from Horn et al., 1969, p. 37.)

above it may often be a good strategy to start by slightly underestimating the need for practice and repetition, but to be aware of the need to extend the practice and repetition material as soon as student data show this to be desirable. Overdosage of material is difficult to detect, whereas underdosage is more easy to spot and adjust.

(2) *Vary repetition*! Routine drill with direct repetition of the same assignments is seldom desirable, partly because going through the material in this manner can easily become boring, partly also because the programmed sequences are worked out for those who have no elementary knowledge and when repeated must be assumed to function less effectively. The practice should instead consist of illuminating and applying the acquired conceptions in new contexts or with different examples. It is often a good idea in this connection to integrate repetition of old material with the introduction of new. In this way repetition monotony is avoided, the area for meaningful associations is increased, and desirable generalizations are facilitated.

(3) *Spread repetition*! As has been noted above, it is true that a concentration of learning can be effective from the point of view of speed but at least in the case of more comprehensive instruction material and long retention periods a certain spreading out of repetition should be desirable. It is thereby possible, for example, to treat the same idea first in a series of consecutive didules and later to allow the idea to turn up again at certain intervals (perhaps shorter in the beginning and successively with greater infrequency later on). A "distribution plan" could then take the principal form sketched in Figure 12.2 below (p. 211).

(4) *Individualize repetition as much as possible*! The most usual procedure, that of allowing the student to pass from one assignment to the next whether he has answered correctly or incorrectly, without returning to it later, has certain disadvantages. As mentioned above in our discussion of various "flow models", a "re-directing" to differentiated repetition (of assignments answered incorrectly at an earlier stage) may sometimes be worth recommending. Skinner's disc machine (also referred to above) functions in just that way, and Holland & Porter (1961) were able to demonstrate that such a method can improve the final result of the student. These methods are especially suitable for learning "subject-matter items" (as, for example, in learning vocabulary in a foreign language), where this differentiated re-direction does not break the continuity. Those types of machines which function according to the "skimming"-principle can be useful here, but simple card collections are often equally effective. In these cases every didule can be noted on an assignment card (with the answer on the reverse side). Those questions which the student answers incorrectly can be placed by him in a special pile. He can then easily go through these once more (or as many times as is necessary until he has performed all assignments correctly).

12.4 Motivation

Reading a long, continuous text without "built-in" work assignments or listening to an extensive oral exposition can be extremely monotonous for many students. The result can be increased fluctuation in attentiveness with an accompanying reduction in the effectiveness of the instruction. Some of the increase in effectiveness which in many cases has been reported in conjunction with the use of programmed study material seems to have some connection with the less monotonous *work dynamics* in the didule system (rather than with the sometimes too greatly stressed reinforcement effects of feedback presentation). The student experiences a constant task variation:

(a) he reads the information and the demand for an answer
(b) he works through to an answer
(c) he writes down the answer
(d) he checks his answer and prepares to go on to the next assignment.

This dynamic variation, the play between tension and relaxation (which we discussed in connection with readability), can here perform an important function, and the *differences* in the activities listed under *a, b, c,* and *d* are probably of importance. It is a reasonable hypothesis that points *a* and *b* ordinarily signify a rising curve of tension (with the summit at *b*), while points *c* and *d* represent a certain psychic relaxation during the phases with more predominant motor activities (writing and machine manipulation). Both the subjective experience of the dynamic alternation and possible psycho-physiological consequences would be worth a special research effort.

But even if the programmed study material because of this inherent alternation of tasks is less monotonous than a running text or a continuous oral presentation, it is quite natural that the student can experience a certain monotony also in the programmed study material if, for a longer period of time or in several different connections, he works with the same type of small presentation units (as long as we have only a few and/or short programs there is relatively little danger of this). Several of the measures mentioned earlier for promoting the building of an integrated field of knowledge for the students can also be useful in reducing the dangers of monotony: for example, work with integrating supplemental material in appendix form or going through built-in test sections. Other methods of counter-acting monotony can be to alternate types of answer (certain sections perhaps without demand for an explicit answer), or to incorporate more comprehensive student tasks (directing the students to various source material; a technique termed above "the intermittent model"). There is a risk that, through exaggerated respect for one special method, we fail to try the united effect of different methods. We must keep in mind to avoid this risk. "A change is as good as a rest" is an old saying worth remembering; it is basically sound in many situations.

That the experience of achievement is of great importance for the student's motivation should be indisputable, but in reality the problem is more complicated than some programmers usually describe it. We must take into consideration the great individual variations of earlier achievement experiences and the current aspiration levels as well as some more stable personality characteristics which may be of importance in this connection (for example, what McClelland and others have called "need Achievement"). The fact that such complications do not require much attention in the world of rats and pigeons (and some programmers always seem to think they will find the solutions to problems of the psychology of learning right in the rat laboratory), should not keep us from being aware of them in human learning situations.

We should consider at least two aspects of the problem complex. On the one hand we should note the fact that the learning effectiveness of an instruction material is often greater when there is a high frequency of positive feedback. This was one of the chief viewpoints of the early programmer group inspired by Skinner, and it was usually assumed that the error frequency should be low (perhaps under 5 %). On the other hand, the maintenance of motivation in the long run (persistence in work) also seems related to whether demands are high enough in relation to ability. Individuals with high "need Achievement" and good learning technique can, for example, find very boring a long series of far too easy tasks, and this, reasonably enough, may decrease their interest in efficiently working with the material.

In this event we should perhaps try to make use of a "*multiple success strategy*". This can mean that while we work fairly constantly with a high probability of correct answers to separate tasks, we combine that procedure with "extra success effects"—for example, the possibility of rapid-track progression and/or the satisfaction of being able to answer correctly without clues (individualized offering of clues as in teaching machine Didak 501). Becker (1963) who proposes such a method of procedure compares this strategy with that which is used in certain lotteries or chewing gum machines. For one's "contribution" (a coin) one always receives a certain "prize" (a piece of chewing gum), but there is also the chance of getting a larger "prize" (an attractive object). A play of this kind on two planes of success should—*mutatis mutandis*—be serviceable in teaching material and might perhaps better do full justice to the varying individual needs.

The reviewer cannot, naturally, make too radical changes in the total structure (these should be allowed to wait until the empirical data also are available). But he should try to detect characteristics of the study material which can encourage boredom or discourage motivation and suggest counter-measures. Any possible monotony can ordinarily be eased through small changes in working methods. And if the reviewer finds that the primary material provides all too little scope for the ambitious student to feel that he can achieve something on a par with his ability, then the addition of "extra success effects" should not be too difficult.

12.5 Various Aids in the Checking Phase

The fact that successive empirical try-outs of the materials are the final and most important steps in the evaluation process does not mean, of course, that we have to rush into premature data collection with hastily produced and unpolished versions of the study material. While an arbitrary reading through of the material may be fairly inefficient, a systematic mapping of certain apparent characteristics of the material, on the other hand, may be very fruitful. We may call this examination of *apparent characteristics,* the mapping of the "*pheno-structure*" of didactic sequences (as distinguished from the mapping of the "*effect-structure*" that might be carried out during the empirical try-outs later on).

In the present section several aids for this mapping process will be described and discussed, including check lists, diagrams of the relations between terminal objectives and the single didactic units, and various kinds of unit-charting protocols. It is felt that the examination is considerably facilitated by summarizing aids of these kinds. The risk of forgetting some important aspects of the examination is reduced, and a long series of questions about the material can be answered much more easily on the basis of a summarizing protocol than on the basis of the non-aided perusal of a long sequence of material, in which the different parts cannot be kept in sight at the same time.

It should be stated from the beginning that many different types of aids are possible, of course, and that each programmer should design his working tools to suit the particular problems of each program. The following descriptions should therefore be looked upon only as illustrations of various possibilities.

12.5.1 *Examination by Means of Check Lists*

The simplest way of remembering the important aspects that should be examined is probably to make up a fairly detailed list of questions to be answered for each self-instructional study material and to use this list for checking off systematically the answers for each separate part of the course material. An example of such a list of questions is given in Box 12.2. (It should perhaps be added that some of the questions in this list are such that only the subsequent empirical try-out can give a more *definite* answer. Nevertheless, it is often possible to make intelligent guesses in advance, and thereby to save some steps in the revision process.)

The check-list illustrated requires a reviewer who is equally sophisticated in

Box 12.2 Check list for pre-test examination: An illustration

1. *Examination of goal relevance and content:*

1.1 Does the program contain all that it should according to the initial goal statements?

1.2 Has all irrelevant material been eliminated? (Irrelevant materials are those that are neither included in the goal statements, nor fill any clear-cut instructional function as aids in the process of reaching these goals.)

1.3 Have all those points been eliminated that, according to the target population analysis, the students have already mastered?

1.4 Does the program avoid giving any single subject-matter aspect a coverage that, according to the goal statements, could be considered unreasonably large or unreasonably small?

1.5 Has all changeable information been checked, so that the students are given maximally up-to-date information?

1.6 In the judgment of subject-matter experts, is the content free from factual errors?

2. *Examination of the "procedural instruction" of the program:*

2.1 Are the "procedural instructions" of the program to the student (instructions about the ways of handling the material during study etc.) complete, clear and easy to follow?

2.2 Is the student given a sufficient amount of training in how to give answers or handle the teaching machine in the beginning of the program (as well as in other places where perhaps a new answering technique is introduced)?

3. *Examination of the organization and sequence of content:*

3.1 Does the program try systematically to establish a connection between those experiences or concepts that the students already have in their repertoires and the new knowledge that is introduced?

3.2 Is the program constructed to use—where this is possible and appropriate—the sequential approaches that are usually referred to by phrases such as "from the simple to the complex", "from the easy to the difficult"?

3.3 Are the units with material for repetition adequately spaced (in the beginning sufficiently near the first presentation to make correct answers possible and after that with increasing and sufficient intervals to maintain retention over large enough periods of time)?

4. *Examination of the stimule-function of the single didules:*

4.1 Have irrelevant and distracting details been removed, so that the attention of the student is clearly focused on the central part of the information of the didule?

4.2 Is the communication presented in a sufficiently life-like and concrete way? For instance, have pictures and supplementary demonstration materials been used where such aids can supply the intended information more effectively than verbal description?

4.3 Are the examples given sufficiently varied so that the student does not get a wrong and one-sided picture of the principle or concepts being treated?

4.4 Is the position of information appropriate, so that, for instance, important information has not been placed after the response request?

4.5 Has the programmer remembered to vary the prompting techniques used?

4.6 Has unnecessary prompting been avoided?

4.7 As a rule, has meaningful prompting (by means of logical induction, parallel exemplification etc.) been chosen where appropriate rather than unnecessary formal prompting of a kind that may distract the student's attention and divert it to unimportant aspects of the communication?

5. *Examination of the respule-function of the single didules:*

5.1 As a rule, can the questions be answered on the basis of the information that the student has received?

5.2 As a rule, have response requests been avoided that can be answered *without* understanding of the content of the didule (by formal-linguistic pattern completion etc.)?

5.3 Has the response request been designed so as to give a reasonable guarantee that the student has understood the *essential* communication of the particular didule? In other words: Are the response requests relevant to the aim of the particular didule (always assuming that each didule has a specifiable aim)?

5.4 Does the program activate varying types of response behavior (writing, drawing, calculating, comparing, etc.)?

5.5 Do the alternatives of a multiple-choice question represent all reasonable, non-trivial sources of misunderstanding? In other words: Is it difficult to think of typical student errors not included among the alternatives listed?

5.6 Are the alternatives in a multiple-choice question so designed that the student's choice is not a pseudo-choice (e.g., so that the incorrect alternatives are not clearly absurd or formally incongruent with the main question)?

5.7 Does the program request the student to give those types of answers that the terminal situation will demand from him (so that, for instance, the program does not merely train the student to recognize correct decisions, if in the terminal situation the student's ability spontaneously to make correct decisions is also going to be tested)?

6. *Examination of the integrative function of the program:*

6.1 Is the student given an opportunity of applying concepts and principles, first presented stepwise, to problem-solving of a kind that forces him to activate and operate upon several concepts or principles at the same time?

6.2 Are integrating materials in the form of reference tables, reference diagrams, reference maps or reference texts utilized where appropriate?

6.3 Does the program help the student to obtain an adequate initial organization ("Gestalt in advance", "properly structured expectations") as well as an adequate final organization ("final Gestalt", e.g., by means of "information maps")?

6.4 If a programmed textbook is used, does the student get a table of contents outlining the broad scope and structure of the total contents?

6.5 Are there adequate indices that make it easy for the student to brush up his knowledge afterwards within specific areas of information, if he so desires?

7. *Examination of the motivating function of the program:*

7.1 Have the programmers tried to provide a sufficient degree of variation in the review items?

7.2 Does the difficulty level of the program appear, throughout the program, to be so adapted to the particular student group under consideration that there is a fair probability that the students will be neither bored nor discouraged?

7.3 Have the examples and illustrations—to the extent that seems possible—been made interesting and relevant to the experiences and needs of the particular student groups?

7.4 Do the possibilities of individualization within the program (available branching arrangements) correspond closely enough to the results of the initial analyses of the target population, so that, for instance, students with considerable previous knowledge of the subject matter are not forced to go through the same material as students without any previous knowledge?

8. *Examination of the external form of the program: Language*

8.1 Do the level of vocabulary and the structure of sentences seem to be sufficiently well adapted to the linguistic habits of the particular student group so as not to be an unnecessary barrier to communication of the main contents?

8.2 Is the meaning of new terms defined or otherwise demonstrated clearly enough as soon as they are introduced?

8.3 Is the language of the program always clear and unambiguous?

8.4 Does the language always have an optimal degree of precision as judged from the goal statements of the program (that is, neither with too low a degree of precision, including sloppy everyday terms where precision is needed, nor with an unnecessarily high degree of precision, such as various scientific distinctions not to be further utilized in the desired terminal behavior)?

8.5 Is the use of numbering, punctuation, abbreviation etc. both correct and consistent?

9. *Examination of the external form of the program: Other aspects*

9.1 Is the general lay-out of the program both educationally appropriate and economically defensible?

9.2 Is the typography sufficiently clear for the intended student group and also designed to emphasize points that should be emphasized?

9.3 Are illustrations of various kinds, both within the program proper and in possible appendices to be used as reference material, so designed technically that they can be expected to result in the best possible communication effect?

program construction as the original programmer. Many programmers prefer to have a subject-matter expert as editor and many need a language editor. There is a danger implicit in all kinds of editorial work by persons not sufficiently experienced in the programming process and not familiar with the student group that the editor will make wrong judgements about what is right for the students. In an attempt to clean up the syntax, for instance, a language editor may unintentionally alter the task radically. Hence, all editorial suggestions for change should normally be returned to the main programmer for review and final acceptance or rejection.

12.5.2 *Examination by Means of "T-D Diagrams" Depicting the Relations between Terminal Objectives and Single Didactic Units*

Even during the writing process proper many programmers find that it makes the work easier to draw simple diagrams of the relations between the terminal objectives as codified in the goal statements on the one hand and the single didactic units (the didules) as appearing in the written program on the other. Very often the program writer arranges both the specific goal statements and the single didule texts on separate cards in a card catalogue. This means that the diagrammatic survey often takes the form of a series of relational diagrams, from which it is easy to see which didule cards (D_1, D_2, etc.) are related to each single terminal card (T_1, T_2, etc.). During the post-writing phase it is easy to examine, with the aid of diagrams of this kind, whether or not certain parts of the total goal structure have been given too much or too little attention in the program. Similarly, it can easily be seen whether or not enough attempts seem to have been made to reach an integrated structure of knowledge. Figure 12.1 shows an example of such a diagram. The numbers of terminal objectives and didules included in the figure (T- and D-numbers) refer to the program fragment in Box 12.3.

If we deal with a so-called scrambled book, the diagram should include not only information about the main part of any particular didule (the page with go-ahead signal and new information), but also information about the error-treatment pages (the pages that explain errors and refer the student back to the main pages again). As a rule, in these cases the programmer should also use a separate "pagination control list" for checking off page numbers used. The reason is, of course, that the programmer and the post-writing examiner have to keep an eye on the scrambling system, sometimes fairly complicated, in order to ensure a suitable sequence of pages, that is, a sequence which is instructionally adequate as well as economical with respect to time and space. (No pages should be left empty; the student should not need to turn too many pages each time; tasks that might make the answer easier than intended or that would otherwise interfere with each other should not be placed side by side on the same two-page fold-up of the book, etc.)

12.5.3 *Examination by Means of Didule Protocols*

A didule protocol is a device which makes it easier to make the examination both complete and systematic. Examination by means of general checklists aids the examiner in covering many aspects, but it may not by itself help him to cover every single part of the program in a systematic way. As a rule didule protocol includes, for each didule, a separate examination column, in which—depending on the particular aim—various kinds of questions may be answered

Symbols:

= a terminal objective ("goal statement")

= a sequence of didules, all related to the same terminal objective

= a single didule

= a simple T-D connection (relation between a terminal objective and one or more didules)

= an integrating T-D connection (two or more terminal objectives are given an integrative treatment in the same didule)

= the working sequence of the student

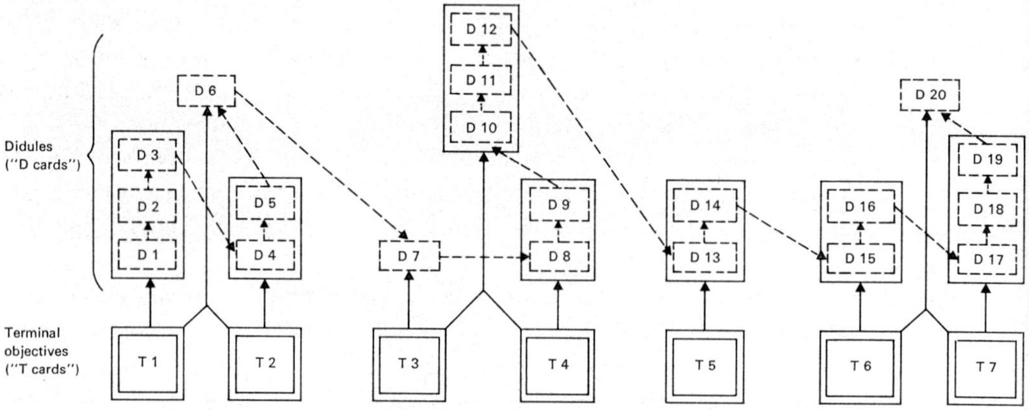

Figure 12.1 An example of a T-D diagram (mapping the program fragment in Box 12.2)

when this particular didule is examined. Three general types of such protocols may perhaps be distinguished: subject-matter protocols, methodological protocols, and combined protocols studying both subject-matter distribution and the methodological approaches used. (Related discussions will be found, for example, in Bjerstedt, 1963, 1964, Anschütz, 1965, Zifreund, 1965, von Voigt, 1970.)

12.5.3.1 *Subject-Matter Protocols*

The main aim of the subject-matter protocol is to some extent similar to the aim of the T-D diagrams described above, viz. to facilitate the examination of the distribution of the subject-matter over the didule sequence. A square-ruled paper may be a good starting-point. The numbers of the didules are written in numerical order along the top of the paper. The various subject matter units that are to be examined are listed down the left-hand margin. For instance, these units may be single conceptual units or conceptual relations

Box 12.3 Terminal descriptions (T cards) and didules (D cards) from a program fragment on programmed instruction (as supplemental material to the T-D diagram in Figure 12.1)

Topic: Introductory course on programmed instruction

Subjects: Teacher students

Note: This fragmentary illustration contains 20 didules (D), covering 7 specific terminal objectives (T)—focusing, in turn, on 3 fairly basic "principles".

T 1. The student should be able to state some acceptable reason for the emphasis on self-pacing in self-instructional materials.
(Principle 1)

T 2. The student should be able to recognize and recall the term "self-pacing".
(Principle 1)

T 3. The student should be able to state some acceptable argument for the emphasis on "overt responses" in self-instructional materials.
(Principle 2)

T 4. The student should be able to recognize and recall the terms "overt response" and "covert response".
(Principle 2)

T 5. Given a set of instructional items, the student should be able to differentiate between items demanding "overt" and "covert" responses.
(Principle 2)

T 6. The student should be able to state some acceptable argument for the emphasis on low error-rate in self-instructional materials.
(Principle 3)

T 7. The student should be able to state some specific characteristics in self-instructional materials that make low error-rate possible, including, at least, the two notions of "small steps" and "careful sequencing".
(Principle 3)

D 1. In the classroom, the teacher most often works with the total class. If so, all students have to progress at the same speed—for instance, at the speed of the average child. This rate often tends to make the work (more/less) interesting to the bright and quick-working child.
(Cf T 1) /less/

D 2. What would you guess about the effect on the slow learners of following the average student's speed?
Probably, they (will/will not) grasp enough of the material presented in the time allowed.
(Cf T 1) /will not/

D 3. If the slow learner does not grasp enough of the material presented, he will easily develop a (positive/neutral/negative) attitude towards classroom learning.
(Cf T 1) /negative/

D 4. Students working at their own speed are said to follow the principle of "self-pacing".
Presumably, the slow learner would be able to grasp more fully the material to be studied, if he were allowed to work at his own speed. Consequently, he would probably also develop a more positive attitude toward classroom learning, if the principle of ____________ were used.
(Cf T 2) /self-pacing/

D 5. Since the quick learner is less likely to lose interest in the work (less likely to get bored), when allowed to proceed as quickly as he is able to, the principle of ____________ also favors the bright and quick pupils.
(Cf T 2) /self-pacing/

D 6. To sum up, then, there is reason to believe that "teacher-pacing" is (more/less) likely to be a favorable learning condition than "__________".
(Cf T 1 & T 2) /less; self-pacing/

D 7. The student who actually works through a statistical calculation is (more/less) likely to learn effectively than a student who merely reads a description of what to do.
(Cf T 3) /more/

D 8. When a student learns, he may make both *overt* and *covert responses.* Those activities we can easily observe (like writing or manipulating a machine) we call overt response. Those activities we cannot observe (like thinking) we call ____________ responses.
(Cf T 4) /covert/

D 9. Using our technical terms "overt" and "covert" responses, we may say that the student of statistics who merely reads a discription of what to do, makes ____________ responses to the text, where as the student who works out the calculation in writing in addition shows ________________ responses.
(Cf T 4) /covert; overt/

D 10. A person who tries to learn cooking from a book just by reading may be said to make only ____________ responses to the text. There is reason to believe that this is normally a (more/less) adequate way of learning cooking than actual practice.
(Cf T 3 & T 4) /covert; less/

D 11. (Observable/Non-observable) reactions are, of course, a better guarantee that the student has actively responded to all the important aspects of the materials than are (overt/covert) reactions.
(Cf T 3 & T 4) /Observable; covert/

D 12. To sum up, then, covert responses are (more/less) likely to be effective in learning than are ____________ responses.
(Cf T 3 & T 4) /less; overt/

D 13. Look back to the three sentences of item 8 above. In which sentence were you expected to make an overt response? Answer: In the ____________ sentence.
(Cf T 5) /third/

D 14. Look at the four items in Panel I. Put checkmarks in the list below to indicate the kind of response expected in each case from the student.

Item	Covert only	Overt
A		
B		
C		
D		

(Cf T 5) /Note. Panel I is excluded from the present illustration/

D 15. A student who is anxious or uninterested in the work may not be motivated to continue working. A student who makes very many errors may get anxious or uninterested in the work. A student who makes very many errors, therefore, (is/is not) likely to be motivated to keep on working.
(Cf T 6) /is not/

D 16. If we make an error, we tend to remember the error, if it is not corrected. If we give a correct answer, we tend to remember the correct answer. In the first case we have to "unlearn" the error. In the second case we "learn" directly. Consequently, learning might become more efficient, if we could arrange the study material so that the students made (many/few) errors.
(Cf T 6) /few/

D 17. If the student is going to reach the goal we have set without making many errors, we have to arrange the study material in (small/large) steps.
(Cf T 7) /small/

D 18. If the goal is to teach the student ITEM A and ITEM B, and ITEM X is something the student needs to know before he can learn ITEM A and ITEM B, we should begin his sequence of items with ITEM ______
(Cf T 7) /X/

D 19.	In order to make sure that the student makes few errors only, it would seem reasonable to recommend the use of ________ steps and a careful ________ of items. (Cf T 7) /small; sequence/
D 20.	To sum up, if we use small steps and a careful sequence of items, we are likely to get (more/fewer) errors. In that case motivation to keep on working will usually be (higher/lower) and the learning will proceed (more/less) efficiently. (Cf T 6 & T 7) /fewer; higher; more/

which have been listed during the pre-writing phase as important key points to be covered in the program. Sometimes it is more natural to use psychological units than logical units, that is, to start out from a series of stimulus-response connections rather than from concepts and conceptual relations. Whatever the particular kind of units used, however, the general examination process will be similar. By means of some kind of check marks in the appropriate cells, we report in which of the didules a particular subject-matter unit is treated (cf. Figure 12.2).

Among the questions that may be answered with the aid of such a protocol, the following may be mentioned: (a) Is each single basic subject-matter unit represented to a sufficient degree in the program? (b) Are some of the didules totally irrelevant to the main subject-matter to be covered? (c) Is the treatment of the single subject-matter units appropriately distributed (for instance, an intensive series of didules at the first presentation, followed later on by separate repetition items at gradually increasing intervals)? (d) To what extent have attempts been made to integrate the separate units into meaningful structures, and are these attempts made at optimal points in the sequence (for instance, where the separate concepts are sufficiently well treated and practised)?

When answering the last question, for instance, the examiner will study to what extent the same didule column contains check marks referring to several different subject-matter units. It is usually desirable that this is the case in many didules in order to facilitate integrated structures of knowledge. At the same time the examiner of the program studies at what specific points in the didule sequence the new subject-matter units are first presented. Often it may be confusing to the student, if several *new* subject-matter units are introduced in the same didule. An integrating didule therefore usually contains *either* a series of units introduced earlier in the program *or* one new unit of subject-matter in combination with one or more units introduced earlier.

As mentioned above it is sometimes maintained that integration of knowl-

Subject-matter units	Didules																			
	1	2	3	4	5	6	7	8	9	10	11	12	13	14	15	16	17	18	19	20
C_1		X	X	X			X					X							X	
C_2					X	X	X			X				X						X
C_3								X	X	X				X						X
C_4											X	X	X	X						X
C_5															X	X	X	X	X	X
Unrelated	X																			

Figure 12.2 An example of a subject-matter protocol (didule protocol, type A)

Reading key: Subject-matter unit C_1 is treated in didules 2, 3, 4 and later on also in didules 7, 12 and 19. Subject-matter unit C_2 is treated in didules 5, 6, 7 and later on also in didules 10, 14 and 20. Etc.

Comments: The present example shows a subject-matter distribution often considered by programmers to be favorable. Only the introductory didule is unrelated to the subject-matter to be covered (such an introductory item is likely to be an explanation of procedure). Each new subject-matter unit is introduced through a number of didules in sequence and is later on repeated, first after a short interval, then after increasing intervals. The repetitions are at the same time arranged so as to include integration with other subject-matter units.

edge may be facilitated by specific patterns of didules, such as systematic alternation ("counterpoint"), systematic overlapping, chronological accumulation, or reversed accumulation of temporal behavior sequences (cf. section 12.2). Further research is needed on these and other patterns of didules recommended for integration purposes. In this experimentation it is, of course, valuable to be able to examine, by means of subject-matter protocols, the appearance of the various patterns under study. It is then easy for the examiner to observe inadvertencies and to correct arrangements which have been left in a less than optimal shape during the writing process. (A few examples of typical patterns referred to by the terms used above are given in Figure 12.3.)

12.5.3.2 *Methodological Protocols*

The purpose of the methodological protocols is to facilitate the examination of various methodological approaches and make it possible to answer systematically questions of the following types:

(a) Has the programmer got stuck in certain working routines with the accompanying risk that the student finds the program monotonous?

a. *Systematic alternation ("counterpoint")*

	D_1	D_2	D_3	D_4	D_5	D_6
C_a	X		X		X	
C_b		X		X		X

b. *Overlapping*

	D_1	D_2	D_3	D_4	D_5	D_6	D_7	D_8	D_9	D_{10}
C_a	X	X	X		X		X			
C_b				X		X		X	X	X

c. *Chronological accumulation*

	D_1	D_2	D_3	D_4
C_1	X	X	X	X
C_2		X	X	X
C_3			X	X
C_4				X

d. *Reversed accumulation*

	D_1	D_2	D_3	D_4
C_1				X
C_2			X	X
C_3		X	X	X
C_4	X	X	X	X

Figure 12.3 Examples of special types of didule sequences as reflected in a subject-matter protocol

Note: C = "concept" or subject-matter unit; D = "didule" or unit of the study material.— In this figure, *numbers* have been given to subject-matter units that make up a connected temporal chain, whereas *letters* have been given to subject-matter units that are not temporally related to each other. The small arrow below the didule number (in diagrams c and d) shows the order in which different parts appear within a single didule.

(b) Are the educational techniques used of such a kind that, besides facilitating the student's learning of certain subject-matter facts, they also contribute to educationally desirable side-effects (such as good working habits, positive study attitudes, etc.)?

The protocol sheets will be similar to the ones used for subject-matter protocols, that is, square-ruled papers with didule numbers along the top. However, questions about the educational approach or key-terms for different methodological categories (instead of subject-matter units) are now written down the left-hand margin. If the question is answered by "yes" for a certain didule, the examiner puts a check mark in the appropriate cell (where the didule column and the row of the question intersect). Similarly, he inserts a check mark whenever the didule under study can be classified under the methodological category listed in the margin.

A very simple question that may be included for study in a protocol of this type is the following: Where has the student to go in order to find a solution to the task set for him in the didule? Among the various possible sub-categories representing different groups of conceivable answers to this question, we may mention the following:

(1) The solution can be found directly in the text of the same didule ("internal-explicit" source).
(2) The solution can be indirectly deduced (through a process of drawing conclusions etc.) from the new information that is given in the same didule ("internal-implicit" source).
(3) The solution can be found in the information presented earlier in the program ("external-proximal" source).
(4) The solution cannot be found within the program, but can be constructed in some way, usually with the aid of the student's background experience and/or his ability to use logical reasoning (or mathematical operations) ("external-distal" source).

At first sight, a subdivision of this type may seem to represent an unnecessary and pedantic eagerness for box-sorting. However, the observation of "response sources" is a very important part of the didule examination, and many existing programs would probably have looked quite different and been more effective, if the programmer had been made aware early enough of one-sided techniques utilized. The special terminological labels used ("internal-explicit" etc.) should not, of course, be taken too seriously, but a brief and handy term may be useful in writing out these protocols as well as in discussing these phenomena.

Some of the categories mentioned above can be further subdivided, if desirable. The third category, for instance, may be divided into maximally proximal cases (when the answer is to be found in the immediately preceding didule) and other cases (when the answer is found earlier in the program). Separate "appendices" (or "panels") as response sources can, when appropriate, be listed as a separate category, etc.

Such simple mapping gives the examiner quick information about the possible monotony of a sequence, showing, for instance, whether or not the programmer has used exclusively "internal-explicit" sources (which seems very often to be the case in some published programs). Each technique may serve an important function. The internal-explicit approach focuses the attention of the student on the key points in the immediate text and seems to be of particular value when new terms and concepts are introduced. The external-proximal method contributes to the gradual training of retention and may also be used in the process of integration. In order to promote valuable educational side-effects (good working habits etc.), the programmer will probably often find it most profitable to use either an internal-implicit or an external-distal technique.

Other questions that can be studied in a similar way, are: What type of activity is expected from the student (for instance, copying, guessing, analogous exemplification, induction from own experiences, logical conclusions)? What kind of prompting is used? How is the answer related to earlier answers and to the key-points of the didule? What is the linguistic structure of the didule? (For instance, how high is the "density" of information-loaded words?) Etc. etc. (For further illustrations, cf. Figure 12.4.)

In certain cases it might be desirable to calculate some index score covering the "instructional variation" (the distribution of didules with respect to a series of sub-categories related to a certain methodological question), or some index score covering the proportion of didules including certain instructional features probably resulting in desirable side effects (when some of the sub-categories belonging to a certain methodological question are thought to be educationally more desirable than the other sub-groups). Such calculations should not, of course, be used too routinely, nor with too great a confidence in the exactness of the scores obtained. Nevertheless, they can serve an important function as general warning signals, telling the examiner, in fact: "The program ought not to look like this. Revision urgently needed!" The methodological protocol can then show more exactly which particular points should be revised.

12.5.3.3 *Combined Protocols*

Combined protocols register both subject-matter distribution and particular methodological approaches in some kind of combination. In many cases it is not enough to see whether the subject-matter is suitably divided over the didules, and whether the methods used are sufficiently varied. We also want to make sure that the various methods enter at the most appropriate points in the subject-matter sequence. Sometimes we consider certain methodological approaches more suitable when a new concept is introduced than when the concept is already relatively well incorporated in the behavior repertoire of the student. The types of prompting techniques that we are perhaps reluctant to accept when we deal with a terminology that is well known to the student (for instance, prompting of a wholly formal-mechanistic type), we may sometimes find acceptable, or even natural, when we introduce a new term. In addition,

Methodology:	Didules									
	1	2	3	4	5	6	7	8	9	10
1. *Response sources:*										
1.1 internal-explicit	X	X	X	X	X		X	X	X	
1.2 internal-implicit										
1.3 external-proximal						X				X
1.4 external-distal										
2. *Types of prompting:*										
2.1 word-form prompts	X	X	X	X	X		X	X	X	
2.2 formal emphasis	X	X	X	X	X		X	X	X	
2.3 syntactic controls	X	X	X	X	X		X	X	X	
2.4 parallel exemplification										
2.5 induction from experience										
2.6 logical conclusion										

Figure 12.4 An example of a methodological protocol (didule protocol, type B)

Reading key: In didule 1 the student can obtain the information needed for his answer directly from what is said within this didule ("internal-explicit" response source), and the answer is facilitated by strong formal prompting (word-form prompts, emphasizing the key words, and syntactic controls). Etc.

Comments: The example shows a one-sided use of "internal-explicit" response sources as well as formal prompting. In two cases, however, there is no prompting at all, but the student is expected to recall material from earlier didules (no. 6 and no. 10). In no case is use made of parallel exemplification, induction from experience, or logical conclusion. If the one-sidedness illustrated here continues over a larger material, there is the risk of both monotony and other side-effects (lack of training in appropriate study techniques).

we sometimes want to make sure that we do not connect a certain subject-matter area too closely with a certain method in the student's behavioral repertoire. Not only do we want to have an overall methodological variation, but now and then we also have to check that we use a methodologically varied technique in the treatment of each single subject-matter area.

What is implied here is a multi-method approach. We might add, in passing, that a multi-media approach may sometimes be indicated for similar reasons. The medium should usually be regarded as unessential, corresponding to details in particular examples that we hope will fade away, leaving the main conceptual image untouched. As stated by Pikas (1971), "the more media used

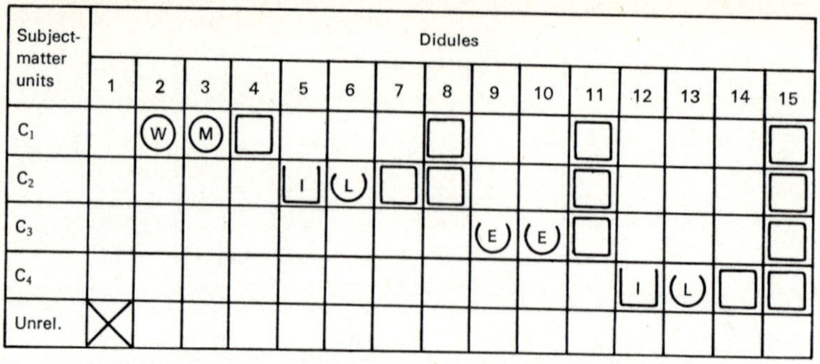

Figure 12.5 An example of a combined protocol (didule protocol, type C)

Reading key:

Symbols for response sources:

= internal-explicit

= internal-implicit

= external-proximal

= external-distal

Symbols for prompting types:

W = word-form prompts

M = formal emphasis

I = induction from experience

L = logical conclusion

E = parallel exemplification

The protocol is read in the following way: The subject matter unit C_1 is treated in the didules 2, 3, 4 and later on also in numbers 8, 11 and 15. In didules 2 and 3 the student obtains his answer within the same didule (first with the aid of word-form prompts, then with the aid of formal emphasis). In the other cases with C_1 the student has to rely on memory. Etc.

Comment:

In general, the didule sequence seems to be well constructed. The micro sequences go from fairly easy tasks (with prompting) to more difficult ones (without prompting); non-formal prompting is frequently used, and the sequences contain problems that contribute to the integration of knowledge as final elements (number 8, 11 and 15).

in order to reach high applicability, defined as great transfer, the more the effects of separate media will be eliminated. We counteract the medium's being the message".

In some respects, the combined protocols are very similar to the subject-matter protocols: a square-ruled arrangement with didule numbers along the top and subject-matter units listed down the left-hand margin. However, instead of the simple check-marking process, we now use a series of different symbols for various methodological categories (cf. Figure 12.5).

12.5.4 *A Final Note*

It should be mentioned that protocols and diagrams of these types may often be good training instruments for persons wanting to train their ability to observe educationally important differences between various published programs (or other similar training materials). Hence, in courses about self-instructional materials and programming, protocols of these and similar types seem to be well suited to make the practical training of the study group more effective and efficient. However, the main aim of these protocols is, of course, to be an aid in the process of constructing a program, making the programmer or an independent examiner aware of possible faults in the program even before the first empirical try-out. As stated above, it is hoped that this will reduce the work and cost involved in the final phase of successive revision.

As our scientific knowledge of the self-instructional learning process is gradually increased, the questions studied by means of these check lists, diagrams and protocols will be more specific, and the evaluation will be more securely founded on hard facts. This will probably mean that the careful study of "pheno-structures" by means of aids of these kinds will gradually become more important and more economical. The empirical try-outs with subsequent revisions will probably always remain an important final control process, but the amount of work involved in it will decrease, and at the same time it will be possible and natural to pay increased attention to the post-writing, pre-testing examination. It may be added that some of the analytical procedures presented in this section may also be used in the construction phase as guidelines for the writing of exercises.

13. The Procedure of Successive Evaluations

13.1 Introductory Viewpoints

A comparison between different types of instruction (for example, lecture, conventional classroom instruction, group work, private tutoring, and programmed instruction) using a systematic examination of various characteristics (for instance, presence or absence of disturbance effects, the degree of data storage, and the degree of feedback from student system to teacher system) seems to give several points of departure for a discussion of educational effectiveness (cf. Figure 13.1). Especially notable seems to be that the programmed instruction is the only situation which combines (1) continuous feedback from student system to educator system with (2) complete data storage.

Among other things this means that the response residuals in the used-up programs give good starting-points for revisions (cf. also Figure 13.2). Usually, therefore, the construction of self-instructional material is a pragmatic procedure in which one considers and acts upon the feedback information. That

Figure 13.1 The role of feedback and data storage in various types of instructional systems

	Symbol explanations:
————————»	= the function of subject-matter presentation (normal educator function)
- - - - - - - - -»	= partial educator function
————————>	= continuous feedback from educand (student) to educator (teacher or machine and/or instructional material with instructor function)
- - - - - - - - ->	= partial feedback
════════⇒	= continuous data storage[1]
= = = = = = = = =⇒	= partial data storage[1]
=:=:=:=:=:⇒	= rudimentary data storage[1]
┼┼┼┼┼┼┼┼┼┼┼┼	= disturbance effect

[1] Quantitative values for what is hereby to be considered "continuous", "partial", or "rudimentary" can hardly be given, but most judges will still be able to agree on the classification of the typical cases over this rough scale.

A. *"Lecture"*

(*No feedback; no data storage* via the educator system; no obvious disturbance effects)

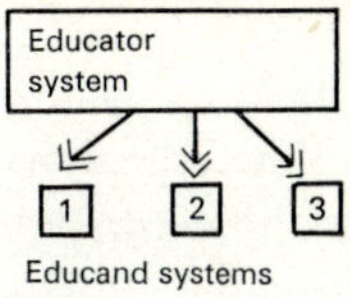

B. *"Classroom instruction"*

(*Partial feedback* from educand to educator; *rudimentary data storage* via the educator system; disturbance effects between the educand systems)

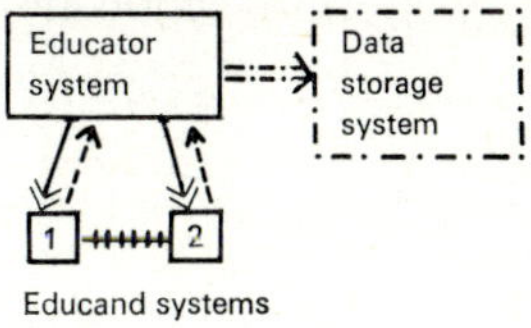

C. *"Group work"*

(*Partial feedback* from educand to educator; *rudimentary*[1] *data storage* via the educator system; disturbance effects, but also partial educator effects between educand systems)

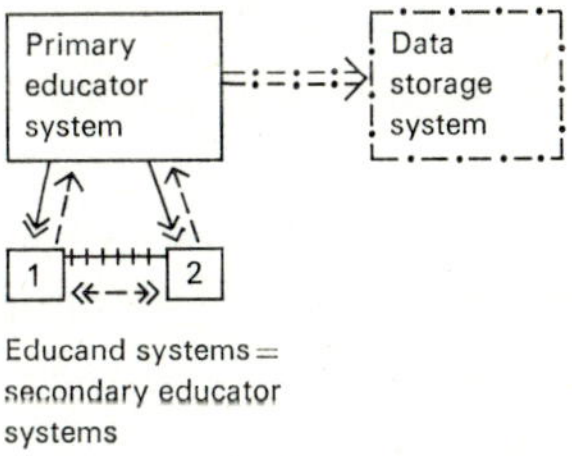

D. *"Private tutoring"*

(*Continuous feedback* from educand to educator; educator systems highly flexible and different from each other in an unsystematic way; *partial data storage*; no disturbance effects)

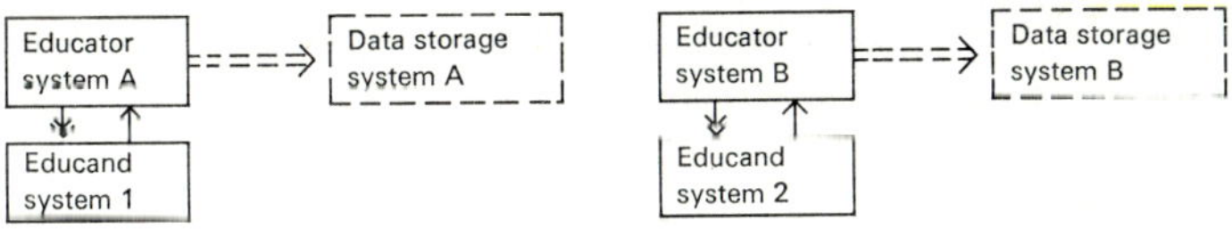

E. *"Programmed instruction"*

(*Continuous feedback* from educand to educator; educator systems often with no or low flexibility, either totally identical or identical in case of identical educand reactions; *total data storage*; no disturbance effects)

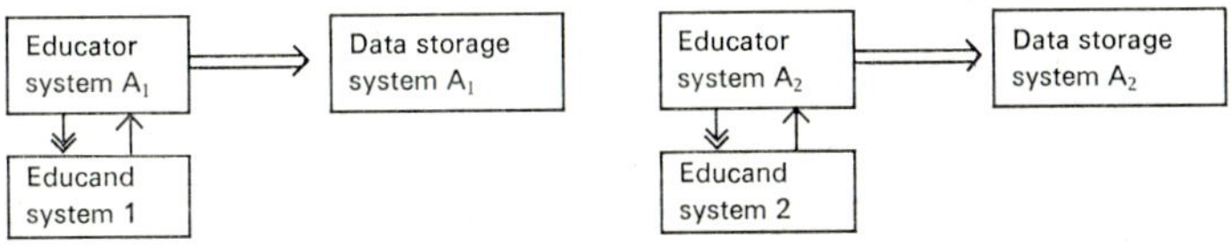

[1] In certain forms of group work with successive work reports, the term "partial data storage" may be more adequate.

which functions well is retained, but that which does not function satisfactorily is taken away or changed. Another way of stating the basic characteristic of this way of acting in the system control phase is: A program is not really a program until it works. Or even more drastically: One should not be surprised that programmed instruction works. It works *per definitionem*!

The examination of the actual interaction between student and program is therefore of basic importance. This means, on a small scale, a Copernican revolution in the way of looking at student achievement. Traditionally many people look at student achievement in the first place as a measure of student ability, and those students who do not seem to achieve much are sorted out from the school system. In the evaluation of self-instructional materials, on the other hand, student achievement is considered primarily as a measure of the effectiveness of the teaching materials, and instructional units which do not seem to lead to good student achievement are sorted out or replaced. (Of course, probably nobody believes that all students are able to learn everything. But a program evaluation with successive revisions based on feedback information means a serious attempt to adapt the method to the individual, thereby trying to reach more individuals in a more effective way.) Programmed instruction has been one of the major influences behind the increased interest in what is now often called mastery learning (cf. Bloom, 1971).

13.2 The Main Stages of the Empirical Evaluation

Revision work and the final testing can be carried out in many different ways. The main principle is an alternating sequence of empirical tests and revisions. The following are some of the most usual work stages.

13.2.1 *First Phase: Explorative Testing of Program Sections on Individual Students*

The first testing stage is usually considered one of the most exciting moments in programming. The program is tried out on individual students. It is one of those moments when the programmer's self-esteem can receive the most unpleasant jolts, namely, if it is shown that working sequences, on which he has devoted a great deal of intensive work and which he himself believes to be well-nigh perfect, do not in fact work at all. In order not to be kept in suspense for too long many programmers consider it appropriate not to keep back this explorative and individual try-out until the whole program is ready. Instead, it may prove good strategy to test out small sections during the actual work of composition, before going any further.

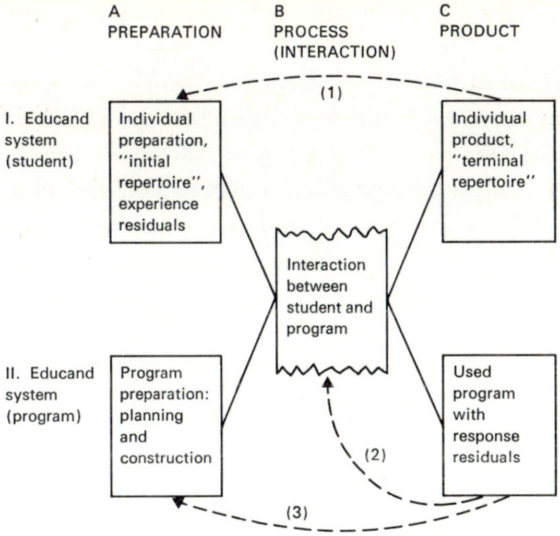

Figure 13.2 The three main phases in the interaction between student and program and three types of feedback effects

Three feedback effects:

(1) "individual effect": addition to or change of the experience residuals of the individual, which means that the initial repertoire is different when confronted with a new educator system

(2) "feedback to the program": in *adaptive* educator systems the information on the individual's responses influence the program's contribution to the next phase of the interaction

(3) "feedback to the programmer": the response residuals in the used-up program give indications of where and/or how to revise, that is lead to reconstruction in the preparation phase.

The students selected for this first try-out should, from a knowledge and intelligence point of view, be fairly typical of the group to whom the program will subsequently be directed, but preferably they should not be too docile and timid. Students who are not afraid to criticize and proclaim their opinion are those who will prove most valuable in this first test stage. The intention here is not that the material should necessarily be gone through under "field conditions". The most important aim is to get as detailed an idea as possible of the student's way of reacting to the details of the program. For this reason the try-out should preferably take place with one student at a time. As a preliminary, one ought—possibly with special tests—to make certain that the student does not know the material in advance. One should also make clear to the student that the try-out applies to the study material not to him. Such a frank declaration usually creates favorable conditions for free and untrammelled communication without unnecessary anxiety. A quiet testing room and plenty of time are also recommended.

The first try-out is often made orally with student comments for each didule and with a detailed follow-up interview. However much the programmer values his own program, he must take care not to be on the defensive during these interviews. His task is not to defend himself, but to collect reaction data. Should we begin to argue, we risk the student becoming unwilling to express his points of view. If we are dealing with adult students, the comments can sometimes be given in writing. The student, for instance, is given the instructional units in the shape of a collection of cards, and he writes his responses on a response-sheet, on which there is also space for marginal side-comments (e.g., a sheet with three columns, one for responses and two for comments and suggestions; cf. Box 13.1 and Leedham & Unwin, 1965, p. 89). Moreover, the student can possibly fill in a special questionnaire. As soon as the instruction has been tested with one or more students, the first revisions can be made. Ambiguities are removed, better examples are chosen, illustrations are made clearer, extra units are added, and so forth. At this stage the *number* of students is less important than the detailed analysis of how well the communication "penetrates". A small number of carefully studied students is often of greater value than a larger number whose reactions are more superficially studied.

Box 13.1 Example of answer sheet for students during early try-outs

Item No.	(1) Answer	(1 b)	(2) Comments	(2 b)	(3) Suggestions	(3 b)

Note: In column 1 the student always gives his response. In Column 2 and 3 he may add comments (question not clear) and/or suggestions (use more simple language). In the adjacent b-columns the experimenter may introduce brief scoring or category marks to aid him in synthesizing the information. Columns 2 and 3 might often have a double effect: (a) they add to the experimenter's information (pinpointing inadequacies), and (b) they make the task more interesting and motivating to the subject (reducing his feelings of anxiety, making him feel more like an important co-worker).

13.2.2 *Second Phase: Successive Testing of the Entire Program on Larger Groups of Students*

When we consider that most of the obvious obstacles have been cleared away, the testing of the total program is begun under normal educational conditions (and with presentation aids intended for use in the field). A sufficiently large group is used so that a certain amount of fairly reliable information can be obtained concerning, for instance, the percentage of mistakes in the individual instructional units. Pre- and post-tests of knowledge are carried out in order to assess the total learning effect. The program is revised on the basis of analysis of mistakes within the program and the terminal effects. Individual units are discarded, additional tasks are inserted, the sequence of units is altered. Perhaps it is shown that extra branchings are necessary. After revision a new try-out on a new group of students is made. The procedure can be repeated several times. In principle, the group try-outs should be continued, until those values of error data and, above all, of terminal performance data have been attained that are considered desirable and agree with the objectives of the course. In order to forestall confusion and, in addition, in order not to give a false impression of having a fully adequate material, the program versions which are used in these preliminary try-outs, should have suitably unambiguous headings such as "Experimental edition 2", "Experimental edition 3" or something similar. (A more detailed discussion of evaluation criteria will be given below.)

13.2.3 *Third Phase: Terminal Field Testing*

When revisions are no longer considered necessary, the time is ripe for the final field testing. In this the demands on the representativeness of the student groups and on the "normality" of the field conditions are more severe. Exhaustive data on pre-knowledge, intelligence, time spent and final results are collected. Pre-knowledge and final results are often measured best by parallel tests. In view of the student being able to learn something also from the pre-test, and taking into consideration that the student can learn a great deal from the study material without on that account attaining the same level of knowledge as a student taught by another material, it is often desirable to use the pre- and post-tests, for the sake of comparison, also in a control group (with a corresponding student group, but taught in a different manner). Another reason to use a control group for the pre-test is that this test can have a certain motivating effect, in that the student gains advance information about his own future possibilities after the end of the course. (A comparison between the first and the third testing stages is given in Box 13.2; an example of a planning schedule is shown in Box 13.3.)

Box 13.2 A comparison between the first and third main stage in the successive try-out work

	First Stage	Third Stage
Aims	Explorative tests of the ability of the program to communicate and teach	Collection of data for final "declaration of ingredients" for program consumers
Time	Several times during developmental work	Not until entire program is in terminal state
Main responsibility	Program constructor	Expert of investigation methods in behavioral sciences
Test persons	A small number of persons typical of the target population	A larger number of persons, an unbiased sample of the target population
Test conditions	Fairly informal with good prospects for relaxed communication and intensive observation	Strictly reproducible conditions, demands for detailed information re student characteristics, demands for the situation to correspond to the conditions under which the program will be used
Follow-up measures	Revision of program	Tabulation and analysis of data re program's effect; no revision

After this field test no alteration of the program should occur. Data of this test's conditions and results will, namely, constitute an essential part of the basic information about the program's character for teachers and administrators. This information should normally be published in the form of a special "program manual", which can be said to be the program producer's "declaration of ingredients" for potential program consumers. (We will return to this final task of the programmer in Chapter 16.)

Box 13.3 Planning and realization schedule: An example

Note: Preparation, construction and follow-up work demand exhaustive planning. Here a planning schedule can be of great use. It should—in addition to the designations for the different work stages—include the names of those responsible for the different work stages as well as the date when the stage's work should be finished (PT = planned time), and when it actually was finished (AT = actual time). The latter details can give a sounder foundation for the planning of the next programming project.

Project ______________	Project leader ______________		
Task:	Responsible:	PT	AT
1. Main direction of goal analysis is established			
2. Goal analysis, including detailed terminal descriptions and terminal tests			
3. Student group identified and analyzed			
4. Enlarged terminal chart and modified tests			
5. Situation analysis			
6. Subject-matter analysis: logical structuring			
7. Subject-matter analysis: psychological supplementation			
8. Choice of presentation media			
9. Points 1—8 are co-ordinated and tabulated in the form of detailed directives to the program author, supplemented with T-catalogue, C-catalogue, etc.			
10. Examination of already existing didactic material. Possible decision on project alteration			
11. Preparatory sequential decisions: Choice of "flow model"			
12. Preparatory subject-matter structuring, possibly in the form of a didactoplan			

Task:	Responsible:	PT	AT
13. Version 1 is completed			
14. Version 1 is re-examined			
15. Version 1 is modified			
16. Version 2 is subjected to preliminary try-out with individual observations			
17. Version 2 is modified			
18. Decision on further preliminary try-outs			
19. Version x is group-tested			
20. Version x is modified			
21. Decision on further group tests for modification purposes			
22. Editorial final examination			
23. Printing (or the like) of final version			
24. Field testing			
25. Writing of program manual with data from field testing			

14. Evaluation Criteria and Evaluation Aids: Some Examples of Relevant Variables and Systematic Mapping Devices

14.1 Introductory Points of View: Different Types of Educational Measurement

In general, educational measurements can be made of conditions *before, during,* and/or *after* a particular instructional sequence, and they can aim at an evaluation both of the *individual* and of the *instructional system* (as is outlined in Figure 14.2).

In the past, work on educational measurement has above all dealt with problems concerning cell 3 in our figure: how one constructs measurement instruments that give as reliable and valid a picture as possible of the final competence of the individual, mostly in comparison to some "norm group". This is, of course, an important aspect. However, other measurement aspects have by comparison been underdeveloped. First, it should be of interest not only to assess the status of the individual but also to evaluate the instructional system he is confronted with. How good are our systems (constructed to bring forth an optimal sequence of behavioral changes in accordance with given goal descriptions among the largest possible number of relevant students)? Second, it can well be said that so far we have been too often satisfied to obtain evaluations afterwards only (cell 3 and 6), in which case we primarily get com parisons between individuals or comparisons between systems, while a combination of measurements during and after the instruction (2 + 3 or 5 + 6) would often give more "useful" information. By useful information we then mean such data that directly serve to localize weak links in the instructional system: single parts that should be improved.

Programmed instruction is one of the fields of recent educational activity that have served to turn the interest of educational measurement specialists in new directions and broaden the focus. When successive revisions of the materials are made, one is guided both by the behavior of the students in the instructional situation (to what extent the student succeeds and how he reacts to single didules) and by their terminal achievements (their ability to reach the goals as measured by terminal tests).

	Before instruction	During instruction	After instruction
Focusing on a single individual	(1) Establishment of initial level	(2) Stepwise testing for successive feedback, e.g., to guide choice of instructional alternatives	(3) Establishment of terminal level; report on "competence"
Focusing on the "system"	(4) Studying relationship between actual student level and difficulty level of the system	(5) Localization of defects in function; control of relevance of branching system	(6) Assessment of total effectiveness and efficiency of system in relation to goal catalogue

Figure 14.1 General examples of various types of educational measurements

14.2 Terminal Variables: Final Achievements

The terminal achievements are naturally enough the most important indicators. If we get good final results, then we need not bother so much about the previous behavior during the instructional situation. However, should we obtain a less satisfactory final achievement, then this is an important indicator that something is not in order, but this piece of information usually gives the programmer rather little specific guidance as to where and how improvements should be made. In this case, then, study of the didule behavior (correct and incorrect reactions on single instructional units) is far more informative.

The character of the final tests is obviously very important. If the test is unsatisfactory (unreliable or not representative as far as the goal of the course is concerned), then we are severely misguided when we try to assess the effectiveness of our study material. The final tests should therefore always be worked out in close cooperation with experts in psychological and educational testing and with reasonable attention paid to appropriate measurement criteria.

There are, of course, many textbooks on educational measurement to which the reader may be referred for further information on these topics. Nevertheless, a warning may also be appropriate. Many research workers have made the point that most conventional techniques used in testing depend on wide variation in the student groups. Given an effective program which enables almost everyone to succeed, these measures will not be adequate. A new subdiscipline of test construction is building up, but its full extent and consequences are not yet evident. We will return to this question below.

Here we would like to emphasize three desirable characteristics of our measurement instruments. They should:

(a) be so designed and so related to the specific instructional system that the results obtained in using them will have clear and meaningful consequences for further planning;

(b) have a broad coverage, rather than be one-sidedly perfect;

(c) be clearly goal-related, rather than content-related or norm-related.

The first condition mentioned was already touched upon above in our brief discussion on Figure 14.1, and we will return to concrete examples of this below. The second point may seem self-evident, but nevertheless is sometimes too easily forgotten. One should keep in mind the total goal area of a course, so that one does not rest satisfied with too narrow a test instrument. The temptation to do this often derives from the fact that certain behaviors are more easily tested than others. If, for example, retention over longer periods of time or a certain kind of transfer effect are important parts of the goal area, one should try to assess these things, even though they may be difficult to measure.

Our measurement techniques are comparatively advanced as long as we deal with the cognitive field. Nevertheless, there is a risk that we rest satisfied with tests dealing primarily with simple recall of separate items of knowledge (since such tests are so easy to construct), in spite of the fact that we really want to cover more complicated abilities (such as application, analysis, or synthesis of knowledge items). In order to help us remember which aspects we intend to cover, it may often be worth while to use a test construction matrix of the kind presented in Figure 14.2. In the headings of the columns the various cognitive functions we want to deal with are entered (for example, using the terms of the well-known taxonomy of the Bloom group; Bloom, 1956), while the rows represent the various subject-matter areas. Such a simple cell system may be a good aid for the test constructor in not forgetting any important type of test item. (Cf., for example, Payne, 1968.) This does not mean, of course, that it is always easy to construct items which correspond to all the cells of such a matrix. We may find it especially difficult when we are interested in including not only cognitive, but also non-cognitive fields (see, e.g., Krathwohl et al., 1964), as we still have very few good test instruments available in these areas. For a recent summary of the state of the art of evaluating learning in relation to taxonomies, we refer the reader to Bloom, Hastings & Madaus, 1971.

In our third and last point on desirable characteristics we touched upon the frame of reference of the evaluation or the criteria used for comparison when we make our assessment. We may distinguish three main categories of such assessments:

	Behavioral dimension:						
Content areas:	Knowledge	Interpretation	Application	Analysis	Synthesis	Evaluation	Sum
Subject-matter area 1							
Subject-matter area 2							
Subject-matter area 3							
⋮	⋮	⋮	⋮	⋮	⋮	⋮	⋮
Subject-matter area n							
Sum							

Figure 14.2 Test construction matrix as an aid in avoiding one-sidedness in item choice

(a) *Goal-oriented assessments.* The assessment of the instructional result is then related to a specific series of goal descriptions. ("Out of the available test items, designed to cover the demands of our goal descriptions, Student S_1 has been able to pass 90 %.")

(b) *Process-oriented (or content-related) assessments.* The assessment of the instructional result is related to some specification of what has been presented during a course. ("Out of the available test items, designed to be a representative sample of the content of the course—as this is seen from a particular book or summary of lectures—Student S_2 has been able to pass 89 %.")

(c) *Product-group oriented (or norm-related) assessments.* The assessment of the instructional result is related to information about results of other individuals. ("On the tests used Student S_3 has obtained a result which places him in the best 25 %.")

All three methods can give valuable information in some situations—and sometimes, in addition, rather similar information. In other cases, however, the similarities are less marked, and then there is reason to ask which of the methods is most meaningful for one's particular aim. It might first be noted that the third type of assessment is most clearly different from the other two in being more relative in character. Thus, we may talk about "absolute" or "criterion-related" assessment on the one hand (and to this group we may then refer both the *a* and the *b* type) vs. "relative" or "norm-related" assessments on the other (the *c* type; cf. for example the dichotomy in Glaser, 1963).

Earlier educational measurement was usually dominated by norm-related measurements. Then the main aim was to differentiate among individuals, for example, in order to make individual predictions of future study success. Test results are thus mainly seen as prognostic instruments (we predict from cell 3—cf. Figure 14.1—at time 1 to cell 3 at time 2 etc.). But for many other purposes, especially when we are interested in the effectiveness of a particular instructional material, this type of information is not specific enough. It is not very informative to know that a certain person has passed through a study material A and done somewhat better than the average student. It would often be much more interesting to know *what* he is able to do.

If this is what we want, the two other criterion-related assessments, type *a* and *b,* come into focus. The difference between them is sometimes not very large, and the distinction is often overlooked. If the particular course has started from and closely kept to a given goal description, then the difference should usually not be of importance (if the main goal is not quite outside the scope of the subject-matter; there may be courses where the subject-matter is more or less irrelevant, but where the goal is to teach the students a particular study technique, for example; this may not explicitly be seen from the particular course material used). The reason why it is important to distinguish between type *a* and type *b* is, however, primarily that many courses lack a clear relation between a specified goal description and a closely related course content. It may be easy and tempting to choose a textbook of a course and "make a test on it" without pondering upon the relation of the book to a given goal description or a goal conception behind it. Then, however, we will lose our chance of detecting defects in the goal-relatedness of the course.

In general then, goal-oriented assessments are in many cases to be preferred to the other two types: they are definitely more informative than the norm-related ones, and they are often more relevant than the process-oriented ones. When we deal with programmed instruction, it is quite obvious that we should usually prefer to work with goal-oriented assessments, very closely connected with the original terminal analyses. This statement may seem rather self-evident, but it has certain consequences that may not be so obvious and even seem a little unusual to a person used to the routines of educational measurements.

The fact is that some of the measurement routines that have been built up are closely related to the aims of norm-related measurements, and—as we noted briefly above—that these are not equally meaningful in the construction of goal-related instruments. For instance, when we deal with norm-related tests, it has often been natural to increase the discriminatory power of the items by screening away such test items that show an especially high or especially low frequency of correct solutions. If one has the general aim of obtaining a clear dispersion in one's group, this is a natural procedure. In a goal-related test, however, one's main demand is that a test item should be clearly relevant to a specific sub-goal of the goal catalogue, and that the test item should differentiate between those who, in a terminal situation, are able to reach this particular sub-goal and those who are not. Let us suppose that we have a test item which fulfils the demands just mentioned. Should such an item get a very high frequency of correct solutions, then this cannot be an argument to remove it: the high frequency shows only that the instruction has been effective in this respect. Should the item get a low frequency of correct solutions, on the other hand, then this fact cannot be a reason for screening it out either: this may rather be an important indicator that the instruction on this point has to be improved. The discriminatory power of the items in the particular product group is thus not an adequate basis for screening out items, when we deal with goal-oriented tests; it is more important that the items discriminate between groups about which one knows, from other sources of information, that they have/do not have abilities which correspond to the goal description (cf. Glaser, 1963 and Marton, 1969). For example: Empirical evidence should show (1) that students can *not* as a rule pass the post-test before instruction, and (2) that known "experts" *can* pass it with an acceptable score.

In general, then, we do not choose test items with general predictive symptom value, but items which are closely related to specific goal descriptions; and we do not necessarily weed out items which most students are able to solve after going through the course.

When *experimental comparisons* are carried out between different programs using, for example, different techniques in order to reach the same objectives, a series of problems is encountered in finding *fair indices of learning and efficiency.* As indices of learning we often find raw post-test scores or gain scores. As an index of efficiency (effectiveness in relation to learning time) post-test scores are sometimes simply divided by learning time. All the three examples of measurements given have very obvious shortcomings and may sometimes lead to quite wrong conclusions. Using raw post-test scores as indices of learning would be justifiable when the groups compared both have no previous knowledge (or possibly when pre-test means are equal); these conditions are rarely valid. The simple use of gain scores presupposes that elevations of scores means the same on all points of the scale, which is seldom true; for example, the high-scorer (in the pre-test) is often penalized in so far that there are fewer items left for him to learn (and these will often be more difficult than the others). The division of post-test scores by the learning time, finally, implies equality of units in the test (seldom to be found in educational instruments). For further discussion of these problems and some possible solutions we refer the reader to a paper by Wheatley (1969). A related, but more general, presentation is found in Davies (1969).

14.3 Medial Variables: Behavior in the Instructional Situation

The behavior in the instructional situation is studied in detail during the explorative, individual try-out phase and from certain points of view (for example, with respect to correct vs. incorrect response behavior on individual instructional units) also during the group try-outs and in the final field study.

14.3.1 *Medial Variables of Achievement Character: Analysis of Correct and Incorrect Responses during the Work with the Program*

Among the most common aspects of the examination of student behavior in working with programmed materials, is *error analysis.* This is very reasonable both from a common sense point of view and from the viewpoint of Skinnerian theory. The risk is that the programmer stresses the counting of errors more than the analysis of errors.

Instructional micro-units ("didules") that have caused many errors should not be discarded *without further investigation* (in some cases and for certain purposes a somewhat higher percentage than usual may be acceptable and educationally meaningful), but these error-causing units should always be carefully examined, so that the programmer can come to as realistic conclusions as possible about the reasons for the increased error frequency. Some of the most common reasons are, of course, that the response demand has been ambiguous, that the language has been poorly adapted to the particular student group, or that the background behavior, built up earlier in the program, has not been trained to a sufficiently high level of stability and precision to ensure a correct solution in the specific task under study. In all these cases a revision seems to be the appropriate next step for the programmer.

Even though the study of errors is important, we should never forget that the error reaction alone does not necessarily tell us very much about the effectiveness of the specific didule where the error occurred. One of the reasons is, of course, that the correct answers are usually given as feedback. We have no simple one-to-one correspondence between the dichotomy "correct versus incorrect response" on the one hand, and the dichotomy "understanding of the task versus lack of understanding" on the other hand.

During the first individual try-out phase, at least, it may therefore be advisable (Gordon, 1963) to have the students mark off the units that they do not quite understand (whether they have answered the questions involved correctly or not). A simple question mark in the margin of the text or on a special sheet of comments would usually be adequate. This gives us four categories of student reactions: (1) "error with remaining doubt", (2) "error without remaining doubt", (3) "no error, but doubt", and (4) "neither error nor doubt". It is obvious that didules of the first type have to be revised. On the other hand, the second type may sometimes be educationally fruitful. (Once in a while the most effective instruction *may* result from the student's being allowed to make an incorrect response and having it clearly classified as wrong; this may be the case when we are dealing with a "spontaneous error tendency", caused by strong interference from earlier response patterns.) The main advantage of this analysis probably lies in the fact that we can identify those units where the students have answered correctly, but where they nevertheless register lack of understanding (the third category above). In these cases the programmer may, for instance, have used too strong prompting techniques, a fault that a simple error analysis unfortunately cannot demonstrate. Such units should usually be revised, too.

This kind of analysis is useful not only for linear programs, but also for the error-treatment program of the scrambled book type. The lack of correspondence between understanding and correct answers may be quite frequent in some of these programs, if no extra checks are made. It is quite possible that the student chooses the correct answer immediately in a multiple-choice situation, without understanding the correct answer (the other alternatives may be too obviously wrong, for instance). There is also no guarantee that the final correct answer given by the student is connected with understanding. It may

Units / Students	U_1	U_2	U_3	U_4	U_5	U_6	...	U_n
S_1			E?		?		...	
S_2	E?	E	E		?		...	E
S_3			E?				...	
S_4			E		?		...	
S_5			E?				...	
S_6							...	
⋮	⋮	⋮	⋮	⋮	⋮	⋮	⋮	⋮
S_n			E		?		...	

Reading key:
E = error
? = lack of understanding

Figure 14.3 Typical structure of a simple survey table ("Error-and-doubt distribution")

In this simple hypothetical example we find a clear error concentration on unit 3 on the one hand (for almost all subjects) and for Subject 2 on the other hand (for almost all units). We also find a relatively large number of question marks for unit 5 in spite of the fact that this unit has not attracted any errors at all. These kinds of information are obviously better starting-points for revision than overall error percentages for total programs. For more detailed discussion, cf. the text.

simple be the only alternative left after the student has passed through all the error branches (without having understood enough of the error treatment given).

If we try our program on one student at a time and simply extend the number of steps at each point where errors occur, there is a considerable risk that we end up with a very large (and inefficient) program. On the other hand, if we feel content with overall error percentage (making no revisions at all if these percentages fall within certain pre-established limits), we do not fully utilize the information collected. The first approach places too much weight on the behavior of single individuals which may or may not be atypical (and is too much influenced by chance), whereas the second approach gives us too little information about individual items. Instead, a systematic mapping of error distributions and error types would usually be preferable, and as a rule this mapping should also include subject reports on understanding. A natural starting point is then a simple survey table, including both errors and reports of lack of understanding. A square-ruled background grid with students as row headings and didule numbers as column headings would be a simple but adequate design (cf. Figure 14.3). This survey table should be supplemented with a frequency list of deviant responses.

These aids are good starting-points when the programmer has to answer questions of the following types: (1) Do the errors concentrate on certain specific program units ("column comparison")? (2) Is there any good educational reason for this, or is it simply an indication that these particular units or some immediately preceding units should be revised? (3) Do the errors concentrate on specific individuals ("row comparison")? (4) Are these errors of such a systematic character that some preparatory additional course (remedial branching after a filtering test) would probably reduce their number considerably? (5) Do the same error types occur repeatedly for some individuals? (6) Could this best be avoided by more complete information in the main program or by utilizing special branching for remedial instruction?

For a summary discussion on the relation between item difficulty and learning effect we may refer to Jacobs (1963). Jacobs's main thesis is that many variables influence the degree of difficulty without influencing the learning effect and vice versa, and that it may therefore be misleading to concentrate the study one-sidedly on item difficulty (in terms of error frequency) as the only evaluation criterion. Our examples above point in the same direction.

Among those who have emphasized the importance of studying not only error frequency, but also error type is Landa (1969 a). Error type is then seen as diagnostic indicator of what went wrong in the student's thought pattern. Just informing the student that he is wrong or what the correct answer is, can be quite insufficient; asking him to start from the beginning again is a very imprecise and inefficient method of treatment. Instead, specific remedial exercises focusing on the particular error type may often be strongly indicated.

It should be added that the technique of having students note, without giving reasons, tasks that are doubtful may not always give enough information for error type analysis. The student is often unable to remember later what confused him. Perhaps the point has been clarified at a later stage, and he no longer experiences the confusion he did at that moment. This is one reason for "talking" the first students through the program, that is, letting them say aloud what they think at the moment it occurs to them.

14.3.2 *Medial Variables of Experience Character: Analyses of Attitude Development and the Degree of Subjective Difficulty*

In addition to such evaluation variables that deal with the final learning result (the terminal behavior) and such that deal with correct vs. incorrect behavior during the study process, it is often also desirable to examine the *development of attitudes* in the instruction situation (or, to use another word, the general "climate of work"). Successive observations of the study behavior during the course as well as direct attitude questioning at certain points of time are natural methodological approaches. Among questions in which one would usually be interested in such studies are: How does the student experience the self-instructional work situation? Is this felt to be more or less stimulating than the traditional teaching the student is used to? And if it should be experienced as more stimulating: Is this only a temporary phenomenon, some kind of novelty effect, or is it more stable, observable during a longer period? What attitudes to the particular subject-matter do we find under the particular conditions of programmed instruction? Can we find any influence on the students' attitudes towards studying in general?

In the debate on programmed instruction, particularly during the early years, many participants seemed to have clear-cut and general answers to such questions. Unfortunately, however, they were often more emphatic and certain than unanimous. Probably such questions can only to a very limited extent be given general answers. The answer for a given situation will depend both on the particular study course under work (there are stimulating and dull programs just as there are stimulating and dull textbooks) and on the other experiences of the particular student group (the "comparison" criteria). It should be no hindrance to our study of attitudes, however, that the answers only seldom can be generalized. On the contrary: it will be so much more important to evaluate the specific course material, as experienced by a particular target group, not only from the point of view of achievement but also from the point of view of attitude development.

It might be added that surveys of student attitudes should usually be conducted by someone not committed to the particular program, in order to avoid influencing effects ("halo enthusiasm"). Moreover, there is rather general agreement that, while student reports may be a cheap and easy way of determining something about attitude, a powerful measure is to observe the student under conditions in which he has a free choice. If he continues work on a program when he does not have to or chooses it in preference to some other activity, he apparently approves of the program.

Side by side with the attitude variables proper, it may sometimes be of value to study other "experience variables", especially the "subjective difficulty level" of the items. When constructing tests one commonly defines the difficulty of an item in terms of frequency of correct solutions, but difficulty defined in this way is obviously not meaningful in the individual case. Let us suppose that the calculating tasks (1) $2 \times 21 =$; (2) $3 \times 34 =$; (3) $11 \times 13 =$; and (4) $145 \times 112 =$; for the four students A, B, C and D result in the following distribution of correct and incorrect solutions:

	1	2	3	4
A	C	C	C	C
B	C	C	C	E
C	C	C	E	E
D	C	E	E	E

C = correct solution
E = error

We note that Task 1 is solved correctly by all. Hence, it has the p-value of 1.00 and is then, using common test-construction terminology, an "easy" task. But is it as easy for student D as for student A? If we define difficulty level in terms of frequency of solution, the answer is 'yes'—or rather: then the question is meaningless. But very probably the degree of "subjective difficulty" is greater for student D than for student A. We might get some idea about whether or not we are correct in making this guess, by examining the amount of time for solution and/or by means of direct student ratings on difficulty, and it should be of interest to relate such variables to both achievement variables and common attitude variables. (Our discussion of this point follows ideas in Jacobs, 1963).

14.3.3 *Special Aids: Didactograms*

If the program is non-linear (for instance, using parallel tracks, remedial loops, by-pass arrangements, etc.), the simple survey table is sometimes not the best possible starting-point for a study of error frequencies on various items. There are two main reasons for this: (1) Error frequencies should usually be considered in close connection with their position within the branching system, and (2) we also need information on *frequency* of use for the various tracks or branches in the system. Hence, in these cases, it is often useful to draw special diagrams.

The basic outline of such a diagram will be stable for a particular program version, irrespective of the student reactions, and will show the sequence of the didules, including all available branching possibilities. As starting-point for these diagrams it is often suitable to use the "didactoplan" constructed earlier during the preliminary decisions on sequence (cf. above). On this background diagram we may fill in information about the individual's actual working route as well as his working results on the single units (correct and incorrect responses symbolized, for instance, by means of plus and minus signs). Such a program outline, filled in with student behavior registrations, might be called a "didactogram", and it gives us a relatively surveyable map of the interaction between the instructional system of the program and an individual (cf. Figure 14.4).

Data from several individual diagrams can be brought together in a "*group diagram*", on which information about the percentage of correct solutions for each single response demand, as well as information about the number of individuals using various possible tracks within the branching system, can be registered (cf. Figure 14.5).

Such a diagram can be used by the programmer for many different kinds of decisions. To take only one example; it may often be shown that some of the branching possibilities have not been used at all. If so, it is a natural task of

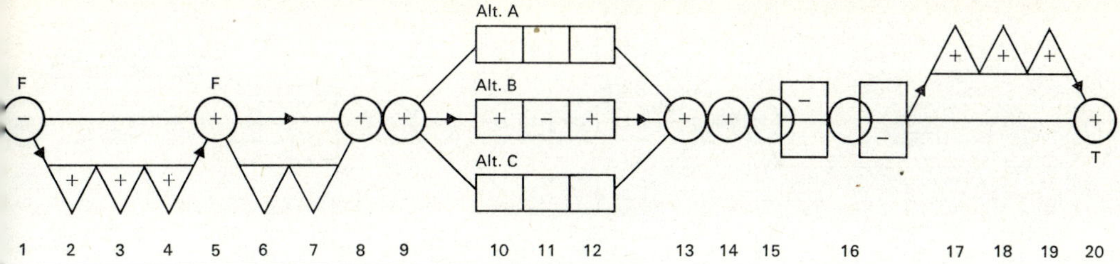

Figure 14.4 A diagram of branching use and response correctness for a single student ("individual didactogram"): An example

Background symbols:

(The background structure is the same in all diagrams representing the same course version)

F = filter function
T = terminal testing function
○ = a didule that all students should go through
▽ = a didule in a special, additional course with remedial function
△ = a didule in a special, additional course containing optional "enrichment"
□ = a didule in a parallel branching system
= a didule with connected error treatment (two error alternatives)

Working symbols (individual data):

→ = the route followed
\+ = correct solution
− = incorrect solution

The diagram is read in the following way:

The subject gives a wrong answer to the introductory filter unit (no. 1) and is then directed to go through the special remedial items 2—4, the response demands of which he answers correctly. Since he also gives a correct response to unit 5, he does not need any further remedial treatment, but is allowed to proceed directly to no. 8. Among the possible parallel tracks (covering units 10—12) he chooses the one called Alternative B. He makes one error choice in each of the multiple-choice tasks (15 and 16). He chooses to go through the optional enrichment sequence (17—19). After that he solves the terminal test item correctly.

revision to get rid of these tracks or give them some other form. Such an analysis is important, for instance, when we work with multiple-choice arrangements and subsequent error instruction connected with the various possible error choices. Perhaps some of the error choices never attract the attention of the students, and the special error instruction included within the program is then dead wood. Unfortunately there is seldom any evidence that the productive authors of scrambled books have examined their often very bulky error instruction in this way.

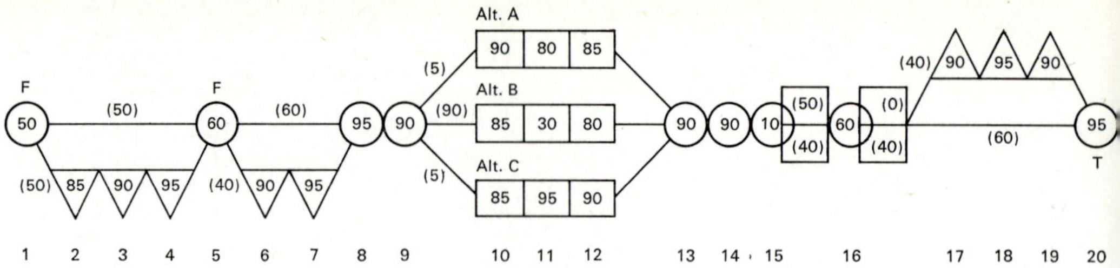

Figure 14.5 A group diagram of branching use and response correctness ("group didactogram"): An example

Background symbols: See Figure 14.4

Working symbols: Figures *without* parenthesis give the percentage of correct responses ("frequency of correctness"). Figures *with* parenthesis give the percentage of students who have used a specific passage ("frequency of use").

The diagram is read in the following way: 50 per cent. of the students answer unit 1 correctly, and these students are instructed to go forward directly to number 5. The rest of the students go through the remedial items 2—4 (in which the resulting correctness percentages are respectively 85, 90 and 95 per cent.) On item 5, correct answers are given by 60 per cent of the students; these students are allowed to go directly to number 8. The remaining 40 per cent. proceed through numbers 6 and 7, etc.

Comments: The *correctness percentage* is fairly high for most of the units. An exception is number 11 in Alternative B; this unit should therefore be given special attention. The units with filter function (1 and 5) have a moderate correctness percentage, which usually can be considered to be adequate (if all students should answer a filter unit correctly, the appended remedial sequence would be unnecessary). The error-treatment units 15 and 16 give uneven values (D 15 has few correct answers, and D 16 has uneven distribution between error alternatives) and should therefore be especially examined. Finally, it is, of course, a good sign that the terminal unit with testing function (20) has a high correctness percentage.—*Frequency of use*: The optional choice of parallel sequences gives an uneven distribution (almost all students choose Alternative B). Here revision is probably indicated. The distribution in the choice of enrichment courses, however, does not seem to give any reason for revision.

14.4 Analyzing Relationships Between Student Behavior Within and Outside the Program

The final criterion of the effectiveness of a program is, of course, the student's terminal behavior. As was stated above: If this reaches acceptable levels within reasonable time periods, we need usually not be so concerned about the details of the behavior within the program.[1] However, when the terminal behavior

[1] It may be added that the student's terminal behavior as determined by a final test may sometimes be regarded as "pseudo-terminal". The *ultimate* criterion for industrial programmers is normally the student's performance on the job. A learner may get 100 % correct on a immediate and specific terminal test, but be unable to put the knowledge

is not fully adequate or when the time used seems too long, an analysis of the student's behavior within the program is needed to show us the place where revision is most indicated. About these general ideas there seems now to be a fair degree of agreement among programmers. However, two deficiencies stand out in many reports on program development. Sometimes the programmers are so exclusively interested in the error percentages within the program that all other considerations, even those concerning the terminal behavior, seem to be forgotten. In other cases attention is paid both to final tests and to the error frequencies within the program, but the programmer does not care to study any particular relationships between student behaviors within and outside the program, even when these relationships should give him important additional information (such as, for instance, would often be the case in branching programs). In the following we will give a few brief illustrations of relationships between student behaviors within the program and outside the program that should be of interest to the programmer.

14.4.1 *Information Density and Information Speed of a Program*

As has been pointed out (Björkman, 1963) the information value of a unit of information can be defined as the difference between the probability of correct answer before and after the communication. Since the single units (didules) of a program often do not contain complete terminal reactions, however, but have other purposes as steps on the way towards such terminal reactions, it is often unrewarding to study the information value (in this sense) of the single units. (This value may be maximal in the stated operational meaning without any guarantee that we have come closer to any of the terminal reactions.) On the other hand, it should be quite meaningful to study the special tasks, sometimes called "criterion problems", which test the student's terminal behavior after he has gone through an instructional sequence of related units. Even when formally built into the program proper, these criterion problems are equivalent to test items and may be considered to represent "behavior outside the program" in the sense intended here. If we examine the ability of the students to solve these criterion problems *before* going through the instructional sequence (error percentage A) as well as their ability to solve them in their natural context, that is, *after* going through the sequence (error percentage B), we shall obtain more meaningful measurements of "uncertainty reduction" (error percentage A—error percentage B).

Let us assume that, for each new concept we introduce, we have at least one instructional sequence, and at least one criterion problem. The uncertainty

to work. Where "real-life" criteria are available, studies of relations between immediate terminal tests and such ultimate criteria are important.

reduction of the criterion problem divided by the number of units (didules) included in the sequence then gives us a measure of the "information density" of that particular sequence. The information density of the total program may then be defined, in principle, as an average of the density of the separate micro sequences:

$$\frac{\frac{A_1 - B_1}{D_1} + \frac{A_2 - B_2}{D_2} + \frac{A_3 - B_3}{D_3} + \ldots + \frac{A_n - B_n}{D_n}}{n}$$

A_i = the error percentage of the student group under examination on criterion problem *i* before the relevant instructional material has been studied.

B_i = the error percentage of the student group under examination on criterion problem *i* after going through the instructional material.

D_i = number of units (didules) in the micro sequence that leads up to criterion problem *i* (and the purpose of which is to teach the student the concept C_i).

C_i = basic concept (represented in the program by the ith criterion problem and the ith instructional sequence).

n = number of basic concepts included in the program.

Note. Obviously a formula of this type only gives *one* aspect of the complex phenomenon of information density as intuitively conceptualized. For instance, it does not consider the fact that various conceptual units can make widely differing demands on the "intermediary processes". If these demands could be expressed quantitatively (and average judgments from a group of raters might perhaps be used in this connection—at least for a first approximation), a weighting of each quotient $(A_i - B_i)/D_i$ with respect to the demands on the intermediary processes might "improve" the formula, that is, mean that one more possible criterion of step size has been taken into consideration.

If we exchange the information about the number of units (didules) in the micro sequences (D_1, D_2, D_3, . . . D_n) against the *time* the micro sequences take (T_1, T_2, T_3, . . . T_n), we would obtain a measure of "information speed" instead of a measure of "information density". Since one of the most basic criteria of educational effectiveness is how much information the student absorbs per unit of time (not how much information has been poured out from the mouth of the teacher or otherwise been potentially available for absorption!), such a formula would give us *one* starting-point in our assessment of the educational effectiveness of the program. In any case it ought to be of interest to be able to compare this measure with other data about a program. It is hoped that comparisons between different operational program characteristics will gradually give us a clearer picture of what is essential and what is less essential in program construction.

14.4.2 *Choice-Point Relationships (Survey Tables of the Distribution of Achievement Patterns in Filter Units)*

The measure of "information speed" just mentioned combines information about time used (a "medial" variable) with information about probabilities of correct responses before and after the study ("initial" and "terminal" variables). Another combined evaluation criterion will be of interest when examining branching programs where the students, on the basis of their achievement at a choice-point (in a filter unit), are led different ways through the program. Simple error frequency data for these filter units are, of course, insufficient as a basis for the revision, since we are not here concerned merely with minimizing the number of errors. Instead, in these cases the aim is to lead the student, by means of the diagnostic indications given by the filter unit, to the particular study material that is most appropriate to *him*. This means that the student's achievement on initial test (pre-test) filter unit, and terminal test have to be examined together. It is obvious that certain combinations ("achievement patterns") are acceptable, whereas others show faults in the program and, hence, indicate where revisions are needed. (A demonstration of this was given by Markle, 1963. Some of Markle's ideas will be incorporated in the following illustration.)

As an aid in this examination the programmer can utilize a survey table of the general kind demonstrated in Figure 14.6. The eight possible "achievement patterns" are placed as row headings, and the filter units of the program as column headings. The distribution of the students over the various achievement patterns is then built up within the table by entering tally marks.

Let us take a brief look at some typical achievement patterns when the program contains filter units of the general type that sort the students into two sub-categories at each choice-point, one of which passes through only part of the total number of units included in the total programs. This formulation is a very general one, describing a formal branching structure, and it therefore covers at least two main situations that the educator will often consider to be quite different. In the first of these, the main group of students goes through all units, while a smaller group of students is found at the choice-point to know already some of the material that will be treated and is therefore directed to skip some part of the program ("shortening of learning sequence for high-achievement group"). In the other situation, the main group of students goes through the shorter sequence, while a smaller group of students is found at the choice-points *not* to know enough about materials covered in some earlier program and is therefore directed to go through an additional "remedial loop" ("lengthening of learning sequence for low-achievement group"). The pattern symbols used in the following are explained in Figure 14.6. Only some of the patterns included in the figure will be commented upon here, and, for the

Achievement patterns:	FD_1	FD_2	FD_3	...	FD_n
A. I_r FD_r T_r				...	
B. I_r FD_r T_w				...	
C. I_r FD_w T_r				...	
D. I_r FD_w T_w				...	
E. I_w FD_r T_r				...	
F. I_w FD_r T_w				...	
G. I_w FD_w T_r				...	
H. I_w FD_w T_w				...	

Reading key:
I = initial test
FD = filter unit (filter didule)
T = terminal test
r = right
w = wrong

Figure 14.6 Possible table arrangement in analyzing the distribution of achievement patterns in filter units ("choice-point relations table")

sake of brevity, only faults of the program proper are mentioned (that is, we assume that pre- and post-tests are reliable and valid):

A. I_r FD_r T_r

In this case the student answers correctly (r) both in the filter unit (FD) within the program and in the corresponding parts of initial test (I) and terminal test (T). Students with this pattern will skip the special part of the program immediately following the particular filter unit. In other words, they go on the quicker track (whether this is considered to be the main track or a track for selected minority of high-achievers). No criticism can, of course, be directed against the fact that this pattern appears. *One* indication for revision may come up, however. If the number of students with this pattern approach 100 per cent in a representative sample of the target population, the additional part of the program is superfluous.

C. I_r FD_w T_r

If the tests are assumed to be valid (an assumption we made above for brevity of discussion), this particular pattern indicates that we have had an inadequate filter unit which directed the student through an extra part of study material that he did not need. The response demands in the filter unit may have been formulated in such a way as to lead the student astray, or the filter unit may simply be too difficult for its purpose. Hence, in this case the revision should focus on the filter unit.

F. I_w FD_r T_w

This combination can be an important indicator of insensitivity on the part of the filter unit. The student who does not know the pertinent facts from the beginning is not correctly sorted by the filter unit and, hence, does not get the additional study he needs. This may happen quite often, for instance, if the filter unit uses multiple-choice techniques with less adequate alternatives (or if, in the filter unit, the student is tested on discrimination behavior only, whereas he is tested on construction behavior in the terminal tests). As was the case in pattern C, the revision should be directed at the filter unit, but in pattern F the revision has the opposite purpose of *in*creasing the difficulty of the filter problem.

G. I_w FD_w T_r

This combination is usually a good sign. The student shows error in the initial test and in the filter unit, but he can solve the terminal problem after the additional training supplied by the extra part of the program. *One* possibility of revision should, however, be kept in mind. The programmer should ask himself whether or not the "additional" program part ought to be incorporated within the main part of the program. If the number of students with G patterns approaches 100 per cent in a representative sample, such an incorporation is clearly indicated.

The tabular and diagrammatic arrangements demonstrated in this chapter should be considered only as examples. Many other types are possible and suitable to aid the programmer in his attempts to deal systematically with the data from the try-out phase, and each programmer should, of course, design his aiding devices to fit his particular needs in each specific situation. Our main purposes have been (a) to emphasize the relative complexity of the evaluation task and the risk of using one-sided criteria in the try-out process, and (b) to show some of the possible ways in which the programmer can equip himself with simple aids in order to make his evaluations more systematic, complete, and efficient. It is felt that a more widespread use of such systematic and comprehensive evaluation schemes would also considerably enhance the accumulation of basic knowledge in the programmed learning field.

15. Examples of Procedures in Modification of Programs

We have already discussed a series of steps in system modification, arising from different test results, when we were dealing with the various evaluation criteria above. In the present section we shall briefly review different combinations of criteria which to a greater or lesser degree call for modification and also mention a few special measures which can occasionally be indicated.

15.1 Survey of Preliminary Indications for Revision from Certain Combinations of Criteria

Figure 15.1 gives a simplified survey of the extent to which different combinations of criteria indicate modification. Such a survey must obviously be fairly schematic. In practice, it is not always easy to determine what are "high" or "low" error rates or decide, for example, how a "limited revision" should be designed. But as a theoretical outline such a schematic survey can perhaps nevertheless give a lead and counterbalance the one-sided consideration of a single criterion of which some programming theoreticians are guilty.

Let us comment briefly on some of the criteria combinations. (For abbreviations used, see the explanations in Figure 15.1.)

All combinations with a high terminal error rate (TE_h) obviously definitely indicate need for change. In these cases the goal set has not been attained. The program is, to use very obvious terminology, simply not "finished". If, in addition, we consider the student's attitudes, we get yet another indicator, and the difference made in the survey between "maximal" and "strong" indication for change is directly dependent on the difference between programs as experienced by students with negative and positive attitudes respectively.

A program which not only misses its performance goal but also creates an unpleasant study situation does not justify its existence. In this case it makes no difference whether the error rate is high (as in the first criteria combination) or low (as in the second). Programmers who discuss modifications only on the basis of the students' errors during the course of the program risk

Criteria combination:	Preliminary indication:
1. $ME_hA_nTE_h$	Maximal indication for change
2. $ME_lA_nTE_h$	Maximal indication for change
3. $ME_hA_pTE_h$	Modification strongly indicated
4. $ME_lA_pTE_h$	Modification strongly indicated
5. $ME_hA_nTE_l$	Limited modification indicated
6. $ME_lA_nTE_l$	Limited modification indicated
7. $ME_hA_pTE_l$	Modification not indicated
8. $ME_lA_pTE_l$	Modification not indicated

Figure 15.1 Outline of principle indications for modification in certain criteria combinations

Symbols:
ME = medial error rate (% of errors during the instructional program)
TE = terminal error rate (% of errors in final test)
A = attitude
h, l = high, low
p, n = positive, negative

accepting a program of the type $ME_lA_nTE_h$, which is here shown as indicating a maximal need of change.

Everyone would agree that criteria combination 8 ($ME_lA_pTE_l$) is advantageous, and that a program with these characteristics scarcely needs modifying. (For the sake of simplicity, we are disregarding certain other variables, e.g. teaching time, which is in many cases important, but which is less so than the final performance and working climate.) We have also accepted criteria combination 7 ($ME_hA_pTE_l$). The error rate during the working of the program is admittedly high, but this has resulted neither in bad performance nor a negative attitude. The difficulties can have resulted from a low degree of support stimulation or a teaching method which failed to explain errors satisfactorily, but these difficulties are not such as to have an overwhelmingly deterrent effect. It is possible that this combination is comparatively rare, but when it does occur, it should hardly be rejected, despite the ME_h factor.

Finally, combinations 5 and 6 are characterized by a negative attitude together with a good final result. In one case, ($ME_hA_nTE_l$), the negative attitude is probably connected with the error-reaction frequency. Here it is possible that a limited modification to reduce the error rate would also produce a better attitude climate. In the other case, it is more probable that the negative attitude is related to the fact that the program is experienced as monotonous and uninspiring. In this situation, an attempt should be made to increase motivation and reduce monotony (cf. our discussion on motivation above).

In a particular situation, the occurrence of different combinations depends not only on the character of the program, but also on the general working climate of the classroom or school and on the student as an individual. Some programs probably give rise to widely different criteria combinations for different individuals which may be of interest, for example, from the point of view of personality research and social psychology. From the point of view of educational technology, however, the general aim must be to construct the program or system in such a way that as many of the target students as possible come up with combinations 7 or 8.

15.2 Special Procedures

15.2.1 *The Question of the Student's Capacity for Independent Work and the Possible Alteration of the Boundary between Educand-System and Educator-System*

As is shown in Figure 15.2, the change from one type of teaching situation to another often involves a shift of the boundary between the educator system and the educand system. An extended educator system may be valuable for the rapid learning of a certain subject-matter. On the other hand, when it is a question of developing the capacity to cope independently with subject-matter which is hard to learn, a comprehensive educator system might often be a hindrance. If the try-out shows that the learning of certain subject-matter takes more time than is desirable, one should consider changing over from a less detailed learning process to a more rigidly controlled one. If the aim is to induce the ability to treat subject-matter independently, and if the try-out seems to indicate that this goal is not being reached, a shift of the boundary between the educator system and the educand system in the opposite direction would be indicated.

15.2.2 *The Question of How the Student Accustoms Himself to Active Cognitive Handling of Subject-Matter and Possible Limitation of the Number of External Response Reactions*

External response reactions are considered valuable as a guarantee that the student actively handles the subject-matter presented to him. Is there a possible

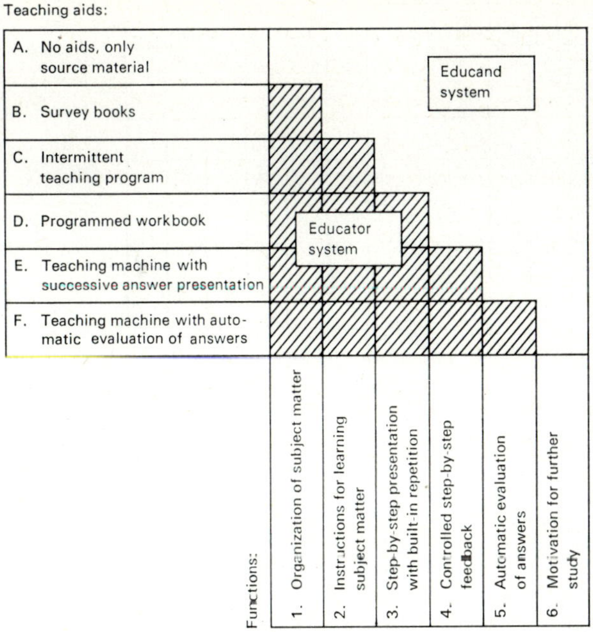

Figure 15.2 Outline sketch of the varying boundary between educator system and educand system

risk that the student gets so accustomed to the special working technique that he avoids active cognitive working when there is *no* explicit response demand? Can the technique sometimes involve an unnecessary loss of time (for those with already established habits of study)?

If the try-out indicates a positive answer to one or both of these questions, one should possibly try a technique which is a compromise between the program's continual demand for external response reactions and the ordinary textbook's lack of such a demand. The program can, for example, be so constructed that a response which generally need only be covert (implicit) is demanded of the student. From time to time (at irregular intervals), however, a demand for an overt statement occurs. Cook (1962), who suggested this type of technique, thinks that by this means the individual might be forced to keep his covert responses alert and so save time.

A schematic diagram of the reaction between student and program when using such a technique (with partial demands for explicit statement of responses) is given in Figure 15.3.

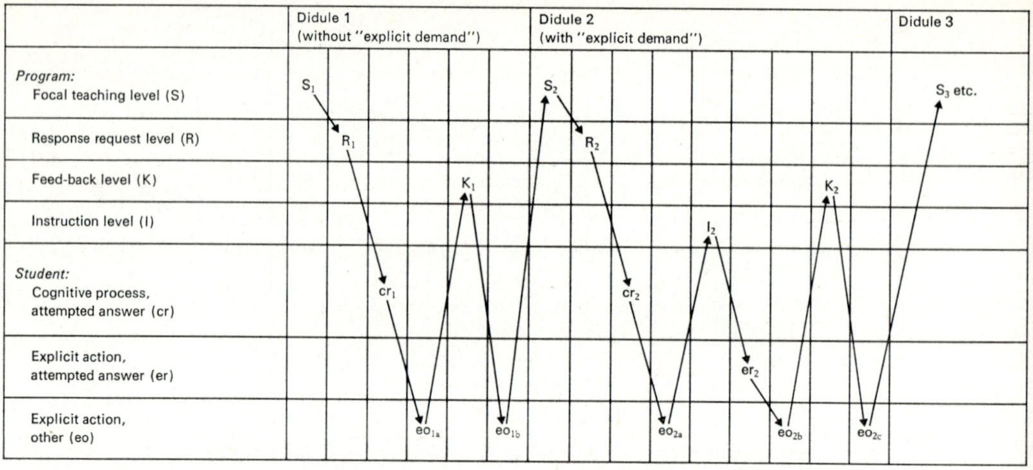

Figure 15.3 Schematic diagram of interaction between student and program demanding only partial explicit response reaction

Note: The other actions, shown as *eo,* here indicate manipulation of the machine. In Didule 1 the student thinks of the answer (cr_1), turns the machine forward one frame (eo_{1a}) and gets the correct answer (K_1). In Didule 2, however, when he turns the machine forward (eo_{2a}), he gets instead the instruction to write down the answer (I_2). Only after he has done this (er_2) is he given, after a further manipulation of the machine, the correct answer (K_2).

15.2.3 *Special Measures against "Boredom"*

We discussed above some general steps which could be taken to reduce monotony and increase motivation. Should investigation show that the students find the program monotonous and boring, the revision should aim at an even greater use of these tactics to give variety. In this section we shall give a few brief hints on other possibilities.

(1) *Adaptation to the students' previous knowledge* has perhaps not been worked out with sufficient care. As illustrated in Figure 15.4, the student's attainment of the skills relevant to a certain goal is seen as a continuous process, which has already gone on, to some extent, before he is faced with the particular study material. If he is aware that he is being taught about things he already knows, he will very often experience boredom. In this case a more thorough student analysis should form the background for a modification of the program.

It may become apparent that the previous knowledge of the target population has been seriously underestimated, and then the program should be shortened—either by cutting out certain sections in the more elementary parts

For the individual student S:

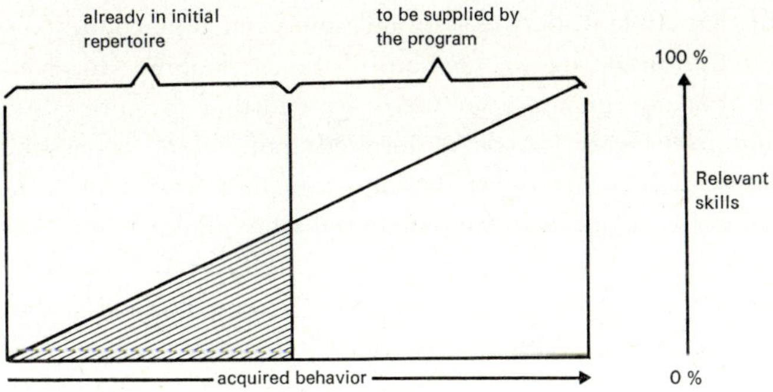

In the total group of students G:

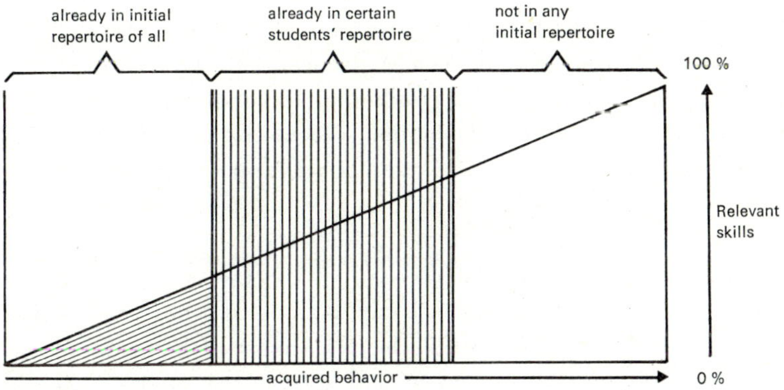

Figure 15.4 Theoretical illustration of relation between initial repertoire and contribution of the program

of the program or by "increasing the size of the steps" (reducing the number of application and practice tasks). But it can also happen that the underestimation applies only to part of the target population and in that case consideration should be given to changing from a linear to a branching program.

The most effective teaching should, in theory, be that which starts out from an *individual analysis of the initial repertoire,* i.e. which begins by testing and analyzing the individual's previous knowledge and tendency to errors and then teaching only those points which are shown to be lacking—with emphasis on individual difficulties. The fact that the programmer for practical reasons finds it difficult to follow such a procedure completely does not prevent him from *approaching* this technique, since the number of individual variations important for teaching is relatively limited in most groups of students. (One works then with a number of "streams" in which the students are placed after an initial filter test.)

It may be thought that student analysis is troublesome and time-consuming, and it is often neglected in preparing the contents of the curriculum. However, the amount of work that one imagines one saves by omitting this procedure will be lost over and over again, partly in lowered motivation among the students, with the consequent lower effort they put into their work, partly in an unnecessary expenditure of time and study-material when one teaches what the students already know.

Individualization plays an important role in several current research and development projects working on methods-and-materials systems. These projects often use a complex system of diagnosis and individual prescription, with the testing being an integral part of the teaching for each student (cf., e.g., the Swedish IMU Project on individualized mathematics teaching: Öreberg, 1966; Jivén & Öreberg, 1968; or the project at the University of Pittsburgh called Individually Prescribed Instruction: see Lindvall & Bolvin, 1967).

(2) *Alteration of tempo of presentation.* As far as the tempo of presentation is concerned there are three main possibilities: student-controlled speed, machine-controlled speed and the combination student-and-machine-controlled speed. Student-controlled speed is the most usual, and it has the obvious advantage that each student has as much time as he needs to think. However, one can imagine (especially when it is not a question of concept-learning or problem-solving activity, but of a motor skill) that the student-controlled tempo involves a risk that the student will stay too long at a low level of skill. This is likely to lead to boredom, since clearly increasing demands are not continually being made on the student. Should a try-out show this to be the case, a situation should be considered in which the student is spurred on to greater efforts by a machine-controlled increase in speed, or which uses a student-machine system where the average speed of the machine is regulated by the student's skill (cf. SAKI).

(3) *Variation of didule components.* We normally work with a fixed series of didule components and student responses: information or "stimule" (S), response-demand or "respule" (R), student response or "response" (r), feedback of correct answer or "corrule" (K). This in itself, as we pointed out above, gives a good dynamic variety (S-R-r-K, S-R-r-K etc.), with greater variation than the usual text's monotonous: S-S-S-S-S etc. However, if we work only with series of the type S-R-r-K, even this can naturally gradually become monotonous and boring. There is a particularly great risk that this will happen when, in addition, there is a great number of consecutive didules which contain very similar S, which is often necessary in the training of skills (e.g. in languages), where the student, by persistent practice, has to get as close as possible to the ideal performance (e.g. perfect pronunciation). If in-

vestigation shows that boredom is experienced by the students, one should consider interrupting the working sequence at suitable places with differently arranged component sequences. If, for example, in training of skills, we occasionally intensify the r-K combination by "extended" sequences, this can serve a useful purpose both for effective work (the ideal performance is attained more easily perhaps when the whole task need not be repeated) and for the students' need of "something different". This type of sequence—e.g. S-R-r-K-r-K-r-K—is, of course, only *one* of many possible variations.

16. Compiling the Program Manual

It may be worthwile to look upon the instructional design process as a series of cycles or iterations (as has been sketched in Figure 16.1). The main stages of each cycle would then be: analysis, synthesis, and operation (try-out). The analysis of the first cycle is a comprehensive and many-faceted task (including analysis of goals, students, subject-matter, media, and various aspects of the situation); this problem area was dealt with in some detail in Part II of the present book. The synthesis of the first cycle includes the specification of the first version of the instructional system (dealt with in Part III). In cycle II, analysis focuses upon evaluation, and synthesis focuses upon modification. This type of process is then iterated (cycle III being similar to cycle II, etc.), until the terminal goal is reached (or until the designer judges the terminal goal to be as well approximated as is possible under the circumstances). Then, as a final task, the designer should describe the history and outcome of his labors in a manual. This should help consumers of programs (instructional systems) to choose their material.

It is naturally not a great deal of use to describe in detail what such a manual should contain. The most suitable choice will vary greatly from program to program. But certain categories of information are usually necessary in one form or another:

(A) *Description of goal and students*

The aim of the program and the use planned for it should be clearly stated. An attempt to attract customers among a wide and varying public by using vague and all-embracing headings is easily seen through and is not a good advertisement for the vendor of the program. The previous knowledge needed is stated and preferably specified by means of a pre-test. Similarly, the purpose of the course is clearly defined by the final test. (For pre- and post-tests, see E below.)

(B) *Character of development work*

(a) *Those responsible for the programming and testing* should be named.
(b) *The goal analysis* on which the program is based should be presented.
(c) A summary of the other stages of the *preliminary work* can give valuable information. (To what extent has a thorough student analysis been carried out? Etc.)

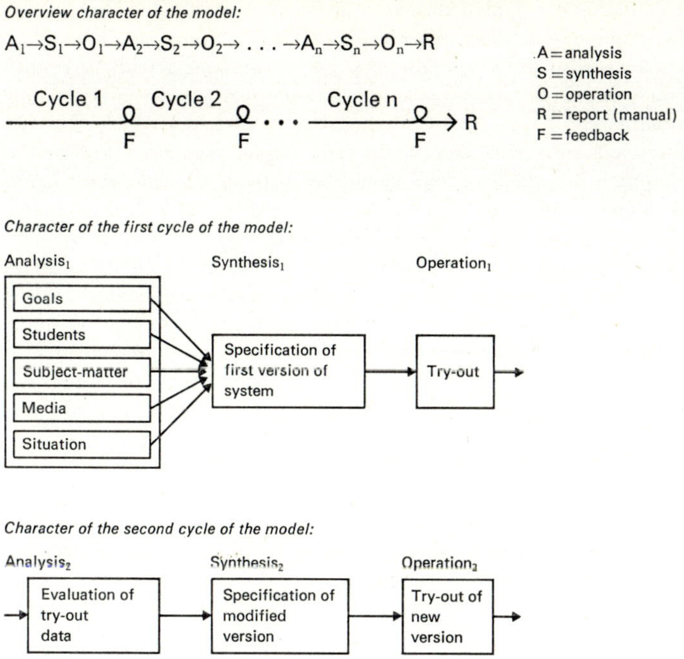

Figure 16.1 A general model for the development of instructional systems

(d) *The examination and try-out processes* should be given in outline.

(C) *The structural characteristics of the program*

should be briefly described and illustrated with extracts from the program. It is possible that in time a standard set of descriptive categories may be used as a basis for such a description. Fry (1963, p. 199 ff.) exemplifies a series of possible bases for classification. Some of those it would be of interest to give are:

(a) *sequence characteristics,* including main flow structure,

(b) *general didule characteristics,* and

(c) *special characteristics of the components,* i.e. of stimules, respules and corrules.

(D) *Characteristics of the subject-matter*

It should be stated here to what degree the program concurs with the curricula concerned, and also how far and in what way it differs from already existing textbooks (or programs) in content.

(E) *Program effects*

This is, in a way, the most important category of information. It is here that the intending purchaser of the program is informed of the demonstrated teaching effectiveness of the program and of the conditions under which this empirical demonstration was carried out. In other words, the manual should contain the following information:

(a) *Scope and conditions of the field try-out.* This should be stated in some detail and comprise not only information about the *research sample* (its size, age of students, intelligence, previous knowledge etc.), but also *external circumstances* both as regards the teaching situation (e.g., how time was allotted, possible teacher co-operation) and as regards the test situations.

(b) *The preliminary and final tests* used in the field try-out should be described in the manual and in addition the complete tests should be available from the constructors or the publishers if desired. (Tests are sometimes sold together with self-instructional material. According to "Programs '63", there were then final tests for 46 % of commercially available programs, but preliminary tests for only 14 %. Were the publishers afraid that the tests might show that the student did not need the program in question?)

(c) *The final results of the field try-out* should obviously be clearly stated. It would be an advantage to give this both verbally and in the form of adequate statistics. It should be possible to compare the students' final performance with their previous knowledge, and there should be supplementary information about the amount of study time used. If other aims than simply the learning of subject-matter have been mentioned in the description of the goal of the course, the manual should also give an account of results of the try-out which confirm that these aims have been attained. Otherwise, the manual should clearly state that these points in the general goal description have not yet been confirmed by empirical results, and that therefore the effect of the program as far as they are concerned is, for the time being, hypothetical.

The task of producing a program manual is the responsibility of the program producer and publisher. This can hardly be considered an excessive burden, provided that the program constructor has really developed his program empirically and carried out a proper field-test. Unfortunately, this kind of account is at present supplied with very few of the commercially available programs. This is not just due to an unwillingness to do the extra work involved in preparing the manual. It is mainly because many of these programs have obviously *not* had a thorough try-out in the field, a fact which may well be obscured by a flood of sales-talk about continuing research and delighted students, but which would look bad in print. When, in one enquiry, publishers of programs in the USA were asked about the size of the groups on which the programs had been tried out, over 80 % avoided answering precisely that question! (Cf. "Programs '63", p. xiii.) In an examination of about 700 programs in 1967 at Northeastern University, it was found that only about 30 % were accompanied by any information about field tests. (Cf. Markle, 1968, p. 17.)

Educators and publishers do not yet seem to be sufficiently aware of or willing to accept the new demands for hard data on effectiveness. Susan M. Markle who knows the U.S. programming scene from within makes these comments:

"A more recent bibliography of 'programed' math materials for elementary school showed 4 % claiming empirical testing at all—usually of one trial of the finished product. The situation in this country is, in other words, appalling. Our educators have shown no tendency to be at all selective—quite the opposite. The million-copy seller (English

2600) was never tested. One publisher who had data sold several thousand orders for a program and received two requests for the data. The average educator is not empirically oriented, does not know how to evaluate data, and knows almost nothing about evaluating the conditions under which the data were collected, which would involve knowing about objectives, about good testing practices, and especially the relation between teaching and testing that enables one to conclude that the programer did not simply 'teach the test'—which everyone agrees is a bad thing. Publishers, with rare exceptions such as Wiley and Sons, do not wonder at all. It means absolutely nothing for their sales. In fact, it tends to be in their favor since the materials are cheaper, having been more cheaply produced, and the author expects less in royalties, having invested less of his time in the tedious development process." (Personal communication, 1971.)

So it is important that program consumers are made more aware of the demands they should make, and that they do not hesitate to make them. Bibliographical reviews giving the nature and scope of any try-out should be more widely used and promoted by central school authorities. Publishers who are forced to leave a blank as far as try-out is concerned can scarcely avoid wondering what it will mean for their sales if their competitors can give fuller information. In addition to such survey lists, a standard forum for critical reviewing would be desirable. To take an example from a somewhat different field, one can point to the influence which Buros' "Mental Measurements Yearbooks" have had with their persistent pointing out of lack of reliability and validity checks.

But apart from this, every buyer of a program naturally has the right to demand detailed information from the seller. Advertising generalisations are not much use to the consumer. The Bulletin of the National Association of Secondary School Principals (Belton, 1962) gives examples of a number of questions which a head teacher should put to a program salesman who has no program manual to show. Their tone and general tendency can be seen from the following (considerably shortened and modified) version:

"We thank you for your offer to demonstrate at our school the programmed study courses which your company is at present marketing. Our study material committee will be glad to see you next Monday at 3:30 p.m. Our time, however, is limited, and we should appreciate it if, when you visit us, you would be prepared to answer briefly the following questions about each of the programmed courses you intend to demonstrate:

1. Is there a teacher's manual or guidebook with instructions for using the course?
2. Are the goals stated in detail in a description of the course?
3. Has the course material been produced as a result of a series of try-outs and modifications? If this is the case, where can we find a description of this development work?
4. Who were those responsible for the development and trying out of the course? What are their qualifications?
5. To what extent has the completed course been tried out in the field, and where can we find an account of how the field trial was arranged and the results of it?

6. Which schools or organizations can we ask about their experiences in using the course?
7. Is the course accompanied by a pre-test and a post-test, or can such pre- and post-tests be ordered separately from your company? Where can we find out about the construction and evaluation of these tests?
8. What is the approximate average time taken for a student to complete the whole course?
9. Is the study material available both in book form and for machine presentation? Is the study material consumable, or can it be used again?
10. What is the cost of the material per student hour? Does your company allow a discount for a first purchase to try out the material?

When we have this information, we should be in a better position to decide on purchasing."

If, after receiving such a letter, programs salesmen with deficient programs fail to turn up for the proposed demonstration, no harm will have been done.

17. Assessment and Comparison of Existing Programs

We have previously studied self-instructional material mainly from the point of view of the constructor and how the teaching program is successively re-examined, tried out and modified. Finally, we shall treat the program in its finished state, above all with the following question in mind: How can we decide whether a teaching program fulfils reasonable demands and fits into a certain teaching situation?

This is mainly the program consumer's concern, but the question is also one for the program constructor. It usually turns up when the programming group has reached the point when analysis of pre-requisites has been made, i.e. when one is clear what the goal is and what type of students one will be dealing with. The questions one should ask oneself at this stage (but scarcely before) are: Is there already a program on the market which corresponds to the goal which has been specified and which is aimed at the same group of students? Is there nevertheless sufficient reason for a new program?

(Figure 17.1 shows schematically some factors in the situation about which the programming group has to make a decision.)

In the evaluation of a program, two kinds of judgment have to be made: (1) judgments based on the program's "pheno-characteristics" which can be observed by a visual examination and (2) judgments based on the program's "functional characteristics", i.e. on experience of how the program works in practice.

Questions about "pheno-criteria" in their turn are of two types: (a) Has the *content* of the program just those qualities which make it fit for the teaching purpose in question? (b) Does the *structure* of the program conform with the "theory" of programmed teaching (or with our knowledge of the principles of human learning)?

Obviously, in judging a program, one can easily come to certain conclusions by looking through it oneself. A new program should always be examined as throughly as a new textbook and primarily with regard to its *contents* and *scope*.

On the other hand (as Rothkopf, 1962, among others, has emphasized), one

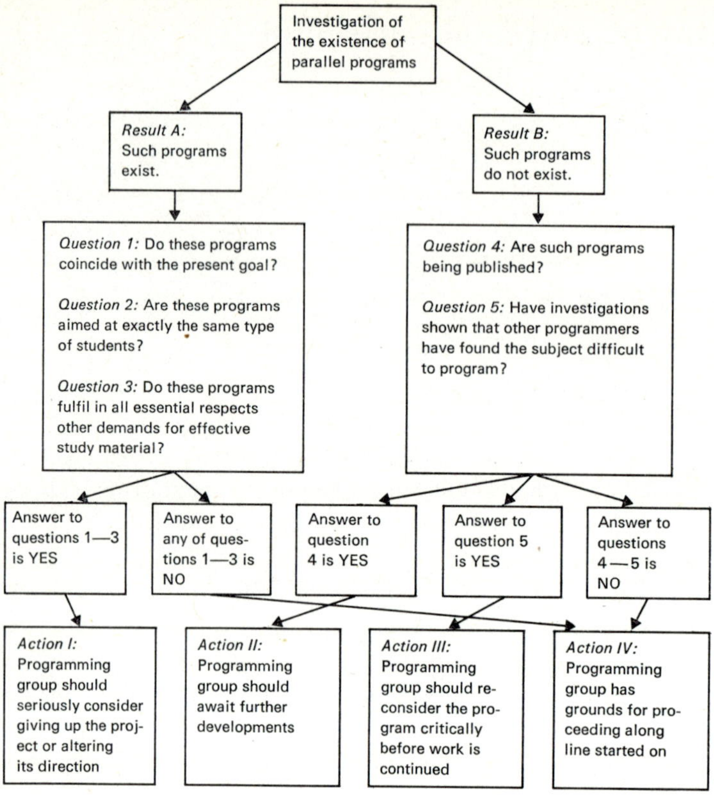

Figure 17.1 Existence of parallel programs: A situation in which a decision must be taken during programming

should beware of the idea that a program can be *adequately* judged merely by a visual examination of its *structural characteristics.* There are several reasons for this. (a) Firstly, there is scarcely a "theory" of what a maximally effective teaching program should look like, reliable enough to enable us to come to any definite conclusions. We have a certain body of general principles, but empirical investigations have given contradictory results on many points of detail. (b) Secondly, even if such principles were relatively clearly established, they cannot be a sufficient basis for an evaluation, since there are a whole series of other factors (e.g. organization of material) which affect effectiveness. (c) Thirdly, even if the principles of programming were both clearly established and could in some way be shown to outweigh all other reasons for variation, a visual examination would still give insufficient information about the value of a program, for the simple reason that many of these principles cannot be directly observed. A low percentage of error is an example of a programming variable which can only be determined by empirical methods. (The expert in a subject often guesses wrongly about this. Precisely because of his expert knowledge, he considers the steps to be extremely "small" and consequently estimates the percentage of error as "lower" than empirical methods show it to be.)

Instead of discussing whether the teaching material conforms to certain programming principles, the experiment has been made of getting experienced teachers to judge its probable effectiveness. One must, however, allow for the fact that, because of lack of training in judging these new types of material, they can go seriously astray. In one study (Rothkopf, 1963) the results even showed a negative correlation (– 0.75) between teacher-estimated and real effectiveness!

To sum up, we can say, then, that while a visual examination is always of interest, it must not be the *only* basis for the consumer's evaluation of a teaching program. He must rely primarily upon how the program has been shown to work in practice, not upon what it looks like. Possibly, in the future, we shall know so much more about the factors which produce an effective program that we shall not always need to proceed via empirical demonstration. But in the present state of programming technique this is the only reliable way.

When the consumer wishes to examine a program thoroughly, both visually and by studying the information given in the manual, it is advisable to use some form of *check-list*. This makes the task easier and also avoids a one-sided examination. The contents of the list can vary according to the needs of the particular teaching situation. We shall now give examples—partly based on American checklists for selecting programs—of questions one often finds it necessary to put (cf. AERA-APA-DAVI Joint Committee, 1963, 1966; see also e.g. Cox et al., 1962; Standards Committee of the NSPI, 1963; Tracey, 1963; Wark, 1963; and Vanderschmidt, 1964). The questions are so formulated that the answer "yes" usually gives the better alternative. In other words, a large number of positive answers is a better indication than few positive answers. However, some questions are obviously more important than others. These must naturally be given the greatest weight in drawing the final conclusion.

1. *Goal and curriculum:*

1.1. Does the publisher or constructor give a clearly formulated description (in the form of observable behavior changes) of what the course is intended to teach?

1.2. Does a visual examination show that the description of the goal is fully covered by the course?

1.3. Does the goal of the programmed course (as it appears in points 1.1 and 1.2) coincide in all essential respects with the curriculum or general goal for your special teaching situation?

1.4. If there is any divergence, is it of such a character that it is pedagogically advantageous and would therefore be accepted as a meaningful change in the course?

1.5. Is there reliable information about the time taken for the course by students of the type you meet in your teaching situation?

1.6. Will your students be able to get through the course, or as much of it as is desirable, in the time at your disposal?

To sum up: Does the general goal of the course sufficiently coincide with the demands of your teaching situation?

2. *Student characteristics:*

2.1. To get the best out of a course, certain skills and previous knowledge are often needed. Are these "starting requirements" clearly described?

2.2. Is there a pre-test, which can show whether a student has the required skills and knowledge to start the course?

2.3. Do these starting requirements coincide with what you could reasonably expect of a student in your teaching situation?

2.4. Is there a pre-test which will show how much a student already knows of the material the course is intended to teach?

2.5. Is the course material so organized that the student with such previous knowledge can start the course at some other point than the beginning or otherwise go through the material in a way suited to his special qualifications?

To sum up: Does the general design of the course reasonably suit the group of students you are teaching?

3. *Specific instructional effectiveness of the study material:*

3.1. Is there a detailed and reliable report of the field try-out of the material in its finished state on representative groups of students (including pre- and post-tests)?

3.2. Are the results of this field try-out satisfactory?

3.3. Were the conditions in the try-out sufficiently like those of your own teaching situation for you to be able to assume a similar result in your own case?

3.4. Has a test been published with which you can check, by a satisfactory measuring procedure, whether the goal of the course has been achieved?

3.5. Are there grounds for assuming that the knowledge and skills acquired during the course are retained for a reasonable time afterwards (i.e. has the try-out also studied retention after a certain interval, with satisfactory results)?

To sum up: Are there both (a) good grounds for supposing that the study material gives the desired specific results with typical groups of students and (b) the possibility of checking in your own teaching situation (suitable final tests)?

4. *General educational character of study material:*

4.1. Does the material give the student training in desirable study behavior (e.g. does it involve more logical reasoning and induction from experience than copying and formal mechanical working)?

4.2. Does the material give the student sufficient opportunity for varied repetition (as against both insufficient and routine repetition)?

4.3. Does the material give the student sufficient opportunity to integrate his knowledge (e.g. by problems which promote integration, work with supplementary and source material etc.)?

4.4. Is there a teacher's handbook which gives examples of how to integrate the self-instructional material with other teaching methods?

4.5. Are there interim tests built into or accompanying the course which will be a good basis for possible additional help or teaching during the course?

4.6. Are there grounds (as a result of the field try-out or research) for supposing that the material created an interest for the subject?

To sum up: Has the study material such educationally desirable characteristics that, in addition to its specific instructional effect, it also promotes such "fringe benefits" as good study technique, positive attitude to further study etc.?

5. *Economic questions:*

5.1. Is the cost of the complete material, including the necessary accessories such as teaching machines and/or printed forms for answers, covered by available resources?

5.2. Will it be easy for you to attend to the storage and upkeep of the material?

5.3. If an expensive machine is necessary for the presentation of the material, will it be possible for you to use it for other courses?

To sum up: Is the purchase of the course material economically defensible?

In certain cases the consumer may consider it desirable to try out the material himself. This is perfectly legitimate, if the program is thought to fulfil all the consumers's requirements, but has been tried out on a group of students which differs essentially from those for whom the teacher intends to use it. In such a case, it is good strategy to try it out on a smaller group before the program is introduced on a large scale.

References

AERA-APA-DAVI Joint Committee on Programed Instruction and Teaching Machines. Criteria for assessing programed instructional materials. *Audiovisual Instruction,* 1963, *8,* 84—89.

AERA-APA-DAVI Joint Committee on Programmed Instruction and Teaching Machines. Recommendations for reporting the effectiveness of programmed-instruction materials. *NSPI J.,* 1966, *5* (3), 3—9.

Anderson, R. C., Kulhavy, R. W. & Andre, Th. Feedback procedures in programmed instruction. *J. educ. Psychol.,* 1971, *62,* 148—156.

Anschütz, H. Die Verteilung der Begriffe in Lehrprogrammtexten. In: H. Frank (Ed.), *Lehrmaschinen in kybernetischer und pädagogischer Sicht, 3.* Stuttgart: Klett, 1965. Pp. 104—113.

Balson, M. The effect of sequence presentation and operant size on rate and amount of learning. *Progr. Learn. educ. Technol.,* 1971, *8,* 202—205.

Barlow, J. A. Conversational chaining in teaching machine programs. *Psychol. Rep.,* 1960, *7,* 187—193.

Basescu, B. More on multiple-choice frames. *Programed Instruction,* 1962, *2* (1), 3.

Becker, J. L. *A programmed guide to writing auto-instructional programs.* Camden, N. J.: RCA, 1963.

Belton, J. R. Programmed learning—20 questions. *The Bulletin of the National Association of Secondary School Principals,* 1962, *46* (No. 278), 77—78.

Berman, M. L. Simultaneous maximization of speed and accuracy on programmed materials through the use of adjusting conjunctive schedules of reinforcement. *NSPI J.,* 1968, *7* (5), 15—18.

Bjerstedt, Å. *Självinstruerande studiematerial.* Lund: Uniskol, 1963.

Bjerstedt, Å. Mapping the pheno-structure of didactic sequences. *Didakometry* (Malmö: School of Education), No. 1, 1964.

Björkman, M. Inlärningspsykologiska principer i programmerad undervisning — några frågetecken. In: Skolöverstyrelsen, *Utredningar i skolfrågor, 11,* 1963. Pp. 96—105.

Bloom, B. S. (Ed.) *Taxonomy of educational objectives. Handbook I: Cognitive domain.* New York: Longmans, 1956.

Bloom, B. S. Individual differences in school achievement: A vanishing point? (Address, AERA, New York, Febr. 1971.)

Bloom, B. S., Hastings, J. Th. & Madaus, G. F. *Handbook on formative and summative evaluation of student learning.* New York: McGraw-Hill, 1971.

Boeckmann, K. Basaltext und operationale Lernzieldefinition — Eine vergleichende Betrachtung ihre Möglichkeiten. In: B. Rollett & K. Weltner (Eds.), *Fortschritte und Ergebnisse der Unterrichtstechnologie.* München: Ehrenwirth, 1971. Pp. 17—25.

Brown, J. L. Effects of logical and scrambled sequences in mathematical materials on learning with programmed instruction materials. *J. educ. Psychol.,* 1970, *61,* 41—45.

Bushnell, D. D. & Allen, D. W. (Eds.) *The computer in American education.* New York: Wiley, 1967.

Cartmell, A. E. The use of CCTV in the assessment of teacher effectiveness. *Progr. Learn. educ. Technol.,* 1971, *8,* 173—185.

Cavanagh, P. & Jones, C. (Eds.) *Programmes in print 1966.* London: Association for Programmed Learning, 1966.

Cavanagh, P. & Jones, C. (Eds.) *Yearbook of educational and instructional technology 1969/70.* London: Cornmarket, 1969.

Center for Programed Instruction. *Programs, '62. A guide to programed instructional materials available to educators by September 1962.* Washington, D.C.: U.S. Government Printing Office, 1962.

Center for Programed Instruction. *Programs, '63. A guide to programed instructional materials available to educators by September 1963.* Washington, D.C.: U.S. Government Printing Office, 1963.

Center for Programed Instruction. *Programed instruction materials 1964—'65. A guide to programed instruction materials available for use in elementary and secondary schools as of April, 1965.* New York: CPI, Columbia Univer., 1965.

Cook, D. A. Behavior theory and the automation of instruction. In: J. E. Coulson (Ed.), *Programmed learning and computer-based instruction.* New York: Wiley, 1962. Pp. 120—128.

Cox, A. et al. Suggested criteria for selection of programed materials. In: *Summary Report of the Eighth Lake Okoboji Audiovisual Leadership Conference.* Iowa City: State Univ. Iowa, 1962. Pp. 80—88.

Cram, D. *Explaining "teaching machines" and programming.* San Francisco: Fearon, 1961.

Crutchfield, R. S. & Covington, M. V. Programed instruction and creativity. *Programed Instruction,* 1965, *4* (4), 1—10.

Dahllöf, U. *The contents of education with regard to demands for different jobs and for further studies.* (2nd ed., mimeo.) Stockholm: School of Education, 1965.

Davies, I. K. Some aspects of measurement in educational technology. In: A. P. Mann & C. K. Brunstrom (Eds.), *Aspects of educational technology, Vol. 3.* London: Pitman, 1969. Pp. 50—56.

Deterline, W. A. et al. Programmed instruction today. *Educational Technology,* 1970, *10* (7), 29—47.

Deutsch, W. Programed learning: An overview of personnel and financial requirements. In: S. Margulies & L. D. Eigen (Eds.), *Applied programed instruction.* New York: Wiley, 1962. Pp. 208—211.

Eigen, L. D. & Margulies, S. Response characteristics as a function of information level. *Journal of programed Instruction,* 1963, *2* (1), 45—54.

Espich, J. E. & Williams, B. *Developing programmed instructional materials.* Palo Alto, Calif.: Fearon, 1967.

Evans, J. L., Glaser, R. & Homme, L. E. An investigation of "teaching machine" variables using learning programs in symbolic logic. *J. educ. Res.,* 1962, *55,* 433—452.

Evans, J. L., Homme, L. E. & Glaser, R. The Ruleg system for the construction of programmed verbal learning sequences. *J. educ. Res.,* 1962, *55,* 513—518.

Flechsig, K.-H. et al. Probleme der Entscheidung über Lernziele. *Programmiertes Lernen,* 1970, *7,* 1—32.

Fry, E. B. *Teaching machines and programmed instruction.* New York: McGraw-Hill,

1963.
Gagné, R. M. *The conditions of learning*. New York: Holt, 1965. (2nd ed., 1970.)
Gagné, R. M. Relations of learned capabilities to instructional objectives. (Paper read at the XVIIth International Congress of Applied Psychology, Liège, 1971.)
Geis, G. L. Some considerations in the evaluation of programs. *AV Communication Review,* 1962, *10,* 64—69.
Gensch, G. Konzeption und Weiterentwicklung des Gruppenlehrautomaten. In: B. Rollett & K. Weltner (Eds.), *Fortschritte und Ergebnisse der Unterrichtstechnologie.* München: Ehrenwirth, 1971. Pp. 255—259.
Gerlach, V. S. Empirische Methoden der Lehrzielfeststellung. In: B. Rollett & K. Weltner (Eds.), *Fortschritte und Ergebnisse der Unterrichtstechnologie.* München: Ehrenwirth, 1971. Pp. 39—45.
Gestrelius, K. *Utbildningsplanering med befattningsanalytiska metoder.* Lund: Uniskol, 1970.
Gestrelius, K. Lärarutbildares arbetsuppgifter, Del I—II. *Pedagogisk-psykologiska problem* (Malmö: School of Education), Nos. 151—152, 1971.
Gilbert, Th. F. *Mathetics: An explicit theory for the design of teaching programmes.* (Rev. educ. Cybernetics & appl. Linguistics, Supplement 1.) London: Longmac, 1969.
Glaser, R. Some research problems in automated instruction. In: J. E. Coulson (Ed.), *Programmed learning and computer-based instruction.* New York: Wiley, 1962. Pp. 67—85.
Glaser, R. Instructional technology and the measurement of learning outcomes: Some questions. *Amer. Psychologist,* 1963, *18,* 519—521.
Gordon, J. M. The evaluative response: A rate problem. *AID,* 1963, *3,* 240.
Grace, H. A. Programming and readability. *Calif. J. educ. Res.,* 1963, *14,* 164—166.
Greenberg, M. Conversational chaining in programmed instruction. *Progr. Learn. educ. Technol.,* 1968, *5,* 115—121.
Guilford, J. P. A system of psychomotor abilities. *Amer. J. Psychol.,* 1958, *71,* 164—174.
Holland, J. G. & Porter, D. The influence of repetition of incorrectly answered items in a teaching-machine program. *Journal of the experimental Analysis of Behavior,* 1961, *4,* 305—307.
Horn, R. E. et al. *Information mapping for learning and reference.* Cambridge, Mass.: Information Resources, 1969.
Hughes, J. L. *Programed instruction for schools and industry.* Chicago: Science Research Associates, 1962.
Husén, T. & Dahllöf, U. *Mathematics and communication skills in school and society.* Stockholm: The Industrial Council for Social and Economic Studies, 1960.
Härnqvist, K. & Grahm, Å. *Vägen genom gymnasiet.* Stockholm: SOU, 1963.
Jacobs, P. I. Item difficulty and programed learning. *Journal of programed Instruction,* 1963, *2* (2), 21—38.
Jenkins, J. R. & Deno, S. L. A model for instructional objectives. *Educational Technology,* 1970, *10* (12), 11—16.
Jivén, L. M. & Öreberg, C. The IMU Project. *Didakometry* (Malmö: School of Education), No. 22, 1968.
Klaus, D. J. & Lumsdaine, A. A. Some economic realities of teaching machine instruction. In: S. Margulies & L. D. Eigen (Eds.), *Applied programed instruction.* New York: Wiley, 1962. Pp. 198—207.
Klingberg, G. A scheme for the classification of educational objectives. *Res. Bull., Dept. Educ. Res., Gothenburg School of Educ.,* No. 5, 1970.
Kopstein, F. F. & Cave, R. T. *Preliminary cost comparison of technical training by*

conventional and programmed learning methods. Wright-Patterson Air Force Base, Ohio: MRL, 1962.

Krathwohl, D. R., Bloom, B. S. & Masia, B. B. *Taxonomy of educational objectives. Handbook II: Affective domain.* New York: McKay, 1964.

Lahn, W. Ein Beitrag zum didaktischen Programmieren: Das Entwickeln der Programmstruktur aus einer Analyse des Lehrgegenstandes durch ein Satzgerüst in Folgesatzen. *Progr. Lernen, Unterrichtstechnol. u. Unterrichtsforschung,* 1971, *8,* 65—81.

Landa, L. N. Algorithms and programmed learning. In: K. Bung (Ed.), *Programmed learning and the language laboratory,* 1. London: Longmac, 1968. Pp. 57—135.

Landa, L. N. *Algorithmierung im Unterricht.* (Transl. fr. Russian). Berlin: Volk u. Wissen, 1969. (a)

Landa, L. N. The construction of algorithmic and heuristic models of thinking activity and some problems in programmed learning. In: W. R. Dunn & C. Holroyd (Eds.), *Aspects of educational technology, Vol. 2.* London: Methuen, 1969. Pp. 133—141. (b)

Larsson, I. Tyska språket i delar av svenskt näringsliv: En studie i enkätmetodik och en undersökning av språkbehoven. *Pedagogisk-psykologiska problem* (Malmö: School of Education), No. 101, 1969.

Leedham, J. & Unwin, D. *Programmed learning in schools.* London: Longmans, 1965.

Lehnert, U. (Ed.) *Elektronische Datenverarbeitung in Schule und Ausbildung.* München: Oldenbourg, 1970.

Leith, G. O. M. et al. *A handbook of programmed learning.* (2nd ed.) Birmingham, England: University of Birmingham, 1966.

Leith, G. O. M. *Second thoughts on programmed learning.* London: National Council for Educational Technology, 1969.

Lewis, B. N. & Pask, G. The theory and practice of adaptive teaching systems. In: R. Glaser (Ed.), *Teaching machines and programed learning, II.* Washington, D.C.: NEA, 1965. Pp. 213—266.

Lewis, D. G. & Whitwell, M. N. The effects of reinforcement and response upon programmed learning in mathematics. *Progr. Learn. educ. Technol.,* 1971, *8,* 186—195.

Lindell, E. A system of study materials for the teaching of foreign languages: Principles and examples. *Didakometry & Sociometry,* 1969, *1,* 91—124.

Lindsten, C. Elevpreferenser vid stoffval i hembygdskunskap, årskurs 3. *Pedagogisk-psykologiska problem* (Malmö: School of Education), No. 95, 1969.

Lindvall, C. M. & Bolvin, J. O. Programed instruction in the schools: An application of programing principles in "Individually Prescribed Instruction". In: Ph. C. Lange (Ed.), *Programed instruction.* (NSSE Yearbook LXVI, Part II.) Chicago: Univer. Chicago Pr., 1967. Pp. 217—254.

Little, J. K. Results of use of machines for testing and for drill upon learning in educational psychology. *J. exp. Educ.,* 1934, *3,* 45—49.

Lublin, S. C. Reinforcement schedules, scholastic aptitude, autonomy need, and achievement in a programmed instruction course. *J. educ. Psychol.,* 1965, *56,* 295—302.

Löfqvist, G. Analys av officiella texter för bestämning av kraven på ämneslärarbefattningen. *Pedagogisk-psykologiska problem* (Malmö: School of Education), No. 103, 1969.

Löfqvist, G. Läroplanerna för grundskolan 1962 och 1969. *Pedagogisk-psykologiska problem* (Malmö: School of Education), No. 136, 1971.

Mager, R. F. *Preparing objectives for programmed instruction.* San Francisco: Fearon, 1961.

Mager, R. F. Deriving objectives for the high school curriculum. *NSPI J.,* 1968, *7* (3), 7—22.

Mager, R. F. & Clark, C. Explorations in student-controlled instruction. In: G. D. Ofiesh & W. C. Meierhenry (Eds.), *Trends in programmed instruction.* Washington, D.C.: NEA, 1964. Pp. 235—238.

Markle, S. M. *A programed primer on programing. Vol. II. Practical problems.* New York: Center for Programed Instruction, 1961.

Markle, S. M. Faulty branching frames: A model for maximizing feedback to the programer. *Programed Instruction,* 1963, *3* (1), 4—8.

Markle, S. M. Five answers in search of the right questions: The bibliographies of programed instruction. *NSPI J.,* 1968, *7* (3), 15—21.

Markle, S. M. *Good frames and bad.* (2nd ed.) New York: Wiley, 1969.

Markle, S. M. et al. *A programed primer on programing. Vol. I. Principles.* New York: Center for Programed Instruction, 1961.

Markle, S. M. & Tiemann, Ph. W. Problems of conceptual learning. *Journal of educational Technology,* 1970, *1,* 52—62.

Marton, F. Evaluering av evalueringar. *Rapporter från Pedag. inst., Göteborgs univer.,* No. 42, 1969.

Niedermeyer, F. C. The relevance of frame sequence in programmed instruction. *AV Communication Review,* 1968, *16,* 301—317.

Noble, G. What instructional skills can intrinsic programmed instruction teach, with and without teacher implementation? In: A. P. Mann & C. K. Brunstrom (Eds.), *Aspects of educational technology, Vol. 3.* London: Pitman, 1969. Pp. 78—84.

O'Day, E. F. et al. *Programmed instruction: Techniques and trends.* New York: Appleton-Century-Crofts, 1971.

Payne, D. A. *The specification and measurement of learning outcomes.* Waltham, Mass.: Blaisdell, 1968.

Payne, D. A., Krathwohl, D. R. & Gordon, J. The effect of sequence on programmed instruction. *Amer. educ. Res. J.,* 1967, *4,* 125—132.

Pennington, D. F. & Slack, C. W. The mathetical design of effective lessons. In: S. Margulies & L. D. Eigen (Eds.), *Applied programed instruction.* New York: Wiley, 1962. Pp. 298—310.

Pierleoni, R. G. & Lysaught J. P. A decision ladder for predicting programmer success. *NSPI J.,* 1970, *9* (5), 6—18.

Pikas, A. Dimensions for developing beyond expository tasks: Planning for greater transfer and increased pupil-teacher interaction in educational technology. (Paper based on a contr. to Symposium on Educational Technology. XVIIth Int. Congress of Applied Psychology, Liège.) Manuscript, 1971.

Popham, W. J. et al. *Instructional objectives.* Chicago: Rand McNally, 1969.

Porter, D. Some effects of year-long teaching machine instruction. In: E. Galanter (Ed.), *Automatic teaching: The state of the art.* New York: Wiley, 1959. Pp. 85—90.

Randell, G. A. 'Adaptive' teaching machines. In: *Programmierter Unterricht und Lehrmaschinen.* Berlin: Pädag. Zentrum, 1964. Pp. 111—117.

Richter, H. Lehrautomaten — Beispiele und Entwicklungstendenzen. In: B. Rollett & K. Weltner (Eds.), *Fortschritte und Ergebnisse der Unterrichtstechnologie.* München: Ehrenwirth, 1971. Pp. 173—192.

Roe, A. Automated teaching methods using linear programs. *J. appl. Psychol.,* 1962, *46,* 198—201.

Rothkopf, E. Z. Criteria for the acceptance of self-instructional programs. In: A. E. Traxler (Ed.), *Improving the efficiency and quality of learning.* Washington, D.C.: Amer. Council on Educ., 1962. Pp. 30—38.

Rothkopf, E. Z. Some observations on predicting instructional effectiveness by simple

inspection. *Journal of programed Instruction.* 1963, *2* (2), 19—20.
Sassenrath, J. M. & Yonge, G. D. Effects of delayed information feedback and feedback cues in learning on delayed retention. *J. educ. Psychol.,* 1969, *60,* 174—177.
Schaefer, H. H. A vocabulary program using "language redundancy". *Journal of programed Instruction,* 1963, *2* (3), 9—16.
Schröter, G. Das zweistufige Programm als integrierender Übergang vom linearen zum verzweigten System. In: B. Rollett (Ed.), *Praxis und Theorie des programmierten Unterrichtes.* Stuttgart: Klett, 1970. Pp. 32—36.
Shay, C. B. Relationship of intelligence to step size on a teaching machine program. *J. educ. Psychol.,* 1961, *52,* 98—103.
Shettel, H. H. & Lindley, R. H. *An experimental comparison of two types of self-instructional programs.* Pittsburgh: AIR, 1961.
Silberman, H. F. et al. Fixed sequence versus branching auto-instructional methods. *J. educ. Psychol.,* 1961, *52,* 166—172.
Skinner, B. F. The science of learning and the art of teaching. *Harvard educ. Rev.,* 1954, *24,* 86—97.
Skinner, B. F. Reflections on a decade of teaching machines. In: R. Glaser (Ed.), *Teaching machines and programed learning, II.* Washington, D.C.: NEA, 1965. Pp. 5—20.
Sorenson, A. G. The use of teaching machines in developing an alternative to the concept of intelligence. *Educ. psychol. Measmt,* 1963, *23,* 323—329.
Standards Committee of the NSPI. Checklist for selecting programs. *NSPI J.,* 1963, 2 (6), 4.
Stolurow, L. M. Application of psychology to educational technology. (Paper read at the XVIIth Int. Congress of Applied Psychology, Liège, 1971.)
Stolurow, L. M. & Davis, D. Teaching machines and computer-based systems. In: R. Glaser (Ed.), *Teaching machines and programed learning, II.* Washington, D.C.: NEA, 1965. Pp. 162—212.
Swets, J. A. & Feurzeig, W. Computer-aided instruction. *Science,* 1965, *150,* 572—576.
Tennyson, R. D. & Boutwell, R. C. A quality control design for validating hierarchical sequencing of programmed instruction. *NSPI J.,* 1971, *10* (4), 5—10.
Tennyson, R. D. & Merrill, M. D. Hierarchical models in the development of a theory of instruction: A comparison of Bloom, Gagné, and Merrill. *Educational Technology,* 1971, *11* (9), 27—31.
Thiagarajan, S. et al. The design and development of grouprograms. *NSPI J.,* 1970, *9* (4), 5—18.
Thomas, C. A. et al. *Programmed learning in perspective.* Barking, Essex: Adelphi, 1963.
Thorndike, E. L. *Education.* New York: Macmillan, 1912.
Tickton, S. G. (Ed.) *To improve learning. An evaluation of instructional technology. Vol. I.* New York: Bowker, 1970.
Tingsten, H. *Gud och fosterlandet. Studier i hundra års skolpropaganda.* Stockholm: Norstedt, 1969.
Tracey, W. K. Content and construction review. *NSPI J.,* 1963, *2* (10), 13—14.
Travers, R. M. W., Van Wagenen, R. K., Haygood, D. H. & McCormick, M. Learning as a consequence of the learner's task involvement under different conditions of feedback. *J. educ. Psychol.,* 1964, *55,* 167—173.
Trittipoe, W. J., Trittipoe, T. G. & Hahn, C. P. The effectiveness of three programed-learning frame styles. *Journal of programed Instruction,* 1963, *2* (1), 35—43.
Vanderschmidt, H. Validation data for programmed texts: A checklist for evaluation of testing. In: G. D. Ofiesh & W. C. Meierhenry (Eds.), *Trends in programmed instruc-*

tion. Washington, D.C.: NEA, 1964. Pp. 210—212.

von Voigt, H. Strukturanalytische Diagramme — ihre Möglichkeiten und Grenzen bei der Erstellung und Beurteilung von Lehrprogrammen. In: B. Rollett (Ed.), *Praxis und Theorie des programmierten Unterrichtes*. Stuttgart: Klett, 1970. Pp. 43—47.

Wark, D. et al. Checklist comments and criticism. *NSPI Newsletter,* 1963, *2* (1), 7—8.

Weltner, K. Der Shannonsche Ratetest in der Praxis der programmierten Instruktion. In: H. Frank (Ed.), *Lehrmaschinen in kybernetischer und pädagogischer Sicht, 4*. Stuttgart: Klett, 1966. Pp. 40—53.

Weltner, K. *Informationstheorie und Erziehungswissenschaft*. Quickborn: Schnelle, 1970. (a)

Weltner, K. Video-Trainer. In: B. Rollett (Ed.), *Praxis und Theorie des programmierten Unterrichtes*. Stuttgart: Klett, 1970. Pp. 41—42. (b)

Weltner, K. Lernziele unter dem Aspekt der Informationstheorie. In: B. Rollett & K. Weltner (Eds.), *Fortschritte und Ergebnisse der Unterrichtstechnologie*. München: Ehrenwirth, 1971. Pp. 26—35.

Weltner, K., Heinrich, P.-B. & Heinze, N. Über den Zusammenhang der verschiedenen Verfahren zur Messung der subjektiven Information. In: B. Rollett & K. Weltner (Eds.), *Fortschritte und Ergebnisse der Unterrichtstechnologie*. München: Ehrenwirth, 1971. Pp. 288—293.

Wheatley, R. A. Measurement in programmed learning experiments—Problems encountered and some possible solutions. In: A. P. Mann & C. K. Brunstrom (Eds.), *Aspects of educational technology, Vol. 3*. London: Pitman, 1969. Pp. 115—120.

Zielke, W. *Programmierte Instruktion in der Wirtschaft*. München: Verlag Moderne Industrie, 1970.

Zielke, W. Stichwortschaubild und Faktenanalyse als Hilfsmittel rationellerer Lernprogrammerstellung. In: B. Rollett & K. Weltner (Eds.), *Fortschritte und Ergebnisse der Unterrichtstechnologie*. München: Ehrenwirth, 1971. Pp. 75—86.

Zifreund, W. Ein strukturanalytisches Diagramm als Hilfsmittel bei der Herstellung und kritischen Analyse von Lehrprogrammen. In: H. Frank (Ed.), *Lehrmaschinen in kybernetischer und pädagogischer Sicht, 3*. Stuttgart: Klett, 1965. Pp. 114—135.

Öreberg, C. Material för individualiserad matematikundervisning. *Pedagogiska Meddelanden,* 1966, *3* (7), 23—28.

Öreberg, C. et al. IMU-projektet: Målbeskrivning för ett självinstruerande studiematerial i matematik för grundskolans högstadium. *Pedagogisk-psykologiska problem* (Malmö: School of Education), No. 43, 1966.

Appendix

Appendix 1

The Terminology of Programmed Instruction and Educational Technology: A Selective List

Some terms within the area of educational technology and programmed instruction are listed with brief definitions. Naturally, complete coverage is not aimed at. Instead, some attempt has been made to include the major terms used in the present survey together with a small sample of frequent words from similar contexts.

Adaptive instructional system An instructional system which can adjust itself to varying student behavior by, for example, giving simpler tasks if the student has not been successful, and more difficult tasks when the student *is* successful.

Algorithm General and non-ambiguous prescription for solving problems within a specific problem area. Part of the subject-matter analysis (as one step in the pre-writing phase when constructing self-instructional study material) may be focused upon the questions: to what extent is it possible to formulate algorithms for the subject-area involved, and to what extent can and should these influence the instructional sequence and method?—The concepts "algorithm for teaching" and "teaching of algorithms" should be distinguished, however. A teaching algorithm is a controlled program for interaction between educator and educand. (In a sense, then, programmed instruction in general presupposes the existence of teaching algorithms, but it does not necessarily demand that algorithms are taught to the students. In other words, a teaching algorithm may be aimed either at the teaching of an algorithm or at the teaching of non-algorithmic processes. Cf. discussion in Landa, 1968.)

Amplified T-tabulation A "T-tabulation" (see that term) to which, besides the usual data from the goal analysis, has been added a list of items of information about the target population with point of departure from the student analysis. Reports on the special preliminary knowledge and existing skills of the students have then been added, as well as possibly a judgment as to how the ordinary occupation of the students *after* their specific educational training can affect the results of the instructional program in the long run. An influence of this kind can naturally be both a support and a hindrance; hence, an appraisement in this respect can modify the programmer's treatment of the question of repetition and overlearning. (For illustration, see chapter 6 above.)

Anschütz diagram A diagrammatic method (developed by H. Anschütz) for the evaluation and comparison of instructional programs, utilizing an examination of the distribution of concepts over the instructional micro-units. (For details, see Anschütz,

1965.)

Branching model A course layout which makes it possible for different categories of students (for example, students with different preparatory knowledge) to take separate paths through the study material.

C-catalogue A collection of fundamental concepts (C) in a certain subject area. Systematizing these logical "basic units" within a hierarchial system results in a "*structured C-catalogue*". (A card file with the separate units on separate cards is often a practical set-up for such a catalogue.)

C.C-catalogue (or "C×C-catalogue") A collection of instructionally interesting relationships between the logical "basic units" (C) within a certain subject area. A catalogue of this type (which in concrete form is ordinarily set up as a card file) can be made up with the help of a "C-matrix" (see that word).

Chain model ("*conversational chaining*") A course layout in which the individual instructional units are linked together in such a way that the feedback component of the preceding instructional unit is incorporated as a part of the stimule component of the following unit. In other words, the key answer is not given a separate presentation, but is embedded in the next unit, ordinarily as one or more words printed in italics.

C-matrix An aid in mapping the instructionally interesting relationships between various fundamental concepts within a certain subject area. In principle it consists of a square-ruled diagram, the row and column headings of which are the key words for the various "basic units" in the C-catalogue, and every cell in the matrix is thought to symbolize all possible relationships between two such units. The constructor can, for example, go through the matrix cell by cell and ask himself questions of this type: What connection is there between these two concepts, and is this connection such that it can and should be used pedagogically? (For illustration, see chapter 7 above.)

Computer-assisted instruction Usually a special case of programmed instruction, viz., the case when a computer handles information storage, registerering, response comparison and feedback, during a highly individualized instructional program.

Conjunctive schedule A conjunctive schedule of reinforcement is a schedule in which two criteria must be met to receive reinforcement. For example, the subject has to complete a specific item sequence (including, say, 60 responses) within 6 minutes or less and make 2 errors or less to receive reinforcement (cf. Berman, 1968).

Correlative stimuli Information, instructions and evaluations, which in an instructional situation are presented in close connection with the principal points of the content but are not themselves meant to be learned. When these correlative stimuli have the chief function of facilitating the learning of certain other items, they can be called "prompts". (Compare "Focal informative stimuli".)

Corrule See "Didule".

Crowder model A course layout which combines a *branched flow-model* (in which the student's working path is successively determined by his accomplishments) with use of *multiple-choice responses.* The model has been realized partly in book form (see the term "Scrambled book"), partly in the form of mechanical presentation (e.g. Auto-Tutor, Mark II). Crowder's most frequent use of the branching technique seems to be for explanation of an error just made.

Density of information A measure of the effective communication of information ("reduction of uncertainty" for the student; compare this word) in relation to some quantitative characteristic of the study material, e.g., the number of instructional units. For example, the fewer "didules" (see that word) which are used to present a certain amount of information to the student, the greater the density of information can be said to be.

Didactogram A diagram (used during the empirical testing of instructional programs) showing one or several students' progress through a programmed study material. As background pattern for the didactogram, the previously worked out "didactoplan" may sometimes be used (see word "Didactoplan"), after the necessary revisions and specifications have been incorporated. On such a pattern (showing the basic structure of the study material) are presented the behavior data: in part, information as to the study routes used; in part, information as to right and wrong performances. (For illustrations, see chapter 14 above; especially Figures 14.4 and 14.5.)

Didactoplan A graphic visualization (mainly made use of during the pre-writing phase) of the internal order in which one plans to bring up different subject-matter units (e.g., concepts) in the auto-instructional study material. By the use of special symbols, it can be shown on the chart which points in the material will be gone through by all, and which will be presented only to certain students.

Didule The fundamental instructional unit in programmed study material, ordinarily consisting of three components: the "stimule" (the information component), the "respule" (the response request), and the "corrule" (the feedback component). The didule can be said to represent the contribution of the program to the fundamental unit of interaction between the pupil and the program.—The didule is an *instructional unit* in programmed study material, that is, it is *not* identical with a *presentation unit.* (The most nearly equivalent term "frame" has the disadvantage of being used both for the concept 'instructional unit' and for the concept 'presentation unit'.)

Didule protocol An aid in the examination of an instructional program. The protocol consists of a chart in which each separate didule has a matching review column and the different review points are entered as row headings. (For illustrations, see chapter 12 above, especially Figures 12.2—12.5.)

Educand The individual who is subjected to educational influence (instruction, attitudinal influence etc.). The "receiving" component in an educational process. In school, "educand" = "student", but "educand" is a more general term.

Educator Someone or something which causes educational influence (instruction, attitudinal influence etc.). The "sending" component in an educational process. In school, "educator" often = "teacher", but "educator" is sometimes used in a more general sense, referring also to non-personal sources of influence (self-instructional materials-and-methods systems etc.).

Egrul See "Ruleg".

Error rate The percentage of incorrect responses on a single instructional unit or a set of such units when tested on a group of students. Low error rate during work on programs has often been considered desirable, but can also be obtained by non-desirable design (such as overprompting) and cannot therefore be used as an evaluation criterion by itself.

Fading Successive diminishing of the number of elements in a stimulus complex. In programmed teaching the term is used in two contexts: (1) = Successive cutting down of prompts (so that the student gradually can give a correct answer without help, while he was able to give the correct answer in the beginning only with the help of certain clues; "fading of correlative stimuli").—(2) = Successive disconnecting of separate parts of a larger stimulus complex, which is meant to be learned as a whole ("fading of focal stimuli"). Example: The student learns a poem by repeated recitations. As a support for his memory he has a text for use in recital, which successively is cut down as words and sentences are deleted.—For meaning (2) the term "vanishing" is sometimes used.

Feedback technique The interplay between the student and the study material, which tells the student how far he has succeeded with each separate task. Ordinarily the feedback takes the form of a key answer presentation, but simple information as to whether the student response was right or wrong, or more detailed error explanations occur in some arrangements. It is typical of programmed instruction that feedback is almost immediate and very frequent.

Filter didule A unit in the study material which informs us as to the best possible working track (branch) for the individual student. Depending on what the more specific purpose is, we can speak of "pre-controlling" or "post-controlling" didules (see these words).

Focal informative stimuli The main points in the content which in an instructional situation are presented to a student to be "learned" (compare "Correlative stimuli").

Formal prompts Stimuli, which provide knowledge about the form of the expected response and thereby make it easier for the student to give the correct answer. The student can, for example, be allowed to see the first letter of the correct answer word or to know how many letters are in the word. (Since overuse of this type of clue technique *can* promote thoughtless answering with an inadequate direction of attention, it should as a rule be used sparingly.)

Goal adjustment Successive changes of earlier goal descriptions guided by empirical controls of the realism of the goal level (in concrete cases where the initial behavioral repertoire of the target group and certain resources are defined). Is sometimes considered to be the final phase of a complete goal-analytic process (cf. "Goal seeking" and "Goal focusing").

Goal analysis Analysis of instructional objectives. A careful and detailed review of what knowledge and skills the students should be able to display after going through a certain study material. (Compare "Terminal behavior repertoire".) Sub-components: "goal seeking", "goal focusing", and "goal adjustment".

Goal focusing Decisions about and formulation of the specific components of a goal description. "Goal focusing" can often be regarded as an intermediate link between "goal seeking" and "goal adjustment" in a total goal-analytic procedure.

Goal-related assessment See "Norm-related assessment".

Goal seeking Collecting of data as a basis for goal decisions and goal formulation. Normally, the goal seeking should involve empirical data collections, be as many-sided as possible, and also give starting-points for priority ranking among various sub-goals.

Horizontal panel-book A programmed textbook in which the pages are divided into panels which are not read in the usual reading sequence (from top to bottom) but from page to page (or from sheet to sheet). The student reads, in other words, the top part of the pages through the whole book (or a large part of the book) before he goes over to another section of the same pages. The key answer for a given task does not usually appear in the same section or on the same page, but separately on the back of the section or in connection with the next information unit.

Integrator A teaching aid which offers the student a constantly *alternating* sequence of (a) *presentation* of material and (b) the possibility of response *reaction*. Programmed textbooks and teaching machines are typical examples. An integrator, through this double function, is different from the much more usual aids in conventional teaching, which *either* have just the function of "presenting" *or* only give the student an opportunity for a response reaction. The term "*presenter*" describes an aid in teaching, the chief task of which is to present to the student a stimulus-sequence prepared in advance (an ordinary textbook or educational film would be typical examples). The term "*reactor*", on the other hand, refers to a teaching aid, the chief function of which is to offer the student opportunities to give response reactions. (Example: Question lists.)

Intermittent model A layout of the auto-instructional material which demands a fairly independent treatment of the material by the student. He is presented with a "guide-book" containing a detailed study plan and self-correcting part tests, but the main material is collected by the student from different sources outside the guide-book. If the result of a test is good, the student is directed to new material. If it is not good, he is sent back to the same source (or one parallel to it). This shifting between instructions, independent study, and diagnostic review tests places the intermittent model somewhere between a completely programmed course and Pressey's "tail model" (see that word).

Iteration model A course layout in which the student always goes through the various instructional micro-units in a pre-established order, the same for all students, but where he is directed to repeat single units (or groups of units) under certain achievement conditions.

Linear model A course layout with the same task sequence for all students.

Mathetics A systematic approach to the analysis of instructional components and the construction of instructional units and sequences, devised by T. Gilbert.

Micro-branching model A "branching model" in which a certain amount of student differentiation may take place *within* the separate instructional unit (e.g., different error explanation), while these units as a whole are taken in the same order by all students. Most scrambled books, for instance, are of this type. (See "Branching model" and "Scrambled books".)

Multiple success strategy An attempt to create a dual motivation (possibly for different categories of students simultaneously). This can mean, for example, that on the one hand the student works through the study material with a high probability of getting the correct answer to separate tasks ("sure winner"), while on the other hand he is offered "extra success possibilities" (for example, possibilities for fast-track procedure and/or the satisfaction of answering correctly without clues, "individualized clue feeding").

Norm-related assessment An assessment of the instructional result in which the single student's result is related to information about other students' results. (For example: "On this test, student A has obtained a result which places him in the best 25 % of group G.") In contrast, "goal-related assessments" relate the instructional result to a specific series of goal descriptions. (For example: "Out of the items of this test, designed to cover all relevant goal descriptions, student B has mastered 80 %.")

Objective A statement describing the behavior the student is expected to acquire from a course.

Parallel track arrangement A branching model (see that word) which allows two or more separate categories of students to go through differently designed study plans with the same final goal. The same principle or group of problems can, for example, be treated from various points of view, depending on the varying preliminary attitudes of the different students.

Passage criterion The lowest possible point which the student can be allowed to reach with reference to a certain terminal behavior. In goal analysis it is important to fix specific values of this kind, as soon as we are dealing with a continuum of skill within a certain area of behavior. Without a clearly defined "minimum for acceptability" it is impossible to judge how well the goal set by the course has been reached. The passage criteria can suitably be included in the "T-tabulations". (Compare "Goal analysis", "Terminal behavior", and "T-tabulation".)

Post-controlling didule A unit in the study material which attempts to ascertain whether the student has learned carefully enough what has just been studied. If his responses show that this is not the case, the student is directed back to a section which has already been gone through or to an alternative repeat section (with similar, although not identical content).

Pre-controlling didule A unit in the study material with which an attempt is made to determine whether the student has sufficient preparatory knowledge to be able to skip a certain section of the course.

Presenter See "Integrator".

Programming Construction of auto-instructional study-material according to a three-phase procedure consisting of (a) preparatory work ("pre-writing" phase) with, among other things, emphasis on goal analysis and subject-matter analysis, (b) composition of a preliminary version utilizing certain psychological principles of learning and (c) a "post-writing phase", including successive empirical try-outs and revisions in the preliminary versions until the goal determined in advance has been reached.

Prompt Some stimulus added to the terminal stimulus to make a correct response more likely during a learning process. Approximate synonyms (at least in some texts): Cue and hint. Sometimes two major types are distinguished: "Formal prompts" and "Thematic prompts" (see these words).

Reactor See "Integrator".

Reduction of uncertainty A measure of the average effectiveness of an instructional material, expressed as a reduction of the number of errors (within a specific student group). If we examine the ability of the students to solve a related terminal test item before going through the material ("error percentage A"), as well as their ability to solve the problem after going through the material ("error percentage B"), then the measure of reduction of uncertainty would be "error percentage A—error percentage B". (Compare terms "Speed of information" and "Density of information".)

Response request That part of an instructional micro-unit which presents the student with the task of giving an active response reaction (to solve a problem in mathematics, to fill in a word which has been left blank, choose the right alternative from several which have been presented, etc.). It is typical of programmed instruction that these response requests are very frequent and continually alternate with the presentation of new material.

Respule See "Didule".

Reverse accumulation A system for practising a temporal behavior sequence as follows: the final phase of the series is practised first, after this the next to the last *plus* the last, etc. Besides the fact that the student practises sequences (instead of separate phases only), the advantage of this arrangement is that the student experiences a motivation in being able, at an early stage, to perform the final phase in a behavior series. This is especially true if this final phase has the character of a desirable goal.

Ruleg (1) A sequence in programmed study material in which new information is introduced according to the formula: first general rule (law, principle, definition or the like), then a complete example, then an incomplete example for the student to work with. That is, the "ru" (rule) precedes the "eg's" (examples). (2) The term is also used (and originally) for a special system of constructing self-instructional study material, developed by Evans, Homme & Glaser (1962), in which the use of the sequence type mentioned above is an important part, but that also has a series of other typical characteristics.—The term "Egrul" is sometimes used for the more inductive sequence (leading the student through some examples before letting him try to formulate the rule himself); hence, the opposite of Ruleg (1).

Scrambled book A programmed textbook characterized by branches incorporated for the purpose of explaining errors. After going through the first information unit, the student must answer a multiple-choice question as control. The answer he chooses determines the page to which he is directed next. If he has chosen the right answer, the new page presents new information and a new task. If his choice has been wrong, on the other hand, he is given an explanation of his error on the new page and as a rule is directed back to the original task page with the instruction to choose a better answer.

Skinner model A course layout which combines a non-branching flow model (linear model where all students go through the same study material in the same order) with a demand for self-constructed responses. The name derives from B. F. Skinner but is somewhat misleading, since Skinner worked with other models also (among them models with extreme individualization of the repetition procedure).

Speed of information A measure of the effective communication of information ("reduction of uncertainty" for the student; compare this word) in relation to the period of time needed for learning. A measure which indicates, in other words, how much effective information the students assimilate per time unit in going through a certain instructional program, and which thereby gives us one meaningful point of departure in evaluating the quality of the program.

Spiral progression A sequence of material set up in such a way that the student goes through different subject-matter areas at a lower grade of difficulty before going on to these different areas of material at a higher level of difficulty.

Stimule See "Didule".

Student-paced flow of information The fact that in programmed instruction the student himself most often decides when a new information unit shall be presented to him (as opposed to lesson and lecture teaching where the flow of information is directed by the teacher).

Surplus learning An extra dividend in the learning result, over and above the specific knowledges and skills. Acquired study techniques, attitudes to a certain field of knowledge and the like may be considered "surplus learning".

System analysis A general term for various types of studies on the different components of a system. A system analysis is usually a very important preparatory phase of work in constructing an instructional methods-and-materials system and then includes such things as goal analysis, student analysis, situation analysis, subject-matter analysis and media analysis.

System synthesis A general term for putting together the components of a system. In constructing a methods-and-materials system for instruction, we usually start with an analytic phase (studying the pre-requisites one by one) and follow up with a system synthesis in constructing a preliminary version.

"*Tail model*" A layout of auto-instructional material which presupposes that the student has already in some other way acquired the main points of the study material (for instance, in an ordinary textbook). The auto-instructional material functions then as post-study control and remedial teaching where needed. The foremost advocate of this partial type of auto-instruction has been S. L. Pressey.

Target population That group of students to which a certain study material is directed.

Terminal behavior or terminal behavior repertoire The knowledge and skill which the student should be able to display after going through a certain study material. A careful mapping of the desired terminal behavior is an important part of the preliminary work in drawing up a programmed course. (Compare "Goal analysis".)

Terminal stimulus The unprompted question or problem to which the student is taught to respond. (Compare the word "prompt".)

Terminal test An examination which makes it possible to ascertain whether a student who has gone through a given study material can demonstrate the knowledge and skill which are specified in the goal description of the course. (Also: "criterion test".)

Thematic prompts Stimuli which with the help of meaningful (content-related) associations make it easier for the student to give the correct answer. Examples and logical deductions can be counted as belonging to this group of hints.

T-tabulation A tabulation (used as an aid in goal analysis), with the help of which the programmer gets a survey of (a) the specific "terminal behaviors" (see that word) which the student should display at the end of the course as well as (b) under which detailed conditions this is to take place. The T-tabulation consists of a cross-classification chart of specific terminal behaviors on the one side and a list of "specifications" (which describe approved aids, acceptable minimum speed, maximum tolerance of error etc.) on the other. (For illustration, see chapter 5 above.)

Tutofor A general term for an aid in presenting a teaching program to a student. This aid, or tool, can take the form of a printed book, which we then refer to as a "programmed textbook" (or "tutoprint"). But it can also be of mechanical character, and we then speak of a "teaching machine" (or "tutomat").

Vertical panel-book A programmed textbook, in which the pages are divided into panels which (in contrast to the case of the "horizontal panel-book", compare that word) are read in the usual reading sequence (from top to bottom of the page). Each panel usually contains a short information unit to which is linked a response request. A key answer is also usually part of the instructional micro-unit, and this can be placed in the same panel ("simple marginal-key"), in connection with a later panel ("delayed marginal-key"), or also on the back of the information page.

Weltner technique A technique for assessment of the instructional effect of a particular program, utilizing the difference in subjective information of a basic text before and after the instruction. The difference is established by means of a specific technique of text predictions, similar to one introduced by C. E. Shannon. (For details, see Weltner, 1966.)

Zig-zag book A programmed textbook in which the pages are divided into cut sections which can be turned forward and backward independently of each other. This provides a better stimulus situation than that offered by the ordinary forms of horizontal and vertical panel-books. That is, the key answer is not in the visual field when the student answers the problem, but both the problem and the key answer are in the visual field *after* the student has answered. (For illustration, see chapter 8 above, especially Figures 8.7 and 8.8.)

Appendix 2

Programmed Instruction and Educational Technology: A Selective Bibliographic Guide

Introductory note

The present bibliographic guide is selective, that is, it does not at all aim at being comprehensive. Instead, we have tried to cover a number of basic topics and, within each of these, to list a sample of pertinent references. For some of the categories we have also attempted to give some further guidance by means of brief comments.

Outline of contents

1. Survey Publications

1.1 *Integrated Surveys in Book Form*

Becker, J. L. *A programed guide to writing auto-instructional programs.* Camden, N.J.: RCA, 1963.

Bernmalm, S. *Programmerad undervisning: En granskning och sammanställning av amerikanska forskningsrapporter.* Göteborg: IPU, 1965.

Bjerstedt, Å. *Programmerad undervisning, språklaboratorier och gruppdynamisk kartläggning.* (4th ed.) Lund: Gleerups, 1968.

Bjerstedt, Å. *Självinstruerande studiematerial.* (Rev. ed.) Lund: Uniskol, 1969.

Brethower, D. M. et al. *Programmed learning: A practicum.* Ann Arbor, Mich.: Ann Arbor Publishers, 1965.

Commission on Instructional Technology. *To improve learning.* Washington, D.C.: U.S. Government Printing Office, 1970.

Davies, I. K. *The management of learning.* London: McGraw-Hill, 1971.

Filby, Y. *Teaching machines. A review of theory and research.* Copenhagen: Munksgaard, 1961.

Fischer, M. *Wege zur inneren Differenzierung des Unterrichts durch programmierte Arbeitsmittel.* Weinheim: Beltz, 1968.

Fry, E. B. *Teaching machines and programmed instruction. An introduction.* New York: McGraw-Hill, 1963.

Garner, W. L. *Programed instruction.* New York: Center for Applied Research in Education, 1966.

Green, E. J. *The learning process and programmed instruction.* New York: Holt, 1962.

Hughes, J. L. *Programed instruction for schools and industry.* Chicago: Science Research Associates, 1962.

Kay, H., Dodd, B. & Sime, M. *Teaching machines and programmed instruction.* Harmondsworth: Penguin Books, 1968.

Klotz, G. *Programmierter Unterricht — ein Verfahren für morgen.* München: Kösel-Verlag, 1969.

Leedham, J. & Unwin, D. *Programmed learning in schools.* London: Longmans, 1965.

Leith, G. O. M. et al. *A handbook of programmed learning.* (Rev. ed.) Birmingham, England: University of Birmingham, 1966.

Leith, G. O. M. *Seconds thoughts on programmed learning.* London: NCET, 1969.

Lysaught, J. P. & Williams, C. M. *A guide to programmed instruction.* New York: Wiley, 1963.

Markle, S. M., Eigen, L. D. & Komoski, P. K. *A programed primer on programing. Vol. I. Principles.* New York: Center for Programed Instruction, 1961.

Markle, S. M. *A programed primer on programing. Vol. II. Practical problems.* New York: Center for Programed Instruction, 1961.

Markle, S. M. *Good frames and bad.* (2nd ed.) New York: Wiley, 1969.

O'Day, E. F. et al. *Programmed instruction: Techniques and trends.* New York: Appleton-Century-Crofts, 1971.

Ofiesh, G. D. *Programed instruction: A guide for management.* New York: Amer. Management Ass., 1965.

Rowntree, D. *Basically branching. A handbook for programmers.* London: MacDonald, 1966.

Saettler, P. *A history of instructional technology.* New York: McGraw-Hill, 1968.

Schiefele, H. & Huber, G. L. *Programmierte Unterweisung — programmiert.* München: Ehrenwirth, 1969.

Schramm, W. *Programed instruction today and tomorrow.* New York: The Fund for the Advancement of Education, 1962.

Shirley-Smith, K. *Programmed learning in integrated industrial training.* London: Gower Pr., 1968.

Silvern, L. C. *Fundamentals of teaching machine and programmed learning systems.* Los Angeles: Education and Training Consultants, 1964.

Skinner, B. F. *The technology of teaching.* New York: Appleton-Century-Crofts, 1968.

Stiernborg, M. *Programmerad undervisning — analys och översikt.* Stockholm: Dept. Educ., 1966.

Stolurow, L. M. *Teaching by machine.* Washington, D.C.: U.S. Government Printing Office, 1961.

Taber, J. I., Glaser, R. & Schaefer, H. H. *Learning and programmed instruction.* Reading, Mass.: Addison-Wesley, 1965.

Thomas, C. A. et al. *Programmed learning in perspective. A guide to programme writing.* Barking, Essex: Adelphi, 1963.

Undervisningsmaskiner och programmerat studiematerial. Skolöverstyrelsen: Utredningar i skolfrågor 11, 1963.

Zielinski, J. & Schöler, W. *Methodik des programmierten Unterrichts.* Ratingen: Henn, 1965.

Zielke, W. *Programmierte Instruktion in der Wirtschaft.* München: Verlag Moderne Industrie, 1970.

Note: Some of these books are elementary and popular in style; whereas others—for instance, the publications by Filby and Stolurow—are more adapted to readers with some familiarity of the terminology and style of scientific psychology. In some cases the presentation form is that of a programmed textbook and, hence, functions both as introduction and illustration (for instance, Becker, 1963; Markle, 1969; Schiefele & Huber, 1969). Those who are most interested in the program construction process will find Fry (1963), Lysaught & Williams (1963), and Markle (1969) to be some of the important references. The aspects of learning theory are given special emphasis by Green (1962). In this section some books are included that are not only out-of-print, but that would also be considered—even by their authors—to be out-of-date. While readers who want to get an up-to-date introduction should, of course, choose among books from later years, for those who are interested in informing themselves about the rapid development of the field we have retained some of the "older" sources available in libraries.

1.2 *Survey Articles*

Holland, J. G. Research on programming variables. In: R. Glaser (Ed.), *Teaching machines and programed learning, II.* Washington, D.C.: NEA, 1965. Pp. 66—117.

Klaus, D. J. An analysis of programming techniques. In: R. Glaser (Ed.), *Teaching machines and programed learning, II.* Washington, D.C.: NEA, 1965. Pp. 118—161.

Leib, J. W. et al. Teaching machines and programmed instruction. *Psychol. Bull.,* 1967, *67,* 12—26.

Lumsdaine, A. A. Instruments and media of instruction. In: N. L. Gage (Ed.), *Handbook of research on teaching.* Chicago: Rand McNally, 1963. Pp. 583—682.

Skinner, B. F. Why we need teaching machines. *Harvard educ. Rev.,* 1961, *31,* 377—398.

Skinner, B. F. Reflections on a decade of teaching machines. In: R. Glaser (Ed.), *Teaching machines and programed learning, II.* Washington, D.C.: NEA, 1965. Pp. 5—20.

Spaulding, S. Advanced educational technologies. *Prospects in Education* (Unesco), 1970, *1* (3), 9—19.

1.3 *Introductory Films and Filmstrips*

"*Example of a teaching machine program.*" Filmstrip prepared by D. H. Luxton & R. E. Corrigan. Color, 69 frames. Pasadena, Calif.: Basic Skill Films.

"*Learning and behavior.*" Interviews with B. F. Skinner and R. J. Herrnstein at Harvard's Psychological Laboratory (CBS). B & w, 16 mm sound, 27 min. New York: Carousel Films.

"*One step at a time.*" Produced by D. Klaus et al., American Institute for Research. Color, 16 mm sound, 28 min. Pittsburgh, Penna.: AIR.

"*Programming is a process.*" Filmstrip (color, 80 frames) and sound tape. Produced by S. M. Markle and Ph. W. Tiemann. Chicago: Tiemann Associates.

"*Selection and use of programmed materials.*" Filmstrip (color, 64 frames) and sound record, 16 min. Washington, D.C.: NEA.

"*Teaching machines.*" Filmstrip prepared by W. H. Allen. Techn. advisor: A. A. Lumsdaine. Color, 62 frames. Pasadena, Calif.: Basic Skill Films.

"*Teaching machines and programmed learning.*" Demonstrations and comments by B. F. Skinner, A. A. Lumsdaine, and R. Glaser (NEA). B & w, 16 mm sound, 29 min. Washington, D.C.: Norwood Films.

1.4 *Inventory-Type Surveys*

Note: Many bibliographical surveys have appeared, but they too often have the disadvantage of becoming obsolete almost before leaving the printing press, due to the rapid increase in literature. Only some examples are therefore listed here. For information about the most recent publications, the reader should consult the latest issues of the journals in the field, where surveys and reviews often appear.—As is apparent from the titles, the inventories cover different things. Inventories of machines (not quite up to date any longer, of course) are given by Finn & Perrin and by Ross, whereas program inventories are presented in "Programs, '62", "Programs, '63" etc. and in Cavanagh & Jones, Hendershot and Hintermaier, for example. Finished research is presented in Schramm. A more general bibliographic aim is represented by Gee and Schmidt. (For a discussion of the problems involved in constructing informative inventories of instructional program, see Markle, S. M. Five answers in search of the right questions: The bibliographies of programed instruction. *NSPI J.*, 1968, *7* (3), 15—21).

Bjerstedt, Å. The terminology of programmed instruction. *Didakometry* (Malmö: School of Education), No. 13, 1966.

Cavanagh, P. & Jones, C. (Eds.) *Programmes in print 1966*. London: Association for Programmed Learning, 1966.

Cavanagh, P. & Jones, C. (Eds.) *Yearbook of educational and instructional technology 1969/70*. London: Cornmarket, 1969.

Center for Programed Instruction. *Programs, '62. A guide to programed instructional materials available to educators by September 1962*. Washington, D.C.: U.S. Government Printing Office, 1962.

Center for Programed Instruction. *Programs, '63. A guide to programed instructional materials available to educators by September 1963*. Washington, D.C.: U.S. Government Printing Office, 1963.

Center for Programed Instruction. *Programed instruction materials 1964—'65. A guide to programed instruction materials available for use in elementary and secondary schools as of April, 1965*. New York: CPI, Columbia Univer., 1965.

Centre de Documentation sur l'Enseignement Programmé. *Bibliographie sur l'enseignement programmé et les machines à enseigner. I—II.* Paris: Institut Pédagogique National, 1966.

Centre de Documentation sur l'Enseignement Programmé. *Catalogue analytique des cours programmés.* (Langue française.) Paris: Institut Pédagogique National, 1967.

Committee for Out-of-school Education, Council for Cultural Co-operation. *Programmed instruction: Institutions and their activities.* Strasbourg: Council of Europe, 1970.

Committee for Out-of-school Education, Council for Cultural Co-operation. *Programmed instruction: Survey of projects.* Strasbourg: Council of Europe, 1970.

Deutschsprachige Lehrprogramme. Stand: Mai 1969. Berlin: Pädagogisches Zentrum, 1969.

Eraut, M. & Squires, G. *An annotated select bibliography of educational technology.* London: NCET, 1971.

Finn, J. D. & Perrin, D. G. *Teaching machines and programed learning. A survey of the industry.* Washington, D.C.: U.S. Government Printing Office, 1962.

Gee, R. D. *Teaching machines and programmed learning. A guide to the literature.* Hatfield: HERTIS, 1965.

Gesellschaft für programmierte Instruktion. *Kontakt-Register der pädagogischen Technik.* (3. Aufl.) Quickborn: Schnelle, 1970.

Hendershot, C. H. *Programmed learning: A bibliography of programs and presentation devices.* (4th ed. & suppl. 1—6.) Bay City, Mich.: Author, 1970.

Hintermaier, R. (Ed.) *Lernprogramme "70.* München: Ehrenwirth, 1970.

Müller, D. D. *Kybernetik-Automation. Band I: Unterrichtstechnologie, Grenzgebiete.* Berlin: Elwert u. Meurer, 1970.

National Society for Programmed Instruction. *Directory of members.* San Antonio, Texas: NSPI, 1971.

Programmed instruction guide. (2nd ed.) Newburyport, Mass.: Entelek, 1968.

Programmed learning and teaching machines: Bibliographical references. Antwerpen: International Audio-Visual Technical Centre. (Undated issues.)

Ross, W. L. m.fl. *Teaching machines: Industry survey and buyers' guide.* New York: Center for Programed Instruction, 1962.

Schmidt, H. *Bibliographie zum programmierten Lernen und zum Einsatz schulbezogener Arbeitsmittel. Zeitschriftennachweis 1947—1967.* (Erziehungswissenschaftliche Dokumentation, Band 5.) Weinheim: Beltz, 1969.

Schramm, W. *The research on programed instruction.* Washington, D.C.: U.S. Government Printing Office, 1964.

Spaulding, S. *Programmed instruction: An international directory.* Paris: Unesco, 1967.

2. Collections

2.1 *Collections of Articles in Book Form*

Aagaard, K., Dohn, H. & Marckmann, W. (Eds.) *Konference om programmeret undervisning.* Copenhagen: Lærerforeningernes Materialudvalg, 1968.

Bajpai, A. C. & Leedham, J. F. (Eds.) *Aspects of educational technology, Vol. 4.* London: Pitman, 1970.

Bung, K. (Ed.) *Programmed learning and the language laboratory (1).* London: Longmac, 1968.

Correll, W. (Ed.) *Zur Theorie und Praxis des programmierten Lernens.* Darmstadt: Wissenschaftliche Buchgesellschaft, 1969.

Coulson, J. E. (Ed.) *Programmed learning and computer-based instruction.* New York: Wiley, 1962.

Dahllöf, U. & Wallin, E. (Eds.) *Läromedelsforskning och undervisningsplanering.* Stockholm: Nord. utredningsserie, 1969.

DeCecco, J. P. (Ed.) *Educational technology. Readings in programmed instruction.* New York: Holt, 1964.

Dolmatch, Th. B. et al. (Eds.) *Revolution in training. Programed instruction in industry.* New York: American Management Ass., 1962.

Dunn, W. R. & Holroyd, L. (Eds.) *Aspects of educational technology, Vol. 2.* London: Methuen, 1969.

Filep, R. T. (Ed.) *Prospectives in programing.* New York: Macmillan, 1963.

Frank, H. (Ed.) *Lehrmaschinen in kybernetischer und pädagogischer Sicht, 1—4.* München: Oldenbourg, 1963—66.

Galanter, E. (Ed.) *Automatic teaching: The state of the art.* New York: Wiley, 1959.

Glaser, R. (Ed.) *Teaching machines and programed learning, II: Data and directions.* Washington, D.C.: NEA, 1965.

Goldsmith, M. (Ed.) *Mechanisation in the classroom. An introduction to teaching machines and programmed learning.* London: Souvenir Pr., 1963.

Goodman, E. H. (Ed.) *Automated education handbook.* Detroit, Mich.: Automated Education Center, 1965.

Hughes, J. L. (Ed.) *Programed learning: A critical evaluation.* Chicago: Educational Methods, 1963.

Lambert, Ph. (Ed.) *The teacher and the machine.* Madison, Wisc.: Dembar, 1962.

Lange, P. (Ed.) *Programmed instruction.* (66th NSSE Yearbook, Part II.) Chicago: Univer. Chicago Pr., 1967.

La recherche en enseignement programmé. Paris: Dunod, 1969.

Lehnert, U. (Ed.) *Elektronische Datenverarbeitung in Schule und Ausbildung.* München: Oldenbourg, 1970.

Lumsdaine, A. A. (Ed.) *Student response in programmed instruction.* Washington, D.C.: National Academy of Sciences, 1961.

Lumsdaine, A. A. & Glaser, R. (Eds.) *Teaching machines and programmed learning: A source book.* Washington, D.C.: NEA, 1960.

Lysaught, J. P. (Ed.) *Programmed learning. Evolving principles and industrial applications.* Ann Arbor, Mich.: The Foundation for Research on Human Behavior, 1961.

Mann, A. P. & Brunstrom, C. K. (Eds.) *Aspects of educational technology, Vol. 3.* London: Pitman, 1969.

Margulies, S. & Eigen, L. D. (Eds.) *Applied programed instruction.* New York: Wiley, 1962.

Merrill, M. D. (Ed.) *Instructional design.* Englewood Cliffs, N.J.: Prentice-Hall, 1971.

Ofiesh, G. D. & Meierhenry, W. C. (Eds.) *Trends in programmed instruction.* Washington, D.C.: NEA, 1964.

Praxis und Perspektiven des programmierten Unterrichts. (Referate des 3. Nürtinger Symposions über Lehrmaschinen.) Quickborn: Schnelle, 1965.

Praxis und Perspektiven des programmierten Unterrichts, Band II. (Referate des V. Symposions über Lehrmaschinen.) Quickborn: Schnelle, 1967.

Programmierter Unterricht und Lehrmaschinen. Bericht. Internationale Konferenz. Berlin: Pädag. Zentrum, 1964.

Rollett, B. (Ed.) *Praxis und Theorie des programmierten Unterrichtes.* Stuttgart: Klett, 1970.

Rollett, B. & Weltner, K. (Eds.) *Perspektiven des programmierten Unterrichts.* Wien:

Österreichischer Bundesverlag, 1970.
Rollett, B. & Weltner, K. (Eds.) *Fortschritte und Ergebnisse der Unterrichtstechnologie.* München: Ehrenwirth, 1971.
Roucek, J. S. (Ed.) *Programmed teaching.* New York: Philosophical Library, 1965.
Schestakow, A. W. (Ed.) *Programmiertes Lernen und Lehrmaschinen.* (Transl. fr. Russian.) Berlin: VEB Verlag Technik, 1965.
Smith, W. I. & Moore, J. W. (Eds.) *Programmed learning: Theory and research.* Princeton, N.J.: Nostrand, 1962.
Teal, G. E. (Ed.) *Programmed instruction in industry and education.* Stamford, Conn.: Public Service Research, 1963.
Tickton, S. (Ed.) *To improve learning, I—II.* New York: Bowker, 1970.
Tobin, M. J. (Ed.) *Problems and methods in programmed learning, 1—5.* Birmingham, England: The National Centre for Programmed Learning, 1967.
Unwin, D. & Leedham, J. (Eds.) *Aspects of educational technology, Vol. 1.* London: Methuen, 1967.
Váňă, J. & Tollingerová, D. (Eds.) *Programované učeni.* (Programmed learning and teaching machines. I—II. From the Liblice Conference, 1965.) Praha: Pedagogický ústav JAK CSAV, 1966.
Wallin, E. (Ed.) *Undervisning — konst eller teknik?* Stockholm: Almqvist & Wiksell, 1968.
Zielinski, J. (Ed.) *Aspekte des programmierten Unterrichts.* Frankfurt am Main: Akademische Verlagsgesellschaft, 1971.
Zifreund, W. (Ed.) *Schulmodelle, programmierte Instruktionen und technische Medien.* München: Ehrenwirth, 1968.

Note: Among the many collections of articles available, the early one by Lumdaine & Glaser (1960) is probably still one of the best sources for anyone who wants to have a survey of the brief history of programmed instruction and to read some of the most important early articles by the originators in the field: Pressey, Skinner, Crowder, and others. This book is also a good bibliographic source for "old" publications (up to 1960). A continuation volume, containing among other things a retrospective essay by B. F. Skinner, is Glaser (1965). The development in Great Britain can be followed in, for example, Unwin & Leedham (1967), Dunn & Holroyd (1969), Mann & Brunstrom (1969), and Bajpai & Leedham (1970). The development in German-speaking countries is mirrored in the many reports from the symposia of Gesellschaft für programmierte Instruktion, for example: Frank, 1963—66; Praxis und Perspektiven des programmierten Unterrichts, 1965 and 1967; Rollett, 1970; Rollett & Weltner, 1970 and 1971.

2.2 *Journals and Bulletins*

AID: Auto-Instructional Devices. Has been published by Institute of International Research and Development, Lubbock, Texas. (Discontinued. Cf. NSPI Journal below.)
Audiovisual Instruction. Ten issues a year. Department of Audiovisual Instruction, NEA, Washington, D.C.
Automated Education Letter. Monthly. Automated Education Center, Detroit. (Supplements E. H. Goodman (Ed.), Automated Education Handbook. Detroit: AE Center, 1965.)
AV Communication Review. Quarterly. Department of Audiovisual Instruction, NEA, Washington, D.C.
Bibliographie: Programmierter Unterricht. Pädagogisches Zentrum, Berlin.

British Journal of Educational Technology (Formerly: Journal of Educational Technology). Three times a year. Journal of the National Council for Educational Technology, England (Councils and Education Press, London).

Deutsche Lehrprogramme für Schule und Praxis. Has been published quarterly by Manz Verlag, München, Germany. (Discontinued.)

Didakometry. Mimeographed bulletin. Department of Educational and Psychological Research, Malmö School of Education, Sweden.

Educational Technology. (Formerly: Teaching Aids News.) Monthly. Educ. Technol. Publ., Englewood Cliffs, New Jersey.

Enseignement Programmé. Quarterly. Published by Centre de Documentation sur l'Enseignement Programmé, Paris (Hachette, Paris).

Grundlagenstudien aus Kybernetik und Geisteswissenschaft. Quickborn: Schnelle.

Journal of Programed Instruction. Quarterly. Has been published by Center for Programed Instruction, Teachers College, Columbia University, New York. (Discontinued.)

La Cybernétique et la Pédagogie Cybernétique. L'Association de Pédagogie Cybernétique, Paris.

NSPI Journal. Ten issues a year. The National Society for Programmed Instruction, USA. A combination of AID (cf. above) and the earlier NSPI Newsletter.

Programed Instruction. Nine issues a year. Has been published by Center for Programed Instruction, Teachers College, Columbia University, New York. (Discontinued.)

Programmed Learning and Educational Technology. Association for Programmed Learning and Educational Technology, London.

Programmed Learning Bulletin. Edinburgh, Scotland: Moray House College of Education.

Programmiertes Lernen, Unterrichtstechnologie und Unterrichtsforschung. Quarterly. Cornelsen, Berlin.

Visual Education. Monthly. National Committee for Audio-Visual Aids in Education, London.

Zentralblatt der Gesellschaft für programmierte Instruktion. Abstract journal. Published by GPI, Berlin. (Quickborn: Schnelle.)

Note: As is obvious from the titles, "AV Communication Review" and "Audiovisual Instruction" are designed to cover the total audio-visual field, but these journals have published much material of interest in the area of didactic programming. Several differences in style of presentation are seen in the group of journals mentioned above. For instance, "AV Communication Review", and "Programmed Learning" favor strict scientific reports, whereas "NSPI Journal", for example, has the style of an information bulletin, in which news and brief notes of various kinds take up more space. The journal activity has been very lively, but it has also shown signs of instability. Several of the "early" journals have already been discontinued (e.g., AID, Deutsche Lehrprogramme, Journal of Programed Instruction, and Programed Instruction). Since some of these discontinued journals have played a role in the development of the field and contain important contributions (still available in libraries), they are mentioned in our list in spite of their disappearance from the scene.—For more detailed information on U.S. periodicals within the area of educational technology, see: Assmann, I. Bibliographie amerikanischer Zeitschriften aus dem Bereich der Bildungstechnologie. *Programmiertes Lernen,* 1970, *7,* 174—179.

3. Special-Topic Publications

3.1 *The Pre-Writing Process: Introductory Analyses and Decisions ("System Analysis")*

3.1.1 *Analyses of terminal objectives, target populations, and subject-matter structure*

Aagaard, K. *Om beskrivelse af undervisningsmål.* Vejle, Denmark: Statens erhvervspædag. læreruddannelse, 1971.

Antunes, A. & Lanoux, J. Étude d'une population en enseignement programmé. *Enseignement programmé,* 1970, No. 12, 13—18.

Bjerstedt, Å. Goal seeking, goal focusing, and goal adjustment. *Progr. Learn. educ. Technol.,* 1970, *7,* 268—279.

Bloom, B. J. (Ed.). *Taxonomy of educational objectives.* New York: Longmans, 1956.

Boeckmann, K. Basaltext und operationale Lernzieldefinition — Eine vergleichende Betrachtung ihrer Möglichkeiten. In: B. Rollett & K. Weltner (Eds.), *Fortschritte und Ergebnisse der Unterrichtstechnologie.* München: Ehrenwirth, 1971. Pp. 17—25.

Bullock, D. H. Strukturanalys av en undervisningsenhet. In: E. Wallin (Ed.), *Undervisning — konst eller teknik?* Stockholm: Almqvist & Wiksell, 1968. Pp. 74—87.

Davies, I. K. The mathetics style of programming. In: K. Bung (Ed.), *Programmed learning and the language laboratory (1).* London: Longmac, 1968. Pp. 29—50.

D'Hainaut, L. Un modèle pour la détermination et la sélection des objectifs pédagogiques du domaine cognitif. *Enseignement programmé,* 1970, No. 11, 21—38.

Evans, J. L., Homme, L. E. & Glaser, R. The Ruleg system for the construction of programmed verbal learning sequences. *J. educ. Res.,* 1962, *55,* 513—518.

Flechsig, K.-H. et al. Probleme der Entscheidung über Lernziele. *Programmiertes Lernen,* 1970, *7,* 1—32.

Frank, H. & Graf, K. D. ALZUDI — Beispiel einer formalen Didaktik. *Z. erziehungswiss. Forsch.,* 1967, *1* (1), 27—34.

Gagné, R. M. The analysis of instructional objectives for the design of instruction. In: R. Glaser (Ed.), *Teaching machines and programed learning, II.* Washington, D.C.: NEA, 1965. Pp. 21—65.

Gagné, R. M. Relations of learned capabilities to instructional objectives. (Paper read at the XVII International Congress of Applied Psychology, Liège, 1971.)

Gardner, K. L. A mathematician's approach to the programming of concepts. In: A. P. Mann & C. K. Brunstrom (Eds.), *Aspects of educational technology, Vol. 3.* London: Pitman, 1969. Pp. 57—64.

Gerlach, V. S. Empirische Methoden der Lehrzielfeststellung. In: B. Rollett & K. Weltner (Eds.), *Fortschritte und Ergebnisse der Unterrichtstechnologie.* München: Ehrenwirth, 1971. Pp. 39—45.

Glaser, R. Some research problems in automated instruction: Instructional programming and subject-matter structure. In: J. E. Coulson (Ed.), *Programmed learning and computer-based instruction.* New York: Wiley, 1962. Pp. 67—85.

Harless, J. H. *An ounce of analysis (is worth a pound of objectives).* Falls Church, Virginia: Harless, 1970.

Hartley, J. Factors affecting the efficiency of learning from programmed instruction. *Visual Education,* 1971, May, 33—35.

Horn, R. E. et al. *Information mapping for computer-based learning and reference.* Cambridge, Mass.: Information Resources, 1971.

Jenkins, J. R. & Deno, S. L. A model for instructional objectives. *Educational Technol-*

ogy, 1970, *10* (12), 11—16.

Kibler, R. J., Barker, L. L. & Miles, D. T. *Behavioral objectives and instruction.* Boston: Allyn & Bacon, 1970.

Klingberg, G. & Ågren, B. Objectives stated for the use of literature in school. *Dept. Educ. Res., Gothenburg School of Education, Res. Bull.,* Nos. 8—9, 1971.

König, E. & Riedel, H. *Unterrichtsplanung als Konstruktion.* Weinheim: Beltz, 1970.

Lahn, W. Ein Beitrag zum didaktischen Programmieren: Das Entwickeln der Programmstruktur aus einer Analyse des Lehrgegenstandes durch ein Satzgerüst in Folgesätzen. *Progr. Lernen, Unterrichtstechnol. u. Unterrichtsforschung,* 1971, *8,* 65—81.

Leith, G. O. M. Learning and personality. In: W. R. Dunn & C. Holroyd (Eds.), *Aspects of educational technology, Vol. 2.* London: Methuen, 1969. Pp. 101—110.

Mager, R. F. *Preparing objectives for programmed instruction.* San Francisco: Fearon, 1961.

Mager, R. F. Deriving objectives for the high school curriculum. *NSPI J.,* 1968, *7* (3), 7—22.

Markle, S. M. & Tiemann, Ph. W. Problems of conceptual learning. *Journal of educational Technology,* 1970, *1,* 52—62.

von Mentzer, C. H. *Studier i empirisk målanalys.* Stockholm: School of Education, 1968.

Möller, Ch. *Technik der Lernplanung. Methoden und Probleme der Lernzielerstellung.* Weinheim: Beltz, 1969.

Popham, W. J. Instructional objectives 1960—1970. *NSPI J.,* 1970, *9* (6), 5—16.

Popham, W. J. et al. *Instructional objectives.* Chicago: Rand McNally, 1969.

Riedel, H. *Psychostruktur: Psychostruktur und Lehrprogrammierung.* Quickborn: Schnelle, 1967.

Stolurow, L. M. Application of psychology to educational technology. (Paper read at the XVII International Congress of Applied Psychology.) Liège, 1971.

Weltner, K. Zur Bestimmung der subjektiven Information durch Ratetests. In: *Praxis und Perspektiven des programmierten Unterrichts, Band II.* Quickborn: Schnelle, 1967. Pp. 69—74.

Weltner, K. Information theory and programmed instruction. *Rev. educ. Cybernetics & appl. Linguistics,* 1969, *1* (1), 25—41.

Weltner, K. *Informationstheorie und Erziehungswissenschaft.* Quickborn: Schnelle, 1970.

Weltner, K. Lernziele unter dem Aspekt der Informationstheorie. In: B. Rollett & K. Weltner (Eds.), *Fortschritte und Ergebnisse der Unterrichtstechnologie.* München: Ehrenwirth, 1971. Pp. 26—35.

Yost, M. A strategy for assessing the reliability and validity of behavioral objectives. *NSPI J.,* 1971, *10* (5), 13—22.

Zielke, W. Stichwortschaubild und Faktenanalyse als Hilfsmittel rationellerer Lehrprogramerstellung. In: B. Rollett & K. Weltner (Eds.), *Fortschritte und Ergebnisse der Unterrichtstechnologie.* München: Ehrenwirth, 1971. Pp. 75—86.

3.1.2 *Decisions on stimulus situation*

Ahlström, K.-G. & Amcoff, S. Feedback functions in teaching machines. *Scand. J. Psychol.,* 1967, *8,* 243—249.

Allen, D. & Ryan, K. *Micro teaching.* Reading, Mass.: Addison-Wesley, 1969.

Atkinson, R. C. Learning to read under computer control. *Progr. Learn. educ. Technol.,* 1968, *5,* 25—37.

Bjerstedt, Å. Schwierigkeiten und beobachtungstechnologische Möglichkeiten in der Lehrerausbildung. *Z. erziehungswiss. Forsch.*, 1968, *2*, 59—82.

Bung, K. *Programmed learning and the language laboratory (2): Collected papers.* London: Longmac, 1967.

Bushnell, D. D. *The role of the computer in future instructional systems.* Washington, D.C.: DAVI, 1963.

Dohn, H. *Datamaskineformidlet undervisning i USA.* Vejle, Denmark: Statens erhvervspædag. læreruddannelse, 1971.

Freudenstein, R. Zehn Jahre Sprachlaborarbeit — Rückblick, Stand und Ausblick. *Progr. Lernen, Unterrichtstechnol. u. Unterrichtsforschung,* 1971, *8,* 86—92.

Goldstein, L. S. & Gotkin, L. G. Teaching machines vs. programed textbooks as presentation modes. *Journal of programed Instruction,* 1962, *1,* 29—36.

Hartley, J. Factors affecting the efficiency of learning from programed instruction. *AV Communication Review,* 1971, *19,* 133—148.

Hayes, A. S. *Language laboratory facilities.* Washington, D.C.: U.S. Government Printing Office, 1963.

Hirzel, M. *Partnerarbeit im programmierten Unterricht.* Stuttgart: Klett, 1969.

Hocking, E. *Language laboratory and language learning.* Washington, D.C.: NEA, 1964.

Holling, K. The feedback classroom in use. In: D. Unwin & J. Leedham (Eds.), *Aspects of educational technology, Vol. 1.* London: Methuen, 1967. Pp. 275—306.

Lewis, B. N. & Pask, G. The theory and practice of adaptive teaching systems. In: R. Glaser (Ed.), *Teaching machines and programed learning, II.* Washington, D.C.: NEA, 1965. Pp. 213—266.

Malmquist, E. & Grundin, H. U. Olika former för bjudning av programmerat undervisningsmaterial. *Forskningsrapporter från Statens Försöksskola i Linköping,* Nr 8, 1966.

Richter, H. Lehrautomaten — Beispiele und Entwicklungstendenzen. In: B. Rollett & K. Weltner (Eds.), *Fortschritte und Ergebnisse der Unterrichtstechnologie.* München: Ehrenwirth, 1971. Pp. 173—192.

Rütter, Th. H. *Zeitenregelung im programmgeführten Unterricht.* Aachen: Techn. Hochsch. (Diss.), 1970.

Schorb, A. O. *Unterrichtsmitschau. Fernsehanlagen im Dienste pädagogischer Ausbildung und Forschung.* Bad Godesberg: Verlag Dürrsche Buchhandlung, 1965.

Stolurow, L. M. & Davis, D. Teaching machines and computer-based systems. In: R. Glaser (Ed.), *Teaching machines and programed learning, II.* Washington, D.C.: NEA, 1965. Pp. 162—212.

Strittmatter, P. *Präsentationsmodi von Lehrprogrammen.* Weinheim: Beltz, 1970.

Weltner, K. Video-Trainer. In: B. Rollett (Ed.), *Praxis und Theorie des programmierten Unterrichtes.* Stuttgart: Klett, 1970. Pp. 41—42.

3.2 *Problems Related to the Writing Process ("System Synthesis")*

3.2.1 *The problem of "flow structure"*

Brown, J. L. Effects of logical and scrambled sequences in mathematical materials on learning with programmed instruction materials. *J. educ. Psychol.,* 1970, *61,* 41—45.

Coulson, J. E. et al. Effects of branching in a computer controlled autoinstructional device. *J. appl. Psychol.,* 1962, *46,* 389—392.

Crowder, N. A. On the differences between linear and intrinsic programming. *Phi Delta Kappan,* 1963, *44,* 250—254.

Davies, I. K. Mathetics—a functional approach. In: D. Unwin & J. Leedham (Eds.), *Aspects of educational technology, Vol. 1.* London: Methuen, 1967. Pp. 205—216.

Evans, J. L., Glaser R. & Homme, L. E. An investigation of "teaching machine" variables using learning programs in symbolic logic. *J. educ. Res.,* 1962, *55,* 433—452.

Gilbert, Th. F. *Mathetics: An explicit theory for the design of teaching programmes.* (Rev. educ. Cybernetics & appl. Linguistics. Supplement 1). London: Longmac, 1969.

Graf, K.-D. Algoritmische Zuordningsdidaktik und Dialog-Didaktik. In: U. Lehnert (Ed.), *Elektronische Datenverarbeitung in Schule und Ausbildung.* München: Oldenbourg, 1970. Pp. 64—73.

Holland, J. G. & Porter, D. The influence of repetition of incorrectly answered items in a teaching-machine program. *Journal of the experimental Analysis of Behavior,* 1961, *4,* 305—307.

Jivén, L. M. & Öreberg, C. The IMU Project: Preliminary plan for investigating the effects of a system for individualized mathematics teaching. *Didakometry* (Malmö: School of Education), No. 22, 1968.

Larkin, T. C. & Leith, G. O. M. The effects of linear and branching methods of programmed instruction on learning and retention of a topic in elementary science. *Programmed Learning,* 1964, *1,* 12—16.

Leith, G. O. M. Conflict and interference. *Progr. Learn. educ. Technol.,* 1971, *8,* 41—50.

Mager, R. F. & Clark, C. Explorations in student-controlled instruction. In: G. D. Ofiesh & W. C. Meierhenry (Eds.), *Trends in programmed instruction.* Washington, D.C.: NEA, 1964. Pp. 235—238.

Pennington, D. F. & Slack, C. W. The mathetical design of effective lessons. In: S. Margulies & L. D. Eigen (Eds.), *Applied programed instruction.* New York: Wiley, 1962. Pp. 298—310.

Pressey, S. L. Basic unresolved teaching-machine problems. *Theory into Practice,* 1962, *1,* 30—37.

Pressey, S. L. Autopresentation vs. autoelucidation. *Programed Instruction,* 1963, *2* (4), 6—7.

Richter, E. O. *Programmierter Unterricht und Selbsttätigkeit.* Berlin: Volk u. Wissen, 1969.

Roe, A. A comparison of branching methods for programmed learning. *J. educ. Res.,* 1962, *55,* 407—416.

Schröter, G. Das zweistufige Programm als integrierender Übergang vom linearen zum verzweigten System. In: B. Rollett (Ed.), *Praxis und Theorie des programmierten Unterrichtes.* Stuttgart: Klett, 1970. Pp. 32—36.

Shettel, H. H. *Individual differences in subject matter knowledge and programmed instructional format.* Pittsburgh: AIR, 1963.

Silberman, H. F. et al. Fixed sequence versus branching autoinstructional methods. *J. educ. Psychol.,* 1961, *52,* 166—172.

Smallwood, R. D. *A decision structure for teaching machines.* Cambridge, Mass.: MIT Pr., 1962.

Tennyson, R. D. & Boutwell, R. C. A quality control design for validating hierarchical sequencing of programmed instruction. *NSPI J.,* 1971, *10* (4), 5—10.

Tulodziecki, G. Beiträge der Algorithmenforschung zu einer Unterrichtswissenschaft. In: B. Rollett & K. Weltner (Eds.), *Perspektiven des programmierten Unterrichts.* Wien: Österreich. Bundesverlag, 1970. Pp. 92—96.

3.2.2 *The characteristics of the single instructional units*

Anderson, R. C., Kulhavy, R. W. & Andre, Th. Feedback procedures in programmed instruction. *J. educ. Psychol.,* 1971, *62,* 148—156.

Barlow, J. A. Conversational chaining in teaching machine programs. *Psychol. Rep.,* 1960, *7,* 187—193.

Basescu, B. More on multiple-choice frames. *Programed Instruction,* 1962, *2* (1), 3.

Basescu, B. & Horn, R. E. A response analysis system. *Programed Instruction,* 1964, *4* (3), 6—9.

Brethower, D. M. et al. *Programmed learning: A practicum.* Ann Arbor, Mich.: Ann Arbor Publ., 1965.

Eigen, L. D. & Margulies, S. Response characteristics as a function of information level. *Journal of programed Instruction,* 1963, *2* (1), 45—54.

Goldbeck, R. A. & Campbell, V. N. The effects of response mode and response difficulty on programed learning. *J. educ. Psychol.,* 1962, *53,* 110—118.

Grace, H. A. Programming and readability. *Calif. J. educ. Res.,* 1963, *14,* 164—166.

Horn, R. E. et al. *Information mapping for learning and reference.* Cambridge, Mass.: Information Resources Inc., 1969.

Klaus, D. J. The art of auto-instructional programming. *AV Communication Review,* 1961, *9,* 130—142.

Krumboltz, J. D. & Kiesler, Ch. A. The partial reinforcement paradigm and programed instruction. *Journal of programed Instruction,* 1965, *3* (2), 9—14.

Krumboltz, J. D. & Weisman, R. G. The effect of overt versus covert responding to programed instruction on immediate and delayed retention. *J. educ. Psychol.,* 1962, *53,* 89—92.

Kulic, V. The psychological interpretation of the concept of feedback in learning and problem solving. In: A. C. Bajpai & J. F. Leedham (Eds.), *Aspects of educational technology, Vol. 4.* London: Pitman, 1970. Pp. 125—132.

Landa, L. N. Algorithms and programmed learning. In: K. Bung (Ed.), *Programmed learning and the language laboratory (1).* London: Longmac, 1968. Pp. 57—135.

Lewis, D. G. & Whitwell, M. N. The effects of reinforcement and response upon programmed learning in mathematics. *Progr. Learn. educ. Technol.,* 1971, *8,* 186—195.

Ludwig, E. H. *Die Technik zur Herstellung von Lehrprogrammen.* Ratingen: Henn, 1965.

Margulies, S. Some general rules of frame construction. In: C. D. Ofiesh & W. C. Meierhenry (Eds.), *Trends in programmed instruction.* Washington, D.C.: NEA, 1964. Pp. 185—188.

O'Day, E. F. et al. *Programmed instruction: Techniques and trends.* New York: Appleton-Century-Crofts, 1971.

Roe, A. Automated teaching methods using linear programs. *J. appl. Psychol.,* 1962, *46,* 198—201.

Schaefer, H. H. A vocabulary program using "language redundancy". *Journal of programed Instruction,* 1963, *2* (3), 9—16.

Trittipoe, W. J., Trittipoe, T. G. & Hahn, C. P. The effectiveness of three programed-learning frame styles. *Journal of programed Instruction,* 1963, *2* (1), 35—43.

3.3 *The Post-Writing Process ("System Modification and Evaluation")*

AERA-APA-DAVI Joint Committee on Programed Instruction and Teaching Machines. Criteria for assessing programed instructional materials. *Audiovisual Instruction,* 1963, *8,* 84—89.

AERA-APA-DAVI Joint Committee on Programmed Instruction and Teaching Machines. Recommendations for reporting the effectiveness of programmed-instruction materials. *NSPI J.*, 1966, *5* (3), 3—9.

Bjerstedt, Å. Mapping the effect-structure of self-instructional materials. *Programmed Learning*, 1965, *2*, 99—109.

Bjerstedt, Å. Mapping the pheno-structure of self-instructional materials. *Progr. Learn. educ. Technol.*, 1967, *4*, 87—102.

Bjerstedt, Å. Phäno-Struktur und Effekt-Struktur didaktischer Sequenzen: Beiträge zur Analyse und Beurteilung von Lehrprogrammen. In: H. Frank (Ed.), *Lehrmaschinen in kybernetischer und pädagogischer Sicht, 4*. Stuttgart: Klett, 1966. Pp. 17—39.

Bloom, B. S., Hastings, J. Th. & Madaus, G. F. *Handbook on formative and summative evaluation of student learning.* New York: McGraw-Hill, 1971.

Carroll, J. B. Problems of measurement related to the concept of learning for mastery. In: J. H. Block (Ed.), *Mastery learning: Theory and practice.* New York: Holt, 1971. Pp. 29—46.

Cook, D. A. Studying the performance of a program. *Programed Instruction,* 1962, *2* (2), 4—8.

Glaser, R. Instructional technology and the measurement of learning outcomes: Some questions. *Amer. Psychologist,* 1963, *18,* 519—521.

Gordon, J. M. The evaluative response: A rate problem. *AID,* 1963, *3,* 240.

Holland, J. G. Evaluating teaching machines and programs. *Teachers College Record,* 1961, *63,* 56—65.

Jacobs, P. I. Item difficulty and programed learning. *Journal of programed Instruction,* 1963, *2* (2), 21—38.

Jacobs, P. I., Maier, M. H. & Stolurow, L. M. *A guide to evaluating self-instructional programs.* New York: Holt, 1966.

Lumsdaine, A. A. Some problems in assessing instructional programs. In: R. T. Filep (Ed.), *Prospectives in programing.* New York: Macmillan, 1963. Pp. 228—262.

Lumsdaine, A. A. Assessing the effectiveness of instructional programs. In: R. Glaser (Ed.), *Teaching machines and programed learning, II.* Washington, D.C.: NEA, 1965. Pp. 267—320.

Markle, S. M. Faulty branching frames: A model for maximizing feedback to the programer. *Programed Instruction,* 1963, *3* (1), 4—8.

Markle, S. M. The lowest common denominator: A persistent problem in programing. *Programed Instruction,* 1963, *2* (3), 4—5.

Rollett, B. Untersuchungen zur semantischen Transinformation. In: B. Rollett & K. Weltner (Eds.), *Perspektiven des programmierten Unterrichts.* Wien: Österreich. Bundesverlag, 1970. Pp. 70—76.

Rothkopf, E. Z. Criteria for the acceptance of self-instructional programs. In: A. E. Traxler (Ed.), *Improving the efficiency and quality of learning.* Washington, D.C.: Amer. Council on Educ., 1962. Pp. 30—38.

Rothkopf, E. Z. Some observations on predicting instructional effectiveness by simple inspection. *Journal of programed Instruction,* 1963, *2* (2), 19—20.

Silverman, R. E. The evaluation of programmed instruction: A problem in decision making. *Psychology in the Schools,* 1964, *1,* 74—78.

Thomas, W. Verfahren zur Prüfung von Lernprogrammen an Hand von Ungütekriterien. In: B. Rollett & K. Weltner (Eds.), *Perspektiven des programmierten Unterrichts.* Wien: Österreich. Bundesverlag, 1970. Pp. 86—92.

Vanderschmidt, H. Validation data for programmed texts: A checklist for evaluation of testing. In: G. D. Ofiesh & W. C. Meierhenry (Eds.), *Trends in programmed instruction.* Washington, D.C.: NEA, 1964. Pp. 210—212.

von Voigt, H. Strukturanalytische Diagramme — ihre Möglichkeiten und Grenzen bei der Erstellung und Beurteilung von Lehrprogrammen. In: B. Rollett (Ed.), *Praxis und Theorie des programmierten Unterrichtes.* Stuttgart: Klett, 1970. Pp. 43—47.

Wheatley, R. A. Measurement in programmed learning experiments — problems encountered and some possible solutions. In: A. P. Mann & C. K. Brunstrom (Eds.), *Aspects of educational technology, Vol. 3.* London: Pitman, 1969. Pp. 115—120.

Zielinski, J. Empirisch-pädagogische Aspekte der Programmtestung und -validierung. *Z. erziehungswiss. Forsch.,* 1967, *1* (3), 38—62.

3.4 *Theoretical Discussions*

Björkman, M. Inlärningspsykologiska principer i programmerad undervisning — några frågetecken. In: Skolöverstyrelsen, *Utredningar i skolfrågor, 11,* 1963. Pp. 96—105.

Cook, D. A. Behavior theory and the automation of instruction. In: J. E. Coulson (Ed.), *Programmed learning and computer-based instruction.* New York: Wiley, 1962. Pp. 120—128.

Corrigan, R. E. Programmed instruction as a systems approach to education. In: G. D. Ofiesh & W. C. Meierhenry (Eds.), *Trends in programmed instruction.* Washington, D.C.: NEA, 1964. Pp. 36—45.

Ely, D. P. Toward a philosophy of instructional technology. *Journal of educational Technology,* 1970, *1,* 81—94.

Frank, H. Kybernetik und Lehrmaschinen. In: H. Frank (Ed.), *Lehrmaschinen in kybernetischer und pädagogischer Sicht.* München: Oldenbourg, 1963. Pp. 13—26.

Frank, H. *Kybernetische Grundlagen der Pädagogik, I—II.* (2. Aufl.) Baden-Baden: Agis-Verlag, 1969.

Hilgard, E. R. Issues within learning theory and programmed learning. *Psychology in the Schools,* 1964, *1,* 129—139.

Landa, L. N. Diagnostik und programmierter Unterricht. In: H. Frank (Ed.), *Lehrmaschinen in kybernetischer und pädagogischer Sicht, 4.* Stuttgart: Klett, 1966. Pp. 54—65.

Landa, L. N. *Algorithmierung im Unterricht.* (Transl. fr. Russian.) Berlin: Volk u. Wissen, 1969.

Landa, L. N. The construction of algorithmic and heuristic models of thinking activity and some problems in programmed learning. In: W. R. Dunn & C. Holroyd (Eds.), *Aspects of educational technology, Vol. 2.* London: Methuen, 1969. Pp. 133—141.

Leith, G. O. M. The acquisition of knowledge and mental development of students. *Journal of educational Technology,* 1970, *1,* 116—128.

Newman, S. E. A mediation model for paired-associate learning. In: J. P. De Cecco (Ed.), *Educational technology.* New York: Holt, 1964. Pp. 172—186.

Pressey, L. Teaching machine (and learning theory) crisis. *J. appl. Psychol.,* 1963, *47,* 1—6.

Pressey, S. L. Autoinstruction: Perspectives, problems, potentials. In: *Theories of learning and instruction* (Sixty-third Yearbook). Chicago: The National Society for the Study of Education, 1964. Pp. 354—370.

Skinner, B. F. *Verbal behavior.* New York: Appleton-Century-Crofts, 1957.

Skinner, B. F. *Contingencies of reinforcement: A theoretical analysis.* New York: Apple-

ton-Century-Crofts, 1969.
Skinner, B. F. Contingency management in the classroom. In: A. P. Mann & C. K. Brunstrom (Eds.), *Aspects of educational technology, Vol. 3.* London: Pitman, 1969. Pp. 3—12.
Tennyson, R. D. & Merrill, M. D. Hierarchical models in the development of a theory of instruction. *Educational Technology,* 1971, *11* (9), 27—31.
Thompson, R. L. Programed instruction and reinforcement theory: A view from the laboratory. In: R. T. Filep (Ed.), *Prospectives in programing.* New York: Macmillan, 1963. Pp. 16—35.
Tulodziecki, G. *Beiträge der Algorithmenforschung zu einer Unterrichtsswissenschaft.* Aachen: Techn. Hochsch. (Diss.), 1970.

3.5 *Activities in Various Countries*

Bjerstedt, Å. Auto-instructional methods in Great Britain. *Audio-Visual Media,* 1968, *2* (2), 89—93.
Bjerstedt, Å. Notes on programmed instruction in Sweden. *Didakometry* (Malmö: School of Education), No. 5, 1966.
Bjerstedt, Å. Educational technology in Sweden. *Educational Technology,* 1969, *9* (11), 48—51.
Bremer, W. et al. *Programmierte Instruktion in der Berufsausbildung der USA.* Weinheim: Beltz, 1967.
Buter, E. M. Educational technology in Holland. *Educational Technology,* 1969, *9* (11), 22—25.
Cavanagh, P. & Jones, C. Further trends in programmes in print in the United Kingdom. *Progr. Learn. educ. Technol.,* 1970, *7,* 56—62.
Center for Programed Instruction. *The use of programed instruction in U.S. schools.* Washington, D.C.: U.S. Government Printing Office, 1963.
Connor, D. V. Educational technology in Australia. *Journal of educational Technology,* 1970, *1,* 207—216.
Décoté, G. L'enseignement programmé en France. In: Décoté, G. *Vers l'enseignement programmé.* Paris: Gauthier-Villars, 1963. Chap. IV.
Dohn, H. *Datamaskineformidlet undervisning i USA.* Vejle, Denmark: Statens erhvervspædag. læreruddannelse, 1971.
Hartley, J. Programmed learning in emerging nations. *Programmed Learning,* 1964, *1,* 21—25.
Hawkridge, D. Programmed learning in Africa. *Journal of educational Technology,* 1970, *1,* 217—225.
Hintermaier, R. Situation des PU in deutschsprachigen Ländern. *Didakometry* (Malmö: School of Education), No. 27, 1970.
Issing, L. J. (Ed.) *Der programmierte Unterricht in den USA heute.* Weinheim: Beltz, 1967.
Kishi, T. & Numano, I. The present state of programmed instruction in Japan. *The Science of Learning* (Tokyo), 1967, *3* (1), 1—10.
Komoski, P. K. & Green, E. J. *Programmed instruction in West Africa and the Arab States. A report on two training workshops.* (Educational Studies and Documents, No. 52.) Paris: Unesco, 1964.
Kulkarni, S. S. Educational technology in India. *Educational Technology,* 1969, *9* (11), 28—32.

Landa, L. N. Programmed instruction in the Soviet Union. *Educational Technology,* 1970, 10 (7), 40—45.

Lindner, H. Programmiertes Lernen: Bericht über das 9. Symposion der GPI. (Manuskript, Hamburg, 1971.)

MacKenzie, N. Springboard or scaffold? The Commission on instructional technology in the United States. *Journal of educational Technology,* 1970, *1,* 173—182.

Müller, D. D. Five stages of development of programmed instruction in Germany. *Progr. Learn. educ. Technol.,* 1967, *4,* 216—222.

Romiszowski, A. J. The international conference on educational technology 1971. *Visual Education,* 1971, May, 29—33.

Vogt, H. Programmierte Instruktion und Pädagogische Kybernetik im sowjetischen Bildungswesen. *Progr. Lern. progr. Unterr.,* 1967, *4,* 54—65.

Vogt, H., Zänker, U. & Schellenberg, E. *Pädagogische Kybernetik und programmierte Instruktion in der Sowjetunion und in der DDR.* Weinheim: Beltz, 1968.

3.6 *From the Discussions and Research on Programmed Instruction and Educational Technology in Sweden*

Ahlström, K.-G. SMID — självinstruerande metoder i dövundervisningen. In: E. Wallin (Ed.), *Undervisning — konst eller teknik*? Stockholm: Almqvist & Wiksell, 1968. Pp. 115—126.

Andersson, B.-E., Parknäs, L. & Wallin, E. Erfarenheter från ett försök med programmerad undervisning. *Nordisk Psykologi,* 1962, *14,* 261—269.

Berglund, L. G. & Jivén, L. M. IMU-projektet: Försök i hjälpklass rörande informationsgivning med två typer av svarsbekräftelse i relation till stegstorlek. *Pedagogisk-psykologiska problem* (Malmö: School of Education), No. 86, 1969.

Bernmalm, S. *Programmerad undervisning vid universitet och högskolor: En granskning av förutsättningarna och ett försök med ett program i njurclearance.* Göteborg: Dept. Educ., 1969.

Bjerstedt, Å. *Programmerad undervisning, språklaboratorier och gruppdynamisk kartläggning.* Lund: Gleerups, 1963. (4th rev. ed., 1968.)

Bjerstedt, Å. *Självinstruerande studiematerial.* Lund: Uniskol, 1963. (Rev. ed., 1969.)

Bjerstedt, Å. Mapping the pheno-structure of didactic sequences. *Didakometry* (Malmö: School of Education), No. 1, 1964.

Bjerstedt, Å. Mapping the effect-structure of didactic sequences. *Didakometry* (Malmö: School of Education), No. 2, 1964.

Bjerstedt, Å. *Undervisningsprogrammering och utvärdering.* Stockholm: Sv. Bokförlaget, 1965. (Rev. ed., 1970.)

Bjerstedt, Å. Notes on programmed instruction in Sweden. *Didakometry* (Malmö: School of Education), No. 5, 1966.

Bjerstedt, Å. Phäno-Struktur und Effekt-Struktur didaktischer Sequenzen: Beiträge zur Analyse und Beurteilung von Lehrprogrammen. In: H. Frank (Ed.), *Lehrmaschinen in kybernetischer und pädagogischer Sicht, IV.* Stuttgart: Klett, 1966. Pp. 17—39.

Bjerstedt, Å. Att konstruera undervisningsprogram: En studieguide. *Kompendieserien* (Malmö: School of Education), No. 4, 1967.

Bjerstedt, Å. Konsten att vänta på fakta: Två diskussionsinlägg. *Pedagogisk-psykologiska problem* (Malmö: School of Education), No. 75, 1968.

Bjerstedt, Å. Educational technology in Sweden. *Didakometry* (Malmö: School of Education), No. 23, 1969.

Bjerstedt, Å. *Den pedagogiska processen.* Lund: Gleerups, 1970. (Rev. ed., 1971.)

Bjerstedt, Å. Systematic analyses of instructional objectives. *Didakometry* (Malmö: School of Education), No. 28, 1970.

Bjerstedt, Å. System analysis in instructional programming: The initial phases of the program construction process. *Didakometry* (Malmö: School of Education), No. 30, 1971.

Bjerstedt, Å. System synthesis in instructional programming: The intermediate phases of the program construction process. *Didakometry* (Malmö: School of Education), No. 32, 1971.

Bjerstedt, Å. System modification and evaluation in instructional programming: The final phases of the program construction process. *Didakometry* (Malmö: School of Education), No. 33, 1971.

Bååth, J. A. *Nya vägar inom fjärrundervisningen.* Malmö: Hermods, 1971.

Edfelt, Å. W. Automatic teaching—principiella synpunkter. *Nordisk Psykologi,* 1962, *14,* 6—20.

Eklund, H. Det programmerade studiematerialets plats inom den obligatoriska skolan. *Pedag. Tidskr.,* 1963, *99,* 145—154.

Ekman, B. *Teaching geometry in grade four.* Uppsala: Sv. Bokförlaget, 1968.

Eriksson, B. En utbildningsteknologisk modell. *Undervisningsteknologi,* 1968, *3* (4), 9—17.

Eriksson, B. & Lindskog, E. *Inlärningsprogram i undervisningsteknologi.* Stockholm: Utbildningsförlaget, 1971.

Gestrelius, K. *Utbildningsplanering med befattningsanalytiska metoder.* Lund: Uniskol, 1970.

Gestrelius, K. Lärarutbildares arbetsuppgifter, Del I—II. *Pedagogisk-psykologiska problem* (Malmö: School of Education), Nos. 151—152, 1971.

Grundin, H. U. Svarskrav och facitsvar vid programmerad undervisning. *Forskningsrapport från lärarhögskolan i Linköping* (Linköping: School of Education), 1970.

Holmberg, I. Programmed and conventional classroom instruction in arithmetic compared with respect to certain achievement, attitude, and behavior variables. *Didakometry* (Malmö: School of Education), No. 4, 1965.

Holmberg, I. A combination of programmed instruction and teacher-supervised, small-group instruction compared with conventional classroom method. *Didakometry* (Malmö: School of Education), No. 10, 1966.

Holmberg, I., Holmberg, L., Jivén, L. M. & Svensson, J.-E. *Statistiska grundbegrepp. En programmerad introduktion.* Stockholm: Läromedelsförlagen/Sv. Bokförl., 1964. (Rev. ed., 3rd pr. 1970.)

Husén, T. Inlärningsmaskiner och programmerade hjälpmedel. *Pedagogisk Debatt,* 1962, *10,* 48—57.

Husén, T. Programmerade hjälpmedel i undervisningen. *Kungl. Krigsvetenskapsakademiens Handlingar och Tidskrift,* 1962, Nr 1, 3—21.

Jivén, L. M. (Ed.) IMU-projektet: Rapport från utprövning av IMU-systemet på grundskolans högstadium. *Pedagogisk-psykologiska problem* (Malmö: School of Education), No. 63, 1968.

Jivén, L. M. & Svensson, J.-E. Erfarenheter från programmerad undervisning i statistik. *Pedagogisk-psykologiska problem* (Malmö: School of Education), No. 32, 1966.

Klingberg, G. A scheme for the classification of educational objectives. *Dept. Educ. Res., Gothenburg School of Education, Res. Bull.,* No. 5, 1970.

Klingberg, G. & Ågren, B. Objectives stated for the use of literature in school. *Dept. Educ. Res., Gothenburg School of Education, Res. Bull.,* Nos. 8—9, 1971.

Lane, G. Erfarenheter av ett försök med programmerad undervisning i matematik. *Rapp. Pedag. inst., Göteborgs univer.*, No. 8, 1963.

Lewerth, A. & Stangvik, G. Läsning av socialt viktiga ord. Ett försök med programmerad undervisning för utvecklingsstörda. *Rapp. Pedag. inst., Lärarhögskolan i Göteborg*, No. 9, 1969.

Lindecrantz, N. *Datamaskinförmedlad undervisning*. Lund: Studentlitteratur, 1968.

Lindell, E. (Ed.) Ett försök med självinstruerande material i språklaboratorium och i skriftlig programmering. *Pedagogisk-psykologiska problem* (Malmö: School of Education), No. 53, 1967.

Lindell, E. A system of study materials for the teaching of foreign languages: Principles and examples. *Didakometry & Sociometry*, 1969, *1*, 91—124.

Lindell, E. (Ed.) Att arbeta med ett undervisningssystem: En presentation av UMT-projektets läromedel. *Pedagogisk-psykologiska problem* (Malmö: School of Education), No. 106, 1970.

Lindell, E. *Främmande språk i grundskolan*. Lund: Gleerups, 1971.

Lindmark, L. m.fl. *Datamaskinförmedlad utbildning*. Stockholm: Ecklesiastikdepartementet, 1966.

Lundin, J. E. Utprövning och revision av PI. *Undervisningsteknologi*, 1969, *4* (4), 16—19.

Löfqvist, G. Arbets- och utbildningskrav för ämneslärarkandidater. *Pedagogisk-psykologiska problem* (Malmö: School of Education), No. 156, 1971.

Malmquist, E. Undervisningsmaskiner och deras användning. *Skola och Samhälle*, 1961, *42*, 175—187.

Malmquist, E. Undervisningsmaskiner och programmerat studiematerial. *Svensk Skolledartidning*, 1963, *22*, 130—145.

Malmquist, E. & Grundin, H. U. Olika former för bjudning av programmerat undervisningsmaterial. *Forskningsrapporter från Statens Försöksskola i Linköping*, Nr 8, 1966.

von Mentzer, C. H. *Studier i empirisk målanalys*. Stockholm: School of Education, 1968.

von Mentzer, C. H. Tio delstudier från UME-projektet. En antologi med exempel på problem och metoder i ett "system"-inriktat forsknings- och utvecklingsarbete. *Rapp. Pedag. inst., Lärarhögskolan i Stockholm*, No. 50, 1970.

Pikas, A. Jämförelser mellan traditionell och programmerad undervisning. *Pedagogisk Tidskrift*, 1967, *103*, 1—10, 41—49, 109—116, 151—167.

Pikas, A. Indoctrination of basic ideas of rational conflict solution. *Report, The Institute of Education, Uppsala University*, No. 41, 1969.

Pikas, A. Dimensions for developing beyond expository tasks: Planning for greater transfer and increased pupil-teacher interaction in educational technology. (Paper based on a contr. to Symposium on Educational Technology, XVIIth Int. Congress of Applied Psychology, Liège.) Manuscript, 1971.

Stiernborg, M. *Utbildning av värnpliktiga utbildningsprogrammerare*. Stockholm: Dept. Educ., 1966.

Stukát, K.-G. *Ett försök med programmering av svensk språklära*. Stockholm: Biblioteksförlaget, 1963.

Stukát, K.-G. Construction and field testing of a grammar program. *Programmed Learning*, 1965, *2*, 14—30.

Stukát, K.-G. Ett experiment rörande kännedom om resultatet och stegstorlek i ett språkläreprogram. *Pedagogisk Forskning*, 1965, *9*, 93—102.

Tidland, A. Undersökningar i anslutning till undervisningsprogrammet "Engelsk skrivning". *Rapp. Pedag. inst., Göteborgs univer.*, No. 21, 1966.

Undervisningsmaskiner och programmerat studiematerial. Skolöverstyrelsen: Utredningar i skolfrågor 11, 1963.

Wallin, E. Om målanalys och målformulering. *Rapp. Pedag. inst., Göteborgs univer.*, No. 49, 1970.

Wallin, E. Vad är undervisningsteknologi? *Utbildningstidningen*, 1970, *1* (3), 43—45.

Öreberg, C. IMU-systemet. *Undervisningsteknologi*, 1968, *3* (1—2), 9—14.

Öreberg, C. et al. IMU-projektet: Målbeskrivning för ett självinstruerande studiematerial i matematik för grundskolans högstadium. *Pedagogisk-psykologiska problem* (Malmö: School of Education), No. 43, 1966.